THE SAMURAI SERIES

THE BOOK OF FIVE RINGS, HAGAKURE: THE WAY OF THE SAMURAI, THE ART OF WAR & BUSHIDO: THE SOUL OF JAPAN

- MIYAMOTO MUSASHI
- YAMAMOTO TSUNETOMO
- SUN TZU & INAZO NITOBE

SANAGE
PUBLISHING HOUSE

Paperback: 978-939574199-6

Any references to historical events, real people, or real places are used fictitiously. Names, characters, and places are products of the author's imagination.

Printed by:

Sanage Publishing House LLP
Mumbai, India

sanagepublishing@gmail.com

CONTENTS

THE BOOK OF FIVE RINGS

HAGAKURE: THE BOOK OF THE SAMUARI

THE ART OF WAR

BUSHIDO, THE SOUL OF JAPAN

THE BOOK OF FIVE RINGS

Miyamoto Musashi: Miyamoto Musashi, also known as Shinmen Takezō, Miyamoto Bennosuke or, by his Buddhist name, Niten Dōraku, was an expert Japanese swordsman and rōnin. He was the founder of the Hyōhō Niten Ichi-ryū or Niten-ryū style of swordsmanship and in his final years authored the The Book of Five Rings, a book on strategy, tactics, and philosophy that is still studied today.

INTRODUCTION

I have been many years training in the Way of Strategy, called Ni Ten Ichi Ryu, and now I think I will explain it in writing for the first time.

It is now during the first ten days of the tenth month in the twentieth year of Kanei (1645). I have climbed mountain Iwato of Higo in Kyushu to pay homage to heaven, pray to Kwannon, and kneel before Buddha. I am a warrior of Harima province, Shinmen Musashi No Kami Fujiwara No Genshin, age sixty years. From youth my heart has been inclined to-ward the Way of Strategy.

My first duel was when I was thirteen, I struck down a strategist of the Shinto school, one Arima Kihei. When I was sixteen, I struck down an able strategist Tadashima Akiyama. When I was twenty-one, I went up to the capital and met all manner of strategists, never once failing to win in many contests.

After that I went from province-to-province dueling with strategist of various schools, and not once failed to win even though I had as many as sixty encounters. This was between the ages of thirteen and twenty-eight or twenty-nine. When I reached thirty, I looked back on my past. The previous victories were not due to my having mastered strategy. Perhaps it was natural ability, or the order of heaven, or that other schools' strategy was inferior.

After that I studied morning and evening searching for the principle and came to realize the Way of Strategy when I was fifty.

Since then, I have lived without following any particular Way. Thus, with the virtue of strategy I practice many arts and abilities all things with no teacher. To write this book I did not use the law of Buddha or the teachings of Confucius, neither old war chronicles nor books on martial tactics. I take up my brush to explain the true spirit of this Ichi school as it is mirrored in the Way of heaven and Kwannon. The time is the night of the tenth day of the tenth month, at the hour of the tiger (3-5 a.m.)

CHAPTER 1

THE GROUND BOOK

Strategy is the craft of the warrior. Commanders must enact the craft, and troopers should know this, Way. There is no warrior in the world today who really understands the Way of Strategy.

There are various Ways. There is the Way of salvation by the law of Buddha, the Way of Confucius governing the Way of learning, the Way of healing as a doctor, as a poet teaching the Way of Waka, tea, archery, and many arts and skills. Each man practices as he feels inclined. It is said the warrior's is the twofold Way of pen and sword, and he should have a taste for both Ways.

Even if a man has no natural ability, he can be a warrior by sticking assiduously to both divisions of the Way. Generally speaking, the Way of the warrior is resolute acceptance of death. Although not only warriors but priests, women, peasants, and lowlier folk have been known to die readily in the cause of duty or out of shame, this is a different thing. The warrior is different in that studying the Way of Strategy is based on overcoming men. By victory gained in crossing swords with individuals, or enjoining battle with large numbers, we can attain power and fame for ourselves or our lord. This is the virtue of strategy.

The Way of Strategy

In China and Japan practitioners of the Way have been known as "masters of strategy". Warriors must learn this Way.

Recently there have been people getting on in the world as strategists, but they are usually just sword-fencers. The attendants of the Kashima Kantori shrines of the province Hitachi received instruction from the gods and made schools based on this teaching, traveling from country to country instructing men. This is the recent meaning of strategy.

In olden times strategy was listed among the Ten Abilities and Seven Arts as a beneficial practice. It was certainly an art but as a beneficial practice it was not limited to sword-fencing. The true value of sword-fencing cannot be seen within the confines of sword-fencing technique.

If we look at the world, we see arts for sale. Men use equipment to sell their own selves. As if with the nut and the flower, the nut has become less than the flower. In this kind of Way of Strategy, both those teaching and those learning the way are concerned with colouring and showing off their technique, trying to hasten the bloom of the flower. They speak of "This Dojo" and "That Dojo". They are looking for profit. Someone once said, "Immature strategy is the cause of grief". That was a true saying.

There are four Ways in which men pass through life: as gentlemen, farmers, artisans, and merchants.

The Way of the farmer. Using agricultural instruments, he sees springs through to autumns with an eye on the changes of season.

Second is the Way of the merchant. The wine maker obtains his ingredients and puts them to use to make his living. The Way of the merchant is always to live by taking profit. This is the Way of the merchant.

Thirdly the gentleman warrior, carrying the weaponry of his Way. The Way of the warrior is to master the virtue of his weapons. If a gentleman dislikes strategy he will not appreciate the benefit of weaponry, so must he not have a little taste for this? Fourthly the Way of the artisan. The Way of the carpenter is to become proficient in the use of his tools, first to lay his plans with a true measure and then perform his work according to plan. Thus, he passes through life. These are the four Ways of the gentleman, the farmer, the artisan, and the merchant.

Comparing the Way of the Carpenter to Strategy

The comparison with carpentry is through the connection with houses. Houses of the nobility, houses of warriors, the Four houses, ruin of houses, thriving of houses, the style of the house, the tradition of the house, and the name of the house. The carpenter uses a master plan of the building, and the Way of Strategy is similar in that there is a plan of campaign. If you want to learn the craft of war, ponder over this book. The teacher is as a needle, the disciple is as thread. You must practice constantly.

Like the foreman carpenter, the commander must know natural rules, and the rules of the country, and the rules of houses. This is the Way of the foreman.

The foreman carpenter must know the architectural theory of towers and temples, and the plans of palaces, and must employ men to raise up houses. The Way of the foreman carpenter is the same as the Way of the commander of a warrior house. In the construction of houses, choice of woods is made.

Straight un-knotted timber of good appearance is used for the revealed pillars, straight timber with small defects is used for the inner pillars. Timbers of the finest appearance, even if a little weak, is used for the thresholds, lintels, doors, and sliding doors, and so on. Good strong timber, though it be gnarled and knotted, can always be used discreetly in construction. Timber which is weak or knotted throughout should be used as scaffolding, and later for firewood.

The foreman carpenter allots his men work according to their ability. Floor layers, makers of sliding doors, thresholds and lintels, ceilings and so on. Those of poor ability lay the floor joists, and those of lesser ability carve wedges and do such miscellaneous work. If the foreman knows and deploys his men well the finished work will be good. The foreman should take into account the abilities and limitations of his men, circulating among them and asking nothing unreasonable. He should know their morale and spirit and encourage them when necessary. This is the same as the principle of strategy.

The Way of Strategy

Like a trooper, the carpenter sharpens his own tools. He carries his equipment in his toolbox and works under the direction of his foreman. He makes columns and girders with an axe, shapes floorboards and shelves with a plane, cuts fine openwork and carvings accurately, giving as excellent a finish as his skill will allow. This is the craft of the carpenters. When the carpenter becomes skilled and understands measures, he can become a foreman.

The carpenter's attainment is, having tools which will cut well, to make small shrines, writing shelves, tables, paper lanterns, chopping boards and pot-lids. These are the specialties of the carpenter. Things are similar for the trooper. You ought to think deeply about this.

The attainment of the carpenter is that his work is not warped, that the joints are not misaligned, and that the work is truly planed so that it meets well and is not merely finished in sections. This is essential. If you want to learn this Way, deeply consider the things written in this book one at a time. You must do sufficient research.

Outline of the Five Books of this Book of Strategy

The Way is shown as five books concerning different aspects. These are Ground, Water, Fire, Wind (tradition), and Void (the illusionary nature of worldly things)

The body of the Way of Strategy from the viewpoint of my Ichi school is explained in the Ground book. It is difficult to realize the true Way just through sword-fencing. Know the smallest things and the biggest things, the shallowest things, and the deepest things. As if it were a straight road mapped out on the ground, the first book is called the Ground book.

Second is the Water book. With water as the basis, the spirit becomes like water. Water adopts the shape of its receptacle; it is sometimes a trickle and sometimes a wild sea. Water has a clear blue colour. By the clarity, things of Ichi school are shown in this book. If you master the principles of sword-fencing, when you freely beat one man, you beat any man in the world. The spirit of defeating a man is the same for ten million men. The strategist makes small things into big things, like building a great Buddha from a one-foot model. I cannot write in detail how this is done. The principle of strategy is having one thing, to know ten thousand things. Things of Ichi school are written in this the Water book.

Third is the Fire book. This book is about fighting. The spirit of fire is fierce, whether the fire be small or big and so it is with battles. The Way of battles is the same for man-to-man fights and for ten thousand a side battle. You must appreciate that spirit can become big or small. What is big is easy to perceive: what is small is difficult to perceive. In short, it is difficult for large numbers of men to change position, so their movements can be easily predicted. An individual can easily change his mind, so his movements are difficult to predict. You must appreciate this. The essence of this book is that you must train day and night in order to make quick decisions. In strategy it is necessary to treat training as part of normal life with your spirit unchanging. Thus, combat in battle is described in the Fire book.

Fourthly the Wind book. This book is not concerned with my Ichi school but with other schools of strategy. By Wind I mean old traditions, present-day traditions, and family traditions of strategy. Thus, I clearly explain the strategies of the world. This is tradition.

It is difficult to know yourself if you do not know others. To all Ways there are side-tracks. If you study a Way daily, and your spirit diverges, you may think you are obeying a good Way but objectively it is not the true Way. If you are following the true way and diverge a little, this will later become a large divergence. You must realize this. Other strategies have come to be thought of as mere sword-fencing, and it is not unreasonable that this should be so. The benefit of my strategy, although it includes sword-fencing, lies in a separate principle. I have explained what is commonly meant by strategy in other schools in the Tradition (Wind) book.

Fifthly, the book of the Void. By void I mean that which has no beginning and no end. Attaining this principle means not attaining the principle. The Way of strategy is the Way of nature. When you appreciate the power of nature, knowing rhythm of any situation, you will be able to hit the enemy naturally and strike naturally. All this is the Way of the Void. I intend to show how to follow the true Way according to nature in the book of the Void.

The Name Ichi Ryu Ni to (One school - two swords)

Warriors, both commanders and troopers, carry two swords at their belt. In olden times these were called the long sword and the sword; nowadays they are known as the sword and the companion sword. Let it suffice to say that in our land, whatever the reason, a warrior carries two swords at his belt. It is the Way of the warrior.

"Nito Ichi Ryu" shows the advantages of using both swords.

The spear and the halberd are weapons which are carried out of doors. Students of the Ichi school Way of Strategy should train from the start with the sword and the long sword in either hand. This is a truth: when you sacrifice your life, you must make fullest use of your weaponry. It is false not to do so and to die with a weapon yet undrawn.

If you hold a sword with both hands, it is difficult to wield it freely to left and right, so my method is to carry the sword in one hand. This does not apply to large weapons such as the spear or halberd, but swords and companion swords can be carried in one hand. It is encumbering to hold a sword in both hands when you are on horseback, when running on uneven roads, on swampy ground, muddy rice fields, stony ground, or in a crowd of people. To hold the long sword in both hands is not the true Way, for if you carry a bow or spear or other arms in your left hand you have only one hand free for the long sword. However, when it is difficult to cut an enemy down with one hand, you must use both hands. It is not difficult to wield a sword in one hand; the Way to learn this is to train with two long swords, one in each hand. It will seem difficult at first, but everything is difficult at first. Bows are difficult to draw, halberds are difficult to wield as you become accustomed to the bow so your pull will become stronger. When you become used to wielding the long sword, you will gain the power of the Way and wield the sword well.

As I will explain in the second book, the Water Book, there is no fast way of wielding the long sword. The long sword should be wielded broadly and the companion sword closely. This is the first thing to realize.

According to this Ichi school, you can win with a long weapon, and yet you can also win with a short weapon. In short, the Way of the Ichi school is the spirit of winning, whatever the weapon and whatever its size.

It is better to use two swords rather than one when you are fighting a crowd, and especially if you want to take a prisoner.

These things cannot be explained in detail. From one thing, know ten thousand things. When you attain the Way of Strategy there will not be one thing you cannot see. You must study hard.

The Benefit of the Two Characters Reading "Strategy"

Masters of the long sword are called strategists. As for the other military arts, those who master the bow are called archers, those who master the spear are called spearmen, those who master the gun are called marksmen, those who master the halberd are called halberdiers. But we do not call masters of the Way of the long sword "long swordsmen", nor do we speak of "companion swordsmen". Because bows, guns, spears, and halberds are all warriors' equipment they are certainly part of strategy. To master the virtue of the long sword is to govern the world and oneself, thus the long sword is the basis of strategy. The principle is "strategy by means of the long sword". If he attains the virtue of the long sword, one man can beat ten men. Just as one man can beat ten, so a hundred men can beat a thousand, and a thousand can beat ten thousand. In my strategy, one man is the same as ten thousand, so this strategy is the complete warrior's craft.

The Way of the warrior does not include other Ways, such as Confucianism, Buddhism, certain traditions, artistic accomplishments, and dancing. But even though these are not part of the Way, if you know the Way broadly you will see it in everything. Men must polish their particular Way.

The Benefit of Weapons in Strategy

There is a time and place for use of weapons.

The best use of the companion sword is in a confined space, or when you are engaged closely with an opponent. The long sword can be used effectively in all situations.

The halberd is inferior to the spear on the battlefield. With the spear you can take the initiative; the halberd is defensive. In the hands of one of two men of equal ability, the spear gives a little extra strength. Spear and halberd both have their uses, but neither is very beneficial in confined spaces. They cannot be used for taking a prisoner. They are essentially weapons for the field.

Anyway, if you learn "indoor" techniques, you will think narrowly and forget the true Way. Thus, you will have difficulty in actual encounters.

The bow is tactically strong at the commencement of battle, especially battles on a moor, as it is possible to shoot quickly from among the spearmen. However, it is unsatisfactory in sieges, or when the enemy is more than forty yards away. For this reason, there are nowadays few traditional schools of archery. There is little use nowadays for this kind of skill.

From inside fortifications, the gun has no equal among weapons. It is the supreme weapon on the field before the ranks clash, but once swords are crossed the gun becomes useless. One of the virtues of the bow is that you can see the arrows in flight and correct your aim accordingly, whereas gunshot cannot be seen. You must appreciate the importance of this.

Just as a horse must have endurance and no defects, so it is with weapons. Horses should walk strongly, and swords and companion swords should cut strongly. Spears and halberds must stand up to heavy use, bows and guns must be sturdy. Weapons should be hardy rather than decorative.

You should not have a favourite weapon. To become over-familiar with one weapon is as much a fault as not knowing it sufficiently well. You should not copy others but use weapons which you can handle properly. It is bad for commanders and troopers to have likes and dis-likes. These are things you must learn thoroughly.

Timing in Strategy

There is timing in everything. Timing in strategy cannot be mastered without a great deal of practice.

Timing is important in dancing and pipe or string music, for they are in rhythm only if timing is good. Timing and rhythm are also involved in the military arts, shooting bows and guns, and riding horses. In all skills and abilities there is timing. There is also timing in the Void.

There is timing in the whole life of the warrior, in his thriving and declining, in his harmony and discord. Similarly, there is timing in the Way of the merchant, in the rise and fall of capital. All things entail rising and falling timing. You must be able to discern this. In strategy there are various timing considerations. From the outset you must know the applicable timing and the inapplicable timing, and from among the large and small things and the fast and slow timings find the relevant timing, first seeing the distance timing and the background timing. This is the main thing in strategy. It is especially important to know the background timing, otherwise your strategy will become uncertain.

You win battles with the timing in the Void born of the timing of cunning by knowing the enemies' timing, and thus using a timing which the enemy does not expect.

All the five books are chiefly concerned with timing. You must train sufficiently to appreciate this.

If you practice day and night in the above Ichi school strategy, your spirit will naturally broaden. Thus, is large scale strategy and the strategy of hand-to-hand combat propagated in the world. This is recorded for the first time in the five books of Ground, Water, Fire, Tradition (Wind) and Void. This is the way for men who want to learn my strategy:

1. Do not think dishonestly.

2. The Way is in training.

3. Become acquainted with every art.

4. Know the Ways of all professions.

5. Distinguish between gain and loss in worldly matters.

6. Develop intuitive judgement and understanding for everything.

7. Perceive those things which cannot be seen.

8. Pay attention even to trifles.

9. Do nothing which is of no use.

It is important to start by setting these broad principles in your heart, and train in the Way of Strategy. If you do not look at things on a large scale it will be difficult for you to master strategy. If you learn and attain this strategy you will never lose even to twenty or thirty enemies. More than anything to start with you must set your heart on strategy and earnestly stick to the Way. You will come to be able to actually beat men in fights, and to be able to win with your eye. Also, by training you will be able to freely control your own body, conquer men with your body, and with sufficient training you will be able to beat ten men with your spirit. When you have reached this point, will it not mean that you are invincible?

Moreover, in large scale strategy the superior man will manage many subordinates dexterously, bear himself correctly, govern the country and foster the people, thus preserving the ruler's discipline. If there is a Way involving the spirit of not being defeated, to help oneself and gain honour, it is the Way of strategy.

CHAPTER 2

THE WATER BOOK

The spirit of the Ni Ten Ichi school of strategy is based on water, and this Water Book explains methods of victory as the long-sword form of the Ichi school. Language does not extend to explaining the Way in detail, but it can be grasped intuitively. Study this book; read a word then ponder on it. If you interpret the meaning loosely you will mistake the Way.

The principles of strategy are written down here in terms of single combat, but you must think broadly so that you attain an understanding for ten-thousand-a-side battles.

Strategy is different from other things in that if you mistake the Way even a little you will become bewildered and fall into bad ways.

If you merely read this book, you will not reach the Way of Strategy. Absorb the things written in this book. Do not just read, memorize, or imitate, but so that you realize the principle from within your own heart study hard to absorb these things into your body.

Spiritual Bearing in Strategy

In strategy your spiritual bearing must not be any different from normal. Both in fighting and in everyday life you should be determined though calm. Meet the situation without tenseness yet not recklessly, your spirit settled yet unbiased. Even when your spirit is calm do not let your body relax, and when your body is relaxed do not let your spirit slacken. Do not let your spirit be influenced by your body, or your body be influenced by your spirit. Be neither insufficiently spirited nor over spirited. An elevated spirit is weak, and a low spirit is weak. Do not let the enemy see your spirit.

Small people must be completely familiar with the spirit of large people, and large people must be familiar with the spirit of small people. Whatever your size, do not be misled by the reactions of your own body. With your spirit open and unconstricted, look at things from a high point of view. You must cultivate your wisdom and spirit. Polish your wisdom: learn public justice, distinguish between good and evil, study the Ways of different arts one by one. When you cannot be deceived by men you will have realized the wisdom of strategy.

The wisdom of strategy is different from other things. On the battlefield, even when you are hard-pressed, you should ceaselessly research the principles of strategy so that you can develop a steady spirit.

Stance in Strategy

Adopt a stance with the head erect, neither hanging down, nor looking up, nor twisted. Your forehead and the space between your eyes should not be wrinkled. Do not roll your eyes nor allow them to blink, but slightly narrow them. With your features composed, keep the line of your nose straight with a feeling of slightly flaring your nostrils. Hold the line of the rear of the neck straight: instill vigour into your hairline, and in the same way from the shoulders down through your entire body. Lower both shoulders and, without the buttocks jutting out, put strength into your legs from the knees to the tips of your toes. Brace your abdomen so that you do not bend at the hips. Wedge your companion sword in your belt against your abdomen, so that your belt is not slack, this is called "wedging in".

In all forms of strategy, it is necessary to maintain the combat stance in everyday life and to make your everyday stance your combat stance. You must research this well.

The Gaze in Strategy

The gaze should be large and broad. This is the twofold gaze "Perception and Sight". Perception is strong and sight week.

In strategy it is important to see distant things as if they were close and to take a distanced view of close things. It is important in strategy to know the enemy's sword and not to be distracted by insignificant movements of his sword. You must study this. The gaze is the same for single combat and for large-scale strategy.

It is necessary in strategy to be able to look to both sides without moving the eyeballs. You cannot master this ability quickly. Learn what is written here; use this gaze in everyday life and do not vary it whatever happens.

Holding the Long Sword

Grip the long sword with a rather floating feeling in your thumb and forefinger, with the middle finger neither tight nor slack, and with the last two fingers tight. It is bad to have play in your hands.

When you take up a sword, you must feel intent on cutting the enemy. As you cut an enemy you must not change your grip, and your hands must not "cower". When you dash the enemy's sword aside, or ward it off, or force it down, you must slightly change the feeling in your thumb and forefinger. Above all, you must be intent on cutting the enemy in the way you grip the sword.

The grip for combat and for sword-testing is the same. There is no such thing as a "man-cutting grip".

Generally, I dislike fixedness in both long swords and hands. Fixedness means a dead hand. Pliability is a living hand. You must bear this in mind.

Footwork

With the tips of your toes somewhat floating, tread firmly with your heels. Whether you move fast or slow, with large or small steps, your feet must always move as in normal walking. I dislike the three walking methods known as "jumping-foot", "floating-foot" and "fixed-steps".

So-called "Yin-Yang foot" is important in the Way. Yin-Yang foot means not moving only one foot. It means moving your feet left-right and right-left when cutting, withdrawing, or warding off a cut. You should not move on one foot preferentially.

The Five Attitudes

The five attitudes are: Upper, Middle, Lower, Right Side, and Left Side. These are the give. Although attitude has these five divisions, the one purpose of all of them is to cut the enemy. There are none but these five attitudes.

Whatever attitude you are in, do not be conscious of making the attitude; think only of cutting. Your attitude should be large or small according to the situation. Upper, Lower and Middle attitudes are decisive. Left Side and Right-Side attitudes are fluid. Left and Right attitudes should be used if there is an obstruction overhead or to one side. The decision to use Left or Right depends on the place.

The essence of the Way is this. To understand attitude, you must thoroughly understand the middle attitude. The middle attitude is the heart of attitudes. If we look at strategy on a broad scale, the Middle attitude is the seat of the commander, with the other four attitudes following the commander. You must appreciate this.

The Way of the Long Sword

Knowing the Way of the long sword means we can wield with two fingers the sword we usually carry. If we know the path of the sword well, we can wield it easily. If you try to wield the long sword quickly you will mistake the Way. To wield the long sword well you must wield it calmly.

If you try to wield it quickly, like a folding fan or a short sword, you will err by using "short sword chopping". You cannot cut down a man with a long sword using this method.

When you have cut downwards with the longsword, lift it straight upwards; when you cut sideways, return the sword along a sideways path. Return the sword in a reasonable way, always stretching the elbows broadly. Wield the sword strongly. This is the Way of the longsword.

If you learn to use the five approaches of my strategy, you will be able to wield a sword well. You must train constantly.

The Five Approaches

1. The first approach is the Middle attitude. Confront the enemy with the point of your sword against his face. When he attacks, dash his sword to the right and "ride" it. Or, when the enemy attacks, deflect the point of his sword by hitting downwards, keep your long sword where it is, and as the enemy renews his attack cut his arms from below. This is the first method.

The five approaches are this kind of thing. You must train repeatedly using a long sword in order to learn them. When you master my Way of the long sword, you will be able to control any attack the enemy makes. I assure you, there are no attitudes other than the five attitudes of the long sword of Ni To.

2. In the second approach with the long sword, from the Upper

attitude cut the enemy just as he attacks. If the enemy evades the cut, keep your sword where it is and, scooping up from below, cut him as he renews the attack. It is possible to repeat the cut from here.

In this method there are various changes in timing and spirit. You will be able to understand this by training in the Ichi school. You will always win with the five long sword methods. You must train repetitively.

3. In the third approach, adopt the Lower attitude, anticipating scooping up. When the enemy attacks, hit his hands from below. As you do so he may try to hit your sword down. If this is the case, cut his upper arm(s) horizontally with a feeling of "crossing". This means that from the lower attitudes you hit the enemy at the instant that he attacks.

You will encounter this method often, both as a beginner and in later strategy. You must train holding a long sword.

4. In this fourth approach, adopt the Left Side attitude. As the enemy attacks hit his hands from below. If as you hit his hands, he attempts to dash down your sword, with the feeling of hitting his hands, parry the path of his long sword and cut across from above your shoulder.

This is the Way of the long sword. Through this method you win by parrying the line of the enemy's attack. You must research this.

5. In the fifth approach, the sword is in the Right-Side attitude. In accordance with the enemy's attack, cross your long sword from below at the side to the Upper attitude. Then cut straight from above.

This method is essential for knowing the Way of the long sword well. If you can use this method, you can freely wield a heavy long sword.

I cannot describe in detail how to use these five approaches. You must become well acquainted with my "in harmony with the long sword" Way, learn large-scale timing, understand the enemy's long sword, and become used to the five approaches from the outset. You will always win by using these five methods, with various timing considerations discerning the enemy's spirit. You must consider all this carefully.

The "Attitude No-Attitude" Teaching

"Attitude No-Attitude" means that there is no need for what are known as long sword attitudes.

Even so, attitudes exist as the five ways of holding the long sword. However, you hold the sword it must be in such a way that it is easy to cut the enemy well, in accordance with the situation, the place, and your relation to the enemy. From the Upper attitude as your spirit lessens you can adopt the Middle attitude, and from the Middle attitude you can raise the sword a little in your technique and adopt the Upper attitude. From the lower attitude you can raise the sword and adopt the Middle attitudes as the occasion demands. According to the situation, if you turn your sword from either the Left Side or Right-Side attitude towards the Centre, the Middle or the Lower attitude results.

The principle of this is called "Existing Attitude, Non-existing Attitude".

The primary thing when you take a sword in your hands is your intention to cut the enemy, whatever the means. Whenever you parry, hit, spring, strike or touch the enemy's cutting sword, you must cut the enemy in the same movement. It is essential to attain this. If you think only of hitting, springing, striking or touching the enemy, you will not be able actually to cut him. More than anything, you must be thinking of carrying your movement through to cutting him. You must thoroughly research this.

Attitude in strategy on a larger scale is called "Battle Array". Such attitudes are all for winning battles. Fixed formation is bad. Study this well.

To Hit the Enemy "In One Timing"

"In One Timing" means, when you have closed with the enemy, to hit him as quickly and directly as possible, without moving your body or settling your spirit, while you see that he is still undecided. The timing of hitting before the enemy decides to withdraw, break, or hit is this "In One Timing".

You must train to achieve this timing, to be able to hit in the timing of an instant.

The "Abdomen Timing of Two"

When you attack and the enemy quickly retreats, as you see him tense you must feint a cut. Then, as he relaxes, follow up and hit him. This is the "Abdomen Timing of Two".

It is very difficult to attain this by merely reading this book, but you will soon understand with a little instruction.

No Design, No Conception

In this method, when the enemy attacks and you also decide to attack, hit with your body, and hit with your spirit, and hit from the Void with your hands, accelerating strongly. This is the "No Design, No Conception" cut.

This is the most important method of hitting. It is often used. You must train hard to understand it.

The Flowing Water Cut

The "Flowing Water Cut" is used when you are struggling blade to blade with the enemy. When he breaks and quickly withdraws trying to spring with his long sword, expand your body and spirit and cut him as slowly as possible with your long sword, following your body like stagnant water. You can cut with certainty if you learn this. You must discern the enemy's grade.

Continuous Cut

When you attack and the enemy also attacks, and your swords spring together, in one action cut his head, hands and legs. When you cut several places with one sweep of the long sword, it is the "Continuous Cut". You must practice this cut; it is often used. With detailed practice you should be able to understand it.

The Fire and Stones

Cut The Fires and Stones Cut means that when the enemy's long sword and your long sword clash together you cut as strongly as possible without raising the sword even a little. This means cutting quickly with the hands, body, and legs all three cutting strongly. If you train well enough, you will be able to strike strongly.

The Red Leaves Cut

The Red Leaves Cut [allusion to falling, dying leaves] means knocking down the enemy's long sword. The spirit should be getting control of his sword. When the enemy is in a long sword attitude in front of you and intent on cutting, hitting, and parrying, you strongly hit the enemy's long sword with the Fire and Stones Cut, perhaps in the spirit of the "No Design, No Conception" Cut. If you then beat down the point of his sword with a sticky feeling, he will necessarily drop the sword. If you practice this cut it becomes easy to make the enemy drop his sword. You must train repetitively.

The Body in Place of the Long Sword

Also "the long sword in place of the body". Usually, we move the body and the sword at the same time to cut the enemy. However, according to the enemy's cutting method, you can dash against him with your body first, and afterwards cut with the sword. If his body is immoveable, you can cut first with the long sword, but generally you hit first with the body and then cut with the long sword. You must research this well and practice hitting.

Cut and Slash

To cut and to slash are two different things. Cutting, whatever form of cutting it is, is decisive, with a resolute spirit. Slashing is nothing more than touching the enemy. Even if you slash strongly, and even if the enemy dies instantly, it is slashing. When you cut, your spirit is resolved.

You must appreciate this. If you first slash the enemy's hands or legs, you must then cut strongly. Slashing is in spirit the same as touching. When you realize this, they become indistinguishable. Learn this well.

Chinese Monkey's Body

The Chinese Monkey's Body is the spirit of not stretching out your arms. The spirit is to get in quickly, without in the least extending your arms before the enemy cuts. If you are intent upon not stretching out your arms you are effectively far away, the spirit is to go in with your whole body. When you come to within arm's reach it becomes easy to move your body in. You must research this well.

Glue and Lacquer Emulsion Body

The spirit of "Glue and Lacquer Emulsion Body" is to stick to the enemy and not separate from him. When you approach the enemy, stick firmly with your head, body, and legs. People tend to advance their head and legs quickly, but their body lags behind. You should stick firmly so that there is not the slightest gap between the enemy's body and your body. You must consider this carefully.

To Strive for Height

By "to strive for height" is meant, when you close with the enemy, to strive with him for superior height without cringing. Stretch your legs, stretch your hips, and stretch your neck face to face with him. When you think you have won, and you are the higher, thrust in strongly. You must learn this.

To Apply Stickiness

When the enemy attacks and you also attack with the long sword, you should go in with a sticky feeling and fix your long sword against the enemy's as you receive his cut. The spirit of stickiness is not hitting very strongly but hitting so that the long swords do not separate easily. It is best to approach as calmly as possible when hitting the enemy's long sword with stickiness. The difference between "Stickiness" and "Entanglement" is that stickiness is firm, and entanglement is weak. You must appreciate this.

The Body Strike

The Body Strike means to approach the enemy through a gap in his guard. The spirit is to strike him with your body. Turn your face a little aside and strike the enemy's breast with your left shoulder thrust out. Approach with the spirit of bouncing the enemy away, striking as strongly as possible in time with your breathing. If you achieve this method of closing with the enemy, you will be able to knock him ten or twenty feet away. It is possible to strike the enemy until he is dead. Train well.

Three Ways to Parry His Attack

There are three methods to parry a cut:

First, by dashing the enemy's long sword to your right, as if thrusting at his eyes, when he makes an attack.

Or, to parry by thrusting the enemy's long sword towards his right eye with the feeling of snipping his neck.

Or, when you have a short "long sword", without worrying about parrying the enemy's long sword, to close with him quickly, thrusting at his face with your left hand.

These are the three methods of parrying. You must bear in mind that you can always clench your left hand and thrust at the enemy's face with your fist. For this it is necessary to train well.

To Stab at the Face

To stab at the face means, when you are in confrontation with the enemy, that your spirit is intent of stabbing at his face, following the line of the blades with the point of your long sword. If you are intent on stabbing at his face, his face and body will become rideable. When the enemy becomes as if rideable, there are various opportunities for winning. You must concentrate on this. When fighting and the enemy's body becomes as if rideable, you can win quickly, so you ought not to forget to stab at the face. You must pursue the value of this technique through training.

To Stab at the Heart

To stab at the heart means, when fighting and there are obstructions above, or to the sides, and whenever it is difficult to cut, to thrust at the enemy. You must stab the enemy's breast without letting the point of your long sword waver, showing the enemy the ridge of the blade square-on, and with the spirit of deflecting his long sword. The spirit of this principle is often useful when we become tired or for some reason our long sword will not cut. You must understand the application of this method.

To Scold "Tut-TUT!"

"Scold" means that, when the enemy tries to counter-cut as you attack, you counter-cut again from below as if thrusting at him, trying to hold him down. With very quick timing you cut, scolding the enemy. Thrust up, "Tut!", and cut "TUT!" This timing is encountered time and time again in exchange of blows. The way to scold Tut-TUT is to time the cut simultaneously with raising your long sword as if to thrust the enemy. You must learn this through repetitive practice.

The Smacking Parry

By "smacking parry" is meant that when you clash swords with the enemy, you meet his attacking cut on your long sword with a tee-dum, tee-dum rhythm, smacking his sword and cutting him. The spirit of the smacking parry is not parrying, or smacking strongly, but smacking the enemy's long sword in accordance with his attacking cut, primarily in-tent on quickly cutting him. If you understand the timing of smacking, however hard your long swords clash together, your sword-point will not be knocked back even a little. You must research sufficiently to realize this.

There are Many Enemies

"There are many enemies" applies when you are fighting one against many. Draw both sword and companion sword and assume a wide-stretched left and right attitude. The spirit is to chase the enemies around from side to side, even though they come from all four directions. Observe their attacking order and go to meet first those who attack first. Sweep your eyes around broadly, carefully examining the attacking order and cut left and right alternately with your swords. Waiting is bad. Always quickly re-assume your attitudes to both sides, cut the enemies down as they advance, crushing them in the direction from which they attack. Whatever you do, you must drive the enemy together, as if tying a line of fishes, and when they are seen to be piled up, cut them down strongly without giving them room to move.

The Advantage when Coming to Blows

You can know how to win through strategy with the long sword, but it cannot be clearly explained in writing. You must practice diligently in order to understand how to win.

Oral tradition: "The true Way of Strategy is revealed in the long sword."

One Cut

You can win with certainty with the spirit of "one cut". It is difficult to attain this if you do not learn strategy well. If you train well in this Way, strategy will come from your heart, and you will be able to win at will. You must train diligently.

Direct Communication

The spirit of "Direct Communication" is how the true Way of the Ni To Ichi school is received and handed down.

Oral tradition: "Teach your body strategy."

Recorded in the above book is an outline of Ichi school sword-fighting. To learn how to win with the long sword in strategy, first learn the five approaches and the five attitudes, and absorb the Way of the long sword naturally in your body. You must understand spirit and timing, handle the long sword naturally, and move body and legs in harmony with your spirit. Whether beating one man or two, you will then know values in strategy.

Study the contents of this book, taking one item at a time, and through fighting with enemies you will gradually come to know the principle of the Way.

Deliberately, with a patient spirit, absorb the virtue of all this, from time to time raising your hand in combat. Maintain this spirit whenever you cross swords with and enemy.

Step by step walk the thousand-mile road.

Study strategy over the years and achieve the spirit of the warrior. Today is victory over yourself of yesterday; tomorrow is your victory over lesser men. Next, in order to beat more skillful men, train according to this book, not allowing your heart to be swayed along a side-track. Even if you kill an enemy, if it is not based on what you have learned it is not the true Way.

If you attain this Way of victory, then you will be able to beat several tens of men. What remains is sword-fighting ability, which you can attain in battles and duels.

CHAPTER 3

THE FIRE BOOK

In this the Fire Book of the Ni To Ichi school of strategy I describe fighting as fire.

In the first place, people think narrowly about the benefit of strategy. By using only their fingertips, they only know the benefit of three of the five inches of the wrist. They let a contest be decided, as with the folding fan, merely by the span of their forearms. They specialize in the small matter of dexterity, learning such trifles as hand and leg movements with the bamboo practice sword.

In my strategy, the training for killing enemies is by way of many contests, fighting for survival, discovering the meaning of life and death, learning the Way of the sword, judging the strength of attacks, and understanding the Way of the "edge and ridge" of the sword.

You cannot profit from small techniques particularly when full armour is worn. My Way of Strategy is the sure method to win when fighting for your life one man against five or ten. There is nothing wrong with the principle "one man can beat ten, so a thousand men can beat ten thousand". You must research this. Of course, you cannot assemble a thousand or ten thousand men for everyday training. But you can become a master of strategy by training alone with a sword, so that you can under-stand the enemy's strategy, his strength, and resources, and come to appreciate how to apply strategy to beat ten thousand enemies.

Any man who wants to master the essence of my strategy must research diligently, training morning and evening. Thus, can he polish his skill, become free from self, and realize extraordinary ability. He will come to possess miraculous power.

This is the practical result of strategy.

Depending on the Place

Examine your environment.

Stand in the sun; that is, take up an attitude with the sun behind you. If the situation does not allow this, you must try to keep the sun on your right side. In buildings, you must stand with the entrance behind you or to your right. Make sure that your rear is unobstructed, and that there is free space on your left, your right side being occupied with your side attitude. At night, if the enemy can be seen, keep the fire behind you and the entrance to your right, and otherwise take up your attitude as above. You must look down on the enemy and take up your attitude on slightly higher places. For example, the Kamiza in a house is thought of as a high place.

When the fight comes, always endeavour to chase the enemy around to your left side. Chase him towards awkward places and try to keep him with his back to awkward places. When the enemy gets into an in-convenient position, do not let him look around, but conscientiously chase him around and pin him down. In houses, chase the enemy into the thresholds, lintels, doors, verandas, pillars, and so on, again not letting him see his situation.

Always chase the enemy into bad footholds, obstacles at the side and so on, using the virtues of the place to establish predominant positions from which to fight. You must research and train diligently in this.

The Three Methods to Forestall the Enemy

The first is to forestall him by attacking. This is called Ken No Sen (to set him up).

Another method is to forestall him as he attacks. This is called Tai No Sen (to wait for the initiative).

The other method is when you and the enemy attack together. This is called Tai Tai No Sen (to accompany him and forestall him).

There are no methods of taking the lead other than these three. Because you can win quickly by taking the lead, it is one of the most important things in strategy. There are several things involved in taking the lead. You must make the best of the situation, see through the enemy's spirit so that you grasp his strategy and defeat him. It is impossible to write about this in detail.

The First - Ken No Sen

When you decide to attack, keep calm and dash in quickly, forestalling the enemy. Or you can advance seemingly strongly but with a reserved spirit, forestalling him with the reserve.

Alternatively, advance with as strong a spirit as possible, and when you reach the enemy move with your feet a little quicker than normal, unsettling him and overwhelming him sharply.

Or, with your spirit calm, attack with a feeling of constantly crushing the enemy, from first to last. The spirit is to win in the depths of the enemy. These are all Ken No Sen.

The Second - Tai No Sen

When the enemy attacks, remain undisturbed but feign weakness. As the enemy reaches you, suddenly move away indicating that you intend to jump aside, then dash in attacking strongly as soon as you see the enemy relax. This is one way.

Or, as the enemy attacks, attack still more strongly, taking advantage of the resulting disorder in his timing to win.

This is the Tai No Sen principle.

The Third - *Tai Tai No Sen*

When the enemy makes a quick attack, you must attack strongly and calmly, aim for his weak point as he draws near, and strongly defeat him.

Or, if the enemy attacks calmly, you must observe his movements and, with your body rather floating, join in with his movements as he draws near. Move quickly and cut him strongly.

This is Tai Tai No Sen.

These things cannot be clearly explained in words. You must research what is written here. In these three ways of forestalling, you must judge the situation. This does not mean that you always attack first; but if the enemy attacks first you can lead him around. In strategy, you have effectively won when you forestall the enemy, so you must train well to attain this.

To Hold Down a Pillow

"To Hold Down a Pillow" means not allowing the enemy's head to rise. In-contests of strategy it is bad to be led about by the enemy. You must always be able to lead the enemy about. Obviously, the enemy will also be thinking of doing this, but he cannot forestall you if you do not allow him to come out. In strategy, you must stop the enemy as he attempts to cut you must push down his thrust and throw off his hold when he tries to grapple. This is the meaning of "to hold down a pillow". When you have grasped this principle, whatever the enemy tries to bring about in the fight you will see in advance and suppress it. The spirit is to check his attack at the syllable "at... " when he jumps check his jump at the syllable "ju... " and check his cut at "cu... ".

The important thing in strategy is to suppress the enemy's useful actions but allow his useless actions. However, doing this alone is defensive. First, you must act according to the Way, suppressing the enemy's techniques, foiling his plans and thence command him directly. When you can do this, you will be a master of strategy. You must train well and research "holding down a pillow".

Crossing at a Ford

"Crossing at a ford" means, for example, crossing the sea at a strait, or crossing over a hundred miles of broad sea at a crossing place. I believe this "crossing at a ford" occurs often in man's lifetime. It means setting sail even though your friends stay in harbour, knowing the route, knowing the soundness of your ship and the favour of the day. When all the conditions are meet, and there is perhaps a favourable wind, or a tailwind, then set sail. If the wind changes within a few miles of your destination, you must row across the remaining distance without sail.

If you attain this spirit, it applies to everyday life. You must always think of crossing at a ford.

In strategy also it is important to "cross at a ford". Discern the enemy's capability and, knowing your own strong points, "cross the ford" at the advantageous place, as a good captain crosses a sea route. If you succeed in crossing at the best place, you may take your ease. To cross at a ford means to attack the enemy's weak point, and to put yourself in an advantageous position. This is how to win large-scale strategy. The spirit of crossing at a ford is necessary in both large- and small-scale strategy.

You must research this well.

To Know the Times

"To know the times" means to know the enemy's disposition in battle. Is it flourishing or waning? By observing the spirit of the enemy's men and getting the best position, you can work out the enemy's disposition and move your men accordingly. You can win through this principle of strategy, fighting from a position of advantage.

When in a duel, you must forestall the enemy and attack when you have first recognized his school of strategy, perceived his quality and his strong and weak points. Attack in an unsuspecting manner, knowing his metre and modulation and the appropriate timing.

Knowing the times means, if your ability is high, seeing right into things. If you are thoroughly conversant with strategy, you will recognize the enemy's intentions and thus have many opportunities to win. You must sufficiently study this.

To Tread Down the Sword

"To tread down the sword" is a principle often used in strategy. First, in large scale strategy, when the enemy first discharges bows and guns and then attacks it is difficult for us to attack if we are busy loading powder into our guns or notching our arrows. The spirit is to attack quickly while the enemy is still shooting with bows or guns. The spirit is to win by "treading down" as we receive the enemy's attack.

In single combat, we cannot get a decisive victory by cutting, with a "tee-dum tee-dum" feeling, in the wake of the enemy's attacking long sword. We must defeat him at the start of his attack, in the spirit of treading him down with the feet, so that he cannot rise again to the attack.

"Treading" does not simply mean treading with the feet. Tread with the body, tread with the spirit, and, of course, tread and cut with the long sword. You must achieve the spirit of not allowing the enemy to attack a second time. This is the spirit of forestalling in every sense. Once at the enemy, you should not aspire just to strike him, but to cling after the attack. You must study this deeply.

To Know "Collapse"

Everything can collapse. Houses, bodies, and enemies collapse when their rhythm becomes deranged.

In large-scale strategy, when the enemy starts to collapse, you must pursue him without letting the chance go. If you fail to take advantage of your enemies' collapse, they may recover.

In single combat, the enemy sometimes loses timing and collapses. If you let this opportunity pass, he may recover and not be so negligent thereafter. Fix your eye on the enemy's collapse, and chase him, attacking so that you do not let him recover. You must do this. The chasing attack is with a strong spirit. You must utterly cut the enemy down so that he does not recover his position. You must understand how to utterly cut down the enemy.

To Become the Enemy

"To become the enemy" means to think yourself in the enemy's position. In the world people tend to think of a robber trapped in a house as a fortified enemy. However, if we think of "becoming the enemy", we feel that the whole world is against us and that there is no escape. He who is shut inside is a pheasant. He who enters to arrest is a hawk. You must appreciate this.

In large-scale strategy, people are always under the impression that the enemy is strong, and so tend to become cautious. But if you have good soldiers, and if you understand the principles of strategy, and if you know how to beat the enemy, there is nothing to worry about.

In single combat also you must put yourself in the enemy's position. If you think, "Here is a master of the Way, who knows the principles of strategy", then you will surely lose. You must consider this deeply.

To Release Four Hands

"To release four hands" is used when you and the enemy are contending with the same spirit, and the issue cannot be decided. Abandon this spirit and win through an alternative resource.

In large-scale strategy, when there is a "four hands" spirit, do not give up, it is man's existence. Immediately throw away this spirit and win with a technique the enemy does not expect.

In single combat also, when we think we have fallen into the "four hands" situation, we must defeat the enemy by changing our mind and applying a suitable technique according to his condition. You must be able to judge this.

To Move the Shade

"To move the shade" is used when you cannot see the enemy's spirit. In large-scale strategy, when you cannot see the enemy's position, indicate that you are about to attack strongly, to discover his resources. It is easy then to defeat him with a different method once you see his resources.

In single combat, if the enemy takes up a rear or side attitude of the long sword so that you cannot see his intention, make a feint attack, and the enemy will show his long sword, thinking he sees your spirit. Benefiting from what you are shown, you can win with certainty. If you are negligent, you will miss the timing. Research this well.

To Hold Down a Shadow

"Holding down a shadow" is use when you can see the enemy's attacking spirit.

In large-scale strategy, when the enemy embarks on an attack, if you make a show of strongly suppressing his technique, he will change his mind. Then, altering your spirit, defeat him by forestalling him with a Void spirit.

Or, in single combat, hold down the enemy's strong intention with a suitable timing, and defeat him by forestalling him with this timing. You must study this well.

To Pass On

Many things are said to be passed on. Sleepiness can be passed on, and yawning can be passed on. Time can be passed on also.

In large-scale strategy, when the enemy is agitated and shows an inclination to rush, do not mind in the least. Make a show of complete calmness, and the enemy will be taken by this and will become relaxed. When you see that this spirit has been passed on, you can bring about the enemy's defeat by attacking strongly with a Void spirit.

In single combat, you can win by relaxing your body and spirit and then, catching on to the moment the enemy relaxes, attack strongly and quickly, forestalling him. What is known as "getting someone drunk" is similar to this. You can also infect the enemy with a bored, careless, or weak spirit. You must study this well.

To Cause Loss of Balance

Many things can cause a loss of balance. One cause is danger, another is hardship, and another is surprise. You must research this.

In large-scale strategy it is important to cause loss of balance. Attack without warning where the enemy is not expecting it, and while his spirit is undecided follow up your advantage and, having the lead, defeat him.

Or, in single combat, start by making a show of being slow, then suddenly attack strongly. Without allowing him space for breath to recover form, the fluctuation of spirit, you must grasp the opportunity to win. Get the feel of this.

To Frighten

Fright often occurs, caused by the unexpected.

In large-scale strategy you can frighten the enemy not just by what you present to their eyes, but by shouting, making a small force seem large, or by threatening them from the flank without warning. These things all frighten. You can win by making best use of the enemy's frightened rhythm.

In single combat, also, you must use the advantage of taking the enemy unawares by frightening him with your body, long sword, or voice, to defeat him. You should research this well.

To Soak In

When you have come to grips and are striving together with the enemy, and you realize that you cannot advance, you "soak in" and become one with the enemy. You can win by applying a suitable technique while you are mutually entangled.

In battles involving large numbers as well as in fights with small numbers, you can often win decisively with the advantage of knowing how to "soak" into the enemy, where-as, were you to draw apart, you would lose the chance to win. Research this well.

To Injure the Corners

It is difficult to move strong things by pushing directly, so you should "injure the corners".

In large-scale strategy, it is beneficial to strike at the corners of the enemy's force. If the corners are overthrown, the spirit of the whole body will be overthrown. To defeat the enemy, you must follow up the attack when the corners have fallen.

In single combat, it is easy to win once the enemy collapses. This happens when you injure the "corners" of his body, and thus weaken him. It is important to know how to do this, so you must research deeply.

To Throw into Confusion

This means making the enemy lose resolve.

In large-scale strategy we can use our troops to confuse the enemy on the field. Observing the enemy's spirit, we can make him think, "Here? There? Like that? Like this? Slow? Fast?". Victory is certain when the enemy is caught up in a rhythm which confuses his spirit.

In single combat, we can confuse the enemy by attacking with varied techniques when the chance arises. Feint a thrust or cut or make the enemy think you are going to close with him, and when he is confused you can easily win. This is the essence of fighting, and you must research it deeply.

The Three Shouts

The three shouts are divided thus: before, during and after. Shout according to the situation. The voice is a thing of life. We shout against fires and so on, against the wind and the waves. The voice shows energy.

In large-scale strategy, at the start of battle we shout as loudly as possible. During the fight, the voice is low-pitched, shouting out as we attack. After the contest, we shout in the wake of our victory. These are the three shouts.

In single combat, we make as if to cut and shout "Ei!" at the same time to disturb the enemy, then in the wake of our shout we cut with the long sword. We shout after we have cut down the enemy, this is to announce victory. This is called "sen go no koe" (before and after voice). We do not shout simultaneously with flourishing the long sword. We shout during the fight to get into rhythm. Research this deeply.

To Mingle

In battles, when the armies are in confrontation, attack the enemy's strong points and, when you see that they are beaten back, quickly separate and attack yet another strong point on the periphery of his force. The spirit of this is like a winding mountain path.

This is an important fighting method for one man against many. Strike down the enemies in one quarter, or drive them back, then grasp the timing and attack further strong points to right and left, as if on a winding mountain path, weighing up the enemies' disposition. When you know the enemies' level attack strongly with no trace of retreating spirit.

What is meant by "mingling" is the spirit of advancing and becoming engaged with the enemy, and not withdrawing even one step. You must understand this.

To Crush

This means to crush the enemy regarding him as being weak.

In large-scale strategy, when we see that the enemy has few men, or if he has many men but his spirit is weak and disordered, we knock the hat over his eyes, crushing him utterly. If we crush lightly, he may recover. You must learn the spirit of crushing as if with a handgrip.

In single combat, if the enemy is less skillful than ourself; if his rhythm is disorganized, or if he has fallen into evasive or retreating attitudes, we must crush him straightaway, with no concern for his presence and without allowing him space for breath. It is essential to crush him all at once. The primary thing is not to let him recover his position even a little. You must research this deeply.

The Mountain-Sea Change

The "mountain-sea" spirit means that it is bad to repeat the same thing several times when fighting the enemy. There may be no help but to do something twice, but do not try it a third time. If you once make an attack and fail, there is little chance of success if you use the same approach again. If you attempt a technique which you have previously tried unsuccessfully and fail yet again, then you must change your attacking method.

If the enemy thinks of the mountains, attack like the sea; and if he thinks of the sea, attack like the mountains. You must research this deeply.

To Penetrate the Depths

When we are fighting with the enemy, even when it can be seen that we can win on the surface with the benefit of the Way, if his spirit is not extinguished, he may be beaten superficially yet undefeated in spirit deep inside. With this principle of "penetrating the depths" we can des-troy the enemy's spirit in its depths, demoralizing him by quickly changing our spirit. This often occurs.

Penetrating the depths means penetrating with the long sword, penetrating with the body, and penetrating with the spirit. This cannot be understood in a generalization.

Once we have crushed the enemy in the depths, there is no need to remain spirited. But otherwise, we must remain spirited. If the enemy remains spirited it is difficult to crush him. You must train in penetrating the depths for large-scale strategy and also single combat.

To Renew

"To renew" applies when we are fighting with the enemy, and an entangled spirit arises where there is no possible resolution. We must abandon our efforts, think of the situation in a fresh spirit then win in the new rhythm. To renew, when we are deadlocked with the enemy, means that without changing our circumstance we change our spirit and win through a different technique.

It is necessary to consider how "to renew" also applies in large-scale strategy. Research this diligently.

Rat's Head, Ox's Neck

"Rat's head and ox's neck" means that, when we are fighting with the enemy and both he and we have become occupied with small points in an entangled spirit, we must always think of the Way of Strategy as being both a rat's head and an ox's neck. Whenever we have become preoccupied with small detail, we must suddenly change into a large spirit, interchanging large with small.

This is one of the essences of strategy. It is necessary that the warrior think in this spirit in everyday life. You must not depart from this spirit in large-scale strategy nor in single combat.

The Commander Knows the Troops

"The commander knows the troops" applies everywhere in fights in my Way of strategy. Using the wisdom of strategy, think of the enemy as your own troops. When you think in this way you can move him at will and be able to chase him around. You become the general and the enemy becomes your troops. You must master this.

To Let Go the Hilt

There are various kinds of spirit involved in letting go the hilt. There is the spirit of winning without a sword. There is also the spirit of holding the long sword but not winning. The various methods cannot be expressed in writing. You must train well.

The Body of a Rock

When you have mastered the Way of Strategy you can suddenly make your body like a rock, and ten thousand things cannot touch you. This is the body of a rock.

You will not be moved. Oral tradition.

What is recorded above is what has been constantly on my mind about Ichi school sword fencing, written down as it came to me. This is the first time I have written about my technique, and the order of things is a bit confused. It is difficult to express it clearly.

This book is a spiritual guide for the man who wishes to learn the Way.

My heart has been inclined to the Way of Strategy from my youth onwards. I have devoted myself to training my hand, tempering my body, and attaining the many spiritual attitudes of sword fencing. If we watch men of other schools discussing theory, and concentrating on techniques with the hands, even though they seem skillful to watch, they have not the slightest true spirit.

Of course, men who study in this way think they are training the body and spirit, but it is an obstacle to the true Way, and its bad influence re-mains forever. Thus, the true Way of Strategy is becoming decadent and dying out.

The true Way of sword fencing is the craft of defeating the enemy in a fight, and nothing other than this. If you attain and adhere to the wisdom of my strategy, you need never doubt that you will win.

CHAPTER 4

THE WIND BOOK

In strategy you must know the Ways of other schools, so I have written about various other traditions of strategies in this the Wind Book.

Without knowledge of the Ways of other schools, it is difficult to under-stand the essence of my Ichi school. Looking at other schools we find some that specialize in techniques of strength using extra-long swords. Some schools study the Way of the short sword, known as kodachi. Some schools teach dexterity in large numbers of sword techniques, teaching attitudes of the sword as the "surface" and the Way as the "interior".

That none of these are the true Way I show clearly in the interior of this book all the vices and virtues and rights and wrongs. My Ichi school is different. Other schools make accomplishments their means of livelihood, growing flowers and decoratively colouring articles in order to sell them. This is definitely not the Way of Strategy.

Some of the world's strategists are concerned only with sword-fencing and limit their training to flourishing the long sword and carriage of the body. But is dexterity alone sufficient to win? This is not the essence of the Way.

I have recorded the unsatisfactory point of other schools one by one in this book. You must study these matters deeply to appreciate the benefit of my Ni To Ichi school.

Other Schools Using Extra-Long Swords

Some other schools have a liking for extra-long swords. From the point of view of my strategy these must been seen as weak schools. This is because they do not appreciate the principle of cutting the enemy by any means. Their preference is for the extra-long sword and, relying on the virtue of its length, they think to defeat the enemy from a distance.

In this world it is said, "One inch gives the hand advantage", but these are the idle words of one who does not know strategy. It shows the inferior strategy of a weak spirit that men should be dependent on the length of their sword, fighting from a distance without the benefit of strategy.

I expect there is a case for the school in question liking extra-long swords as part of its doctrine, but if we compare this to real life it is un-reasonable. Surely, we need not necessarily be defeated if we are using a short sword, and have no long sword?

It is difficult for these people to cut the enemy when at close quarters because of the length of the long sword. The blade path is large, so the long sword is an encumbrance, and they are at a disadvantage compared to the man armed with a short companion sword.

From olden times it has been said: "Great and small go together.". So do not unconditionally dislike extra-long swords. What I dislike is the inclination towards the long sword. If we consider large-scale strategy, we can think of large forces in terms of long swords, and small forces as short swords. Cannot few me give battle against many? There are many instances of few men overcoming many.

Your strategy is of no account if when called on to fight in a confined space your heart is inclined to the long sword, or if you are in a house armed only with your companion sword.

Besides, some men have not the strength of others. In my doctrine, I dislike preconceived, narrow spirit. You must study this well.

The Strong Long Sword Spirit in Other Schools

You should not speak of strong and weak long swords. If you just wield the long sword in a strong spirit your cutting will be coarse, and if you use the sword coarsely you will have difficulty in winning.

If you are concerned with the strength of your sword, you will try to cut unreasonably strongly, and will not be able to cut at all. It is also bad to try to cut strongly when testing the sword. Whenever you cross swords with an enemy you must not think of cutting him either strongly or weakly; just think of cutting and killing him. Be intent solely upon killing the enemy. Do not try to cut strongly and, of course, do not think of cutting weakly. You should only be concerned with killing the enemy.

If you rely on strength, when you hit the enemy's sword you will inevitably hit too hard. If you do this, your own sword will be carried along as a result. Thus, the saying, "The strongest hand wins", has no meaning.

In large-scale strategy, if you have a strong army and are relying on strength to win, but the enemy also has a strong army, the battle will be fierce. This is the same for both sides.

Without the correct principle the fight cannot be won. The spirit of my school is to win through the wisdom of strategy, paying no attention to trifles. Study this well.

Use of the Shorter Long Sword in Other Schools

Using a shorter long sword is not the true Way to win.

In ancient times, tachi and katana meant long and short swords.

Men of superior strength in the world can wield even a long sword lightly, so there is no case for their liking the short sword. They also make use of the length of spears and halberds. Some men use a shorter long sword with the intention of jumping in and stabbing the enemy at the unguarded moment when he flourishes his sword. This inclination is bad.

To aim for the enemy's unguarded moment is completely defensive, and undesirable at close quarters with the enemy. Furthermore, you can-not use the method of jumping inside his defense with a short sword if there are many enemies. Some men think that if they go against many enemies with a shorter long sword they can unrestrictedly frisk around cutting in sweeps, but they have to parry cuts continuously, and eventually become entangled with the enemy. This is inconsistent with the true Way of Strategy.

The sure Way to win thus is to chase the enemy around in confusing manner, causing him to jump aside, with your body held strongly and straight. The same principle applies to large-scale strategy. The essence of strategy is to fall upon the enemy in large numbers and bring about his speedy downfall. By their study of strategy, people of the world get used to countering, evading, and retreating as the normal thing. They become set in this habit, so can easily be paraded around by the enemy. The Way of Strategy is straight and true. You must chase the enemy around and make him obey your spirit.

Other Schools with many Methods of using the Long Sword

Placing a great deal of importance on the attitudes of the long sword is a mistaken way of thinking. What is known in the world as "attitude" applies when there is no enemy. The reason is that this has been a precedent since ancient times, and there should be no such thing as "This is the modern way to do it" in dueling. You must force the enemy into inconvenient situations.

Attitudes are for situations in which you are not to be moved. That is, for garrisoning castles, battle array, and so on, showing the spirit of not being moved even by a strong assault. In the Way of dueling, however, you must always be intent upon taking the lead and attacking. Attitude is the spirit of awaiting an attack. You must appreciate this.

In duels of strategy, you must move the opponent's attitude. Attack where his spirit is lax, throw him into confusion, irritate and terrify him. Take advantage of the enemy's rhythm when he is unsettled, and you can win.

I dislike the defensive spirit known as "attitude". Therefore, in my Way, there is something called "Attitude, No Attitude".

In large-scale strategy we deploy our troops for battle bearing in mind our strength, observing the enemy's numbers, and noting the details of the battlefield. This is at the start of the battle.

The spirit of attacking first is completely different from the spirit of being attacked. Bearing an attack well, with a strong attitude, and parrying the enemy's attack well, is like making a wall of spears and halberds. When you attack the enemy, your spirit must go to the extent of pulling the stakes out of a wall and using them as spears and halberds. You must examine this well.

Fixing the Eyes in Other Schools

Some schools maintain that the eyes should be fixed on the enemy's long sword. Some schools fix the eyes on the hands. Some fix the eyes on the face, and some fix the eyes on the feet, and so on. If you fix the eyes on these places your spirit can become confused, and your strategy thwarted.

I will explain this in detail. Footballers do not fix their eyes on the ball, but by good play on the field they can perform well. When you become accustomed to something, you are not limited to the use of your eyes. People such as master musicians have the music score in front of their nose, or flourish swords in several ways when they have mastered the Way, but this does not mean that they fix their eyes on these things specifically, or that they make pointless movements of the sword. It means that they can see naturally.

In the Way of Strategy, when you have fought many times, you will easily be able to appraise the speed and position of the enemy's sword and having mastery of the Way you will see the weight of his spirit. In strategy, fixing the eyes means gazing at the man's heart.

In large-scale strategy the area to watch is the enemy's strength. "Perception" and "sight" are the two methods of seeing. Perception consists of concentrating strongly on the enemy's spirit, observing the condition of the battlefield, fixing the gaze strongly, seeing the progress of the fight and the changes of advantages. This is the sure way to win.

In single combat you must not fix the eyes on the details. As I said before, if you fix your eyes on details and neglect important things, your spirit will become bewildered, and victory will escape you. Research this principle well and train diligently.

Use of the Feet in Other Schools

There are various methods of using the feet: floating foot, jumping foot, springing foot, treading foot, crow's foot, and such nimble walking methods. From the point of view of my strategy, these are all unsatisfactory.

I dislike floating foot because the feet always tend to float during the fight. The Way must be trod firmly.

Neither do I like jumping foot, because it encourages the habit of jumping, and a jumpy spirit. However much you jump, there is no real justification for it so, jumping is bad.

Springing foot causes a springing spirit which is indecisive.

Treading foot is a "waiting" method, and I especially dislike it.

Apart from these, there are various fast walking methods, such as crow's foot, and so on.

Sometimes, however, you may encounter the enemy on marshland, swampy ground, river valleys, stony ground, or narrow roads, in which situations you cannot jump or move the feet quickly.

In my strategy, the footwork does not change. I always walk as I usually do in the street. You must never lose control of your feet. According to the enemy's rhythm, move fast or slowly, adjusting your body not too much and not too little.

Carrying the feet is important also in large-scale strategy. This is because, if you attack quickly and thoughtlessly without knowing the enemy's spirit, your rhythm will become deranged, and you will not be able to win. Or, if you advance too slowly, you will not be able to take advantage of the enemy's disorder, the opportunity to win will escape, and you will not be able to finish the fight quickly. You must win by seizing upon the enemy's disorder and derangement, and by not according to him even a little hope of recovery. Practice this well.

Speed in Other Schools

Speed is not part of the true Way of Strategy. Speed implies that things seem fast or slow, according to whether or not they are in rhythm. Whatever the Way, the master of strategy does not appear fast.

Some people can walk as fast as a hundred or a hundred and twenty miles in a day, but this does not mean that they run continuously from morning till night. Unpracticed runners may seem to have been running all day, but their performance is poor.

In the Way of dance, accomplished performers can sing while dancing, but when beginners try this, they slow down, and their spirit becomes busy. The "old pine tree" melody beaten on a leather drum is tranquil, but when beginners try this, they slow down, and their spirit becomes busy. Very skillful people can manage a fast rhythm, but it is bad to beat hurriedly. If you try to beat too quickly you will get out of time. Of course, slowness is bad. Really skillful people never get out of time, and are always deliberate, and never appear busy. From this example, the principle can be seen.

What is known as speed is especially bad in the Way of Strategy. The reason for this is that depending on the place, marsh, or swamp and so on, it may not be possible to move the body and legs together quickly. Still less will you be able to cut quickly if you have a long sword in this situation. If you try to cut quickly, as if using a fan or short sword, you will not actually cut even a little. You must appreciate this.

In large-scale strategy also, a fast busy spirit is undesirable. The spirit must be that of holding down a pillow, then you will not be even a little late.

When your opponent is hurrying recklessly, you must act contrarily and keep calm. You must not be influenced by the opponent. Train diligently to attain this spirit.

"Interior" and "Surface" in Other Schools

There is no "interior" nor "surface" in strategy.

The artistic accomplishments usually claim inner meaning and secret tradition, and "interior" and "gate", but in combat there is no such thing as fighting on the surface or cutting with the interior. When I teach my Way, I first teach by training in techniques which are easy for the pupil to understand, a doctrine which is easy to understand. I gradually endeavour to explain the deep principle, points which it is hardly possible to comprehend, according to the pupil's progress. In any event, because the way to understanding is through experience, I do not speak of "interior" and "gate".

In this world, if you go into the mountains, and decide to go deeper and yet deeper, instead you will emerge at the gate. Whatever the Way, it has an interior, and it is sometimes a good thing to point out the gate. In strategy, we cannot say what is concealed and what is revealed.

Accordingly, I dislike passing on my Way through written pledges and regulations. Perceiving the ability of my pupils, I teach the direct Way, remove the bad influence of other schools, and gradually introduce them to the true Way of the warrior.

The method of teaching my strategy is with a trustworthy spirit.

You must train diligently. I have tried to record an outline of the strategy of other schools in the above nine sections. I could now continue by giving a specific account of these schools one by one, from the "gate" to the "interior", but I have intentionally not named the schools or their main points. The reason for this is that different branches of schools give different interpretations of the doctrines. In as much as men's opinions differ, so there must be differing ideas on the same matter. Thus no one man's conception is valid for any school.

I have shown the general tendencies of other schools on nine points. If we look at them from an honest viewpoint, we see that people always tend to like long swords or short swords and become concerned with strength in both large and small matters. You can see why I do not deal with the "gates" of other schools.

In my Ichi school of the long sword there is neither gate nor interior. There is no inner meaning in sword attitudes. You must simply keep your spirit true to realize the virtue of strategy.

CHAPTER 5

THE BOOK OF THE VOID

The Ni To Ichi Way of Strategy is recorded in this the Book of the Void. What is called the spirit of the void is where there is nothing. It is not

included in man's knowledge. Of course, the void is nothingness. By knowing things that exist, you can know that which does not exist. That is the void.

People in this world look at things mistakenly and think that what they do not understand must be the void. This is not the true void. It is bewilderment.

In the Way of Strategy, also, those who study as warriors think that whatever they cannot understand in their craft is the void. This is not the true void.

To attain the Way of Strategy as a warrior you must study fully other martial arts and not deviate even a little from the Way of the warrior. With your spirit settled, accumulate practice day by day, and hour by hour. Polish the twofold spirit heart and mind and sharpen the twofold gaze perception and sight. When your spirit is not in the least clouded, when the clouds of bewilderment clear away, there is the true void.

Until you realize the true Way, whether in Buddhism or in

common sense, you may think that things are correct and in order. However, if we look at things objectively, from the viewpoint of laws of the world, we see various doctrines departing from the true Way. Know well this spirit, and with forthrightness as the foundation and the true spirit as the Way. Enact strategy broadly, correctly, and openly.

Then you will come to think of things in a wide sense and, taking the void as the Way, you will see the Way as void.

In the void is virtue, and no evil. Wisdom has existence, principle has existence, the Way has existence, spirit is nothingness.

Twelfth day of the fifth month, second year of Shoho (1645). Teruro Magonojo

SHINMEN MUSASHI

HAGAKURE: THE BOOK OF THE SAMURAI

Yamamoto Tsunetomo: Yamamoto Tsunetomo, Buddhist monastic name Yamamoto Jōchō (June 11, 1659 – November 30, 1719), was a samurai of the Saga Domain in Hizen Province under his lord Nabeshima Mitsushige. He became a Zen Buddhist priest and relayed his experiences, memories, lessons, ideas, and aphorisms to the samurai Tashiro Tsuramoto, who compiled them under the title Hagakure.

INTRODUCTION

Hagakure is the essential book of the Samurai. Written by Yamamoto Tsunetomo, who was a Samurai in the early 1700s, it is a book that combines the teachings of both Zen and Confucianism. These philosophies are centered on loyalty, devotion, purity and selflessness, and Yamamoto places a strong emphasis on the notion of living in the present moment with a strong and clear mind.

The Samurai were knights who defended and fought for their lords at a time when useful farming land was scarce and in need of protection. They believed in duty and gave themselves completely to their masters. The Samurai believed that only after transcending all fear could they obtain peace of mind and yield the power to serve their masters faithfully and loyally even in the face of death.

The word Hagakure literally translates as hidden beneath the leaves and also fallen leaves. Perhaps it was named this because at the time that it was written, the way of the samurai was becoming obsolete.

The Hagakure has been rewritten in modern terms by one of Japan's famous writers, Yukio Mishima. His own views were very similar to those of Yamamoto, particularly the philosophy of cultivating the self. His characters all had self-sufficiency in common and did not rely upon anyone else for completion.

Although the Hagakure was written centuries ago for a breed of warriors that no longer exist, the philosophies and wisdom within are still practical, even in our modern times.

CHAPTER ONE

Although it stands to reason that a samurai should be mindful of the Way of the Samurai, it would seem that we are all negligent. Consequently, if someone were to ask, "What is the true meaning of the Way of the Samurai?" the person who would be able to answer promptly is rare. This is because it has not been established in one's mind beforehand. From this, one's Un-mindfulness of the Way can be known.

Negligence is an extreme thing.

The Way of the Samurai is found in death. When it comes to either/ or, there is only the quick choice of death. It is not particularly difficult. Be determined and advance. To say that dying without reaching one's aim is to die a dog's death is the frivolous way of sophisticates. When pressed with the choice of life or death, it is not necessary to gain one's aim.

We all want to live. And in large part we make our logic according to what we like. But not having attained our aim and continuing to live is cowardice. This is a thin dangerous line. To die without gaming, one's aim is a dog's death and fanaticism. But there is no shame in this. This is the substance of the Way of the Samurai. If by setting one's heart right every morning and evening, one is able to live as though his body were already dead, he pains freedom in the Way. His whole life will be without blame, and he will succeed in his calling.

A man is a good retainer to the extent that he earnestly places importance in his master. This is the highest sort of retainer. If one is born into a prominent family that goes back for generations, it is sufficient to deeply consider the matter of obligation to one's ancestors, to lay down one's body and mind, and to earnestly esteem one's master. It is further good fortune if, more than this, one has wisdom and talent and can use them appropriately. But even a person who is good for nothing and exceedingly clumsy will be a reliable retainer if only he has the determination to think earnestly of his master. Having only wisdom and talent is the lowest tier of usefulness.

According to their nature, there are both people who have quick intelligence, and those who must withdraw and take time to think things over. Looking into this thoroughly, if one thinks selflessly and adheres to the four vows of the Nabeshima samurai, surprising wisdom will occur regardless of the high or low points of one's nature.

People think that they can clear up profound matters if they consider them deeply, but they exercise perverse thoughts and come to no good because they do their reflecting with only self-interest at the center.

It is difficult for a fool's habits to change to selflessness. In confronting a matter, however, if at first you leave it alone, fix the four vows in your heart, exclude self-interest, and make an effort, you will not go far from your mark.

Because we do most things relying only on our own sagacity, we become self-interested, turn our backs on reason, and things do not turn out well. As seen by other people this is sordid, weak, narrow, and inefficient. When one is not capable of true intelligence, it is good to consult with someone of good sense. An advisor will fulfill the Way when he makes a decision by selfless and frank intelligence because he is not personally involved. This way of doing things will certainly be seen by others as being strongly rooted. It is, for example, like a large tree with many roots. One man's intelligence is like a tree that has been simply stuck in the ground.

We learn about the sayings and deeds of the men of old in order to entrust ourselves to their wisdom and prevent selfishness. When we throw off our own bias, follow the sayings of the ancients, and confer with other people, matters should go well and without mishap. Lord Katsushige borrowed from the wisdom of Lord Naoshige. This is mentioned in the Ohanashikikigaki. We should be grateful for his concern.

Moreover, there was a certain man who engaged a number of his younger brothers as retainers, and whenever he visited Edo or the Kamigata area, he would have them accompany him. As he consulted with them every day on both private and public matters, it is said that he was without mishap.

Sagara Kyuma was completely at one with his master and served him as though his own body were already dead. He was one man in a thousand.

Once there was an important meeting at Master Sakyo's Mizugae Villa, and it was commanded that Kyuma was to commit seppuku. At that time in Osaki there was a teahouse on the third floor of the suburban residence of Master Taku Nut. Kyuma rented this and gathering together all the good-for-nothings in Saga he put on a puppet show, operating one of the puppets himself, carousing and drinking all day and night. Thus, overlooking Master Sakyo's villa, he carried on and caused a great disturbance. In instigating this disaster, he gallantly thought only of his master and was resolved to committing suicide.

Being a retainer is nothing other than hemp a supporter of one's lord, entrusting matters of good and evil to him, and renouncing self-interest. If there are but two or three men of this type, the fief will be secure.

If one looks at the world when affairs are going smoothly, there

72

are many who go about putting in their appearance, being useful by their wisdom, discrimination, and artfulness. However, if the lord should retire or go into seclusion, there are many who will quickly turn their backs on him and ingratiate themselves to the man of the day. Such a thing is unpleasant even to think about. Men of high position, low position, deep wisdom, and artfulness all feel that they are the ones who are working righteously, but when it comes to the point of throwing away one's life for his lord, all get weak in the knees. This is rather disgraceful. The fact that a useless person often becomes a matchless warrior at such times is because he has already given up his life and has become one with his lord. At the time of Mitsushige's death there was an example of this. His one resolved attendant was I alone. The others followed in my wake. Always the pretentious, self-asserting notables turn their backs on the man just as his eyes are closing in death.

Loyalty is said to be important in the pledge between lord and retainer. Though it may seem unobtainable, it is right before your eyes. If you once set yourself to it, you will become a superb retainer at that very moment.

To give a person one's opinion and correct his faults is an important thing. It is compassionate and comes first in matters of service. But the way of doing this is extremely difficult. To discover the good and bad points of a person is an easy thing, and to give an opinion concerning them is easy, too. For the most part, people think that they are being kind by saying the things that others find distasteful or difficult to say. But if it is not received well, they think that there is nothing more to be done. This is completely worthless. It is the same as brining shame to a person by slandering him. It is nothing more than getting it off one's chest.

To give a person an opinion one must first judge well whether that person is of the disposition to receive it or not. One must become close with him and make sure that he continually trusts one's word. Approaching subjects that are dear to him, seek the best way to speak and to be well understood. Judge the occasion and determine whether it is better by letter or at the time of leave-taking. Praise his good points and use every device to encourage him, perhaps by talking about one's own faults without touching on his, but so that they will occur to him. Have him receive this in the way that a man would drink water when his throat is dry, and it will be an opinion that will correct faults.

This is extremely difficult. If a person s fault is a habit of some years prior, by and large it won't be remedied. I have had this experience myself. To be intimate with alt one's comrades, correcting each other's faults, and being of one mind to be of use to the master is the great compassion of a retainer. By bringing shame to a person, bow could one expect to make him a better man?

It is bad taste to yawn in front of people. When one unexpectedly has to yawn, if he rubs his forehead in an upward direction, the sensation will stop. If that does not work, he can lick his lips while keeping his mouth closed, or simply hide it with his hand or his sleeve in such a way that no one will know what he is doing. It is the same with sneezing. One will appear foolish. There are other things besides these about which a person should use care and training.

When a certain person was saying that present matters of economy should be detailed, someone replied that this is not good at all.

It is a fact that ash will not live where the water is too clear. But if there is duckweed or something, the fish will hide under its shadow and thrive. Thus, the lower classes will live in tranquility if certain matters are a bit overlooked or left unheard. This fact should be understood with regard to people's conduct.

Once when Lord Mitsushige was a little boy and was supposed to recite from a copybook for the priest Kaion, he called the other children and acolytes and said, "Please come here and listen. It's difficult to read if there are hardly any people listening." The priest was impressed and said to the acolytes, "That's the spirit in which to do everything."

Every morning one should first do reverence to his master and parents and then to his patron deities and guardian Buddhas. If he will only make his master first in importance, his parents will rejoice and the gods and Buddhas will give their assent. For a warrior there is nothing other than thinking of his master. If one creates this resolution within himself, he will always be mindful of the master's person and will not depart from him even for a moment.

Moreover, a woman should consider her husband first, just as he considers his master first.

According to a certain person, a number of years ago Matsuguma Kyoan told this story:

In the practice of medicine there is a differentiation of treatment according to the Yin and Yang of men and women. There is also a difference in pulse. In the last fifty years, however, men's pulse has become the same as women's. Noticing this, in the treatment of eye disease I applied women's treatment to men and found it suitable. When I observed the application of men's treatment to men, there was no result. Thus, I knew that men's spirit had weakened and that they had become the same as women, and the end of the world had come. Since I witnessed this with certainty, I kept it a secret.

When looking at the men of today with this in mind, those who could be thought to have a woman's pulse are many indeed, and those who seem like real men few. Because of this, if one were to make a little effort, he would be able to take the upper hand quite easily. That there are few men who are able to cut well in beheadings is further proof that men's courage has waned. And when one comes to speak of kaishaku, it has become an age of men who are prudent and clever at making excuses. Forty or fifty years ago, when such things as matanuki were considered manly, a man wouldn't show an unscarred thigh to his fellows, so he would pierce it himself.

All of man's work is a bloody business. That fact, today, is considered foolish, affairs are finished cleverly with words alone, and jobs that require effort are avoided. I would like young men to have some understanding of this.

The priest Tannen used to say, "People come to no understanding because priests teach only the doctrine of 'No Mind.' What is called 'No Mind' is a mind that is pure and lacks complication.' This is interesting.

Lord Sanenori said, "In the midst of a single breath, where perversity cannot be held, is the Way. " If so, then the Way is one. But there is no one who can understand this clarity at first. Purity is something that cannot be attained except by piling effort upon effort.

There is nothing that we should be quite so grateful for as the last line of the poem that goes, "When your own heart asks." It can probably be thought of in the same way as the Nembutsu, and previously it was on the lips of many people.

Recently, people who are called "clever" adorn themselves with superficial wisdom and only deceive others. For this reason, they are inferior to dull-wilted folk. A dull- wilted person is direct. If one looks deeply into his heart with the above phrase, there will be no hidden places. It is a good examiner. One should be of the mind that, meeting this examiner, he will not be embarrassed.

The word gen means "illusion" or "apparition." In India, a man who uses conjury is called a genjutsushi ["a master of illusion technique"]. Everything in this world is but a marionette show. Thus, we use the word gen.

To hate injustice and stand on righteousness is a difficult thing. Furthermore, to think that being righteous is the best one can do and to do one's utmost to be righteous will, on the contrary, brig many mistakes. The Way is in a higher place then righteousness. This is very difficult to discover, but it is the highest wisdom. When seen from this standpoint, things like righteousness are rather shallow. If one does not understand this on his own, it cannot be known. There is a method of getting to this Way, however, even if one cannot discover it by himself. This is found in consultation with others. Even a person who has not attained this Way sees others front the side. It is like the saying from the game of go: "He who sees from the side has eight eyes." The saying, "Thought by thought we see our own mistakes," also means that the highest Way is in discussion with others. Listening to the old stories and reading books are for the purpose of sloughing off one's own discrimination and attaching oneself to that of the ancients.

A certain swordsman in his declining years said the following:

In one's life. there are levels in the pursuit of study. In the lowest level, a person studies but nothing comes of it, and he feels that both he and others are unskillful. At this point he is worthless. In the middle level he is still useless but is aware of his own insufficiencies and can also see the insufficiencies of others. In a higher level he has pride concerning his own ability, rejoices in praise from others, and laments the lack of ability in his fellows. This man has worth. In the highest level a man has the look of knowing nothing.

These are the levels in general; But there is one transcending level, and this is the most excellent of all. This person is aware of the endlessness of entering deeply into a certain Way arid never thinks of himself as having finished. He truly knows his own insufficiencies and never in his whole life thinks that he has succeeded. He has no thoughts of pride but with self-abasement knows the Way to the end. It is said that Master Yagyu once remarked, "I do not know the way to defeat others, but the way to defeat myself."

Throughout your life advance daily, becoming more skillful than yesterday, more skillful than today. This is never-ending.

Among the maxims on Lord Naoshige's wall there was this one: "Matters of great concern should be treated lightly." Master Ittei commented, "Matters of small concern should be treated seriously." Among one's affairs there should not be more than two or three matters of what one could call great concern. If these are deliberated upon during ordinary times, they can be understood. Thinking about things previously and then handling them lightly when the time comes is what this is all about. To face an event anew solve it lightly is difficult if you are not resolved beforehand, and there will always be uncertainty in hitting your mark. However, if the foundation is laid previously, you can think of the saying, "Matters of great concern should be treated lightly," as your own basis for action.

A certain person spent several years of service in Osaka and then returned home. When he made his appearance at the local bureau, everyone was put out and he was made a laughingstock because he spoke in the Kamigata dialect. Seen in this light, when one spends a long time in ado or the Kamigata area, he had better use his native dialect even more than usual.

When in a more sophisticated area it is natural that one's disposition be affected by different styles. But it is vulgar and foolish to look down upon the ways of one's own district as being boorish, or to be even a bit open to the persuasion of the other place's ways and to think about giving up one's own. That one's own district is unsophisticated and unpolished is a great treasure. Imitating another style is simply a sham.

A certain man said to the priest Shungaku, "The Lotus Sutra Sect's character is not good because it's so fearsome." Shungaku replied, "It is by reason of its fearsome character that it is the Lotus Sutra Sect. If its character were not so, it would be a different sect altogether." This is reasonable.

At the time when there was a council concerning the promotion of a certain man, the council members were at the point of deciding that promotion was useless because of the fact that the man had previously been involved in a drunken brawl. But someone said, "If we were to cast aside every man who had made a mistake once, useful men could probably not be come by. A man who makes a mistake once will be considerably more prudent and useful because of his repentance. I feel that he should be promoted."

Someone else then asked, "Will you; guarantee him?" The man replied, "Of course I will."

The others asked, "By what will you guarantee him?"

And he replied, "I can guarantee him by the fact that he is a man who has erred once. A man who has never once erred is dangerous." This said, the man was promoted.

At the time of a deliberation concerning criminals, Nakane Kazuma proposed making the punishment one degree lighter than what would be appropriate. This is a treasury of wisdom that only he was the possessor of. At that time, though there were several men in attendance, if it had not been for Kazuma alone, no one would have opened his mouth. For this reason, he is called Master Commencement and Master Twenty-five Days.

A certain person was brought to shame because he did not take revenge. The way of revenge lies in simply forcing one's way into a place and being cut down. There is no shame in this. By thinking that you must complete the job you will run out of time. By considering things like how many men the enemy has, time piles up; in the end you will give up. No matter if the enemy has thousands of men, there is fulfillment in simply standing them off and being determined to cut them all down, starting from one end. You will finish the greater part of it.

Concerning the night assault of Lord Asano's ronin, the fact that they did not commit seppuku at the Sengakuji was an error, for there was a long delay between the time their lord was struck down and the time when they struck down the enemy. If Lord Kira had died of illness within that period, it would have been extremely regrettable. Because the men of the Kamigata area have a very clever sort of wisdom, they do well at praiseworthy acts but cannot do things indiscriminately, as was done in the Nagasaki fight.

Although all things are not to be judged in this manner, I mention it in the investigation of the Way of the Samurai. When the time comes, there is no moment for reasoning. And if you have not done your inquiring beforehand, there is most often shame. Reading books and listening to people's talk are for the purpose of prior resolution.

Above all, the Way of the Samurai should be in being aware that you do not know what is going to happen next, and in querying every item day and night. Victory and defeat are matters of the temporary force of circumstances. The way of avoiding shame is different. It is simply in death.

Even if it seems certain that you will lose, retaliate. Neither wisdom nor technique has a place in this. A real man does not think of victory or defeat. He plunges recklessly towards an irrational death. By doing this, you will awaken from your dreams.

There are two things that will blemish a retainer, and these are riches and honor. If one but remains in strained circumstances, he will not be marred.

Once there was a certain man who was very clever, but it was his character to always see the negative points of his jobs. In such a way, one will be useless. If one does not get it into his head from the very beginning that the world is full of unseemly situations, for the most part his demeanor will be poor, and he will not be believed by others. And if one is not believed by others, no matter how good a person he may be, he will not have the essence of a good person. This can also be considered as a blemish.

There was a man who said, "Such and such a person has a violent disposition, but this is what I said right to his face... This was an unbecoming thing to say, and it was said simply because he wanted to be known as a rough fellow. It was rather low, and it can be seen that he was still rather immature. It is because a samurai has correct manners that he is admired. Speaking of other people in this way is no different from an exchange between low class spearmen. It is vulgar.

It is not good to settle into a set of opinions. It is a mistake to put forth effort and obtain some understanding and then stop at that. At first putting forth great effort to be sure that you have grasped the bastes, then practicing so that they may come to fruition is something that will never stop for your whole lifetime. Do not rely on following the degree of understanding that you have discovered, but simply think, "This is not enough."

One should search throughout his whole life how best to follow the Way. And he should study, setting his mind to work without putting things off. Within this is the Way.

These are from the recorded sayings of Yamamoto Jin'-emon:

• If you can understand one affair, you will understand eight.

• An affected laugh shows lack of self-respect in a man and lewdness in a woman.

• Whether speaking formally or informally, one should look his listener in the eye. A polite greeting is done at the beginning and finished. Speaking with downcast eyes is carelessness.

• It is carelessness to go about with one's hands inside the slits in the sides of his hakama.

• After reading books and the like, it is best to burn them or throw them away. It is said that reading books is the work of the Imperial Court, but the work of the House of Nakano is found in military valor, grasping the staff of oak.

• A samurai with no group and no horse is not a samurai at all.

• A kusemono is a man to rely upon.

• It is said that one should rise at four in the morning, bathe and arrange his hair daily, eat when the sun comes up, and retire when it becomes dark.

• A samurai will use a toothpick even though he has not eaten. Inside the skin of a dog, outside the hide of a tiger.

How should a person respond when he is asked, "As a human being, what is essential in terms of purpose and discipline?" First, let us say, "It is to become of the mind that is right now pure and lacking complications." People in general all seem to be dejected. When one has a pure and uncomplicated mind, his expression will be lively. When one is attending to matters, there is one thing that comes forth from his heart. That is, in terms of one's lord, loyalty; in terms of one's parents, filial piety; in martial affairs, bravery; and apart from that, something that can be used by all the world.

This is very difficult to discover. Once discovered, it is again difficult to keep in constant effect.

There is nothing outside the thought of the immediate moment.

Every morning, the samurai of fifty or sixty years ago would bathe, shave their foreheads, put lotion in their hair, cut their fingernails and toenails rubbing them with pumice and then with wood sorrel, and without fail pay attention to their personal appearance. It goes without saying that their armor in general was kept free from rust, that it was dusted, shined, and arranged.

Although it seems that taking special care of one's appearance is similar to showiness, it is nothing akin to elegance. Even if you are aware that you may be struck down today and are firmly resolved to an inevitable death, if you are slain with an unseemly appearance, you will show your lack of previous resolve, will be despised by your enemy, and will appear unclean. For this reason, it is said that both old and young should take care of their appearance.

Although you say that this is troublesome and time-consuming, a samurai's work is in such things. It is neither busy- work nor time-consuming. In constantly hardening one's resolution to die in battle, deliberately becoming as one already dead, and working at one's job and dealing with military affairs, there should be no shame. But when the time comes, a person will be shamed if he is not conscious of these things even in his dreams, and rather passes his days in self-interest and self-indulgence. And if he thinks that this is not shameful and feels that nothing else matters as long as he is comfortable, then his dissipate and discourteous actions will be repeatedly regrettable.

The person without previous resolution to inevitable death makes certain that his death will be in bad form. But if one is resolved to death beforehand, in what way can he be despicable? One should be especially diligent in this concern.

Furthermore, during the last thirty years customs have changed; now when young samurai jeer together, if there is not just talk about money matters, loss and gain, secrets, clothing styles or matters of sex, there is no reason to gather together at all. Customs are going to pieces. One can say that formerly when a man reached the age of twenty or thirty, he did not carry despicable things in his heart, and thus neither did such words appear. If an elder unwittingly said something of that sort, he thought of it as a sort of injury. This new custom probably appears because people attach importance to being beautiful before society and to household finances. What things a person should be able to accomplish if he had no haughtiness concerning his place in society!

It is a wretched thing that the young men of today are so contriving and so proud of their material possessions. Men with contriving hearts are lacking in duty. Lacking in duty, they will have no self-respect.

According to Master Ittei, even a poor penman will become substantial in the art of calligraphy if he studies by imitating a good model and puts forth effort. A retainer should be able to become substantial too, if he takes a good retainer as his model.

Today, however, there are no models of good retainers. In light of this, it would be good to make a model and to learn from that. To do this, one should look at many people and choose from each person his best point only. For example, one person for politeness, one for bravery, one for the proper way of speaking, one for correct conduct and one for steadiness of mind. Thus, will the model be made.

An apprentice will not be up to his teacher's good points in the world of the arts either but will receive and imitate only his bad ones. This is worthless. There are people who are good at manners but have no uprightness. In imitating someone like this, one is likely to ignore the politeness and imitate only the lack of uprightness. If one perceives a person's good points, he will have a model teacher for anything.

When delivering something like an important letter or other written materials, grasp it firmly in your hand as you go and do not release it once, but hand it over directly to the recipient.

A retainer is a man who remains consistently undistracted twenty-four hours a day, whether he is in the presence of his master or in public. If one is careless during his rest period, the public will see him as being only careless.

Regardless of class, a person who does something beyond his social standing will at some point commit mean or cowardly acts. In the lower classes there are even people who will run away. One should be careful with menials and the like.

There are many people who, by being attached to a martial art and taking apprentices, believe that they have arrived at the full stature of a warrior. But it is a regrettable thing to put forth much effort and, in the end, become an "artist." In artistic technique it is good to learn to the extent that you will not be lacking. In general, a person who is versatile in many things is considered to be vulgar and to have only a broad knowledge of matters of importance.

When something is said to you by the master, whether it is for your good or bad fortune, to withdraw in silence shows perplexity. You should have some appropriate response. It is important to have resolution beforehand.

Moreover, if at the time that you are asked to perform some function you have deep happiness or great pride, it will show exactly as that on your face. This has been seen in many people and is rather unbecoming. But another type of person knows his own defects and thinks, "I'm a clumsy person but I've been asked to do this thing anyway. Now how am I going to go about it? I can see that this is going to be much trouble and cause for concern." Though these words are never said, they will appear on the surface. This shows modesty.

By inconsistency and frivolity, we stray from the Way and show ourselves to be beginners. In this we do much harm.

Learning is a good thing, but more often it leads to mistakes. It is like the admonition of the priest Konan. It is worthwhile just looking at the deeds of accomplished persons for the purpose of knowing our own insufficiencies. But often this does not happen. For the most part, we admire our own opinions and become fond of arguing.

Last year at a great conference there was a certain man who explained his dissenting opinion and said that he was resolved to kill the conference leader if it was not accepted. His motion was passed. After the procedures were over the man said, "Their assent came quickly. I think that they are too weak and unreliable to be counselors to the master."

When an official place is extremely busy and someone comes in thoughtlessly with some business or other, often there are people who will treat him coldly and become angry. This is not good at all. At such times, the etiquette of a samurai is to calm himself and deal with the person in a good manner. To treat a person harshly is the way of middle-class lackeys.

According to the situation, there are times when you must rely on a person for something or other. If this is done repeatedly, it becomes a matter of importuning that person and can be rather rude. If there is something that must be done, it is better not to rely on others.

There is something to be learned from a rainstorm. When meeting with a sudden shower, you try not to pet wet and run quickly along the road. But doing such things as passing under the eaves of houses, you still get wet. When you are resolved from the beginning, you will not be perplexed, though you still get the same soaking. This understanding extends to everything.

In China there was once a man who liked pictures of dragons, and his clothing and furnishings were all designed accordingly. His deep affection for dragons was brought to the attention of the dragon god, and one day a real dragon appeared before his window. It is said that he died of fright. He was probably a man who always spoke big words but acted differently when facing the real thing.

There was a certain person who was a master of the spear. When he was dying, he called his best disciple and spoke his last injunctions:

I have passed on to you all the secret techniques of this school, and there is nothing left to say. If you think of taking on a disciple yourself, then you should practice diligently with the bamboo sword every day. Superiority is not just a matter of secret techniques.

Also, in the instructions of a renga teacher, it was said that the day before the poetry meeting one should calm his mind and look at a collection of poems. This is concentration on one affair. All professions should be done with concentration.

Although the Mean is the standard for all things, in military affairs a man must always strive to outstrip others. According to archery instructions the right and left hands are supposed to be level, but the right hand has a tendency to go higher. They will become level if one will lower the right hand a bit when shooting. In the stories of the elder warriors, it is said that on the battlefield if one wills himself to outstrip warriors of accomplishment, and day and night hopes to strike down a powerful enemy, he will grow indefatigable and fierce of heart and will manifest courage. One should use this principle in everyday affairs too.

There is a way of bringing up the child of a samurai. From the time of infancy, one should encourage bravery and avoid trivially frightening or teasing the child. If a person is affected by cowardice as a child, it remains a lifetime scar. It is a mistake for parents to thoughtlessly make their children dread lightning, or to have them not go into dark places, or to tell them frightening things in order to stop them from crying.

Furthermore, a child will become timid if he is scolded severely.

One should not allow bad habits to form. After a bad habit is ingrained, although you admonish the child he will not improve. As for such things as proper speaking and good manners, gradually make the child aware of them. Let him not know avarice. Other than that, if he is of a normal nature, he should develop well by the way he is brought up.

Moreover, the child of parents who have a bad relationship will be unfilial. This is natural. Even the birds and beasts are affected by what they are used to seeing and hearing from the time they are born. Also, the relationship between father and child may deteriorate because of a mother's foolishness. A mother loves her child above all things and will be partial to the child that is corrected by his father. If she becomes the child's ally, there will be discord between father and son. Because of the shallowness of her mind, a woman sees the child as her support in old age.

You will be tripped up by people when your resolution is lax. Moreover, if at a meeting you are distracted while an- other person is speaking, by your carelessness you may think that he is of your opinion and you will follow along saying, "Of course, of course," even though he is saying something that is contrary to your own feelings, and others will think that you are in agreement with him. Because of this, you should never be distracted even for an instant when meeting with others.

When you are listening to a story or being spoken to, you should be mindful not to be tripped up; and if there is something that you do not agree with, to speak your mind, to show your opponent his error, and to grapple with the situation. Even in unimportant affairs mistakes come from little things. One should be mindful of this. Moreover, it is better not to become acquainted with men about whom you have formerly had some doubts. No matter what you do, they will be people by whom you will be tripped up or taken in, to be certain of this fact you must have much experience.

The saying, "The arts aid the body," is for samurai of other regions. For samurai of the Nabeshima clan the arts bring ruin to the body. In all cases, the person who practices an art is an artist, not a samurai, and one should have the intention of being called a samurai.

When one has the conviction that even the slightest artful ability is harmful to the samurai, all the arts become useful to him. One should understand this sort of thing.

Ordinarily, looking into the mirror and grooming oneself is sufficient for the upkeep of one's personal appearance. This is very important. Most people's personal appearance is poor because they do not look into the mirror well enough.

Training to speak properly can be done by correcting one's speech when at home.

Practice in letter writing goes to the extent of taking care in even one-line letters.

It is good if all the above contain a quiet strength. Moreover, according to what the priest Ryozan heard when he was in the Kamgala area, when one is writing a letter, he should think that the recipient will make it into a hanging scroll.

It is said that one should not hesitate to correct himself when he has made a mistake. If he corrects himself without the least bit of delay, his mistakes will quickly disappear. But when he tries to cover up a mistake, it will become all the more unbecoming and painful. When words that one should not use slip out, if one will speak his mind quickly and clearly, those words will have no effect and he will not be obstructed by worry. If there is, however, someone who blames a person for such a thing, one should be prepared to say something like, "I have explained the reason for my careless speech. There is nothing else to be done if you will not listen to reason. Since I said it unwittingly, it should be the same as if you didn't hear it. No one can evade blame." And one should never talk about people or secret matters. Furthermore, one should only speak according to how he judges his listener's feelings.

The proper manner of calligraphy is nothing other than not being careless, but in this way one's writing will simply be sluggish and stiff. One should go beyond this and depart from the norm. This principle applies to all things.

It is said, "When you would see into a person's heart, become ill." When you are sick or in difficulties, many of those who were friendly or close to you in daily life will become cowards. Whenever anyone is in unhappy circumstances, you should above all inquire after them by visiting or sending some gift. And you should never in your whole life be negligent toward someone from whom you have received a favor.

By such things the consideration of others can be seen. In this world the people who will rely on others when they are in difficulties and afterwards not give them a thought are many.

You cannot tell whether a person is good or bad by his vicissitudes in life. Good and bad fortune are matters of fate. Good and bad actions are Man's Way. Retribution of good and evil is taught simply as a moral lesson.

Because of some business, Morooka Hikoemon was called upon to swear before the gods concerning the truth of a certain matter. But he said, "A samurai's word is harder than metal. Since I have impressed this fact upon myself, what more can the gods and Buddhas do?" and the swearing was cancelled. This happened when he was twenty-six.

Master Ittei said, "Whatever one prays for will be granted. Long ago there were no matsutake mushrooms in our province. Some men who saw them in the Kamigata area prayed that they might grow here, and nowadays they are growing all over Kitagama. In the future I would like to have Japanese cypress grow in our province. As this is something that everyone desires, I predict it for the future. This being so, everyone should pray for it."

When something out of the ordinary happens, it is ridiculous to say that it is a mystery or a portent of something to come. Eclipses of the sun and moon, comets, clouds that flutter like flags, snow in the fifth month, lightning in the twelfth month, and so on, are all things that occur every fifty or one hundred years. They occur according to the evolution of Yin and Yang. The fact that the sun rises in the east and sets in the west would be a mystery, too, if it were not an everyday occurrence.

It is not dissimilar. Furthermore, the fact that something bad always happens in the world when strange phenomena occur is due to people seeing something like fluttering clouds and thinking that something is going to happen. The mystery is created in their minds, and by waiting for the disaster, it is from their very minds that it occurs. The occurrence of mysteries is always by word of mouth.

Calculating people are contemptible. The reason for this is that calculation deals with loss and pain, and the loss and gain mind never stops. Death is considered loss and life is considered gain. Thus, death is something that such a person does not care for, and he is contemptible.

Furthermore, scholars and their like are men who with wit and speech hide their own true cowardice and greed. People often misjudge this.

Lord Naoshige said, "The Way of the Samurai is in desperateness. Ten men or more cannot kill such a man. Common sense will not accomplish great things. Simply become insane and desperate.' "In the Way of the Samurai, if one uses discrimination, he will fall behind. One needs neither loyalty nor devotion, but simply to become desperate in the Way. Loyalty and devotion are of themselves within desperation."

The saying of Shida Kichinosuke, "When there is a choice of either living or dying, as long as there remains nothing behind to blemish one's reputation, it is better to live," is a paradox. He also said, "When there is a choice of either going or not going, it is better not to go." A corollary to this would he, "When there is a choice of either eating or not eating, it is better not to eat. When there is a choice of either dying or not dying, it is better to die."

When meeting calamities or difficult situations, it is not enough to simply say that one is not at all flustered. When meeting difficult situations, one should dash forward bravely and with joy. It is the crossing of a single barrier and is like the saying, "The more the water, the higher the boat."

It is spiritless to think that you cannot attain to that which you have seen and heard the masters attain. The masters are men. You are also a man. If you think that you will be inferior in doing something, you will be on that road very soon. Master Ittei said, "Confucius was a sage because he had the will to become a scholar when he was fifteen years old. He was not a sage because he studied later on." This is the same as the Buddhist maxim, "First intention, then enlightenment."

A warrior should be careful in all things and should dislike to be the least bit worsted. Above all, if he is not careful in his choice of words, he may say things like, "I'm a coward," or "At that time I'd probably run," or "How frightening," or "How painful." These are words that should not be said even in jest, on a whim, or when talking in one's sleep. If a person with understanding hears such things, he will see to the bottom of the speaker's heart. This is something that should be carefully thought about beforehand.

When one's own attitude on courage is fixed in his heart, and when his resolution is devoid of doubt, then when the time comes, he will of necessity be able to choose the right move. This will be manifested by one's conduct and speech according to the occasion. One's word is especially important. It is not for exposing the depths of one's heart. This is something that people will know by one's everyday affairs.

After I took up the attitude of a retainer, I never sat sloppily whether at home or in some other place. Neither did I speak, but if there was something that could not be done properly without words, I made an effort to settle things by putting ten words into one. Yamazaki Kurando was like this.

It is said that even after one's head has been cut off, he can still perform some function. This fact can be known from the examples of Nitta Yoshisada and Ono Doken. How shall one man be inferior to another? Mitani Jokyu said, "Even if a man be sick to death, he can bear up for two or three days."

In the words of the ancients, one should make his decisions within the space of seven breaths. Lord Takanobu said, "If discrimination is long, it will spoil." Lord Naoshige said, "When matters are done leisurely, seven out of ten will turn out badly. A warrior is a person who does things quickly."

When your mind is going hither and thither, discrimination will never be brought to a conclusion. With an intense, fresh, and undelaying spirit, one will make his judgments within the space of seven breaths. It is a matter of being determined and having the spirit to break right through to the other side.

In admonishing the master, if one is not of the proper rank to do so, it shows great loyalty to have someone who is of that rank speak and have the master correct his mistakes. To be on a footing to do this one must be on cordial terms with everyone. If one does this for his own sake, it is simply flattery. One does this, rather, in his concern to support the clan on his own. If one will do it, it can be done.

Bad relations between retired and present rulers, father and son, and elder and younger brothers develop from selfish motives. The proof of this is that there are no such bad relations between master and retainer.

It is unthinkable to be disturbed at something like being ordered to become a ronin. People at the time of Lord Katsushige used to say, "If one has not been a ronin at least seven times, he will not be a true retainer. Seven times down, eight times up."

Men like Narutomi Hyogo have been ronin seven times. One should understand that it is something like being a self- righting doll. The master is also apt to give such orders as a test.

Illnesses and the like become serious because of one's feelings. I was born when my father was seventy-one years old and was hence a rather sickly child. But because I have had the great desire to be of use even in old age, when the chance came, I improved my health and haven't been sick since.

And I have abstained from sex and have consistently taken moxa cautery. There are things that I feel have definitely had effect.

There is a saying that even though one burns up a mamushi seven times, it will return each time to its original form. This is my great hope. I have always been obsessed with one idea: to be able to realize my heart's desire, which is that, though I am born seven times, each time I will be reborn as a retainer of my clan.

Yamamoto Jin'emon once said that it is best for a samurai to have good retainers. Military affairs are not matters for one person alone, regardless of how useful he tries to be. Money is something that one can borrow from people, but a good man cannot suddenly be come by. One should sustain a man kindly and well from the first. And in having retainers it will not do to nourish oneself alone. If you divide what you have and feed your lower ranks, you will be able to hold good men.

A person with a bit of wisdom is one who will criticize the times. This is the basis of disaster. A person who is discreet in speaking will be useful during the good times and will avoid punishment during the bad.

Being superior to others is nothing other than having people talk about your affairs and listening to their opinions. The general run of people settle for their own opinions and thus never excel. Having a discussion with a person is one step in excelling him, A certain person discussed with me the written materials at the clan office. He is better than someone like me in writing and researching. In seeking correction from others, you excel them.

It is bad when one thing becomes two. One should not look for anything else in the Way of the Samurai. It is the same for anything that is called a Way. Therefore, it is inconsistent to hear something of the Way of Confucius or the Way of the Buddha and say that this is the Way of the Samurai. If one understands things in this manner, he should be able to hear about all Ways and be more and more in accord with his own.

For a samurai, a simple word is important no matter where he may be. By just one single word martial valor can be made apparent. In peaceful times words show one's bravery. In troubled times, too, one knows that by a single word his strength or cowardice can be seen. This single word is the flower of one's heart. It is not something said simply with one's mouth.

A warrior should not say something fainthearted even casually. He should set his mind to this beforehand. Even in trifling matters the depths of one's heart can be seen.

No matter what it is, there is nothing that cannot be done. If one manifests the determination, he can move heaven and earth as he pleases. But because man is pluck less, he cannot set his mind to it. Moving heaven and earth without putting forth effort is simply a matter of concentration.

A person who is said to be proficient at the arts is like a fool. Because of his foolishness in concerning himself with just one thing, he thinks of nothing else and thus becomes proficient. He is a worthless person.

Until the age of forty it is best to gather strength. It is appropriate to have settled clown by the age of fifty.

When discussing things with someone, it is best to speak appropriately about whatever the subject may be. No matter how good what you are saying might be, it will dampen the conversation if it is irrelevant.

When someone is giving you his opinion, you should receive it with deep gratitude even though it is worthless. If you don't, he will not tell you the things that he has seen and heard about you again. It is best to both give and receive opinions in a friendly way.

There is a saying that great genius matures late. If something is not brought to fruition over a period of twenty to thirty years, it will not be of great merit. When a retainer is of a mind to do his work hurriedly, he will intrude upon the work of others and will be said to be young but able. He will become over-enthusiastic and will be considered rather rude. He will put on the airs of someone who has done great works, will become a flatterer and insincere, and will be talked about behind his back. In the pursuit of one's development, if he does not make great effort and is not supported by others in his advancement in the world, he will be of no use.

When one is involved in the affairs of a warrior such as being a kaishaku or making an arrest within one's own clan or group, people will notice when the time comes if he has resolved beforehand that no one can take his place. One should always take the attitude of standing above others in martial valor, always feel that he is inferior to no one, and always cultivate his courage.

When on the battlefield, if you try not to let others take the lead and have the sole intention of breaking into the enemy lines, then you will not fall behind others, your mind will become fierce, and you will manifest martial valor. This fact has been passed down by the elders. Furthermore, if you are slain in battle, you should be resolved to have your corpse facing the enemy.

If everyone were in accord and left things to Providence, their hearts would be at ease. If they are not in accord, though they would do acts of righteousness, they lack loyalty. To be at odds with one's companions, to be prone to miss even infrequent meetings, to speak only cantankerous words al come from a shallow foolishness of mind. But thinking of the moment of truth, even though it be unpleasant, one should fix it in his mind to meet people cordially at all times and without distraction, and in a way in which one will not seem bored. Moreover, in this world of uncertainties one is not even sure of the present. It would be worthless to die while being thought ill of by people. Lies and insincerity are unbecoming. This is because they are for self-profit.

Though it is not profitable to have others lead the way, or not to be quarrelsome, or not to be lacking in manners, or to be humble, if one will do things for the benefit of others and meet even those whom he has met often before in a first-time manner, he will have no bad relationships. Manners between husband and wife are not different from this. If one is as discreet in the end as he is in the beginning, there should be no discord.

There is a certain priest who is said to be able to get everything accomplished by means of his cleverness. There is not a monk in Japan today who can oppose him. This is not the least bit strange. There is simply no one who sees through to the foundation of things.

Senility is when one goes about doing only that towards which he is most inclined. One is able to suppress and hide this while his vigor is still strong, but when he weakens, the essential strong points of his nature appear and are a shame to him. This manifests itself in several forms, but there is not a man who does not get senile by the time he reaches sixty. And when one thinks that he will not be senile, he is already so, it can be thought that Master Ittei had a senility of argumentation. As if to show that he alone could support the House of Nabeshima, he went about with a senile appearance to prominent people's houses and chatted amiably with them. At the time, everybody thought that it was reasonable, but thinking about it now, it was senility. For myself, with that good example and the feeling that dotage was overtaking me, I declined to participate at the temple on the thirteenth anniversary of Lord Mitsushige's death, and I have decided to stay more and more indoors. One must get a clear view of what lies ahead.

If one is but secure at the foundation, he will not be pained by departure from minor details or affairs that are contrary to expectation. But in the end, the details of a matter are important. The right and wrong of one's way of doing things are found in trivial matters.

According to a story at the Ryutaiji, there was a master of the Book of Changes in the Kamigata area who said that even if a man is a priest, it is useless to give him rank while he is under the ape of forty. This is because he will make many mistakes. Confucius was not the only man to become unperplexed after reaching the age of forty. Upon reaching the age of forty, both wise and foolish have gone through an appropriate amount of experience and will no longer be perplexed.

Concerning martial valor, merit lies more in dying for one's master than in striking down the enemy. This can be understood from the devotion of Sate Tsugunobu.

When I was young, I kept a "Dairy of Regret" and tried to record my mistakes day by day, but there was never a day when I didn't have twenty or thirty entries. As there was no end to it, I gave up. Even today, when I think about the day's affairs after going to bed, there is never a day when I do not make some blunder in speaking or in some activity. Living without mistakes is truly impossible. But this is something that people who live by cleverness have no inclination to think about.

When reading something aloud, it is best to read from the belly. Reading from one's mouth, one's voice will not endure. This is Nakano Shikibu's teaching.

During happy times, pride and extravagance are dangerous. If one is not prudent in ordinary times, he will not be able to catch up. A person who advances during good times will falter during the bad.

Master Ittei said, "In calligraphy it is progress when the paper, brush and ink are in harmony." Yet they are so wont to be disjointed!

The master took a book from its box. When he opened it there was the smell of drying clove buds.

What is called generosity is really compassion. In the Shin'ei it is written, "Seen from the eye of compassion, there is no one to be disliked. One who has sinned is to be pitied all the more." There is no limit to the breadth and depth of one's heart. There is room enough for all. That we still worship the sages of the three ancient kingdoms is because their compassion reaches us yet today.

Whatever you do should be done for the sake of your master and parents, the people in general, and for posterity. This is great compassion. The wisdom and courage that come from compassion are real wisdom and courage. When one punishes or strives with the heart of compassion, what he does will be limitless in strength and correctness. Doing something for one's own sake is shallow and mean and turns into evil. I understood the matters of wisdom and courage some time ago. I am just now beginning to understand the matter of compassion.

Lord Ieyasu said, "The foundation for ruling the country in peace is compassion, for when one thinks of the people as being his children, the people will think of him as their parent." Moreover, can't it be thought that the names "group parent" and "group child" [i.e., group leader and member] are so called because they are attached to each other by the harmonious hearts of a parent-child relationship?

One can understand that Lord Naoshige's phrase, "A faultfinder will come to be punished by others," came from his compassion. His saying, "Principle is beyond reason," should also be considered compassion. He enthusiastically stated that we should taste the inexhaustible.

The priest Tannen said, "A clever retainer will not advance. However, there are no cases of stupid people coming up in the world either."

This was Nakano Shikibu's opinion.

When one is young, he can often bring on shame for a lifetime by homosexual acts. To have no understanding of this is dangerous. As there is no one to inform young men of this matter, I can give its general outline.

One should understand that a woman is faithful to only one husband. Our feelings go to one person for one lifetime. If this is not so, it is the same as sodomy or prostitution. This is shame for a warrior. Ihara Saikaku has written a famous line that goes, "An adolescent without an older lover is the same as a woman with no husband." But this sort of person is ridiculous.

A young man should test an older man for at least five years, and if he is assured of that person's intentions, then he too should request the relationship. A fickle person will not enter deeply into a relationship and later will abandon his lover.

If they can assist and devote their lives to each other, then their nature can be ascertained. But if one partner is crooked, the other should say that there are hindrances to the relationship and sever it with firmness. If the first should ask what those hindrances are, then one should respond that he will never in his life say. If he should continue to push the matter, one should get angry; if he continues to push even further, cut him down.

Furthermore, the older man should ascertain the younger's real motives in the aforementioned way. If the younger man can devote himself and pet into the situation for five or six years, then it will not be unsuitable.

Above all, one should not divide one's way into two. One should strive in the Way of the Samurai.

Hoshino Ryotetsu was the progenitor of homosexuality in our province, and although it can be said that his disciples were many, he instructed each one individually. Edayoshi Saburozaemon was a man who understood the foundation of homosexuality. Once, when accompanying his master to ado, Ryotetsu asked Saburozaemon, "What have you understood of homosexuality?"

Saburozaemon replied, "It is something both pleasant and unpleasant."

Ryotetsu was pleased and said, "You have taken great pains for some time to be able to say such a thing."

Some years later there was a person who asked Saburozaemen the meaning of the above. He replied, "To lay down one's life for another is the basic principle of homosexuality. If it is not so, it becomes a matter of shame. However, then you have nothing left to lay down for your master. It is therefore understood to be something both pleasant and unpleasant."

Master Ittei said, ' 'If one were to say what it is to do good, in a single word it would be to endure suffering. Not enduring is bad without exception."

Until one reaches the ape of forty it is better to put off wisdom and discrimination and excel in vitality. According to the person and the rank, though a person has passed the age of forty, if he has no vitality, he will pet no response from others.

Recently, a certain person on his way to Edo sent home a detailed letter from the first night's inn. Though he was a person who neglected such things when he was busy, he excelled other people in being as attentive as this.

In the judgment of the elders, a samurai's obstinacy should be excessive. A thing done with moderation may later be judged to be insufficient. I have heard that when one thinks he has gone too far, he will not have erred. This sort of rule should not be forgotten.

When one has made a decision to kill a person, even if it will be very difficult to succeed by advancing straight ahead, it will not do to think about going at it in a long roundabout way. One's heart may slacken, he may miss his chance, and by and large there will be no success. The Way of the Samurai is one of immediacy, and it is best to dash in headlong. When a certain man was going to the sutra readings at the Jissoin in Kawakami, one of his pages got drunk on the ferryboat and began to pester one of the sailors. When they landed on the other side, as the page had drawn his sword, the sailor took a pole and struck him on the head. At that time the other sailors all ran up together carrying oars and were at the point of striking the page down. However, as the master passed by with an air of not knowing what was happening, one of the other pages ran back and apologized to the sailors. Then, pacifying his comrade, he accompanied him home. That night the page who had been drunk learned that his sword was being taken away from him.

Now, first of all, it was an insufficiency on the master's part not to have reproved and pacified the drunken page while they were on the boat. Furthermore, even though his page had acted unreasonably, after he had been struck on the head there was no reason for an apology. The master should have approached the sailor and the drunken page in an apologetic manner and cut them both down. Certainly, he was a spiritless master.

The resolution of the men of former times was deep. Those between the ages of thirteen and sixty went to the front lines. For this reason, men of advanced years hid their age.

For serious affairs that bear directly on oneself, if one does not take care of things by making his own judgment his foundation and breaking through headlong, matters will not be brought to a close. In conferring with people about matters of importance, there may be many cases when your affair is thought lightly of, or when people will not speak of the real circumstances. At such times one must use his own judgment. At any rate, it is sufficient to become a fanatic and choose to throw away one's life. At such a time, if one thinks about doing things well, confusion will soon arise, and he will blunder. In many cases one's downfall may be brought about by an ally who is trying to do something for one's benefit, or one may be killed by his friend's kindness. It is the same as when one requests permission to become a monk.

Lord Naoshige said, "An ancestor's good or evil can be determined by the conduct of his descendants." A descendant should act in a way that will manifest the good in his ancestor and not the bad. This is filial piety.

It is a wretched thing that one's family lineage be thrown into confusion with an adoption based on money alone. Such a thing is immoral from the beginning, but it is extreme wickedness to be thus immoral with the excuse that without doing so one will be unable to afford even today's rice.

When Nakano Shogen committed seppuku, the members of his group gathered at Oki Hyobu's place and said various bad things about him. Hyobu said, "One does not speak bad things about a person after his death. And especially since a person who has received some censure is to be pitied, it is the obligation of a samurai to speak something good of him, no matter how little. There is no doubt that in twenty years Shogen will have the reputation of a faithful retainer." These were truly the words of a seasoned man.

To place one's armor out splendidly is a fine discipline, but it is sufficient if it is simply all accounted for. Fukabori Inosuke 's armor is a good example. Men of high rank and with many retainers will also need such things as money to set aside for campaign use. It is said that Okabe Kunai made bags equaling the number of men in his group, affixed a name to each, and put in the appropriate amount of money for a campaign. This sort of discipline is profound. As for men of low rank, if they cannot make the proper preparation at the time, they should rely on assistance from their group leader. To this extent, it is necessary for the group leader to be on intimate terms with his men beforehand. As for men who are under the master's direction, and especially for those who are with him directly, it is better to be without preparation money. At the time of the summer maneuvers at Osaka, a certain person brought along twelve monme of refined silver and went off with Master Taku Zusho. This, of course, would have been fine if he had simply ridden off early. I think that it is better to dispense with such care.

In carefully scrutinizing the affairs of the past, we find that there are many different opinions about them, and that there are some things that are quite unclear. It is better to regard such things as unknowable. Lord Sanenori once said, "As for the things that we don't understand, there are ways of understanding them. Furthermore, there are some things we understand just naturally, and again some that we can't understand no matter how hard we try. This is interesting."

This is very profound. It is natural that one cannot understand deep and hidden things. Those things that are easily understood are rather shallow.

CHAPTER TWO

It is said that much sake, self-pride and luxury are to be avoided by a samurai, there is no cause for anxiety when you are unhappy, but when you become a little elated, these three things become dangerous. Look at the human condition. It is unseemly for a person to become prideful and extravagant when things are going well. Therefore, it is better to have some unhappiness while one is still young, for if a person does not experience some bitterness, his disposition will not settle down. A person who becomes fatigued when unhappy is useless.

Meeting with people should be a matter of quickly grasping their temperament and reacting appropriately to this person and that. Especially with an extremely argumentative person, after yielding considerably one should argue him down with superior logic, but without sounding harsh, and in a fashion that will allow no resentment to be left afterwards. This is a function of both the heart and words. This was an opinion given by a priest concerning personal encounters.

Dreams are truthful manifestations. When I occasionally have dreams of dying in battle or committing seppuku, if I brace myself with courage, my frame of mind within the dream gradually changes.

This concerns the dream I had on the night of the twenty-seventh day of the fifth month.

If one were to say in a word what the condition of being a samurai is, its basis lies first in seriously devoting one's body and soul to his master. And if one is asked what to do beyond this, it would be to fit oneself inwardly with intelligence, humanity, and courage.' The combining of these three virtues may seem unobtainable to the ordinary person, but it is easy. Intelligence is nothing more than discussing things with others. Limitless wisdom comes from this. Humanity is something done for the sake of others, simply comparing oneself with them and putting them in the fore. Courage is gritting one' s teeth; it is simply doing that and pushing ahead, paying no attention to the circumstances. Anything that seems above these three is not necessary to be known.

As for outward aspects, there are personal appearance, one's way of speaking and calligraphy. And as all of these are daily matters, they improve by constant practice. Basically, one should perceive their nature to be one of quiet strength. If one has accomplished all these things, then he should have a knowledge of our area's history and customs. After that he may study the various arts as recreation. If you think it over, being a retainer is simple. And these days, if you observe people who are even a bit useful, you will see that they have accomplished these three outward aspects.

A certain priest said that if one thoughtlessly crosses a river of unknown depths and shallows, he will die in its currents without ever reaching the other side or finishing his business. This is the same as when one is indiscriminately eager in being a retainer without understanding the customs of the times or the likes and dislikes of the master and, as a result, is of no use and brings ruin upon himself. To try to enter the good graces of the master is unbecoming. One should consider first stepping back and getting some understanding of the depths and shallows and then work without doing anything the master dislikes.

If you attach a number of bags of cloves to your body, you will not be affected by inclemency or colds. Some years ago, Nakano Kazuma returned to this province as a messenger by horse in the dead of winter, and though he was an old man, he was not the least bit in pain. It is said that that was because of his having used cloves. Furthermore, drinking a decoction of the feces from a dappled horse is the way to stop bleeding from an injury received by falling off a horse.

A faultless person is one who withdraws from affairs. This must be done with strength.

There is surely nothing other than the single purpose of the present moment. A man's whole life is a succession of moment after moment. If one fully understands the present moment, there will be nothing else to do, and nothing else to pursue. Live being true to the single purpose of the moment.

Everyone lets the present moment slip by, then looks for it as though he thought it were somewhere else. No one seems to have noticed this fact. But grasping this firmly, one must pile experience upon experience. And once one has come to this understanding, he will be a different person from that point on, though he may not always bear it in mind.

When one understands this settling into single-mindedness well, his affairs will thin out. Loyalty is also contained within this single-mindedness.

It is said that what is called "the spirit of an ape' ' is seine- thing to which one cannot return. That this spirit gradually dissipates is due to the world's coming to an end. In the same way, a single year does not have just spring or summer. A single day, too, is the same.

For this reason, although one would like to change today's world back to the spirit of one hundred years or more ago, it cannot be done. Thus, it is important to make the best out of every generation. This is the mistake of people who are attached to past generations. They have no understanding of this point.

On the other hand, people who only know the disposition of the present day and dislike the ways of the past are too lax.

Be true to the thought of the moment and avoid distraction. Other than continuing to exert yourself, enter into nothing else, but go to the extent of living single thought by single thought.

The brave men of old times were for the most part rowdies. As they were of the disposition to be out running amuck, their vitality was strong, and they were brave. When I had doubts about this and asked, Tsunetomo said, "It is understandable that since their vitality was strong, they were generally rough and went about running amuck. These days rowdiness is nonexistent because man's vitality has weakened. Vitality has fallen behind, but man's character has improved. Valor is yet a different thing. Although men have become gentle these days because of the lack of vitality, this does not mean that they are inferior in being crazy to die. That has nothing to do with vitality."

Concerning the military tactics of Lord Naoshige, Ushida Shoemon said that it was characteristic of his retainers to face a situation with no previous knowledge of what was to happen, and for him to freely bring everything to a finish by a single word. When he was at the point of passing from this world, he said nothing, even when his chief retainers came to see him.

Once Lord Ieyasu gamed nothing in a battle, but in a later judgment it was said, "Ieyasu is a general of great courage. Of his retainers who died in battle, not one of them died with his back turned. They all died facing the enemy lines." Since a warrior's daily frame of mind is manifested even after death, it is something that can bring shame to him.

As Yasuda Ukyo said about offering up the last wine cup, only the end of things is important. One's whole life should be like this. When guests are leaving, the mood of being reluctant to say farewell is essential. If this mood is lacking, one will appear bored, and the day and evening's conversation will disappear. In all dealings with people, it is essential to have a fresh approach. One should constantly give the impression that he is doing something exceptional. It is said that this is possible with but a little understanding.

Our bodies are given life from the midst of nothingness. Existing where there is nothing is the meaning of the phrase, "Form is emptiness." That all things are provided for by nothingness is the meaning of the phrase, "Emptiness is form.'" One should not think that these are two separate things.

Uesugi Kenshin said, "I never knew about winning from beginning to end, but only about not being behind in a situation." This is interesting. A retainer will be dumbfounded if he is behind in a situation. In each and every instance one's function or responsiveness will not be shallow if he is not behind.

One should be wary of talking on end about such subjects as learning, morality, or folklore in front of elders or people of rank. It is disagreeable to listen to.

In the Kamigata area they have a sort of tiered lunch box they use for a single day when flower viewing. Upon returning, they throw them away, trampling them underfoot. As might be expected, this is one of my recollections of the capital [Kyoto]. The end is important in all things.

While walking along the road together, Tsunetomo said, "Is not man like a well-operated puppet? It is a piece of dexterous workmanship that he can run, jump, leap, and even talk though there are no strings attached. Will we not be guests at next year's Ben Festival? This world is vanity indeed. People always forget this."

It was once said to one of the young lords that "right now" is "at that time, " and "at that time" is "right now." One will miss the occasion if he thinks that these two are different. For example, if one were called before the master to explain something right away, he would most likely be perplexed. This is proof that he understands the two to be different. If, however, a person makes "right now" and "at that time" one, though he will never be an advisor to the master, still he is a retainer, and in order to be able to say something clearly, whether it be in front of the master, the elders or even the shogun at Edo Castle, it should be practiced beforehand in the corner of one's bedroom.

All things are like this. Accordingly, one should inquire into things carefully. It is the same for martial training as for official business. When one attempts to concentrate things in this manner, won't daily negligence and today's lack of resolve be understood?

Even though one has made some blunder in governmental work, it can probably be excused by pleading clumsiness or inexperience. But what kind of excuse may be given for the failure of the men who were involved in this recent unexpected event?" Master Jin'emon always used to say, "It is enough if a warrior is simply a stalwart," and this is just such a case. If one felt that such a failure were a mortification, it would be the least he could do to cut open his stomach, rather than live on in shame with a burning in his breast and the feeling that he had no place to go, and, as his luck as a warrior had run out, he was no longer able to function quickly and had been given a bad name. But if one regretted losing his life and reasoned that he should live because such a death would be useless, then for the next five, ten or twenty years of his life, he would be pointed at from behind and covered with shame. After his death his corpse would be smeared with disgrace, his guiltless descendants would receive his dishonor for having been born in his line, his ancestors' name would be dragged down, and all the members of his family would be blemished. Such circumstances are truly regrettable.

If one has no earnest daily intention, does not consider what it is to be a warrior even in his dreams, and lives through the day idly, he can be said to be worthy of punishment.

Presumably it can be said that a man who has been cut down was lacking in ability and had run out of luck as a warrior. The man who cut him down, compelled by unavoidable circumstances and feeling that there was nothing else to be done, also put his life on the line, and thus there should be no evidence of cowardice. Being short-tempered is inappropriate, but it cannot be said that two men who face each other are cowards. In this recent event, however, the men who lived and covered themselves with shame were not true warriors.

One should every day think over and make an effort to implant in his mind the saying, "At that time is right now." It is said that it is strange indeed that anyone is able to pass through life by one means or another in negligence. Thus, the Way of the Samurai is, morning after morning, the practice of death, considering whether it will be here or be there, imagining the most slightly way of dying, and putting one's mind firmly in death. Although this may be a most difficult thing, if one will do it, it can be done. There is nothing that one should suppose cannot be done.

Moreover, the influence of words is important in military affairs. It would have been best for stopping the man in this recent event, too. When the situation is too much, one may either cut the man down, or, if the man is escaping, yell something like, "Don't run I Only cowards run!" and thus, according to what the situation demands, achieve one's goals by the influence of words. There was a certain man who was said to be good at judging men's dispositions and formerly had everyone's attention, and he was able to handle such cases. This is proof that "right now" is no different from "when the time comes." The position of yokoza no yari is another example of this.* It is something that should be made one's aim beforehand.

The things to be deeply considered beforehand are many. If there is someone who has killed a man in the lord's mansion and has managed to escape, as one does not know whether he may still be swinging his sword and advancing toward the room next to the lord's, he should cut the man down. Indeed, one may be blamed later in an investigation as a confederate of the killer, or as someone who had a grudge against him. But at that time, one should think only of cutting the man down and not anticipate later blame.

Even if one's head were to be suddenly cut off, he should be able to do one more action with certainty. The last moments of Nitta Yoshisada are proof of this. Had his spirit been weak, he would have fallen the moment his head was severed. Recently, there is the example of Ono Doken. These actions occurred because of simple determination. With martial valor, if one becomes like a revengeful ghost and shows great determination, though his head is cut off, he should not die.

Whether people be of high or low birth, rich or poor, old, or young, enlightened, or confused, they are all alike in that they will one day die. It is not that we don't know that we are going to die, but we grasp at straws. While knowing that we will die someday, we think that all the others will die before us and that we will be the last to go. Death seems a long way off.

Is this not shallow thinking? It is worthless and is only a joke within a dream. It will not do to think in such a way and be negligent. Insofar as death is always at one's door, one should make sufficient effort and act quickly.

It is good to carry some powdered rouge in one's sleeve. It may happen that when one is sobering up or waking from sleep, his complexion may be poor. At such a time it is good to take out and apply some powdered rouge.

There are times when a person gets carried away and talks on without thinking much. But this can be seen by observers when one's mind is flippant and lacking truth. After such an occasion it is best to come face to face with the truth and express it. The truth will then be arrived at in one's own heart too. Even when greeting someone lightly, one should consider the circumstances and after deliberation speak in a way that will not injure the man's feelings.

Furthermore, if there is a person who is criticizing the Way of the Samurai or one's own province, one should speak with him severely, without the least bit of ceremony. One must be resolved in advance.

Although a person who excels in an art regards others as competitors, last year Hyodo Sachu gave up the title of Master of Renga to Yamaguchi Shochin. A praiseworthy act.

The priest Tannen used to hang up wind-bells but said, "It's not because I like the sound. I hang them in order to know the wind conditions in the event of fire, for that is the only worry in having a large temple." When the wind blew, he himself walked about at night. Throughout his whole life the fire in his brazier was never out, and he always put a paper lantern and lighter by his pillow. He said, ' 'People are flustered during an emergency, and there is no one to quickly strike a light."

If one makes a distinction between public places and one's sleeping quarters, or between being on the battlefield and on the tatami, when the moment comes there will not be time for making amends. There is only the matter of constant awareness. If it were not for men who demonstrate valor on the tatami, one could not find them on the battlefield either.

Bravery and cowardice are not things that can be conjectured in times of peace. They are in different categories.

Though it may be said that the gods dislike impurity, if one thinks a bit, he will see that he has not been negligent in his daily worship. Thus, one's previous faithfulness has been exactly for the sake of praying for good fortune in such times as when one is barbed in blood and climbing over the dead. At such a time, if it is a god that turns back when one is defiled, then one should know clearly that praying is ineffective and should worship regardless of defilement.

At times of great trouble or disaster, one word will suffice. At times of happiness, too, one word will be enough. And when meeting or talking with others, one word will do. One should think well and then speak. This is clear and firm, and one should learn it with no doubts. It is a matter of putting forth one's whole effort and having the correct attitude previously. This is very difficult to explain but is something that everyone should work on in his heart. If a person has not learned this in his heart, it is not likely that he will understand it.

Human life is truly a short affair. It is better to live doing the things that you like. It is foolish to live within this dream of a world seeing unpleasantness and doing only things that you do not like. But it is important never to tell this to young people as it is something that would be harmful if incorrectly understood.

Personally, I like to sleep. And I intend to appropriately confine myself more and more to my living quarters and pass my life away sleeping.

I had a dream on the night of the twenty-eighth day of the twelfth month in the third year of Shotoku. The content of the dream changed gradually to the extent that I strengthened my will. The condition of a person is revealed by his dreams. It would be good to make companions of your dreams and to put forth effort.

Shame and repentance are like upsetting a pot of water. When a certain friend of mine listened to the way that a man who had stolen his sword ornament confessed, he felt compassion. If one rectifies his mistakes, their traces will soon disappear.

According to what the Buddhist priest Kaion said, a person becomes more and more prideful if he gains a little understanding because he thinks he knows his own limits and weak points. However, it is a difficult thing to truly know one's own limits and weak points.

At a glance, every individual's own measure of dignity is manifested just as it is. There is dignity in personal appearance. There is dignity in a calm aspect. There is dignity in a paucity of words. There is dignity in flawlessness of manners. There is dignity in solemn behavior. And there is dignity in deep insight and a clear perspective.

These are all reflected on the surface. But in the end, their foundation is simplicity of thought and tautness of spirit.

Covetousness, anger, and foolishness are things to sort out well. When bad things happen in the world, if you look at them comparatively, they are not unrelated to these three things. Looking comparatively at the good things, you will see that they are not excluded from wisdom, humanity, and bravery.

This is according to what Nakano Kazuma Toshiaki said. There are people who feel that using old utensils for the Tea Ceremony is coarse, and that it is better to use new, clean utensils. There are also people who are wont to use old materials because of their lack of gaudiness. Both are mistaken. Old utensils, although they are things that are used by the humble, are also used by the higher classes because of their value. Their value is revered.

A retainer is just like this. A person rises from the humble to the higher classes because he has value. At the same time, to feel that a person of no family cannot do the same work as one of higher family, or that a man who has heretofore been only a foot soldier should not be allowed to become a leader, is entirely wrong thinking. As for a person who has risen from the humble, his value should be prized and especially respected, even more than that of a person who was born into his class.

My father Jin'emon said that when he was young, he was taken from time to time to the entrance of the Chinese settlement in order to be exposed to the atmosphere of the city and to become used to people. From the time he was five years old he was sent as family representative to various people's homes, and in order to make him strong he was made to put on a warrior's straw sandals and visit the temples of his ancestors from the time he was seven.

It is said that one will not be able to do great works if he does not behave with some reserve towards his master, the chief retainers, and elders. What is done casually and freely will not work out well. It is a matter of attitude.

It is unfitting that one be ignorant of the history and origins of his clan and its retainers. But there are times when extensive knowledge becomes a hindrance. One should use discretion. Knowing the circumstances can be an obstruction in everyday affairs, too. One should use discretion.

It is written that the priest Shungaku said, "In just refusing to retreat from something one gains the strength of two men." This is interesting. Something that is not done at that time and at that place will remain unfinished for a lifetime. At a time when it is difficult to complete matters with the strength of a single man, one will bring it to a conclusion with the strength of two. If one thinks about it later, he will be negligent all his life.

"Stamp quickly and pass through a wall of iron" is another interesting phrase. To quickly break in and stamp through directly is the first step of celerity. In connection with this, Hideyoshi can be thought of as the only man who has grasped solidly the chance of a lifetime since the creation of Japan.

People who talk on and on about matters of little importance probably have some complaint in the back of their mind. But in order to be ambiguous and to hide this they repeat what they are saving over and over. To hear something like this causes doubt to arise in one's breast.

One should be careful and not say things that are likely to cause trouble at the time. When some difficulty arises in this world, people get excited, and before one knows it the matter is on everyone's lips. This is useless. If worse comes to worse, you may become the subject of gossip, or at least you will have made enemies by saying something unnecessary and will have created ill will. It is said that at such a time it is better to stay at home and think of poetry.

To talk about other people's affairs is a great mistake. To praise them, too, is unfitting. In any event, it is best to know your own ability well, to put forth effort in your endeavors, and to be discreet in speech.

The heart of a virtuous person has settled down and he does not rush about at things. A person of little merit is not at peace but walks about making trouble and is in conflict with all.

It is a good viewpoint to see the world as a dream. When you have something like a nightmare, you will wake up and tell yourself that it was only a dream. It is said that the world we live in is not a bit different from this.

People with intelligence will use it to fashion things both true and false and will try to push through whatever they want with their clever reasoning. This is injury from intelligence. Nothing you do will have effect if you do not use truth.

In affairs like lawsuits or even in arguments, by losing quickly one will lose in fine fashion. It is like sumo [wrestling]. If one thinks only of winning, a sordid victory will be worse than a defeat. For the most part, it becomes a squalid defeat.

Feeling deeply the difference between oneself and others, bearing ill will and falling out with people, these things come from a heart that lacks compassion. If one wraps up everything with a heart of compassion, there will be no coming into conflict with people.

A person who knows but a little will put on an air of knowledge. This is a matter of inexperience.

When someone knows something well, it will not be seen in his manner. This person is genteel.

When going someplace for a talk or something similar, it is best to let the person know ahead of time, and then go. To go without knowing whether the other party is busy, or when he has some particular anxiety, is awkward. There is nothing that surpasses not going where you have not been invited. Good friends are rare. Even if someone is invited somewhere, he should use understanding. It is difficult to feel deeply the sensitivities of people other than those who go out only rarely. Fiascos at pleasure gatherings are numerous.

However, you should not be brusque towards a person who has come to visit, even if you are busy.

It is bad to carry even a good thing too far. Even concerning things such as Buddhism, Buddhist sermons, and moral lessons, talking too much will bring harm.

The late Jin'emon said that it is better not to bring up daughters. They are a blemish to the family name and a shame to the parents. The eldest daughter is special, but it is better to disregard the others.

The priest Keiho related that Lord Aki once said that martial valor is a matter of becoming a fanatic. I thought that this was surprisingly in accord with my own resolve and thereafter became more and more extreme in my fanaticism.

The late Nakano Kazuma said that the original purpose of the Tea Ceremony is to cleanse the six senses. For the eyes there are the hanging scroll and flower arrangement. For the nose there is the incense. For the ears there is the sound of the hot water. For the mouth there is the taste of the tea. And for the hands and feet there is the correctness of term. When the five senses have thus been cleansed, the mind will of itself be purified. The Tea Ceremony will cleanse the mind when the mind is clogged up. I do not depart from the heart of the Tea Ceremony for twenty-four hours a day, yet this is absolutely not a matter of tasteful living. Moreover, the tea utensils are something that should be in accord with one's social position.

In the poem, "Under the deep snows in the last village/ Last night numerous branches of plum blossomed," the opulence of the phrase "numerous branches" was changed to "a single branch." It is said that this "single branch" contains true tranquility.

When intimate friends, allies, or people who are indebted to you have done some wrong, you should secretly reprimand them and intervene between them and society in a good manner. You should erase a person's bad reputation and praise him as a matchless ally and one man in a thousand. If you wilt thus reprimand a person in private and with good understanding, his blemish will heal, and he will become good. If you praise a person, people's hearts will change, and an ill reputation will go away of itself. It is important to have the single purpose of handling all things with compassion and doing things well.

A certain person said the following.

There are two kinds of dispositions, inward and outward, and a person who is lacking in one or the other is worthless. It is, for example, like the blade of a sword, which one should sharpen well and then put in its scabbard, periodically taking it out and knitting one's eyebrows as in an attack, wiping of the blade, and then placing it in its scabbard again.

If a person has his sword out all the time, he is habitually swinging a naked blade; people will not approach him, and he will have no allies.

If a sword is always sheathed, it will become rusty, the blade will dull, and people will think as much of its owner.

One cannot accomplish things simply with cleverness. One must take a broad view. It will not do to make rash judgments concerning good and evil. However, one should not be sluggish. It is said that one is not truly a samurai if he does not make his decisions quickly and break right through to completion.

Once, when a group of five or six pages were traveling to the capital together in the same boat, it happened that their boat struck a regular ship late at night. Five or six seamen from the ship leapt aboard and loudly demanded that the pages give up their boat's anchor, in accord with the seaman's code. Hearing this, the pages ran forward yelling, "The seaman's code is something for people like you! Do you think that we samurai are going to let you take equipment from a boat carrying warriors? We will cut you down and throw you into the sea to the last man!" With that, all the seamen fled back to their own ship.

At such a time, one must act like a samurai. For trifling occasions, it is better to accomplish things simply by yelling. By making something more significant than it really is and missing one's chance, an affair will not be brought to a close and will be no accomplishment at all.

A certain person who came up with a cash shortage when closing out an account book sent a letter to his section leader saying, "It is regrettable to have to commit seppuku over a matter of money. As you are my section leader, please send some funds." Since this was reasonable, the balance was provided, and the matter was closed. It is said that even wrongdoings can be managed without detection.

By being impatient, matters are damaged and great works cannot be done. If one considers something not to be a matter of time, it will be done surprisingly quickly. Times change. Think about the world fifteen years from now. It should be rather different, but if one were to look into a book of prophecies, I imagine that it would not be that different. In the passing fifteen years, not one of the useful men of today will be left. And even if men who are young now come forth, probably less than half will make it. Worth gradually wanes. For example, if there were a shortage of gold, silver would become treasure, and if there were a shortage of silver, copper would be valued. With changing times and the waning of men's capacities, one would be of suitable worth even if he put forth only slight effort. Something like fifteen years is the space of a dream. If a man but takes care of his health, in the end he will have accomplished his purpose and will be a valuable person. Certainly, in a period when masters are many, one must put forth considerable effort. But at the time when the world is sliding into a decline, to excel is easy.

To put forth great effort in correcting a person's bad habits is the way it should be done. One should be like the digger wasp. It is said that even with an adopted child, if you teach him continually so that he will resemble you, he surely will.

If your strength is only that which comes from vitality, your words and personal conduct will appear to be in accord with the Way, and you will be praised by others. But when you question yourself about this, there will be nothing to be said. The last line of the poem that goes, "When your own heart asks," is the secret principle of all the arts. It is said that it is a good censor.

When you are listening to the stories of accomplished men and the like, you should listen with deep sincerity, even if it's something about which you already know. If in listening to the same thing ten or twenty times it happens that you come to an unexpected understanding, that moment will be very special. Within the tedious talk of old folks are their meritorious deeds.

CHAPTER THREE

Lord Naoshige once said, "There is nothing felt quite so deeply as giri. There are times when someone like a cousin dies, and it is not a matter of shedding tears. But we may hear of someone who lived fifty or a hundred years ago, of whom we know nothing and who has no family ties with us whatsoever, and yet from a sense giri shed tears."

When Lord Naoshige was passing by a place called Chiriku, someone said to him, ' 'In this place there lives a man who is over ninety years old. Since this man is so fortunate, why don't you stop and see him?" Naoshige heard this and said, "How could anyone be more pitiful than this man? How many of his children and grandchildren do you suppose he has seen fall before his very eyes? Where is the good fortune in that?"

It seems that he did not stop to see the man.

When Lord Naoshige was speaking to his grandson, Lord Motoshige, he said, "No matter whether one be of high or low rank, a family line is something that will decline when its trine has come. If one tries to keep it from going to ruin at that time, it will have an unsightly finish. If one thinks that the time has come, it is best to let it go down with good grace. Doing so, he may even cause it to be maintained."

It is said that Motoshige's younger brother heard this from him.

CHAPTER FOUR

When Nabeshima Tadanao was fifteen years old, a manservant in the kitchen committed some rude act and a foot soldier was about to beat him, but in the end the servant cut the soldier down. The clan elders deemed the death sentence appropriate, saying that the man had in the first place erred in matters concerning the ranks of men, and that he had also shed the blood of his opponent. Tadanao heard this and said, "Which is worse, to err in matters concerning the ranks of men or to stray from the Way of the Samurai?"

The elders were unable to answer. Then Tadanao said, "I have read that when the crime itself is unclear, the punishment should be light. Put him in confinement for a while."

Once, when Lord Katsushige was hunting at Shiroishi, he shot a large boar. Everyone came running up to see it and said, "Well, well. You have brought down an uncommonly large one!" Suddenly the boar got up and dashed into their midst. All of them fled in confusion, but Nabeshima Matabet drew his sword and finished it off. At that point Lord Katsushige covered his face with his sleeve and said, "It sure is dusty." This was presumably because he did not want to see the spectacle of his flustered men.

When Lord Katsushige was young, he was instructed by his father, Lord Naoshige, "For practice in cutting, execute some men who have been condemned to death." Thus, in the place that is now within the western gate, ten men were lined up, and Katsushige continued to decapitate one after another until he had executed nine of them. When he came to the tenth, he saw that the man was young and healthy and said, "I'm tired of cutting now. I'll spare this man's life." And the man's life was saved.

Lord Katsushige always used to say that there are four kinds of retainers. They are the "quick, then lapping," the "lagging, then quick," the "continually quick," and the "continually lagging."

The "continually quick" are men who when given orders will undertake their execution quickly and settle the matter well. Fukuchi Kichizaemon and the like resemble this type.

The "lagging, then quick" are men who, though lacking in understanding when given orders, prepare quickly and bring the matter to a conclusion. I suppose that Nakano Kazuma and men similar are like this.

The "quick, then lagging" are men who when given orders seem to be going to settle things but in their preparation take time and procrastinate. There are many people like this.

Other than these, one could say that the rest are "continually lagging."

CHAPTER SIX

When Lord Takanobu was at the Battle of Bungo, a messenger came from the enemy camp bearing's sake and food. Takanobu wanted to partake of this quickly, but the men at his side stopped him, saying, "Presents from the enemy are likely to be poisoned. This is not something that a general should eat."

Takanobu heard them out and then said, "Even if it is poisoned, how much of an effect would that have on things? Call the messenger here!" He then broke open the barrel right in front of the messenger, drank three large cups of sake, offered the messenger one too, gave him a reply, and sent him back to his camp.

Takagi Akifusa turned against the Ryuzoji clan, appealed to Maeda Iyo no kami Iesada, and was sheltered by him. Akifusa was a warrior of matchless valor and was an accomplished and agile swordsman. His retainers were Ingazaemon and Fudozaemon, stalwarts in no way inferior, and they left Akifusa's side neither day nor night. Thus, it happened that a request was sent from Lord Takanobu to Iesada to kill Akifusa. At one point, when Akifusa was seated on the veranda having Ingazaemon wash his feet, Iesada came running up behind him and struck off his head, before his head fell, Akifusa drew out his short sword and turned to strike but cut off Ingazaemon's head. The two heads fell into the wash basin together. Akifusa's head then rose into the midst of those present. This was the sort of magic technique that he consistently had.

The priest Tannen used to say in his daily talks that: A monk cannot fulfill the Buddhist Way if he does not manifest compassion without and persistently store up courage within. And if a warrior does not manifest courage on the outside and hold enough compassion within his heart to burst his chest, he cannot become a retainer. Therefore, the monk pursues courage with the warrior as his model, and the warrior pursues the compassion of the monk.

I traveled about for many years and met men of wisdom but never found the means to the pursuit of knowledge. Therefore, whenever I heard of a man of courage in one place or another, I would go and look for him regardless of the hardships on the way. I have learned clearly that these stories of the Way of the Samurai have been an aid on the road to Buddhism. Now a warrior with his armor will rush into the enemy camp, making that armor his strength. Do you suppose that a monk with a single rosary can dash into the midst of spears and long swords, armed with only meekness and compassion? If he does not have great courage, he will do no dashing at all. As proof of this, the priest offering the incense at a great Buddhist memorial service may tremble, and this is because he has no courage.

Things like kicking a man back from the dead, or pulling all living creatures out of hell, are all matters of courage. Nevertheless, monks of recent times all entertain false ideas and desire to become laudably gentle; there are none who complete the Way. Furthermore, among warriors there are some cowards who advance Buddhism. These are regrettable matters. It is a great mistake for a young samurai to learn about Buddhism. The reason is that he will see things in two ways. A person who does not set himself in just one direction will be of no value at all. It is fine for retired old men to learn about Buddhism as a diversion, but if a warrior makes loyalty and filial piety one load, and courage and compassion another, and carries these twenty-four hours a day until his shoulders wear out, he will be a samurai.

In one's morning and evening worship, and as one goes about his day, he had best recite the name of his master. It is not a bit different from the Buddha's names and holy words. Furthermore, one should be in harmony with his family gods. These are matters of the strength of one's fate. Compassion is like a mother who nurtures one's fate. Examples of the ruin of merciless warriors who were brave alone are conspicuous in both past and present.

There was a certain point in the conversation when a retainer of Lord Nabeshima Naohiro said, "There are no men here upon whom the master can truly rely. Although I am consistently useless, I am the only one who would throw away his life for you."

It is said that Lord Naohiro got outrageously angry, saying, "Among our retainers there is not a one who holds his life in regret! You are talking arrogance!" and he was at the point of striking him when the man was pulled away by others who were there.

Once when Master Tanesada, the founder of the China family, was coming by sea to the island of Shikoku, a strong wind began blowing and the boat was damaged. The boat was saved from sinking by abalone gathering together and covering over the damaged sections. From that time on none of the China family nor any of its retainers ate abalone. If one of them mistakenly ate one, it is said that his body was covered with boils in the shape of abalone.

At the fall of the castle at Arima, on the twenty-eighth day in the vicinity of the inmost citadel, Mitsuse Gender sat down on a levee between the fields. When Nakano Shintohi passed by and asked the reason for this, Mitsuse replied, "I have abdominal pains and can't go a step farther. I have sent the members of my group ahead, so please take command." This situation was reported by the overseer, pronounced to be a case of cowardice, and Mitsuse was ordered to commit seppuku.

Long ago, abdominal pains were called "cowardice grass." This is because they come suddenly and render a person immobile.

At the time of Lord Nabeshima Naohiro's death, Lord Mitsushige forbade Naohiro 's retainers the practice of tsuifuku. His messenger went to Naohiro's mansion and made the declaration, but those who received this news could in no way agree to it. From their midst Ishimaru Uneme (later called Seizaemon) spoke from the lowest seat, "It is improper for me as a younger person to speak out, but I think that what Lord Katsushige has said is reasonable. As a person who received the master's care when I was young, I had whole- heartedly decided on tsuifuku. But hearing Lord Katsushige's dictum and being convinced of his reasoning, no matter what the others may do, I am giving up the idea of tsuifuku and will serve the master's successor." Hearing this, the others all followed suit.

Once Lord Masaie was playing shogi with Lord Hideyoshi and there were a number of daimyo watching. When it came time to withdraw, although Lord Masaie could stand, his feet were numb, and he could not walk. He made his withdrawal crawling away, causing everyone to laugh. Because Lord Masaie was big and obese, he was not ordinarily able to be on his knees. After this event he thought it would not be fitting to be in attendance anymore and began refusing such duties.

Nakano Uemonnosuke Tadaaki was killed on the twelfth day of the eighth month in the sixth year of Eiroku, at the time of the fight between Master Goto and Master Hirai of Suko on the island of Kabashima in the Kishima district. When Uemonnosuke was leaving for the front lines, he emgraced his son Shikibu (later called Jin'emon) in the garden and, although Shikibu was very young, said, "When you grow up, win honor in the Way of the Samurai!"

Even when the children in his family were very young, Yamamoto Jin'emon would draw near to them and say, "Grow up to be a great stalwart, and be of good use to your master." He said, "It is good to breathe these things into their ears even when they are too young to understand."

When Ogawa Toshikiyo's legitimate son Sahei Kiyoji died as a youth, there was one young retainer who galloped up to the temple and committed seppuku.

When Taku Nagato no kami Yasuyori passed away, Kola Yataemon said that he had been unable to repay the master's kindness and committed seppuku.

CHAPTER SEVEN

Narutomi Hyogo said, "What is called winning is defeating one's allies. Defeating one's allies is defeating oneself and defeating oneself is vigorously overcoming one's own body.

"It is as though a man were in the midst of ten thousand allies but not a one were following him. If one hasn't previously mastered his mind and body, he will not defeat the enemy."

During the Shimabara Rebellion, his armor being still at the encampment, Shugyo Echizen no kami Tanenao participated in the fight dressed only in hakama and haori. It is said that he died in battle in this attire.

At the time of the attack on the castle at Shimabara, Tazaki Geki was wearing very resplendent armor. Lord Katsushige was not pleased by this, and after that every time he saw something showy, he would say, "That's just like Geki's armor."

In the light of this story, military armor and equipment that are showy can be seen as being weak and having no strength. By them one can see through the wearer's heart.

When Nabeshima wizen no kami Tadanao died, his attendant Ezoe Kinbei took his remains and had them consecrated at Mt. Kola. Then, confining himself in a hermitage, he carved a statue of his master and another of himself doing reverence before the master. On the first anniversary of Tadanao's death, he returned to his home and committed tsuifuku. Later the statue was taken from Mt. Koya and was placed at the Kodenji.

In the generation of Lord Mitsushige, Oishi Kosuke was at first a foot soldier serving at the side of his master. Whenever Lord Mitsushige was making the trip for his alternate year residence in Edo, Kosuke would make the rounds around the sleeping quarters of his master, and if he thought a certain area to be insecure, he would spread a straw mat and pass through the night awake by himself. In rainy weather he would simply wear a bamboo hat and an oilpaper raincoat and would stand watch while being pelted by the rain. It is said that to the end he never spent a single night in negligence.

When Oishi Kosuke was an uchitonin, a mysterious person sneaked into the area of the maids' chambers late at night.' There was a great commotion from upstairs to down and men and women of all ranks were running about; only Kosuke was not to be seen. While the senior ladies in waiting were searching about, Kosuke yanked his sword from its scabbard and waited quietly in the room next to the master's bedchamber. As all was in confusion, he had felt apprehension for the master and was there to protect him. Because of this it was said that his viewpoint was quite different.

The man who had sneaked in was Narutomi Kichibei. He and his accomplice Hamada Ichizaemon were condemned to death for adultery.

Once when Lord Katsushige was hunting at Nishime, for some reason he got very angry. He drew his sword from his obi, scabbard, and all, and began beating Soejima Zennojo with it, but his hand slipped, and his sword fell into a ravine. Zennojo, in order to stay with the sword, fumbled down into the ravine and picked it up. This done, he stuck the sword in his lapel, crawled up the precipice, and just as he was, offered the sword to his master. In terms of quick-mindedness and reserve this was matchless resource.

Once when Master Sane Ukyo was crossing over the Takao River, the bridge was being repaired and there was one large piling that could not be pulled up. Master Ukyo dismounted, grasped the piling firmly, pave a shout, and began to pull it up. There was a tremendous sound, and although he was able to pull it up to his own height, it would go no further and thereupon sank. After he returned home, he became sick and suddenly died.

At the time of the funeral at the temple in Jobaru, when the funeral procession crossed the Takao Bridge, the corpse leapt from the casket and fell into the river. A sixteen-year- old acolyte from the Shufukuji immediately jumped into the river and took hold of the dead body. Everyone then ran down into the river and pulled up the corpse. The head monk was very impressed and instructed the other acolytes to be guided by this young man. It is said that he later became a very famous monk.

Yamamoto Kichizaemon was ordered by his father Jin'-emon to cut down a dog at the age of five, and at the age of fifteen he was made to execute a criminal. Everyone, by the time they were fourteen or fifteen, was ordered to do a beheading without fail. When Lord Katsushige was young, he was ordered by Lord Naoshige to practice killing with a sword. It is said that at that time he was made to cut down more than ten men successively.

A long time ago this practice was followed, especially in the upper classes, but today even the children of the lower classes perform no executions, and this is extreme negligence. To say that one can do without this sort of thing, or that there is no merit in killing a condemned man, or that it is a crime, or that it is defiling, is to make excuses. In short, can it not be thought that because a person's martial valor is weak, his attitude is only that of trimming his nails and being attractive?

If one investigates into the spirit of a man who finds these things disagreeable, one sees that this person gives himself over to cleverness and excuse making not to kill because he feels unnerved. But Naoshige made it his orders exactly because this is something that must be done.

Last year I went to the Kase Execution Grounds to try my hand at beheading, and I found it to be an extremely good feeling. To think that it is unnerving is a symptom of cowardice.

Among the pageboys in forelocks in Lord Mitsushige's retinue, one Tomoda Shozaemon was in attendance. A rather wanton fellow, he fell in love with a leading actor of the theater by the name of Tamon Shozaemon and changed both his name and his crest to that of the actor. Completely abandoning himself to this affair, he spent everything he had and lost all his clothing and furnishings. And at length, when he had exhausted all his means, he stole Mawatari Rokubei's sword and had a spearman take it to a pawnshop.

The spearman, however, spoke up about this matter, and in the investigation both he and Shozaemon were condemned to death. The investigator was Yamamoto Gorozaemon. When he read the report, he spoke in a loud voice and said, "The man who accuses the defendant is Spearman so and so."

Mitsushige responded quickly, "Put him to death."

When it came time to announce his fate to Shozaemon, Gorozaemon came in and said, "There is now nothing left to be done for you. Prepare yourself for your place of death."

Shozaemon settled himself and said, "Very well. I understand what you have said and am grateful for your words." Due to somebody's trickery, however, while a kaishaku was introduced to Shozaemon, it was arranged that a foot soldier, Naozuka Rokuuemon, was to step from the side and decapitate him.

Repairing to the execution grounds, where the kaishaku stood opposite him, Shozaemon saluted him with extreme calm. But just then, seeing Naozuka drawing his sword, he jumped up and said, "Who are you? I'll never let you cut off my head!" From that point on his peace of mind was shattered and he showed terrible cowardice. Finally, he was brought to the ground, stretched out, and decapitated.

Gorozaemon later said secretly, ' 'If he hadn't been deceived, he would have probably met his death well."

Noda Kizaemon said about the function of kaishaku, "When a man who has come to his place of death loses his wits and is crawling about, it is likely seine damage will be done when it comes time to perform kaishak. At such a time first wait a bit and by some means gather your strength. Then if you cut by standing firm and not missing the chance, you will do well."

In the generation of Lord Katsushige there were retainers who, regardless of high or low rank, were requested to work before the master from the time they were young. When Shiba Kizaemon was doing such service, once the master was clipping his nails and said, "Throw these away." Kizaemon held them in his hand but did not stand up, and the master said, "What's the matter?" Kizaemon said, "There's one missing." The master said, ' 'Here it is," and banded over the one that he had hidden.

Sawabe Heizaemon was ordered to commit seppuku on the eleventh day of the eleventh month in the second year of Tenna. As this became known to him on the night of the tenth, he sent a request to Yamamoto Gonnojo [Tsunetomo] to be kaishaku. The following is a copy of Yamamoto's reply. (Tsunetomo was twenty-four years old at this time.)

I am in accord with your resolution and accept your request for me to function as kaishaku. I instinctively felt that I should decline, but as this is to take place tomorrow there is no time for making excuses and I will undertake the job. The fact that you have chosen me from among many people is a great personal satisfaction to me. Please set your mind at ease concerning all that must follow. Although it is now late at night, I will come to your house to talk over the particulars.

When Heizaemon saw this reply, it is said that he remarked, "This is a matchless letter."

From ages past it has been considered ill-omened by samurai to be requested as kaishaku. The reason for this is that one pains no fame even if the job is well done. And if by chance one should blunder, it becomes a lifetime disgrace.

Once when Tanaka Yahei was attending to affairs in Edo, one of his menials was rather insolent and Yahei scolded him severely. Late that night Yahei heard the noise of someone coming up the stairs. He felt this to be suspicious and quietly got up. With short sword in hand, he asked who was there, and it turned out to be the menial whom he had scolded previously, secretly holding a short sword. Yahei leapt down and with a single stroke cut the man down. I heard many people later state that he had had good luck.

A certain Master Tokuhisa was born quite different from other people and looked to be a bit moronic. Once, a guest was invited and mudfish salad was served. At that time everyone said, "Master Tokuhisa's mudfish salad," and laughed. Later when he was in attendance and a certain person made fun of him by quoting the above remark, Tokuhisa pulled out his sword and cut the man down. This event was investigated, and it was stated to Lord Naoshige, "Seppuku is recommended because this was a matter of rashness within the palace."

When Lord Naoshige heard this, he said, ' 'To be made fun of and remain silent is cowardice. There is no reason to overlook this fact because one is within the palace. A man who makes fun of people is himself a fool. It was his own fault for being cut down."

Once when Nakano Mokunosuke bearded a small boat on the Sumida River to enjoy the coolness, a rogue got in too and committed all manner of rude acts. When Mokunosuke saw that the rogue was relieving himself over the side of the boat, he cut the man's head off and it fell into the river. So that people would not notice this, he quickly covered the body with various things. He then said to the boatman, "This matter should not become known. Row up to the upper reaches of the river and bury the corpse. I shall naturally pay you well."

The boatman did as he was told, but in the lagoon where the body was buried Mokunosuke cut off the head of the boatman and returned directly. It is said that this fact never became known publicly. At that time there was also one young homosexual male prostitute riding in the boat. Mekunosuke said, "That fellow was a man too. It is best to learn how to cut a man while one is still young," and so the man cut the corpse once. Because of that the young man said nothing later on.

It is said that every time Oki Hyobu's group gathered and after all their affairs were finished, he would say, "Young men should discipline themselves rigorously in intention and courage. This will be accomplished if only courage is fixed in one's heart. If one's sword is broken, he will strike with his hands. If his hands are cut off, he will press the enemy down with his shoulders. If his shoulders are cut away, he will bite through ten or fifteen enemy necks with his teeth. Courage is such a thing."

Shida Kichinosuke said, "At first it is an oppressive thing to run until one is breathless. But it is an extraordinarily good feeling when one is standing around after the running. More than that, it is even better to sit down. More than that, it is even better to lie down. And more than that, to put down a pillow and sleep soundly is even better. A man's whole life should be like this. To exert oneself to a great extent when one is young and then to sleep when he is old or at the point of death is the way it should be. But to first sleep and then exert oneself . . . To exert oneself to the end, and to end one's whole life in toil is regrettable." Shimomura Rokurouemon told this story.

A saying of Kichinosuke's that is similar to this is, "A man's life should be as toilsome as possible."

135

When Ueno Rihei was overseer of accounting in Edo, he had a young assistant whom he treated in a very intimate way. On the first night of the eighth month, he went drinking with Hashimoto Taemon, an overseer of foot soldiers, and got so drunk that he lost good sense. He accompanied his young assistant back home, babbling on in a drunken manner, and when they arrived there, Rihei said that he was going to cut the assistant down. The assistant pushed away the tip of Rihei's scabbard. They grappled and both fell into the gutter with the assistant on top pushing Rihei down. At this time, Rihei's servant ran up and asked, "Is Master Rihei on the top or on the bottom?"

When Rihei replied, "I'm on the bottom!" the servant stabbed the assistant once. The assistant got up and, as his wound was light, ran away.

When the affair was brought under investigation, Rihei was put into confinement at the Naekiyama prison and was condemned to capital punishment by beheading. Before this, when he was positioned in Edo and living in a rented house in the merchants' district, a servant had opposed him, and he had cut him down. But he had acted in a good way at that time, and people said that he had acted like a man. This time, however, his actions were outrageous and were certainly unnecessary.

If one thinks about this well from beginning to end, to get so drunk as to draw one's sword is both cowardice and lack of resolve. Rihei's servant was a man from Taku, but his name is not remembered. Though he was a member of the lower classes, he was a brave man. It is said that Taemon committed suicide during the investigation.

In the twelfth section of the fifth chapter of the Ryoankyo there is this story:

In the Province of wizen there was a certain man from Take who, although he had contracted smallpox, was considering joining the forces attacking the castle at Shimabara. His parents earnestly tried to get him to desist, saying, "With such a grave illness, even if you should get there, how could you be of any use?"

He replied, "It would be to my satisfaction to die on the way. After having received the warm benevolence of the master, should I tell myself that I will be of no use to him now?" And he left for the front. Although it was winter camp and the cold was extreme, he did not pay any attention to his health, and neither put on many layers of clothing nor took off his armor day or night. Moreover, he did not avoid uncleanliness, and in the end recovered quickly and was able to fulfill his loyalty completely. So, to the contrary of what you would expect, it cannot be said that one is to despise uncleanliness.

When the teacher, Suzuki Shozo, heard this, he said, "Was it not a cleansing act to throw away his life for his master? For a man who will cut of his life for the sake of righteousness, there is no need to call upon the god of smallpox. All the gods of heaven will protect him. "

Lord Katsushige said, "Whether a man of Hizen holds death in regret or not is not a matter of concern. What I worry about is that people will not take to heart the command to keep the rules of manners and etiquette correctly. I am afraid that the entire clan, our relatives, and elders, out of too much earnestness, will feel that the command to keep correct etiquette is an exaggeration. Up to now there have existed men who were used to these things, and even if etiquette was slightly wrong, they could remember the correct way, and the matter was settled. I have given this command because people are negligent in affairs of this sort."

During the Genroku period there was a samurai of low rank from the Province of Ise by the name of Suzuki Rokubei. He was ill with a severe fever, and his consciousness became dim. At that time a certain male nurse was unexpectedly stricken with greed and was about to open up the ink box and steal the money that was kept in it. Just then the sick man suddenly stirred, took the sword from the base of his pillow, and in a sudden attack cut the man down with one blow. With that, the sick man fell back and died. By this act, Rokubei seemed to be a man of principled disposition.

I heard this story in Edo, but later when I was serving in the same province with a Dr. Nagatsuka, who was also from the Province of Ise, I asked him about it, and indeed he knew the story and said that it was true.

CHAPTER EIGHT

On the night of the thirteenth day of the ninth month in the fourth year of Teikyo, there was a group of ten No actors moon-viewing at the house of Nakayama Mosuke, a foot soldier, in Sayanomoto. Beginning with Naotsuka Kanzaemon they all began to make fun of the foot soldier Araki Kyozaemen because he was so short. Araki became angry, killed Kanzaemon with his sword, and then began striking at the others.

Though he suffered a severed hand, Matsumoto Rokuzaemon came down into the garden, seized Araki from behind with his other hand, and said, "As for the likes of you, I'll twist your head off with one hand!" Grabbing away Araki's sword, he pushed him to the doorsill and pressed him down with his knee, but as he seized him by the neck, he became faint and was quickly overpowered.

Araki quickly sprang back and again began to strike at those around him, but now Master Hayata (later known as Jirozaemon) met him with a spear. In the end he was overpowered by a number of men. Following this, Araki was made to commit seppuku, and the others who were involved were all made ronin on account of their indiscretion, but Hayata was later pardoned.

As Tsunetomo does not remember this story clearly, one should ask around about it.

Some years ago, there was a sutra reading at the Jissoin in Kawakami. Five or six men from Kon'yamachi and the area of Tashiro had gone to the service, and on their way home passed some time drinking. Among them was one of Kizuka Kyuzaemon's retainers who, having some reason for doing so, turned down his companions' invitation to join them and returned borne before nightfall. The others, however, later pot into a fight with some men and cut them all down.

Kyuzaemon's retainer heard of this late that night and went quickly to his companions' quarters. He listened to the details and then said, "In the end I suppose you will have to submit a statement. When you do, you should say that I was there also and assisted in cutting down those men. When I return, I will say as much to Kyuzaemon. Since a fight is a matter involving all concerned, I should meet the same death sentence as you. And that is my deepest desire. The reason is that even if I were to explain to my master that I had returned home early, he would never accept it as the truth. Kyuzaemon has always been a severe man, and even if I were cleared by the investigators, he would probably have me executed as a coward right before his eyes. In such a case, dying with the bad reputation of having run away from a place would be extremely regretful.

"Since the fate of dying is the same, I would like to die being blamed for having killed a man. If you are not in agreement with this, I will cut my stomach open right here."

Having no alternative, his companions spoke as he had requested. Presently, during the inquiry, although the circumstances were explained in the above manner, it became known that the retainer had returned home early. All the investigators were impressed and in fact praised the man. This matter was transmitted to me only in outline, so I will look into the details at a later date.

Once when Nabeshima Aki no kami Shigetake was halfway through his meal, a guest suddenly came to see him, and he left his tray just as it was. Later, a certain retainer of his sat down at the tray and began eating the fried fish that was on it. Just then Lord Aki came back and saw him, and the man became flustered and ran off. Lord Aki yelled out, "What a low-life slave you are to eat something that someone else has been eating!" and sat down and finished what was left.

This is one of Jin'emon's stories. It is said that this retainer was one of those who committed tsuifuku for the master.

Yamamoto Jin'emon always said to his retainers, "Go ahead and gamble and lie. A person who will not tell you seven lies within a hundred yards is useless as a man. " Long ago people spoke in this fashion because they were only concerned with a man's attitude towards military matters and considered that a man who was "correct" would never do great works. They also ignored the misconduct of men and dismissed such matters by saying, "They do good works, too..."

Men like Sagara Kyoma also excused retainers who had committed theft and adultery and trained them gradually. He said, "If it weren't for such persons, we would have no useful men at all."

Ikumo Oribe said, "If a retainer will just think about what he is to do for the day at hand, he will be able to do anything. If it is a single day's work, one should be able to put up with it. Tomorrow, too, is but a single day."

At the time when Lord Nabeshima Tsunashige had still not taken over as heir, he was converted by the Zen priest Kurotakiyama Choon and learned Buddhism from him. Since he had had an enlightenment, the priest was going to confer the seal upon him, and this became known throughout the mansion. At that time Yamamoto Gorozaemon had been ordered to be both Tsunashige's attendant and overseer. When he heard of this, he knew that it absolutely would not do and planned to make a request to Choon, and if he did not assent, kill him. He went to the priest's house in Edo and entered; the priest, thinking that he was someone on a pilgrimage, met him in a dignified manner.

Gorozaemon drew near him and said, ' 'I have some secret thing to tell you directly. Please send out your attendant priests.

"It is said that you will soon award Tsunashige the seal because of his cleverness in Buddhism. Now as you are from Hizen, you should know in large part the customs of the Ryuzoji and Nabeshima clans. Our country is ruled with harmony between high and low because, unlike others, it has had continuous heirs for successive generations. There has never been the taking of a Buddhist seal by the daimyo for ages past. If you present the seal now, Tsunashige will probably think of himself as enlightened and regard what his retainers say as so much dirt. A great man will become vain. Absolutely do not give this award. If you do not agree to this, I too am resolved. This he said with determination.

The priest's color changed, but he said, "Well, well. You have trustworthy intentions, and I see that you under- stand the affairs of your clan well. You are a loyal retainer . . ."

But Gorozaemon said, "No! I understand that ploy. I didn't come here to be praised. Without adding anything else, let me hear clearly whether you plan to cancel the seal or not."

Choon said, "What you say is reasonable. I will definitely not award the seal."

Gorozaemon made sure of this and returned. Tsunetomo heard this story directly from Gorozaemon.

A group of eight samurai all took the same road for some merrymaking. Two of them, Komori Eijun and Otsubo Jin'-emon, went into a teahouse in front of the Kannon temple at Asakusa, got into an argument with the male employees there, and were soundly beaten. This could be heard by the others, who were in an excursion boat, and Mute Rokuemen said, "We should go back and take revenge." Yoshii Yoichiemon and Ezoe Jinbei both agreed to this.

The others, however, dissuaded them, saying, "This will cause trouble for the clan," and they all returned home. When they arrived at the mansion, Rokuemon again said, "We should definitely take revenge!" but the others disuaded him. Although they sustained heavy wounds on their arms and legs, Eijian and Jin'emon cut the teahouse men down, and those who had returned were taken to task by the master.

In due course some thought was given to the details of this event. One person said, "By waiting to get the agreement of others, a matter like taking revenge will never be brought to a conclusion. One should have the resolution to go alone and even to be cut down. A person who speaks vehemently about taking revenge but does nothing about it is a hypocrite. Clever people, by using their mouths alone, are taking care of their reputations for a later date. But a real stalwart is a man who will go out secretly, saying nothing, and die. It is not necessary to achieve one's aim; one is a stalwart in being cut down. Such a person will most likely achieve his purpose."

Ichiyuken was a low-class servant in the kitchen of Lord Takanobu. Because of some grudge he had over a matter of wrestling, he cut down seven or eight men and was hence ordered to commit suicide. But when Lord Takanobu heard of this, he pardoned the man and said, "In these strife-torn times of our country, brave men are important. This man would seem to be a man of bravery." Consequently, at the time of the action around the Uji River, Lord Takanobu took Ichiyuken along, and the latter earned unrivaled fame, advancing deep into the lead, and plundering the enemy every time.

At the battle of Takagi, Ichiyuken went so far into the enemy lines that Lord Takanobu felt regret and called him back. Since the vanguard had been unable to advance, only by quickly dashing out was he able to grab Ichiyuken by the sleeve of his armor. At that time Ichiyuken's head had suffered many wounds but he had stopped them up with preen leaves which he bound with a thin towel.

On the first clay of the attack on Hara Caste, Tsuruta Yashichibei went as a messenger from Lord Mimasaka to Oki Hyobu, but as he was delivering the message, he was shot through the pelvic region by a bullet fired from the castle and instantly fell on his face. He got up again and delivered the rest of the message, was felled a second time, and died. Yashichibei's body was carried back by Taira Chihyoei. When Chihyoei was returning to Hyobu's camp, he too was struck by a rifle ball and died.

Dense was born in Taku and the members of his family living at this time were his elder brother Jirbei, his younger brother and his mother. Around the ninth month Denko's mother took Jirobei's son with her to hear a sermon. When it was time to go home, the child, as he was putting on his straw sandals, accidentally stepped on the foot of the man next to him. The man rebuked the child, and in the end, they pot into a vehement argument and the man unsheathed his short sword and killed him. Jirobei's mother was dumb struck. She clung to the man, and he killed her too. Having done this, the man returned to his house.

This man's name was Gorouemon, and he was the son of a ronin by the name of Nakajima Moan. His younger brother was the mountain ascetic, Chuzobo. Moan was an advisor to Master Mimasaka, and Gorouemon had been given a stipend also.

When the circumstances became known at Jirobei's home, his younger brother set out for Gorouemon's place. Finding that the door was locked from within and that no one would come out, he disguised his voice, pretending to be a visitor. When the door was opened, he shouted his real name and crossed swords with his enemy. Both men fumbled into the rubbish heap, but in the end Gorouemon was killed. At this point, Chuzobo dashed in and cut down Jirobei's younger brother.

Hearing of this incident, Dense went immediately to Jirobei's place and said, "Of our enemies only one has been killed, while we have lost three. This is extremely regret- table, so why don't you strike at

144

Chuzobo?" Jirobei, however, would not comply.

Denko felt that this was indeed shameful, and although a Buddhist priest, he decided on striking at the enemy of his mother, younger brother, and nephew. He knew, nevertheless, that since he was simply an ordinary priest, there was likely to be a reprisal from Master Mimasaka and therefore worked hard, finally gaining eminence as the chief priest of the Ryuunji. He then went to the sword maker Iyonojo and asked him to make both a long and a short sword, offered to be his apprentice, and was even allowed to take part in the work.

By the twenty-third day of the ninth month of the following year, he was ready to make his departure. By chance a guest had come at this time. Giving orders for food to be served, Denko secretly slipped out of the chief priest's headquarters disguised as a layman. He then went to taku and, upon asking about Chuzobo, learned that he was with a large group of people who had gathered to watch the moonrise, and that therefore nothing much could be done. Unwilling to let time pile up, he felt that it would be fulfilling his basic desire to strike at the father, Moan. Going to Moan's house, he forced his way into the sleeping chambers, announced his name, and when the man began to get up, stabbed and killed him. When the people of the neighborhood came running and surrounded him, he explained the situation, threw away both long and short swords, and returned home. News of this preceded him to Saga, and a good number of Denko's parishioners came out quickly and accompanied him on his return.

Master Mimasaka was quite outraged, but as Denko was the chief priest of a Nabeshima clan temple, there was nothing to be done. Finally, through the offices of Nabeshima Toneri, he sent word to Tannen, the chief priest of the Kodenji, saying, "When a priest has killed a man, he should be given a sentence of death." Tannen's reply was, "The punishment for one within the religion will be in accordance with the feelings of the Kodenji. Kindly do not interfere."

Master Mimasaka became even angrier and asked, "What sort of punishment will this be?" Tannen replied, "Although it is profitless for you to know, you are forcing the question, so I will give you an answer. The [Buddhist] Law is that an apostate priest is deprived of his robes and driven out."

Denko's robes were taken from him at the Kodenji, and when he was to be driven out, some novices put on their long and short swords, and a great number of parishioners came to protect him, accompanying him as far as Todoroki. On the road a number of men who looked like hunters appeared and asked if the party had come from Taku. Thereafter Denko lived in Chikuzen, was well received by all, and was on friendly terms with samurai as well. This story was widely circulated, and it is said that he was treated kindly everywhere.

Horie San'emon's misdeed was robbing the Nabeshima warehouse in Edo of its money and fleeing to another prov ince. He was caught and confessed. Thus, it was pronounced, "Because this is a grave crime he should be tortured to death, " and Nakano Daigaku was ordered to be the official who verified the execution. At first all the hairs on his body were burner off and his fingernails were pulled out. His tendons were then cut, he was bored with drills and subjected to various other tortures. Throughout, he did not flinch once, nor did his face change color. In the end his back was split, he was boiled in soy sauce, and his body was bent back in two.

Once when Fukuchi Rokurouemon was leaving the castle, the palanquin of what appeared to be a rather upper-class woman was passing in front of Master Taku's mansion, and a man who was standing there made the proper salutation. A halberd carrier who was with the palanquin procession, however, said to the man, "You didn't bow low enough," and struck him on the head with the handle of his halberd. When the man wiped his head, he found that he was bleeding. In just that condition he stood up and said, "You have committed an outrageous act, even though I was courteous.

A regrettable piece of luck." So, saying, he cut the halberd carrier down with a single blow. The palanquin continued on to wherever it was going, but Rokurouemon unsheathed his spear, stood before the man, and said. "Put away your sword. Within the castle grounds it is forbidden to go about holding a naked blade." The man said, "What happened now was unavoidable, and I was compelled by the circumstances. Certainly, you could see that this was so. Although I would like to sheathe my sword, it is difficult to do so due to the tone of your words. It is unpleasant, but I shall be glad to accept your challenge."

Rokurouemon immediately threw down his spear and said courteously, "What you have said is reasonable. My name is Fukuchi Rokurouemon. I will bear witness that your conduct was quite admirable. Moreover, I will back you up even if it means forfeiting my life. Now put away your sword."

"With pleasure," the man said, and sheathed his sword. On being asked where he was from, the man replied that he was a retainer of Taku Nagato no kami Yasuyori. Therefore, Rokurouemon accompanied him and explained the circumstances. Knowing that the woman in the palanquin was the wife of a nobleman, however, Lord Nagato ordered his retainer to commit seppuku.

Rokurouemon came forward and said, "Because I have given the pro mise of a samurai, if this man is ordered to commit seppuku, then I will commit seppuku first."

It is said that the affair was thus finished without mishap.

Lord Shima sent a messenger to his father, Lord Aki, saying, "I would like to make a pilgrimage to the Atago Shrine in Kyoto." Lord Aki asked, "For what reason?" and the messenger replied, "Since Atago is the pod of archery, my intentions are for the sake of fortune in war." Lord Aki became angry and answered. "That is absolutely worthless! Should the vanguard of the Nabeshimas be making requests to Atago? If the incarnation of Atago were fighting on the enemy's side, the vanguard should be equal to cutting him neatly in two."

Dohaku lived in Kurotsuchibaru. His son was named Gorobei. Once when Goro bei was carrying a load of rice, a ronin of Master Kumashiro Sakyo's by the name of Iwamura Kyunai was coming from the other direction. There was a grudge between the two of them from some former incident, and now Gorobei struck Kyunai with his load of rice, started an argument, beat him, and pushed him into a ditch, and then returned home. Kyunai yelled some threat at Gorobei and returned to his home where he related this event to his older brother Gen'emon. The two of them then went off to Gorobei's to take revenge.

When they got there the door was open just a bit, and Gorobei was waiting behind it with drawn sword. Not knowing this, Gen'emon entered and Gorobei struck at him with a sweep from the side. having received a deep wound, Gen'emon used his sword as a staff and hobbled back outside. Then Kyunai rushed in and struck at Dohaku's son-in-law Katsuemon, who was sitting by the hearth. His sword glanced off the pot hanger, and he cut off half of Katsuemen's face. Dohaku, together with his wife, grabbed the sword away from Kyunai.

Kyunai apologized and said, "I have already achieved my purpose. Please give me back my sword and I will accompany my brother home. But when Dohaku banded it back to him, Kyunai cut him once in the back and severed his neck halfway through. He then crossed swords with Gorobei again and both went outside and fought an even match until he cut off Gorobei's arm.

At this point Kyunai, who also suffered many wounds, shouldered his elder brother Gen'emon and returned home. Gen'emon, however, died on the way back.

Gorobei's wounds were numerous. Although he stopped the bleeding, he died on account of drinking some water. Dohaku's wife suffered some severed fingers. Dohaku's wound was a severed neck bone, and since only his throat remained intact, his head hung down in front. Now boosting his head up with his own hands, Dohaku went off to the surgeons.

The surgeon s treatment was like this: First he rubbed a mixture of pine resin and oil on Dohaku's jaw and bound it in ramie. He then attached a rope to the top of his head and tied it to a beam, sewed the open wound shut, and buried his body in rice so that he would not be able to move.

Dohaku never lost consciousness, nor did he change from his everyday attitude, nor did he even drink ginseng. It is said that only on the third day when there was a hemorrhage did, he use a little medicinal stimulant. In the end the bones mended, and he recovered without incident.

When Lord Mitsushige contracted smallpox at Shimonoseki, Ikushima Sakuan gave him some medicine. It was an exceptionally heavy case of smallpox, and his attendants both high and low were rather tense. Suddenly his scabs turned black. The men who were nursing him lost heart and secretly informed Sakuan, who came immediately. He said, "Well, this is something to be thankful for. The scabs are healing. He should soon make a complete recovery with no complications. I give you, my guarantee."

The people who were at Lord Mitsushige's side heard this and thought, "Sakuan looks a little deranged. This has become all the more hopeless."

Sakuan then set folding screens around, came out after a while, and fed Lord Mitsushige one packet of medicine. Very quickly the patient's scabs healed, and he made a complete recovery. Sakuan later confided to someone, "I gave the master that one packet of medicine resolved that, as I was undertaking this treatment alone, if he did not recover, I would quickly cut open my stomach and die with him."

When Nakano Takumi was dying, his whole house gathered and he said, "You should understand that there are three conditions to the resolution of a retainer. They are the condition of the master's will, the condition of vitality, and the condition of one's death."

Once when a number of men had gathered on the platform of the inner citadel of the castle, a certain man said to Uchida Shouemon, "It is said that you are a teacher of the sword, but judging by your everyday attitude, your teaching must be very wild indeed. If you were requested to perform kaishaku, I can imagine that instead of cutting the neck you'd probably cut the top of the man's head."

Shouemon rejoined, "Such is not the case. Draw a little ink spot on your own neck, and I'll show you that I can cut without being off by a hair."

Nagayama Rokurozaemon was going down the Tokaido and was at Hamamatsu. As he passed by an inn, a beggar faced his palanquin and said, "I am a ronin from Echigo. I am short of money and in difficulties. We are both warriors. Please help me out."

Rokurozaemon got angry and said, "It is a discourtesy to mention that we are both warriors. If I were in your state of affairs, I'd cut my stomach open. Rather than being out of money for the road and exposing yourself to shame, cut your stomach open right where you are!" It is said that the beggar moved off.

In Makiguchi Yohei's life he was kaishaku for many men. When a certain Kanahara was to commit seppuku, Yohei consented to be kaishaku. Kanahara thrust the sword into his belly, but at the point of pulling it across he was unable to go further. Yohei approached his side, yelled "Ei!" and stamped his foot. From this impetus, Kanahara was able to pull his sword straight across his belly. After finishing the kaishaku, it is said that Yohei shed tears and said, "Even though he was formerly a good friend of mine . . ." This is a story of Master Sukeemon's.

At the time of a certain person's seppuku, when the kaishaku a cut off his head, a little bit of skin was left hanging and the head was not entirely separated from the body. The official observer said, "There's some left." The kaishaku got angry, took hold of the head, and cutting it completely off, held it above eye level and said, "Take a look!" It is said that it was rather chilling. This is a story of Master Sukeemon's.

In the practice of past times, there were instances when the head flew off. It was said that it is best to cut leaving a little skin remaining so that it doesn't fly oft in the direction of the verifying officials. However, at present it is best to cut clean through.

A man who had cut off fifty heads once said, "According to the head, there are cases when even the trunk of a body will bring some reaction to you. Cutting off just three heads, at first there is no reaction, and you can cut well. But when you pet to four or five, you feel quite a bit of reaction. At any rate, since this is a very important matter, if one always plans on bringing the head to the ground there should be no mistakes."

When Lord Nabeshima Tsunashige was a child, Iwamura Kuranosuke was ordered to the position of elder. On one occasion Kuranosuke saw that there were gold coins before the young Tsunashige and asked the attending retainer, "For what reason have you brought these out before the young master?" The attendant replied, "The master just now heard that a gift had been brought for him. He said that he had not yet seen it, so I brought it out for him." Kuranosuke scolded the man severely, saying, "To place such base things before a person of importance is the extremity of careless ness. You may also consider them something not to be put before the lord's son. Attending retainers should henceforth be very mindful of this."

Another time, when Lord Tsunashige was about twenty years old, he once went to the mansion at Naekiyama for some diversion. As the party neared the mansion, he asked for a walking stick. His sandal carrier, Miura Jibuzaemon, fashioned a stick and was about to give it to the young lord.

Kuranosake saw this, quickly took the stick from Jibuzaemon, and scolded him severely, saying, ' 'Will you make our important young lord a sluggard? Even if he should ask for a stick, it should not be given to him. This is carelessness on the part of the attending retainer."

Jibuzaernon was later promoted to the rank of teakiyari, and Tsunetomo heard this story directly from him.

CHAPTER NINE

When Shimomura Shoun was on service at the castle, Lord Naoshige said, "How wonderful it is that Katsushige is so vigorous and powerful for his age. In wrestling with his peers, he even beat those who are older than he is."

Shoun replied, "Even though I'm an old man, I'll bet I'm best at seated wrestling." So, saying he jerked up Katsushige and threw him so forcefully that it hurt. He then said, "To be prideful about your strength while your mettle is not yet established is likely to bring you shame in the midst of people. You are weaker than you look." Then he withdrew.

At the time when Matsuda Yohei was an intimate friend of Ishii Jinku's, there developed some bad feelings between the former and Nozoe Jinbei. Yohei sent word to Jinbei saying, "Please come and I will settle this matter once and for all." Then he and Jinku set out together and, coming to the Yamabushi mansion at Kihara, they crossed the only bridge there was and destroyed it. Talking over the circumstances of the discord, they examined them from all sides and found no reason to fight. But when they decided to turn around and go home, there was, of course, no bridge.

While they were looking for an appropriate way of crossing the moat, the men whom the two had challenged could be seen approaching stealthily. Yohei and Jinku saw this and said, "We have passed the point of no return, and may as well fight rather than be disgraced at a later date." The battle lasted for some time. Seriously wounded, Yohei fell down between two fields. Jinbei also received a deep wound, and with blood flowing into his eyes was unable to find Yohei. While Jinbei thus searched about blindly, Yohei was able to hold him off from his prone position and in the end cut him down. But when he attempted to deliver the finishing blow, having no strength left in his hand, he pierced Jinbei's neck by pushing the sword with his foot.

At this point, friends arrived and accompanied Yohei back. After his wounds healed, he was ordered to commit seppuku. At that time, he called his friend Jinku and they drank a farewell cup together.

Okubo Toemon of Shioda ran a wineshop for Nabeshima Kenmotsu. Lord Okura, the son of Nabeshima Kai no kami, was a cripple and confined indoors in a place called Mine. He harbored wrestlers and liked rowdies. The wrestlers would often go to nearby villages and cause disturbances. One time they went to Toemon's place, drank sake, and talked unreasonably, bringing Toemon into an argument. He met them with a halberd, but as there were two of them, he was cut down.

His son, Kannosuke, was fifteen years old and was in the midst of studies at the Jozeiji when he was informed of the incident. Galloping off, he took a short sword about sixteen inches in length, joined combat with the two big men, and in a short time finished them both off. Although Kannosuke received thirteen wounds, he recovered. Later he was called Doko and is said to have become very adept at massage.

It is said that Tokunaga Kichizaemon repeatedly com- plained, "I've grown so old that now, even if there were to be a battle, I wouldn't be able to do anything. Still, I would like to die by galloping into the midst of the enemy and being struck down and killed. It would be a shame to do nothing more than to die in one's bed."

It is said that the priest Gyojaku heard this when he was an acolyte. Gyojaku's master was the priest Yemen, who was Kichizaemon's youngest child.

When Sagara Kyuma was requested to become a chief retainer, he said to Nabeshima Heizaemon, "For some reason I have been increasingly well treated by the master and now have been requested to take a high rank. Not having a good retainer, my affairs are liable to be in disorder. It is my request that you give me your retainer, Takase Jibusaemon." Heizaemon listened to him and consented, saying, "It is very gratifying that you have kept an eye on my retainer. I will therefore do as you ask."

But when he related this to Jibusaemon, the latter said, "I should reply directly to Master Kyuma." He then went to Kyuma's place and talked with him. Jibusaemon told Kyuma, "I know it is a great honor that you have thought well of me and have made this request. But a retainer is a person who cannot change masters. As you are of high rank, if I were to become your retainer my life would be replete, but that repleteness would be a vexation to me. Because her zaemon is of low rank and is hard pressed, we live by eating cheap rice gruel. Yet that is sweet enough. Please think this over."

Kyuma was extremely impressed.

A certain man went off somewhere and on returning home late at night, found that a strange man had slipped into the house and was committing adultery with his wife. He thereupon killed the man. He then broke down a wall and propped up a bale of rice, and by this arrangement submitted to the authorities that he had killed a thief. Thus, it went without mishap. After some time had passed, he divorced his wife, and the affair was finished.

When a certain person returned home from some place or other, he found his wife committing adultery with a retainer in the bedroom. When he drew near the two, his retainer fled through the kitchen. He then went into the bedroom and slew his wife.

Calling the maidservant, he explained what had happened and

155

said, "Because this would bring shame to the children, it should be covered up as death by illness and I will need considerable help. If you think that this is too much for you, I may as well kill you too for your part in this serious crime."

She replied, "If you will spare my life, I will go on as if I don't know anything. " She rearranged the room and set out the corpse in its nightclothes. Then, after sending a man to the doctor's place two or three times saying that there was a sudden illness, they sent a last messenger saying that it was too late and there was no longer any need to come. The wife's uncle was called in and told about the illness, and he was convinced. The entire affair was passed off as death by illness, and to the end no one knew the truth. At a later date the retainer was dismissed. This affair happened in Edo.

At New Year's in the third year of Keicho at a place in Korea called Yolsan, when the armies of the Ming appeared by the hundreds of thousands, the Japanese troops were amazed and watched with bated breath. Lord Naoshige said, "Well, well. That's a great number of men! I wonder how many hundreds of thousands there are?"

Jin'emon said, "In Japan, for something that's numberless we say, 'as many as the hairs on a three-year-old calf.' This would certainly live up to the number of hairs on a three-year-old calf!" It is said that everybody laughed and regained their spirits.

Later, Lord Katsushige was hunting at Ml. Shiroishi and told Nakano Matabei about this. ' 'Except for your father who spoke in such a way, there was no one who said even a word."

Nakano Jin'emon constantly said, "A person who serves when treated kindly by the master is not a retainer. But one who serves when the master is being heartless and unreasonable is a retainer. You should understand this principle well."

When Yamamoto Jin'emon was eighty years old, he became ill. At one point, he seemed to be on the verge of groaning, and someone said to him, "You'll feel better if you groan. Go ahead. *' But he replied, "Such is not the case. The name of Yamamoto Jin'emon is known by everyone, and I have shown up well throughout a whole lifetime. To let people, hear my groaning voice in my last moments would never do." It is said that he did not let out a groan to the very end.

A certain son of Mori Monbei got into a fight and returned home wounded. Asked by Monbei, "What did you do to your opponent?" his son replied, "I cut him down."

When Monbei asked, "Did you deliver the coup de grace?" his son replied, "Indeed I did."'

Then Monbei said, "You have certainly done well, and there is nothing to regret. Now, even if you fled you would have to commit seppuku anyway. When your mood improves, commit seppuku, and rather than die by another's hand, you can die by your father's." And soon after he performed kaishaku for his son.

A man in the same group as Aiura Genzaemon committed some nefarious deed, and so the group leader gave him a note, condemning him to death, which was to be taken to Genzaemon's place. Genzaemon perused the note and then said to the man, "It says here that I should kill you, so I will do away with you on the eastern bank. Previously you have practiced such things as swordsmanship . . . . Now fight with all you've got."

The man replied, "I will do as you say," and with Genzaemon alone accompanying him, they left the house. They had gone about twenty yards along the edge of the moat when a retainer of Genzaernon's yelled out, "Hey, Hey!" from the other side. As Genzaemon was turning around, the condemned man attacked him with his sword. Genzaemon ducked backwards, drew his sword, and cut the man down. He then returned home.

He put the clothes he had been wearing at that time into a chest and locked them up, never showing them to anyone for the rest of his life. After he died the clothes were examined and it was seen that they were rent. This was told by his son, Genzaemon.

Okubo Doko is said to have remarked:

Everyone says that no masters of the arts will appear as the world comes to an end. This is something that I cannot claim to understand. Plants such as peonies, azaleas and camellias will be able to produce beautiful flowers, end of the world or not. If men would give some thought to this fact, they would understand. And if people took notice of the masters of even these times, they would be able to say that there are masters in the various arts. But people become imbued with the idea that the world has come to an end and no longer put forth any effort. This is a shame. There is no fault in the times.

While Fukahori Magoroku was still living as a dependent second son, he once went hunting at Fukahori, and his retainer, mistaking him for a wild boar in the darkness of the undergrowth, fired the rifle, wounding him in the knee and causing him to fall from a great height. The retainer, greatly upset, stripped himself to the waist and was about to commit seppuku. Magoroku said, "You can cut your stomach open later. I don't feel well, so bring me some water to drink." The retainer ran about and obtained some water for his master to drink and in the process calmed down. After that the retainer was again about to commit seppuku, but Magoroku forcibly stopped him. Upon returning they checked in with the man on guard, and Magoroku asked his father, Kanzaemen, to forgive the retainer.

Kanzaemon said to the retainer, "It was an unexpected mistake, so do not be worried. There is no need for reservation. Continue with your work."

A man by the name of Takagi got into an argument with three farmers in the neighborhood, was soundly beaten out in the fields, and returned home. His wife said to him, "Haven't you forgotten about the matter of death?" "Definitely not!" he replied.

His wife then retorted, "At any rate, a man dies only once. Of the various ways of dying -dying of disease, being cut down in battle, seppuku or being beheaded to die ignominiously would be a shame," and went outside. She soon returned, carefully put the two children to bed, prepared some torches, dressed herself for battle after nightfall, and then said, "When I went out to survey the scene a bit earlier, it seemed that the three men went into one place for a discussion. Now is the right time. Let's go quickly!" So, saying they went out with the husband in the lead, burning torches and wearing short swords. They broke into their opponents' place and dispersed them, both husband and wife slashing about and killing two of the men and wounding the other. The husband was later ordered to commit seppuku.

CHAPTER TEN

There was a certain retainer of Ikeda Shingen's who started an argument with a man, grappled him to the ground, thrashed him soundly, and trampled on him until his companions ran up and pulled them apart. The elders conferred over this and said, "The man who was trampled should be punished." Shingen heard this and said, "A fight is something that goes to the finish. A man who forgets the Way of the Samurai and does not use his sword will be forsaken by the gods and Buddhas. As an example, to subsequent retainers, both men should be crucified." The men who had pulled them apart were banished.

In Yui Shosetsu's military instructions, "The Way of the Three Ultimate's," there is a passage on the character of karma.' He received an oral teaching of about eighteen chapters concerning the Greater Bravery and the Lesser Bravery. He neither wrote them down nor committed them to memory but rather forgot them completely. Then, in facing real situations, he acted on impulse and the things that he had learned became wisdom of his own. This is the character of karma.

When faced with a crisis, if one puts some spittle on his earlobe and exhales deeply through his nose, he will overcome anything at hand. This is a secret matter. Furthermore, when experiencing a rush of blood to the head, if one puts spittle on the upper part of one's ear, it will soon go away.

Tzu Ch'an was on the point of death when someone asked him how to govern the country. He replied:

There is nothing that surpasses ruling with benevolence. However, to put into practice enough benevolent governing to rule the country is difficult. To do this lukewarmly will result in neglect. If governing with benevolence is difficult, then it is best to govern strictly. To govern strictly means to be strict before things have arisen, and to do things in such a way that evil will not arise. To be strict after the evil has arisen is like laying a snare. There are few people who will make mistakes with fire after having once been burned. Of people who regard water lightly, many have been drowned.

A certain man said, "I know the shapes of Reason and of Woman." When asked about this, he replied, "Reason is four-cornered and will not move even in an extreme situation. Woman is round. One can say that she does not distinguish between good and evil or right and wrong and tumbles into any place at all."

The basic meaning of etiquette is to be quick at both the beginning and end and tranquil in the middle. Mitani Chizaemon heard this and said, "That's just like being a kaishaku.

Fukae Angen accompanied an acquaintance of his to the priest Tesshu of Osaka, and at first said privately to the priest, "This man aspires to study Buddhism and hopes to receive your teaching. He is a man of rather high determination."

Soon after the interview the priest said, "Angen is a man who does harm to others. He said that this man is a good man, but wherein is his goodness. There was no goodness visible to Tesshu's eyes. It is not a good idea to praise people carelessly. When praised, both wise and foolish become prideful. To praise is to do harm."

When Hotta Kaga no kami Masamori was a page to the shogun, he was so headstrong that the shogun wished to test what was at the bottom of his heart. To do this, the shogun heated a pair of tongs and placed them in the hearth. Masamori's custom was to go to the other side of the hearth, take the tongs, and greet the master. This time, when he unsuspectingly picked up the tongs, his hands were immediately turned. As he did obeisance in his usual manner, however, the shogun quickly pot up and took the tongs from him.

A certain person said, "When a castle is being surrendered, as long as there are one or two men within it who are determined to hold on, the defending forces will not be of one accord, and in the end, no one will hold the castle. "In the taking of the castle, if when the man who is to receive it approaches and the one or two men who are determined to hold on to it lightly fire on him from the shadows, the man will be alarmed, and the battle will be on. In such a case, even though it is unwillingly done, the castle will have to be stormed. This is called being forced to besiege a castle by those besieged."

The Buddhist priest Ryozan wrote down some generalities concerning Takanobu's battles. A certain priest saw this and criticized him, saying, "It is inappropriate for a priest to write about a military commander. No matter how successful his writing style may be, since he is not acquainted with military things, he is liable to be mistaken in understanding a famous general's mind. It is irreverent to pass on misconceptions concerning a famous general to later generations."

A certain person said, "In the Saint's mausoleum there is a poem that goes:

"If in one's heart
He follows the path of sincerity,
Though he does not pray
Will not the gods protect him?
What is this path of sincerity?"
A man answered him by saying, "You seem to like poetry. I will answer you with a poem.
As everything in this world is but a shame,
Death is the only sincerity.

It is said that becoming as a dead man in one's daily living is the following of the path of sincerity."

If you cut a face lengthwise, urinate on it, and trample on it with straw sandals, it is said that the skin will come off. This was heard by the priest Gyojaku when he was in Kyoto. It is information to be treasured.

One of Matsudaira Sagami no kami's retainers went to Kyoto on a matter of debt collection and took up lodgings by renting living quarters in a townhouse. One day while standing out front watching the people go by, he heard a passer-by say, "They say that Lord Matsudaira's men are involved in a fight right now." The retainer thought, "How worrisome that some of my companions are involved in a fight. There are some men to relieve those at Edo staying here. Perhaps these are the men involved." He asked the passer-by of the location, but when he arrived out of breath, his companions had already been cut down and their adversaries were at the point of delivering the coup de grace. He quickly let out a yell, cut the two men down and returned to his lodgings.

This matter was made known to an official of the shogunate, and the man was called up before him and questioned. "You gave assistance in your companions' fight and thus disregarded the government's ordinance. This is true beyond a doubt, isn't it?"

The man replied, "I am from the country, and it is difficult for me to understand everything that Your Honor is saying. Would you please repeat that?"

The official got angry and said, "Is there something wrong with your ears? Didn't you abet a fight, commit bloodshed, disregard the government's ordinance, and break the law?"

The man then replied, "I have at length understood what you are saying. Although you say that I have broken the law and disregarded the government's ordinance, I have by no means done so. The reason

163

for this is that all living things value their lives, and this goes without saying for human beings. I, especially, value my life. However, I thought that to hear a rumor that one's friends are involved in a fight and to pretend not to hear this is not to preserve the Way of the Samurai, so I ran to the place of action. To shamelessly return home after seeing my friends struck down would surely have lengthened my life, but this too would be disregarding the Way. In observing the Way, one will throw away his own precious life. Thus, in order to preserve the Way of the Samurai and not to disregard the Samurai Ordinances, I quickly threw away my life at that place. I beg that you execute me immediately."

The official was very impressed and later dismissed the matter, communicating to Lord Matsudaira, "You have a very able samurai in your service. Please treasure him."

This is among the sayings of the priest Banker. "Not to borrow the strength of another, nor to rely on one's own strength to cut off past and future thoughts, and not to live within the everyday mind . . . then the Great Way is right before one's eyes."

Lord Soma's family genealogy, called the Chiken marokashi, was the best in Japan. One year when his mansion suddenly caught fire and was burning to the ground, Lord Soma said, "I feel no regret about the house and all its furnishings, even if they burn to the very last piece, because they are things that can be replaced later on. I only regret that I was unable to take out the genealogy, which is my family's most precious treasure."

There was one samurai among those attending him who said, "I will go in and take it out."

Lord Soma and the others all laughed and said, "The house is already engulfed in flames. How are you going to take it out?"

Now this man had never been loquacious, nor had he been particularly useful, but being a man who did things from beginning to end, he was engaged as an attendant. At this point he said, "I have never been of use to my master because I'm so careless, but I have lived resolved that someday my life should be of use to him. This seems to be that time." And he leapt into the flames. After the fire had been extinguished the master said, "Look for his remains. What a pity!'"

Looking everywhere, they found his burnt corpse in the garden adjacent to the living quarters. When they turned it over, blood flowed out of the stomach. The man had cut open his stomach and placed the genealogy inside and it was not damaged at all. From this time on it was called the "Blood Genealogy.'

According to a certain person's story, "In the tradition of the I Ching, it is a mistake to think that it is something for divination. Its essence is non-divination. This can be seen by the fact that the Chinese character 'I' is read as 'change.' Although one divines good fortune, if he does evil, it will become bad fortune. And although he divines bad fortune, if he does good it will become good fortune.

"Confucius' saying, 'By setting myself to the task for many years and in the end learning change [I], I should make no big mistakes,' is not a matter of learning the I Ching. It means by studying the essence of change and conducting oneself for many years in the Way of Good, one should make no mistakes."

Hirano Gonbei was one of the Men of Seven Spears who advanced straight up the hill at the battle of Shizugadake. At a later date he was invited to become one of Lord Ieyasu's hatamoto. Once he was being entertained at Master Hosekawa's. The master said, "Master Gonbei's bravery is not a hidden matter in Japan. It is truly a shame that such a man of bravery has been placed in a low rank such as you are in now. This must be contrary to your wishes. If you were to become a retainer of mine, I would give you half the domain."

Giving no answer at all, Gonbei suddenly pot up from his seat, went out to the veranda, stood facing the house, and urinated. Then he said, "If I were the master's retainer, it would never do to urinate from here."

When the priest Daiyu from Sanshu was making a sick call at a certain place, he was told, "The man has just now died." Daiyu said, "Such a thing shouldn't have happened at this time. Didn't this occur from insufficient treatment? What a shame!"

Now the doctor happened to be there at that time and heard what was said from the other side of the shoji. He got extraordinarily angry and came out and said, "I heard Your Reverence say that the man died from insufficient treatment. Since I am a rather bungling doctor, this is probably true. I have heard that a priest embodies the power of the Buddhist Law. Let me see you bring this dead man back to life, for without such evidence Buddhism is worthless."

Daiyu was put out by this, but he felt that it would be un- pardonable for a priest to put a blemish on Buddhism, so he said, "I will indeed show you how to bring his life back by prayer. Fleas' wait a moment. I must go prepare myself," and returned to the temple. Soon he came back and sat in meditation next to the corpse. Pretty soon the dead man began to breathe and then completely revived. It is said that he lived on for another half a year. As this was something told directly to the priest Tannen, there is nothing mistaken about it.

When telling of the way he prayed, Daiyu said, "This is something not practiced in our sect, so I didn't know of any way of prayer. I simply set my heart for the sake of the Buddhist Law, returned to the temple, sharpened a short sword that had been given as an offering to the temple, and put it in my robe. Then I faced the dead man and prayed, 'If the strength of the Buddhist Law exists, come back to life immediately. 'Since I was thus committed, if he hadn't come back to life, I was resolved to the point of cutting open my stomach and dying embracing the corpse."

When Yamamoto Gorozaemon went to the priest Tetsugyu in Edo wanting to hear something about Buddhism, Tetsugyo said,

"Buddhism gets rid of the discriminating mind. It is nothing more than this. I can give you an illustration in terms of the warrior. The Chinese character for "cowardice" is made by adding the character for "meaning" to the character radical for "mind". Now "meaning" is "discrimination," and when a man attaches discrimination to his true mind, he becomes a coward. In the Way of the Samurai can a man be courageous when discrimination arises? I suppose you can get the idea from this."

According to what one of the elders said, taking an enemy on the battlefield is like a hawk taking a bird. Even though it enters into the midst of a thousand of them, it gives no attention to any bird other than the one that it has first marked.

Moreover, what is called a tezuke no kubi is a head that one has taken after having made the declaration, "I will take that warrior wearing such and such armor."

In the Kiyogunkan one person said, "When facing the enemy, I feel as if I have just entered darkness. Because of this I get heavily wounded. Although you have fought with many famous men, you have never been wounded. Why is that?"

The other man answered, "When I have faced the enemy, of course it is like being in the dark. But if at that time I tranquilize my mind, it becomes like a night lit by a pale moon. If I begin my attack from that point, I feel as though I will not be wounded. "This is the situation at the moment of truth.

A rifle ball hitting the water will ricochet. It is said that if one marks it with a knife or dents it with his teeth, it will pass through the water. Moreover, when the master is hunting or some such thing, if one marks the ball with a sign, it will come in handy in case of a mishap.

When Master Owari, Master Kit and Master Mite were around the age of ten, one day Lord Ieyasu was with them in the garden and knocked down a big wasps' nest. A great number of wasps flew out, and Master Owari and Master Kit were frightened and ran away. But Master Mite picked off the wasps that were on his face, threw them away one by one, and did not run away.

Another time, when Lord Ieyasu was roasting a great number of chestnuts in a large hearth, he invited the boys to join him. When the chestnuts got sufficiently hot, they all started to pop out at once. Two of the boys were frightened and moved away. Master Mite, however, not the least bit frightened, picked up the ones that had popped out and threw them back into the hearth.

In order to study medicine Eguchi Than went to old Yoshida Ichian's place in the Bancho area of Edo. At that time, there was in the neighborhood a teacher of swordsmanship, to whom he used to go for training from time to time. There was a ronin pupil there who one day came up to toan and said as a parting remark, "I am now going to realize a lo ngcherished ambition, one I have had for many years. I am informing you of this because you have always been friendly to me." Then he walked away. Then felt uneasy about this, and when he followed him, he could see a man wearing a braided hat coming from the opposite direction.

Now the sword teacher was about eight or ten yards ahead of the ronin, and in passing by the man with the hat he soundly struck the man's scabbard with his own. When the man looked around, the ronin knocked off' the man's hat and announced in a loud voice that his purpose was revenge. With the man's attention being distracted by the confusion, he was easily cut down. A tremendous amount of congratulations came from the nearby mansions and townhouses. It is said that they even brought out money for him. This was a favorite story of Toan's.

Once when the priest Ungo of Matsushima was passing through the mountains at night, he was set upon by mountain bandits. Ungo said, "I am a man of this area, not a pilgrim. I have no money at all, but you can have these clothes if you like. Please spare my life."

The bandits said, "Well, our efforts have been in vain. We don't need anything like clothes," and passed on. They had gone about two hundred yards when Ungo turned back and called to them, "I have broken the commandment against lying. In my confusion I forgot that I had one piece of silver in my moneybag. I am truly regretful I said that I had nothing at all. I have it here now, so please take it." The mountain bandits were deeply impressed, cut off their hair right there, and became his disciples.

In Edo four or five hatamoto gathered together one night for a game of go. At one point one of them got up to go to the toilet, and while he was gone an argument broke out. One man was cut down, the lights were extinguished, and the place was in an uproar. When the man came running back, he yelled, "Everybody calm down I This is really over nothing at all. Put the lamps back on and let me handle this." After the lamps had been relighted and everyone had calmed down, the man suddenly struck off the head of the other man involved in the argument. He then said, "My luck as a samurai having run out, I was not present at the fight. If this were seen as cowardice, I would be ordered to commit seppuku. Even if that didn't happen, I would have no excuse if it were said that I had fled to the toilet, and I would still have no recourse other than seppuku. I have done this thing because I thought I would die having cut down an adversary rather than die having shamed myself alone." When the shogun heard of this matter, he praised the man.

Once a group of ten blind masseuses were traveling together in the mountains and when they began to pass along the top of a precipice, they all became very cautious, their legs shook, and they were in general struck with terror. Just then the leading man stumbled and fell of the cliff. Those that were left all wailed, "Ahh, ahh I How piteous!" But the masseuse who had fallen veiled up from below, "Don't be afraid. Although I fell, it was nothing. I am now rather at ease. Before falling I kept thinking 'What will I do if I fall?' and there was no end to my anxiety. But now I've settled down. If the rest of you want to be at ease, fall quickly!"

Hojo Awa no kami once gathered together his disciples in the martial arts and called in a physiognomist, who was popular in Edo at the time, to have him determine whether they were brave men or cowards. He had them see the man one by one, telling them, "If he determines 'bravery,' you should strive all the more. If it is 'cowardice,' you should strive by throwing away your life. It's something that you're born with, so there's no shame in it."

Hirose Denzaemon was then about twelve or thirteen years old. When he sat down in front of the physiognomist, he said in a bristling voice, "if you read cowardice in me, I'll cut you down with a single blow!"

When there is something to be said, it is better if it is said right away. If it is said later, it will sound like an excuse. Moreover, it is occasionally good to really overwhelm your opponent. Also, in addition to having spoken sufficiently it is the highest sort of victory to teach your opponent some-thing that will be to his benefit. This is in accordance with the Way.

The priest Ryoi said: The samurai of old were mortified by the idea of dying in bed; they hoped only to die on the battlefield. A priest, too, will be unable to fulfill the Way unless he is of this disposition. The man who shuts himself away and avoids the company of men is a coward. Only evil thoughts allow one to imagine that something good can be done by shutting oneself away. For even if one does some good thing by shutting himself away, he will be unable to keep the way open for future generations by promulgating the clan traditions.

Takeda Shingen's retainer, Amari Bizen no kami, was killed in action and his son, Tozo, at the age of eighteen took over his father's position as an armed horseman attached to a general. Once a certain man in his group received a deep wound, and since the blood would not clot, Tozo ordered him to drink the feces of a red-haired horse mixed with water. The wounded man said, "Life is dear to me.

How can I drink horse feces?' Tozo heard this and said, "What an admirably brave warrior! What you say is reasonable. However, the basic meaning of loyalty requires us to preserve our lives and gain victory for our master on the battlefield. Well, then, I'll drink some for you." Then he drank some himself and banded over the cup to the man who took the medicine gratefully and recovered.

CHAPTER ELEVEN

In the "Notes on Martial Laws" it is written that:

The phrase, "Win first, fight later, " can be summed up in the two words, "Win beforehand." The resourcefulness of times of peace is the military preparation for times of war. With five hundred allies one can defeat an enemy force of ten thousand.

When advancing on the enemy's castle and then pulling back, do not retreat by the main road, but rather by the side roads.

One should lay one's dead and wounded allies face down in the direction of the enemy.

It is a matter of course that a warrior's attitude should be to be in the vanguard during an attack and in the rear during a retreat. In approaching for the attack, he does not forget to wait for the right moment. In waiting for the right moment, he never forgets the attack.

A helmet is usually thought to be very heavy, but when one is attacking a castle or something similar, and arrows, bullets, large rocks, great pieces of wood and the like are corning down, it will not seem the least bit so.

Once when Master Yagyu was before the shogun on some business, a number of bamboo swords fell from the ceiling. He quickly clasped his hands above his head and was not struck.

Again, at a certain time when he was summoned, the shogun was waiting behind cover with a bamboo sword ready to strike him. Master Yagyu called out in a loud voice, "This is for your own discipline. Don't look!" As the shogun turned around, Master Yagyu stepped up and took the sword out of his hand.

A person who does not want to be struck by the enemy s arrows will have no divine protection. For a man who does not wish to be hit by the arrows of a common soldier, but rather by those of a warrior of fame, there will be the protection for which he has asked.

Wind-bells are things that are used during campaigns in order to know the direction of the wind. For night attacks, fire can be set windward while the attack can be carried out from the opposite direction. Your allies should be mindful of this also. One should always hang wind-bells in order to know the direction of the wind.

Lord Aki declared that he would not have his descendants learn military tactics. He said, "On the battlefield, once discretion starts it cannot be stopped. One will not break through to the enemy with discretion. Indiscretion is most important when in front of the tiger's den. Therefore, if one were informed of military tactics, he would have many doubts, and there will be no end to the matter. My descendants will not practice military tactics.'

According to Lord Naoshige's words:

There is something to which every young samurai should pay attention. During times of peace when listening to stories of battle, one should never say, "In facing such a situation, what would a person do?" Such words are out of the question. How will a man who has doubts even in his own room achieve anything on the battlefield? There is a saying that goes, "No matter what the circumstances might be, one should be of the mind to win. One should be holding the first spear to strike." Even though you have put your life on the line, there is nothing to be done when the situation doesn't go as planned.

173

Takeda Shingen once said, "If there was a man who could kill Lord Ieyasu, I would give him a handsome reward." Hearing this, a boy of thirteen entered into the service of Lord Ieyasu and one night when he saw that Ieyasu had retired, took a stab at his bedding. Lord Ieyasu was actually in the next room silently reading a sutra, but he quickly grabbed the boy.

When the investigation was held, the boy related the facts honestly, and Lord Ieyasu said, "You seemed to be an excellent young man, so I employed you on friendly terms. Now, however, I am even more impressed by you." He then sent the lad back to Shingen.

One night some samurai from Karatsu gathered together and were playing go. Master Kitabatake was watching the game, and when he offered a suggestion, one man attacked him with a sword. After the people around them had stopped the man, Master Kitabatake pinched out the light of the candle and said, "It was nothing more than my own indiscretion, and I apologize. The sword hit the go case; I was not the least bit wounded."

Then the candle was relighted, but when the man came to reconciliate and offer him a sake cup, Kitabatake cut the man's head off with one blow. Presently he said, "My thigh having been cut through, it was difficult to offer any resistance, but by binding my leg with my coat and supporting myself with the go board, I have done this thing." Having said this, he expired.

There is nothing so painful as regret. We would all like to be without it. However, when we are very happy and become elated, or when we habitually jump into something thoughtlessly, later we are distraught, and it is for the most part because we did not think ahead and are now regretful. Certainly, we should try not to become dejected, and when very happy should calm our minds.

These are teachings of Yamamoto Jin'emon:

• Singlemindedness is all-powerful.

- Tether even a roasted chicken.

- Continue to spur a running horse.

- A man who will criticize you openly carries no connivance.

- A man exists for a generation, but his name lasts to the end of time.

- Money is a thing that will be there when asked for. A good man is not so easily found.

- Walk with a real man one hundred yards and he'll tell you at least seven lies.

- To ask when you already know is politeness. To ask when you don't know is the rule.

- Wrap your intentions in needles of pine.

- One should not open his mouth wide or yawn in front of another. Do this behind your fan or sleeve.

- A straw hat or helmet should be worn tilled toward the front.

It is a principle of the art of war that one should simply lay down his life and strike. If one's opponent also does the same, it is an even match. Defeating one's opponent is then a matter of faith and destiny.

One should not show his sleeping quarters to other people. The times of deep sleep and dawning are very important. One should be mindful of this. This is from a story by Nagahama Inosuke.

When one departs for the front, he should carry rice in a bag. His underwear should be made from the skin of a badger. This way he will not have lice. In a long campaign, lice are troublesome.

When meeting with the enemy, there is a way to determine his strength. If he has his head cast down, he will appear black and is strong. If he is looking upward, he will appear white and is weak. This is from a story by Natsume Toneri.

If a warrior is not unattached to life and death, he will be of no use whatsoever. The saying that "All abilities come from one mind" sounds as though it has to do with sentient matters, but it is in fact a matter of being unattached to life and death. With such non-attachment one can accomplish any feat. Martial arts and the like are related to this insofar as they can lead to the Way.

To calm one's mind, one swallows his saliva. This is a secret matter. When one becomes angry, it is the same. Putting spittle on one's forehead is also good. In the Yoshida school of archery, swallowing one's spittle is the secret principle of the art.

A certain general said, "For soldiers other than officers, if they would test their armor, they should test only the front. Furthermore, while ornamentation on armor is unnecessary, one should be very careful about the appearance of his helmet. It is something that accompanies his head to the enemy's camp."

Nakano Jin'emon said, "Learning such things as military tactics is useless. If one does not strike out by simply closing his eyes and rushing into the enemy, even if it is only one step, he will be of no use." This was also the opinion of Iyanaga Sasuke.

In Natsume Toneri's "Military Stories" it is written: "Look at the soldiers of recent times! Even in long battles there are hardly one or two occasions when blood is washed with blood. One should not be negligent." Toneri was a ronin from the Kamigata area.

To have execution grounds in a place where travelers come and go is useless. The executions in Edo and the Kamigala area are meant to be an example for the whole country. But the executions in one province are only for an example in that province. If crimes are many, it is a province's shame. How would this look to other provinces?

With the passing of time, the criminal will forget the reason for his crime; it is best to execute him on the spot.

Matsudaira Izu no kami said to Master Mizuno Kenmotsu, "You're such a useful person, it's a shame that you're so short."

Kenmotsu replied, "That's true. Sometimes things in this world don't go the way we would like. Now if I were to cut off your head and attach it to the bottom of my feet, I would be taller. But that's something that couldn't be done."

A certain person was passing by the town of Yae when suddenly his stomach began to hurt. He stopped at a house on a side street and asked to use the toilet. There was only a young woman there, but she took him to the back and showed him where it was. Just as he was taking off his hakama and going into the toilet, the woman's husband came home and accused them both of adultery. In the end, it became a public matter.

Lord Naoshige heard the case and said, "Even if this is not a matter of adultery, it is the same as adultery to take off one's hakama without hesitation in a place where there is an unaccompanied woman, and in the woman's case to allow someone to disrobe while her husband is absent from home."

It is said that they were both condemned to death for this act.

In assessing the enemy's castle there is a saying that goes, "Smoke and mist are like looking at a spring mountain. After the rain is like viewing a clear day." There is weakness in perfect clarity.

Among the words spoken by great generals, there are some that were said offhandedly. One should not receive these words in the same manner, however.

People who have an intelligent appearance will not be outstanding even if they do something good, and if they do something normal, people will think them lacking. But if a person who is thought of as having a gentle disposition does even a slightly good thing, he will be praised by people.

On the fourteenth day of the seventh month in the third year of Shotoku, there were some cooks in the midst of preparations for the Ben Festival in the outer citadel of the castle. One of them, Hara Jurozaemon, unsheathed his sword and cut off the head of Sagara Genzaemon. Mawatari Rokuuemon, Aiura Tarobei, Kola Kinbei and Kakihara Riemen all ran away in confusion. When Jurozaemon sighted Kinbei and start ed chasing him, the latter fled to the foot soldiers' gathering area. There, the daimyo's palanquin attendant, Tanaka Takeuemon, stood against Jurozaemon and took away his still drawn sword. Ishirnaru San'emon chased Jurozaemon, and when they came to the foot soldiers' area, assisted Takeuemon.

The punishment was given on the twenty-ninth day of the eleventh month in the same year. Jurozaemon was bound with rope and beheaded. Rokuuemon, Tarobei, Kinbei and Riemon were banished and San'emon was ordered to retire. Takeuemon was rewarded with three pieces of silver.

It was later said that Takeuemon had been slow to act, for he had not bound the man at that time.

Among Takeda Shingen's retainers there were men of matchless courage, but when Katsuyori was killed in the fight at Tenmokuzan, they all fled. Tsuchiya Sozo, a warrior who had been in disfavor for many years, came out alone, however, and said, "I wonder where all the men are who spoke so bravely every day? I shall return the master's favors to me." And he fell alone in battle.

The essentials of speaking are in not speaking at all. If you think that you can finish something without speaking, finish it without saying a single word. If there is something that cannot be accomplished without speaking, one should speak with few words, in a way that will accord well with reason.

To open one's mouth indiscriminately brings shame, and there are many times when people will turn their backs on such a person.

A devotee of the Nembutsu recites the Buddha's name with every incoming and outgoing breath in order never to forget the Buddha. A retainer, too, should be just like this in thinking of his master. Not to forget one's master is the most fundamental thing for a retainer.

Men who did well at the time of their death were men of real bravery. There are many examples of such. But people who talk in an accomplished fashion every day yet are agitated at the time of their death can be known not to have true bravery.

In the secret principles of Yagyu Tajima no kami Munenori there is the saying, "There are no military tactics for a man of great strength." As proof of this, there was once a certain vassal of the shogun who came to Master Yagyu and asked to become a disciple. Master Yagyu said, "You seem to be a man who is very accomplished in some school of martial art. Let us make the master-disciple contract after I learn the name of the school."

But the man replied, "I have never practiced one of the martial arts."

Master Yagyu said, "Have you come to make sport of Tajima no kami? Is my perception amiss in thinking that you are a teacher to the shogun?" But the man swore to it and Master Yagyu then asked, "That being so, do you not have some deep conviction?"

The man replied, "When I was a child, I once became suddenly aware that a warrior is a man who does not hold his life in regret. Since I have held that in my heart for many years, it has become a deep conviction, and today I never think about death. Other than that, I have no special conviction."

Master Yagyu was deeply impressed and said, "My perceptions were not the least bit awry. The deepest principle of my military tactics is just that one thing. Lip until now, among all the many hundreds of disciples I have had, there is not one who is licensed in this deepest principle. It is not necessary for you to take up the wooden sword.

I will initiate you right now." And it is said that he promptly banded him the certified scroll.

This is a story of Muragawa Soden's.

Meditation on inevitable death should be performed daily. Every day when one's body and mind are at peace, one should meditate upon being ripped apart by arrows, rifles, spears, and swords, being carried away by surging waves, being thrown into the midst of a great fire, being struck by lightning, being shaken to death by a great earthquake, falling from thousand-foot cliffs, dying of disease, or committing seppuku at the death of one's master. And every day without fail one should consider himself as dead.

There is a saying of the elders' that goes, "Step from under the eaves and you're a dead man. Leave the gate and the enemy is waiting." This is not a matter of being careful. It is to consider oneself as dead beforehand.

People will become your enemies if you become eminent too quickly in life, and you will be ineffectual. Rising slowly in the world, people will be your allies and your happiness will he assured. In the long run, whether you are fast or slow, as long as you have people's understanding there will be no danger. It is said that fortune that is urged upon you from others is the most effective.

The warriors of old cultivated mustaches, for as proof that a man had been slain in battle, his ears and nose would be cut off and brought to the enemy's camp. So that there would be no mistake as to whether the person was a man or a woman, the mustache was also cut off with the nose. At such a time the head was thrown away if it had no mustache, for it might be mistaken for that of a woman. Therefore, growing a mustache was one of the disciplines of a samurai so that his head would not be thrown away upon his death. Tsunetomo said, "If one washes his face with water every morning, if he is slain his complexion will not change."

The word "person of the north" comes from a tradition of the correct way of upbringing. A couple will put their pillows in the west, and the man, lying on the south side, will face the north, while the woman, lying on the north side, will face the south.

In bringing up a boy, one should first encourage a sense of valor. From the time he is young the child should liken his parents to the master, and learn everyday politeness and etiquette, the serving of other people, the ways of speech, forbearance and even the correct way of walking down the street. The elders were taught in the same fashion. When he does not put effort into things, he should be scolded and made to go the entire day without eating. This is also one of the disciplines of a retainer.

As for a girl, it is most important to teach her chastity from the time she is a child. She should not be in the company of a man at a distance of less than six feet, nor should she meet them eye to eye, nor should she receive things from them directly from hand to hand. Neither should she go sight-seeing or take trips to temples. A woman who has been brought up strictly and has endured suffering at her own borne will suffer no ennui after she is married.

In dealing with younger children, one should use rewards and punishments. If one is lax in being sure that they do as they are told, young children will become self-interested and will later be involved in wrongdoings. It is something about which one should be very careful.

LATE NIGHT IDLE TALK

As a retainer of the Nabeshima clan, one should have the intention of studying our province's history and traditions, but provincial studies are made light of nowadays. The basic reason for this study is to understand the foundation of our clan, and to know that the clan's forefathers established its perpetuity by means of their suffering and compassion. The fact that our clan has perpetually continued in an unrivaled manner up to this very day is due to the humanity and martial valor of Master Ryuzoji Iekane, the charity and faith of Master Nabeshima Kiyohisa, and the appearance of Lord Ryuzoji Takanobu and Lord Nabeshima Naoshige and their might.

I am at a complete loss when it comes to understanding why people of this generation have forgotten these things and respect the Buddhas of other places. Neither the Shakyamuni Buddha, nor Confucius, nor Kusunoki, nor Shingen were ever retainers of the Ryuzojis or the Nabeshimas; hence it cannot be said that they are in harmony with our clan's customs. In times of war or in times of peace it would be sufficient if both the upper and lower classes would worship our ancestors and study their teachings. One worships the head of whatever clan or discipline to which he belongs. Outside learning for retainers of our clan is worthless. One may think that it is fine to study other disciplines as a diversion after his provincial studies are replete. Yet if a person has a good understanding of provincial studies, he will see that there is nothing lacking in them.

Today, if someone from another clan were to ask about the origin of the Ryuzojis and the Nabeshimas, or why the fief was transferred from the former to the latter, or if they were to ask something like, "I have heard that the Ryuzojis and the Nabeshimas are the greatest in Kyushu for deeds of martial valor, but can you tell me some of the particulars?" I suppose that the man with no knowledge of provincial studies would not be able to answer a word.

For a retainer there should be nothing other than doing his own job. For the most part people dislike their own jobs, find those of others more interesting, cause misunderstanding, and bring on utter disasters. Good models of men who performed their duty in their work are Lord Naoshige and Lord Katsushige. The retainers of those times all performed their duties. From the upper classes, men who would be of good use were searched out, while from the lower classes' men desired to be useful. The minds of the two classes were of mutual accord, and the strength of the clan was secure.

In all our generations of masters there has never been a bad or foolish one, and in the end, there has never been one who ranked second or third among the daimyo of Japan. It is truly a wonderful clan; this is due to the faith of its founders. Moreover, they did not send the clan's retainers to other provinces. nor did they invite men from other provinces in. Men who were made ronin were kept within the province, as were the descendants of those who were made to commit seppuku. The wonder of being born into a clan with such a deep pledge between master and servant is an inexpressible blessing, passed down through the apes, for both farmer and townsman. This goes without saying for the retainer.

The foundation of a Nabeshima samurai should be in knowing this fact; in being deeply resolved to return this blessing by being useful; in serving more and more selflessly when treated kindly by the master ; in knowing that being made a ronin or being ordered to commit seppuku are also forms of service and in aiming to be mindful of the clan forever, whether one is banished deep in the mountains or buried under the earth. Although it is unfitting for someone like me to say this, in dying it is my hope not to become a Buddha. Rather, my will is permeated with the resolution to help manage the affairs of the province, though I be reborn as a Nabeshima samurai seven times. One needs neither vitality nor talent. In a word, it is a matter of having the will to shoulder the clan by oneself.

How can one human being be inferior to another? In all matters of discipline, one will be useless unless he has great pride. Unless one is determined to move the clan by himself, all his discipline will come to naught. Although, like a tea kettle, it is easy for one's enthusiasm to cool, there is a way to keep this from happening. My own vows are the following:

• Never to be outdone in the Way of the Samurai.

• To be of good use to the master.

• To be filial to my parents.

• To manifest great compassion, and to act for the sake of Man.

If one dedicates these four vows to the gods and Buddhas every morning, he will have the strength of two men and will never slip backward. One must edge forward like the inchworm, bit by bit. The gods and Buddhas, too, first started with a vow.

THE ART OF WAR

THE OLDEST MILITARY TREATISE IN THE WORLD

Translated from the Chinese with
Introduction and Critical Notes

BY

LIONEL GILES, M.A.

1910

To my brother
Captain Valentine Giles, R.G.

In the hope that a work 2400 years old may yet contain lessons
worth consideration by the soldier of today this translation is
affectionately dedicated.

Sun Tzu: Sun Tzu was a Chinese military general, strategist, philosopher, and writer who lived during the Eastern Zhou period. Sun Tzu is traditionally credited as the author of The Art of War, an influential work of military strategy that has affected both Western and East Asian philosophy and military thinking.

PREFACE BY LIONEL GILES

The seventh volume of *Mémoires concernant l'histoire, les sciences, les arts, les mœurs, les usages, &c., des Chinois* is devoted to the Art of War, and contains, amongst other treatises, "Les Treize Articles de Sun-tse," translated from the Chinese by a Jesuit Father, Joseph Amiot. Père Amiot appears to have enjoyed no small reputation as a sinologue in his day, and the field of his labours was certainly extensive. But his so-called translation of the Sun Tzu, if placed side by side with the original, is seen at once to be little better than an imposture. It contains a great deal that Sun Tzu did not write, and very little indeed of what he did. Here is a fair specimen, taken from the opening sentences of chapter 5:—

De l'habileté dans le gouvernement des Troupes. Sun-tse dit : Ayez les noms de tous les Officiers tant généraux que subalternes; inscrivez-les dans un catalogue à part, avec la note des talents & de la capacité de chacun d'eux, afin de pouvoir les employer avec avantage lorsque l'occasion en sera venue. Faites en sorte que tous ceux que vous devez commander soient persuadés que votre principale attention est de les préserver de tout dommage. Les troupes que vous ferez avancer contre l'ennemi doivent être comme des pierres que vous lanceriez contre des œufs. De vous à l'ennemi il ne doit y avoir d'autre différence que celle du fort au faible, du vide au plein. Attaquez à découvert, mais soyez vainqueur en secret. Voilà en peu de mots en quoi consiste l'habileté & toute la perfection même du gouvernement des troupes.

Throughout the nineteenth century, which saw a wonderful development in the study of Chinese literature, no translator ventured to tackle Sun Tzu, although his work was known to be highly valued in China as by far the oldest and best compendium of military science. It was not until the year 1905 that the first English translation, by Capt. E.F. Calthrop. R.F.A., appeared at Tokyo under the title "Sonshi"(the Japanese form of Sun Tzu). Unfortunately, it was evident that the translator's knowledge of Chinese was far too scanty to fit him to grapple with the manifold difficulties of Sun Tzu. He himself plainly acknowledges that without the aid of two Japanese gentlemen "the accompanying translation would have been impossible." We can only wonder, then, that with their help it should have been so excessively bad. It is not merely a question of downright blunders, from which none can hope to be wholly exempt. Omissions were frequent; hard passages were wilfully distorted or slurred over. Such offences are less pardonable. They would not be tolerated in any edition of a Greek or Latin classic, and a similar standard of honesty ought to be insisted upon in translations from Chinese.

From blemishes of this nature, at least, I believe that the present translation is free. It was not undertaken out of any inflated estimate of my own powers; but I could not help feeling that Sun Tzu deserved a better fate than had befallen him, and I knew that, at any rate, I could hardly fail to improve on the work of my predecessors. Towards the end of 1908, a new and revised edition of Capt. Calthrop's translation was published in London, this time, however, without any allusion to his Japanese collaborators. My first three chapters were then already in the printer's hands, so that the criticisms of Capt. Calthrop therein contained must be understood as referring to his earlier edition. This is on the whole an improvement on the other, thought there still remains much that cannot pass muster. Some of the grosser blunders have been rectified and lacunae filled up, but on the other hand a certain number of new mistakes appear. The very first sentence of the introduction is startlingly inaccurate; and later on, while mention is made of "an army of Japanese commentators" on Sun Tzu (who are these, by the way?), not a word is vouchsafed about the Chinese commentators, who nevertheless, I venture to assert, form a much more numerous and infinitely more important "army."

A few special features of the present volume may now be noticed. In the first place, the text has been cut up into numbered paragraphs, both in order to facilitate cross-reference and for the convenience of students generally. The division follows broadly that of Sun Hsing-yen's edition; but I have sometimes found it desirable to join two or more of his paragraphs into one. In quoting from other works, Chinese writers seldom give more than the bare title by way of reference, and the task of research is apt to be seriously hampered in consequence. With a view to obviating this difficulty so far as Sun Tzu is concerned, I have also appended a complete concordance of Chinese characters, following in this the admirable example of Legge, though an alphabetical arrangement has been preferred to the distribution under radicals which he adopted. Another feature borrowed from "The Chinese Classics" is the printing of text, translation and notes on the same page; the notes, however, are inserted, according to the Chinese method, immediately after the passages to which they refer. From the mass of native commentary my aim has been to extract the cream only, adding the Chinese text here and there when it seemed to present points of literary interest. Though constituting in itself an important branch of Chinese literature, very little commentary of this kind has hitherto been made directly accessible by translation.

I may say in conclusion that, owing to the printing off of my sheets as they were completed, the work has not had the benefit of a final revision. On a review of the whole, without modifying the substance of my criticisms, I might have been inclined in a few instances to temper their asperity. Having chosen to wield a bludgeon, however, I shall not cry out if in return I am visited with more than a rap over the knuckles. Indeed, I have been at some pains to put a sword into the hands of future opponents by scrupulously giving either text or reference for every passage translated. A scathing review, even from the pen of the Shanghai critic who despises "mere translations," would not, I must confess, be altogether unwelcome. For, after all, the worst fate I shall have to dread is that which befell the ingenious paradoxes of George in *The Vicar of Wakefield*.

INTRODUCTION

SUN WU AND HIS BOOK

Ssu-ma Ch'ien gives the following biography of Sun Tzu: [1]

Sun Tzu Wu was a native of the Ch'i State. His Art of War brought him to the notice of Ho Lu, King of Wu. Ho Lu said to him:

"I have carefully perused your 13 chapters. May I submit your theory of managing soldiers to a slight test?"

Sun Tzu replied: "You may."

Ho Lu asked: "May the test be applied to women?"

The answer was again in the affirmative, so arrangements were made to bring 180 ladies out of the Palace. Sun Tzu divided them into two companies, and placed one of the King's favorite concubines at the head of each. He then bade them all take spears in their hands, and addressed them thus: "I presume you know the difference between front and back, right hand and left hand?"

The girls replied: Yes.

Sun Tzu went on: "When I say "Eyes front," you must look straight ahead. When I say "Left turn," you must face towards your left hand. When I say "Right turn," you must face towards your right hand. When I say "About turn," you must face right round towards your back."

Again the girls assented. The words of command having been thus explained, he set up the halberds and battle-axes in order to begin the drill. Then, to the sound of drums, he gave the order "Right turn." But the girls only burst out laughing. Sun Tzu said: "If words of command are not clear and distinct, if orders are not thoroughly understood, then the general is to blame."

So he started drilling them again, and this time gave the order "Left turn," whereupon the girls once more burst into fits of laughter. Sun Tzu: "If words of command are not clear and distinct, if orders are not thoroughly understood, the general is to blame. But if his orders are clear, and the soldiers nevertheless disobey, then it is the fault of their officers."

So saying, he ordered the leaders of the two companies to be beheaded. Now the king of Wu was watching the scene from the top of a raised pavilion; and when he saw that his favorite concubines were about to be executed, he was greatly alarmed and hurriedly sent down the following message: "We are now quite satisfied as to our general's ability to handle troops. If we are bereft of these two concubines, our meat and drink will lose their savor. It is our wish that they shall not be beheaded."

Sun Tzu replied: "Having once received His Majesty's commission to be the general of his forces, there are certain commands of His Majesty which, acting in that capacity, I am unable to accept."

Accordingly, he had the two leaders beheaded, and straightway installed the pair next in order as leaders in their place. When this had been done, the drum was sounded for the drill once more; and the girls went through all the evolutions, turning to the right or to the left, marching ahead or wheeling back, kneeling or standing, with perfect accuracy and precision, not venturing to utter a sound. Then Sun Tzu sent a messenger to the King saying: "Your soldiers, Sire, are now properly drilled and disciplined, and ready for your majesty's inspection. They can be put to any use that their sovereign may desire; bid them go through fire and water, and they will not disobey."

But the King replied: "Let our general cease drilling and return to camp. As for us, We have no wish to come down and inspect the troops."

Thereupon Sun Tzu said: "The King is only fond of words, and cannot translate them into deeds."

After that, Ho Lu saw that Sun Tzu was one who knew how to handle an army, and finally appointed him general. In the west, he defeated the Ch'u State and forced his way into Ying, the capital; to the north he put fear into the States of Ch'i and Chin, and spread his fame abroad amongst the feudal princes. And Sun Tzu shared in the might of the King.

About Sun Tzu himself this is all that Ssu-ma Ch'ien has to tell us in this chapter. But he proceeds to give a biography of his descendant, Sun Pin, born about a hundred years after his famous ancestor's death, and also the outstanding military genius of his time. The historian speaks of him too as Sun Tzu, and in his preface we read: "Sun Tzu had his feet cut off and yet continued to discuss the art of war." [3] It seems likely, then, that "Pin" was a nickname bestowed on him after his mutilation, unless the story was invented in order to account for the name. The crowning incident of his career, the crushing defeat of his treacherous rival P'ang Chuan, will be found briefly related in Chapter V. § 19, note.

To return to the elder Sun Tzu. He is mentioned in two other passages of the Shih Chi:—

In the third year of his reign [512 B.C.] Ho Lu, king of Wu, took the field with Tzu-hsu [i.e. Wu Yuan] and Po P'ei, and attacked Ch'u. He captured the town of Shu and slew the two prince's sons who had formerly been generals of Wu. He was then meditating a descent on Ying [the capital]; but the general Sun Wu said: "The army is exhausted. It is not yet possible. We must wait".... [After further successful fighting,] "in the ninth year [506 B.C.], King Ho Lu addressed Wu Tzu-hsu and Sun Wu, saying: "Formerly, you declared that it was not yet possible for us to enter Ying. Is the time ripe now?" The two men replied: "Ch'u's general Tzu-ch'ang, [4] is grasping and covetous, and the princes of T'ang and Ts'ai both have a grudge against him. If Your Majesty has resolved to make a grand attack, you must win over T'ang and Ts'ai, and then you may succeed." Ho Lu followed this advice, [beat Ch'u in five pitched battles and marched into Ying.] [5]

This is the latest date at which anything is recorded of Sun Wu. He does not appear to have survived his patron, who died from the effects of a wound in 496. In another chapter there occurs this passage:[6]

From this time onward, a number of famous soldiers arose, one after the other: Kao-fan, [7] who was employed by the Chin State; Wang-tzu, [8] in the service of Ch'i; and Sun Wu, in the service of Wu. These men developed and threw light upon the principles of war.

It is obvious enough that Ssu-ma Ch'ien at least had no doubt about the reality of Sun Wu as an historical personage; and with one exception, to be noticed presently, he is by far the most important authority on the period in question. It will not be necessary, therefore, to say much of such a work as the Wu Yueh Ch'un Ch'iu, which is supposed to have been written by Chao Yeh of the 1st century A.D. The attribution is somewhat doubtful; but even if it were otherwise, his account would be of little value, based as it is on the Shih Chi and expanded with romantic details. The story of Sun Tzu will be found, for what it is worth, in chapter 2. The only new points in it worth noting are: (1) Sun Tzu was first recommended to Ho Lu by Wu Tzu-hsu. (2) He is called a native of Wu. (3) He had previously lived a retired life, and his contemporaries were unaware of his ability.

The following passage occurs in the Huai-nan Tzu: "When sovereign and ministers show perversity of mind, it is impossible even for a Sun Tzu to encounter the foe." Assuming that this work is genuine (and hitherto no doubt has been cast upon it), we have here the earliest direct reference for Sun Tzu, for Huai-nan Tzu died in 122 B.C., many years before the Shih Chi was given to the world.

Liu Hsiang (80-9 B.C.) says: "The reason why Sun Tzu at the head of 30,000 men beat Ch'u with 200,000 is that the latter were undisciplined."

Teng Ming-shih informs us that the surname "Sun" was bestowed on Sun Wu's grandfather by Duke Ching of Ch'i [547-490 B.C.]. Sun Wu's father Sun P'ing, rose to be a Minister of State in Ch'i, and Sun Wu himself, whose style was Ch'ang-ch'ing, fled to Wu on account of the rebellion which was being fomented by the kindred of T'ien Pao. He had three sons, of whom the second, named Ming, was the father of Sun Pin. According to this account then, Pin was the grandson of Wu, which, considering that Sun Pin's victory over Wei was gained in 341 B.C., may be dismissed as chronologically impossible. Whence these data were obtained by Teng Ming-shih I do not know, but of course no reliance whatever can be placed in them.

An interesting document which has survived from the close of the Han period is the short preface written by the Great Ts'ao Ts'ao, or

Wei Wu Ti, for his edition of Sun Tzu. I shall give it in full:—

I have heard that the ancients used bows and arrows to their advantage. [10] The Lun Yu says: "There must be a sufficiency of military strength." The Shu Ching mentions "the army" among the "eight objects of government." The I Ching says: "'army' indicates firmness and justice; the experienced leader will have good fortune." The Shih Ching says: "The King rose majestic in his wrath, and he marshaled his troops." The Yellow Emperor, T'ang the Completer

199

and Wu Wang all used spears and battle-axes in order to succor their generation. The Ssu-ma Fa says: "If one man slay another of set purpose, he himself may rightfully be slain." He who relies solely on warlike measures shall be exterminated; he who relies solely on peaceful measures shall perish. Instances of this are Fu Ch'ai [11] on the one hand and Yen Wang on the other. [12] In military matters, the Sage's rule is normally to keep the peace, and to move his forces only when occasion requires. He will not use armed force unless driven to it by necessity.

Many books have I read on the subject of war and fighting; but the work composed by Sun Wu is the profoundest of them all. [Sun Tzu was a native of the Ch'i state, his personal name was Wu. He wrote the Art of War in 13 chapters for Ho Lu, King of Wu. Its principles were tested on women, and he was subsequently made a general. He led an army westwards, crushed the Ch'u state and entered Ying the capital. In the north, he kept Ch'i and Chin in awe. A hundred years and more after his time, Sun Pin lived. He was a descendant of Wu.] [13] In his treatment of deliberation and planning, the importance of rapidity in taking the field, [14] clearness of conception, and depth of design, Sun Tzu stands beyond the reach of carping criticism. My contemporaries, however, have failed to grasp the full meaning of his instructions, and while putting into practice the smaller details in which his work abounds, they have overlooked its essential purport. That is the motive which has led me to outline a rough explanation of the whole.

One thing to be noticed in the above is the explicit statement that the 13 chapters were specially composed for King Ho Lu. This is supported by the internal evidence of I. § 15, in which it seems clear that some ruler is addressed.

In the bibliographic section of the Han Shu, there is an entry which has given rise to much discussion: "The works of Sun Tzu of Wu in 82 p'ien (or chapters), with diagrams in 9 chuan." It is evident that this cannot be merely the 13 chapters known to Ssu-ma Ch'ien, or those we possess today. Chang Shou-chieh refers to an edition of Sun Tzu's Art of War of which the "13 chapters" formed the first chuan, adding that there were two other chuan besides. This has brought forth a theory, that the bulk of these 82 chapters consisted of other writings of Sun Tzu—we should call them apocryphal—similar to the Wen Ta, of which a specimen dealing with the Nine Situations [15] is preserved in the T'ung Tien, and another in Ho Shin's commentary. It is suggested that before his interview with Ho Lu, Sun Tzu had only written the 13 chapters, but afterwards composed a sort of exegesis in the form of question and answer between himself and the King. Pi I-hsun, the author of the Sun Tzu Hsu Lu, backs this up with a quotation from the Wu Yueh Ch'un Ch'iu: "The King of Wu summoned Sun Tzu, and asked him questions about the art of war. Each time he set forth a chapter of his work, the King could not find words enough to praise him." As he points out, if the whole work was expounded on the same scale as in the above-mentioned fragments, the total number of chapters could not fail to be considerable. Then the numerous other treatises attributed to Sun Tzu might be included. The fact that the Han Chih mentions no work of Sun Tzu except the 82 p'ien, whereas the Sui and T'ang bibliographies give the titles of others in addition to the "13 chapters," is good proof, Pi I-hsun thinks, that all of these were contained in the 82 p'ien. Without pinning our faith to the accuracy of details supplied by the Wu Yueh Ch'un Ch'iu, or admitting the genuineness of any of the treatises cited by Pi I-hsun, we may see in this theory a probable solution of the mystery. Between Ssu-ma Ch'ien and Pan Ku there was plenty of time for a luxuriant crop of forgeries to have grown up under the magic name of Sun Tzu, and the 82 p'ien may very well represent a collected edition of these lumped together with the original work. It is also possible, though less likely, that some of them existed in the time of the earlier historian and were purposely ignored by him. [16]

Tu Mu's conjecture seems to be based on a passage which states: "Wei Wu Ti strung together Sun Wu's Art of War," which in turn may have resulted from a misunderstanding of the final words of Ts'ao King's preface. This, as Sun Hsing-yen points out, is only a modest way of saying that he made an explanatory paraphrase, or in other words, wrote a commentary on it. On the whole, this theory has met with very little acceptance. Thus, the Ssu K'u Ch'uan Shu says: "The mention of the 13 chapters in the Shih Chi shows that they were in existence before the Han Chih, and that latter accretions are not to be considered part of the original work. Tu Mu's assertion can certainly not be taken as proof."

There is every reason to suppose, then, that the 13 chapters existed in the time of Ssu-ma Ch'ien practically as we have them now. That the work was then well known he tells us in so many words. "Sun Tzu's 13 Chapters and Wu Ch'i's Art of War are the two books that people commonly refer to on the subject of military matters. Both of them are widely distributed, so I will not discuss them here." But as we go further back, serious difficulties begin to arise. The salient fact which has to be faced is that the Tso Chuan, the greatest contemporary record, makes no mention whatsoever of Sun Wu, either as a general or as a writer. It is natural, in view of this awkward circumstance, that many scholars should not only cast doubt on the story of Sun Wu as given in the Shih Chi, but even show themselves frankly skeptical as to the existence of the man at all. The most powerful presentment of this side of the case is to be found in the following disposition by Yeh Shui-hsin: [17]—

It is stated in Ssu-ma Ch'ien's history that Sun Wu was a native of the Ch'i State, and employed by Wu; and that in the reign of Ho Lu he crushed Ch'u, entered Ying, and was a great general. But in Tso's Commentary no Sun Wu appears at all. It is true that Tso's Commentary need not contain absolutely everything that other histories contain. But Tso has not omitted to mention vulgar plebeians and hireling ruffians such as Ying K'ao-shu, [18] Ts'ao Kuei, [19], Chu Chih-wu and Chuan She-chu [20]. In the case of Sun Wu, whose fame and achievements were so brilliant, the omission is much more glaring. Again, details are given, in their due order, about his contemporaries Wu Yuan and the Minister P'ei. [21] Is it credible that Sun Wu alone should have been passed over?

In point of literary style, Sun Tzu's work belongs to the same school as Kuan Tzu, [22] Liu T'ao, [23] and the Yueh Yu [24] and may have been the production of some private scholar living towards the end of the "Spring and Autumn" or the beginning of the "Warring States" period. [25] The story that his precepts were actually applied by the Wu State, is merely the outcome of big talk on the part of his followers.

From the flourishing period of the Chou dynasty [26] down to the time of the "Spring and Autumn," all military commanders were statesmen as well, and the class of professional generals, for conducting external campaigns, did not then exist. It was not until the period of the "Six States" [27] that this custom changed. Now although Wu was an uncivilized State, it is conceivable that Tso should have left unrecorded the fact that Sun Wu was a great general and yet held no civil office? What we are told, therefore, about Jang-chu [28] and Sun Wu, is not authentic matter, but the reckless fabrication of theorizing pundits. The story of Ho Lu's experiment on the women, in particular, is utterly preposterous and incredible.

Yeh Shui-hsin represents Ssu-ma Ch'ien as having said that Sun Wu crushed Ch'u and entered Ying. This is not quite correct. No doubt the impression left on the reader's mind is that he at least shared in these exploits. The fact may or may not be significant; but it is nowhere explicitly stated in the Shih Chi either that Sun Tzu was general on the occasion of the taking of Ying, or that he even went there at all. Moreover, as we know that Wu Yuan and Po P'ei both took part in the expedition, and also that its success was largely due to the dash and enterprise of Fu Kai, Ho Lu's younger brother, it is not easy to see how yet another general could have played a very prominent part in the same campaign.

Ch'en Chen-sun of the Sung dynasty has the note:—

Military writers look upon Sun Wu as the father of their art. But the fact that he does not appear in the Tso Chuan, although he is said to have served under Ho Lu King of Wu, makes it uncertain what period he really belonged to.

He also says:—

The works of Sun Wu and Wu Ch'i may be of genuine antiquity.

It is noticeable that both Yeh Shui-hsin and Ch'en Chen-sun, while rejecting the personality of Sun Wu as he figures in Ssu-ma Ch'ien's history, are inclined to accept the date traditionally assigned to the work which passes under his name. The author of the Hsu Lu fails to appreciate this distinction, and consequently his bitter attack on Ch'en Chen-sun really misses its mark. He makes one of two points, however, which certainly tell in favor of the high antiquity of our "13 chapters." "Sun Tzu," he says, "must have lived in the age of Ching Wang [519-476], because he is frequently plagiarized in subsequent works of the Chou, Ch'in and Han dynasties." The two most shameless offenders in this respect are Wu Ch'i and Huai-nan Tzu, both of them important historical personages in their day. The former lived only a century after the alleged date of Sun Tzu, and his death is known to have taken place in 381 B.C. It was to him, according to Liu Hsiang, that Tseng Shen delivered the Tso Chuan, which had been entrusted to him by its author. [29] Now the fact that quotations from the Art of War, acknowledged or otherwise, are to be found in so many authors of different epochs, establishes a very strong anterior to them all,—in other words, that Sun Tzu's treatise was already in existence towards the end of the 5th century B.C. Further proof of Sun Tzu's antiquity is furnished by the archaic or wholly obsolete meanings attaching to a number of the words he uses. A list of these, which might perhaps be extended, is given in the Hsu Lu; and though some of the interpretations are doubtful, the main argument is hardly affected thereby. Again, it must not be forgotten that Yeh Shui-hsin, a scholar and critic of the first rank, deliberately pronounces the style of the 13 chapters to belong to the early part of the fifth century. Seeing that he is actually engaged in an attempt to disprove the existence of Sun Wu himself, we may be sure that he would not have hesitated to assign the work to a later date had he not honestly believed the contrary. And it is precisely on such a point that the judgment of an educated Chinaman will carry most weight. Other internal evidence is not far to seek. Thus in XIII. § 1, there is an unmistakable allusion to the ancient system of land-tenure which had already passed away by the time of Mencius, who was anxious to see it revived in a modified form. [30] The only warfare Sun Tzu knows is that carried on between the various feudal princes, in which armored chariots play a large part. Their use seems to have entirely died out before the end of the Chou dynasty. He speaks as a man of Wu, a state which ceased to exist as early as 473 B.C. On this I shall touch presently.

But once refer the work to the 5th century or earlier, and the chances of its being other than a bonâ fide production are sensibly diminished. The great age of forgeries did not come until long after. That it should have been forged in the period immediately following 473 is particularly unlikely, for no one, as a rule, hastens to identify himself with a lost cause. As for Yeh Shui-hsin's theory, that the author was a literary recluse, that seems to me quite untenable. If one thing is more apparent than another after reading the maxims of Sun Tzu, it is that their essence has been distilled from a large store of personal observation and experience. They reflect the mind not only of a born strategist, gifted with a rare faculty of generalization, but also of a practical soldier closely acquainted with the military conditions of his time. To say nothing of the fact that these sayings have been accepted and endorsed by all the greatest captains of Chinese history, they offer a combination of freshness and sincerity, acuteness and common sense, which quite excludes the idea that they were artificially concocted in the study. If we admit, then, that the 13 chapters were the genuine production of a military man living towards the end of the "Ch'un Ch'iu" period, are we not bound, in spite of the silence of the Tso Chuan, to accept Ssu-ma Ch'ien's account in its entirety? In view of his high repute as a sober historian, must we not hesitate to assume that the records he drew upon for Sun Wu's biography were false and untrustworthy? The answer, I fear, must be in the negative. There is still one grave, if not fatal, objection to the chronology involved in the story as told in the Shih Chi, which, so far as I am aware, nobody has yet pointed out. There are two passages in Sun Tzu in which he alludes to contemporary affairs. The first in in VI. § 21:—

Though according to my estimate the soldiers of Yueh exceed our own in number, that shall advantage them nothing in the matter of victory. I say then that victory can be achieved.

The other is in XI. § 30:—

Asked if an army can be made to imitate the shuai-jan, I should answer, Yes. For the men of Wu and the men of Yueh are enemies; yet if they are crossing a river in the same boat and are caught by a storm, they will come to each other's assistance just as the left hand helps the right.

These two paragraphs are extremely valuable as evidence of the date of composition. They assign the work to the period of the struggle between Wu and Yueh. So much has been observed by Pi I-hsun. But what has hitherto escaped notice is that they also seriously impair the credibility of Ssu-ma Ch'ien's narrative. As we have seen above, the first positive date given in connection with Sun Wu is 512 B.C. He is then spoken of as a general, acting as confidential adviser to Ho Lu, so that his alleged introduction to that monarch had already taken place, and of course the 13 chapters must have been written earlier still. But at that time, and for several years after, down to the capture of Ying in 506, Ch'u and not Yueh, was the great hereditary enemy of Wu. The two states, Ch'u and Wu, had been constantly at war for over half a century, [31] whereas the first war between Wu and Yueh was waged only in 510, [32] and even then was no more than a short interlude sandwiched in the midst of the fierce struggle with Ch'u. Now Ch'u is not mentioned in the 13 chapters at all. The natural inference is that they were written at a time when Yueh had become the prime antagonist of Wu, that is, after Ch'u had suffered the great humiliation of 506. At this point, a table of dates may be found useful.

B.C.

514 Accession of Ho Lu.
Ho Lu attacks Ch'u, but is dissuaded from entering Ying,
512 the capital. Shih Chi mentions Sun Wu as general.

511 Another attack on Ch'u.

510 Wu makes a successful attack on Yueh. This is the first war between the two states.

509 or 508 Ch'u invades Wu, but is signally defeated at Yu-chang.
Ho Lu attacks Ch'u with the aid of T'ang and Ts'ai.
506 Decisive battle of Po-chu, and capture of Ying. Last mention of Sun Wu in Shih Chi.

505 Yueh makes a raid on Wu in the absence of its army. Wu is beaten by Ch'in and evacuates Ying.

504 Ho Lu sends Fu Ch'ai to attack Ch'u.

497 Kou Chien becomes King of Yueh.

496 Wu attacks Yueh, but is defeated by Kou Chien at Tsui-li. Ho Lu is killed.

494 Fu Ch'ai defeats Kou Chien in the great battle of Fu-chaio, and enters the capital of Yueh.

485 or 484 Kou Chien renders homage to Wu. Death of Wu Tzu-   hsu.

482 Kou Chien invades Wu in the absence of Fu Ch'ai.

478 to 476 Further attacks by Yueh on Wu.

475   Kou Chien lays siege to the capital of Wu.

473   Final defeat and extinction of Wu.

The sentence quoted above from VI. § 21 hardly strikes me as one that could have been written in the full flush of victory. It seems rather to imply that, for the moment at least, the tide had turned against Wu, and that she was getting the worst of the struggle. Hence we may conclude that our treatise was not in existence in 505, before which date Yueh does not appear to have scored any notable success against Wu. Ho Lu died in 496, so that if the book was written for him, it must have been during the period 505-496, when there was a lull in the hostilities, Wu having presumably exhausted by its supreme effort against Ch'u. On the other hand, if we choose to disregard the tradition connecting Sun Wu's name with Ho Lu, it might equally well have seen the light between 496 and 494, or possibly in the period 482-473, when Yueh was once again becoming a very serious menace. [33] We may feel fairly certain that the author, whoever he may have been, was not a man of any great eminence in his own day. On this point the negative testimony of the Tso Chuan far outweighs any shred of authority still attaching to the Shih Chi, if once its other facts are discredited. Sun Hsing-yen, however, makes a feeble attempt to explain the omission of his name from the great commentary. It was Wu Tzu-hsu, he says, who got all the credit of Sun Wu's exploits, because the latter (being an alien) was not rewarded with an office in the State.

How then did the Sun Tzu legend originate? It may be that the growing celebrity of the book imparted by degrees a kind of factitious renown to its author. It was felt to be only right and proper that one so well versed in the science of war should have solid achievements to his credit as well. Now the capture of Ying was undoubtedly the greatest feat of arms in Ho Lu's reign; it made a deep and lasting impression on all the surrounding states, and raised Wu to the short-lived zenith of her power. Hence, what more natural, as time went on, than that the acknowledged master of strategy, Sun Wu, should be popularly identified with that campaign, at first perhaps only in the sense that his brain conceived and planned it; afterwards, that it was actually carried out by him in conjunction with Wu Yuan, [34] Po P'ei and Fu Kai?

It is obvious that any attempt to reconstruct even the outline of Sun Tzu's life must be based almost wholly on conjecture. With this necessary proviso, I should say that he probably entered the service of Wu about the time of Ho Lu's accession, and gathered experience, though only in the capacity of a subordinate officer, during the intense military activity which marked the first half of the prince's reign. [35] If he rose to be a general at all, he certainly was never on an equal footing with the three above mentioned. He was doubtless present at the investment and occupation of Ying, and witnessed Wu's sudden collapse in the following year. Yueh's attack at this critical juncture, when her rival was embarrassed on every side, seems to have convinced him that this upstart kingdom was the great enemy against whom every effort would henceforth have to be directed. Sun Wu was thus a well-seasoned warrior when he sat down to write his famous book, which according to my reckoning must have appeared towards the end, rather than the beginning of Ho Lu's reign. The story of the women may possibly have grown out of some real incident occurring about the same time. As we hear no more of Sun Wu after this from any source, he is hardly likely to have survived his patron or to have taken part in the death-struggle with Yueh, which began with the disaster at Tsui-li.

If these inferences are approximately correct, there is a certain irony in the fate which decreed that China's most illustrious man of peace should be contemporary with her greatest writer on war.

CHAPTER I. LAYING PLANS

[Ts'ao Kung, in defining the meaning of the Chinese for the title of this chapter, says it refers to the deliberations in the temple selected by the general for his temporary use, or as we should say, in his tent. See. § 26.]

1. Sun Tzu said: The art of war is of vital importance to the State.

2. It is a matter of life and death, a road either to safety or to ruin. Hence it is a subject of inquiry which can on no account be neglected.

3. The art of war, then, is governed by five constant factors, to be taken into account in one's deliberations, when seeking to determine the conditions obtaining in the field.

4. These are:(1) The Moral Law; (2) Heaven; (3) Earth; (4) The Commander; (5) Method and discipline.

[It appears from what follows that Sun Tzu means by "Moral Law" a principle of harmony, not unlike the Tao of Lao Tzu in its moral aspect. One might be tempted to render it by "morale," were it not considered as an attribute of the ruler in § 13.]

5, 6. *The Moral Law* causes the people to be in complete accord with their ruler, so that they will follow him regardless of their lives, undismayed by any danger.

[Tu Yu quotes Wang Tzu as saying: "Without constant practice, the officers will be nervous and undecided when mustering for battle; without constant practice, the general will be wavering and irresolute when the crisis is at hand."]

7. Heaven signifies night and day, cold and heat, times and seasons.

[The commentators, I think, make an unnecessary mystery of two words here.

Meng Shih refers to "the hard and the soft, waxing and waning" of Heaven. Wang Hsi, however, may be right in saying that what is meant is "the general economy of Heaven," including the five elements, the four seasons, wind and clouds, and other phenomena.]

8. Earth comprises distances, great and small; danger and security; open ground and narrow passes; the chances of life and death.

9. The Commander stands for the virtues of wisdom, sincerity, benevolence, courage and strictness.

[The five cardinal virtues of the Chinese are (1) humanity or benevolence; (2) uprightness of mind; (3) self-respect, self-control, or "proper feeling;" (4) wisdom; (5) sincerity or good faith. Here "wisdom" and "sincerity" are put before "humanity or benevolence," and the two military virtues of "courage" and "strictness" substituted for "uprightness of mind" and "self-respect, self-control, or 'proper feeling.'"]

10. By Method and discipline are to be understood the marshaling of the army in its proper subdivisions, the graduations of rank among the officers, the maintenance of roads by which supplies may reach the army, and the control of military expenditure.

11. These five heads should be familiar to every general: he who knows them will be victorious; he who knows them not will fail.

12. Therefore, in your deliberations, when seeking to determine the military conditions, let them be made the basis of a comparison, in this wise:—

13. (1) Which of the two sovereigns is imbued with the Moral law?

[I.e., "is in harmony with his subjects." Cf. § 5.]

(2) Which of the two generals has most ability?

(3) With whom lie the advantages derived from Heaven and Earth?

[See §§ 7, 8]

(4) On which side is discipline most rigorously enforced?

[Tu Mu alludes to the remarkable story of Ts'ao Ts'ao (A.D. 155-220), who was such a strict disciplinarian that once, in accordance with his own severe regulations against injury to standing crops, he condemned himself to death for having allowed his horse to shy into a field of corn! However, in lieu of losing his head, he was persuaded to satisfy his sense of justice by cutting off his hair. Ts'ao Ts'ao's own comment on the present passage is characteristically curt: "when you lay down a law, see that it is not disobeyed; if it is disobeyed the offender must be put to death."]

(5) Which army is stronger?

[Morally as well as physically. As Mei Yao-ch'en puts it, freely rendered, "esprit de corps and 'big battalions.'"]

(6) On which side are officers and men more highly trained?

[Tu Yu quotes Wang Tzu as saying: "Without constant practice, the officers will be nervous and undecided when mustering for battle; without constant practice, the general will be wavering and irresolute when the crisis is at hand."]

(7) In which army is there the greater constancy both in reward and punishment?

[On which side is there the most absolute certainty that merit will be properly rewarded and misdeeds summarily punished?]

14. By means of these seven considerations I can forecast victory or defeat.

15. The general that hearkens to my counsel and acts upon it, will conquer:—let such a one be retained in command! The general that hearkens not to my counsel nor acts upon it, will suffer defeat:—let such a one be dismissed!

[The form of this paragraph reminds us that Sun Tzu's treatise was composed expressly for the benefit of his patron Ho Lu, king of the Wu State.]

16. While heading the profit of my counsel, avail yourself also of any helpful circumstances over and beyond the ordinary rules.

17. According as circumstances are favorable, one should modify one's plans.

[Sun Tzu, as a practical soldier, will have none of the "bookish theoric." He cautions us here not to pin our faith to abstract principles; "for," as Chang Yu puts it, "while the main laws of strategy can be stated clearly enough for the benefit of all and sundry, you must be guided by the actions of the enemy in attempting to secure a favorable position in actual warfare." On the eve of the battle of Waterloo, Lord Uxbridge, commanding the cavalry, went to the Duke of Wellington in order to learn what his plans and calculations were for the morrow, because, as he explained, he might suddenly find himself Commander-in-chief and would be unable to frame new plans in a critical moment. The Duke listened quietly and then said: "Who will attack the first tomorrow—I or Bonaparte?" "Bonaparte," replied Lord Uxbridge. "Well," continued the Duke, "Bonaparte has not given me any idea of his projects; and as my plans will depend upon his, how can you expect me to tell you what mine are?" [1]]

18. All warfare is based on deception.

[The truth of this pithy and profound saying will be admitted by every soldier. Col. Henderson tells us that Wellington, great in so many military qualities, was especially distinguished by "the extraordinary skill with which he concealed his movements and deceived both friend and foe."]

19. Hence, when able to attack, we must seem unable; when using our forces, we must seem inactive; when we are near, we must make the enemy believe we are far away; when far away, we must make him believe we are near.

20. Hold out baits to entice the enemy. Feign disorder, and crush him.

[All commentators, except Chang Yu, say, "When he is in disorder, crush him." It is more natural to suppose that Sun Tzu is still illustrating the uses of deception in war.]

21. If he is secure at all points, be prepared for him. If he is in superior strength, evade him.

22. If your opponent is of choleric temper, seek to irritate him. Pretend to be weak, that he may grow arrogant.

[Wang Tzu, quoted by Tu Yu, says that the good tactician plays with his adversary as a cat plays with a mouse, first feigning weakness and immobility, and then suddenly pouncing upon him.]

23. If he is taking his ease, give him no rest.

[This is probably the meaning though Mei Yao-ch'en has the note: "while we are taking our ease, wait for the enemy to tire himself out." The Yu Lan has "Lure him on and tire him out."]

If his forces are united, separate them.

[Less plausible is the interpretation favored by most of the commentators: "If sovereign and subject are in accord, put division between them."]

24. Attack him where he is unprepared, appear where you are not expected.

25. These military devices, leading to victory, must not be divulged beforehand.

26. Now the general who wins a battle makes many calculations in his temple ere the battle is fought.

[Chang Yu tells us that in ancient times it was customary for a temple to be set apart for the use of a general who was about to take the field, in order that he might there elaborate his plan of campaign.]

The general who loses a battle makes but few calculations beforehand. Thus do many calculations lead to victory, and few calculations to defeat: how much more no calculation at all! It is by attention to this point that I can foresee who is likely to win or lose.

[1] "Words on Wellington," by Sir. W. Fraser.

CHAPTER II. WAGING WAR

[Ts'ao Kung has the note: "He who wishes to fight must first count the cost," which prepares us for the discovery that the subject of the chapter is not what we might expect from the title, but is primarily a consideration of ways and means.]

Sun Tzu said: In the operations of war, where there are in the field a thousand swift chariots, as many heavy chariots, and a hundred thousand mail-clad soldiers,

[The "swift chariots" were lightly built and, according to Chang Yu, used for the attack; the "heavy chariots" were heavier, and designed for purposes of defense. Li Ch'uan, it is true, says that the latter were light, but this seems hardly probable. It is interesting to note the analogies between early Chinese warfare and that of the Homeric Greeks. In each case, the war-chariot was the important factor, forming as it did the nucleus round which was grouped a certain number of foot-soldiers. With regard to the numbers given here, we are informed that each swift chariot was accompanied by 75 footmen, and each heavy chariot by 25 footmen, so that the whole army would be divided up into a thousand battalions, each consisting of two chariots and a hundred men.]

with provisions enough to carry them a thousand *li*,

[2.78 modern li go to a mile. The length may have varied slightly since Sun Tzu's time.]

the expenditure at home and at the front, including entertainment of guests, small items such as glue and paint, and sums spent on chariots and armor, will reach the total of a thousand ounces of silver per day. Such is the cost of raising an army of 100,000 men.

2. When you engage in actual fighting, if victory is long in coming, then men's weapons will grow dull and their ardor will be damped. If you lay siege to a town, you will exhaust your strength.

3. Again, if the campaign is protracted, the resources of the State will not be equal to the strain.

4. Now, when your weapons are dulled, your ardor damped, your strength exhausted and your treasure spent, other chieftains will spring up to take advantage of your extremity. Then no man, however wise, will be able to avert the consequences that must ensue.

5. Thus, though we have heard of stupid haste in war, cleverness has never been seen associated with long delays.

[This concise and difficult sentence is not well explained by any of the commentators. Ts'ao Kung, Li Ch'uan, Meng Shih, Tu Yu, Tu Mu and Mei Yao-ch'en have notes to the effect that a general, though naturally stupid, may nevertheless conquer through sheer force of rapidity. Ho Shih says: "Haste may be stupid, but at any rate it saves expenditure of energy and treasure; protracted operations may be very clever, but they bring calamity in their train." Wang Hsi evades the difficulty by remarking: "Lengthy operations mean an army growing old, wealth being expended, an empty exchequer and distress among the people; true cleverness insures against the occurrence of such calamities." Chang Yu says: "So long as victory can be attained, stupid haste is preferable to clever dilatoriness." Now Sun Tzu says nothing whatever, except possibly by implication, about ill-considered haste being better than ingenious but lengthy operations. What he does say is something much more guarded, namely that, while speed may sometimes be injudicious, tardiness can never be anything but foolish—if only because it means impoverishment to the nation. In considering the point raised here by Sun Tzu, the classic example of Fabius Cunctator will inevitably occur to the mind. That general deliberately measured the endurance of Rome against that of Hannibals's isolated army, because it seemed to him that the latter was more likely to suffer from a long campaign in a strange country. But it is quite a moot question whether his tactics would have proved successful in the long run. Their reversal it is true, led to Cannae; but this only establishes a negative presumption in their favour.]

6. There is no instance of a country having benefited from prolonged warfare.

7. It is only one who is thoroughly acquainted with the evils of war that can thoroughly understand the profitable way of carrying it on.

[That is, with rapidity. Only one who knows the disastrous effects of a long war can realize the supreme importance of rapidity in bringing it to a close. Only two commentators seem to favor this interpretation, but it fits well into the logic of the context, whereas the rendering, "He who does not know the evils of war cannot appreciate its benefits," is distinctly pointless.]

8. The skillful soldier does not raise a second levy, neither are his supply-wagons loaded more than twice.

[Once war is declared, he will not waste precious time in waiting for reinforcements, nor will he return his army back for fresh supplies, but crosses the enemy's frontier without delay. This may seem an audacious policy to recommend, but with all great strategists, from Julius Caesar to Napoleon Bonaparte, the value of time—that is, being a little ahead of your opponent—has counted for more than either numerical superiority or the nicest calculations with regard to commissariat.]

9. Bring war material with you from home, but forage on the enemy. Thus the army will have food enough for its needs.

[The Chinese word translated here as "war material" literally means "things to be used", and is meant in the widest sense. It includes all the impedimenta of an army, apart from provisions.]

10. Poverty of the State exchequer causes an army to be maintained by contributions from a distance. Contributing to maintain an army at a distance causes the people to be impoverished.

[The beginning of this sentence does not balance properly with the next, though obviously intended to do so. The arrangement, moreover, is so awkward that I cannot help suspecting some corruption in the text. It never seems to occur to Chinese commentators that an emendation may be necessary for the sense, and we get no help from them there. The Chinese words Sun Tzu used to indicate the cause of the people's impoverishment clearly have reference to some system by which the husbandmen sent their contributions of corn to the army direct. But why should it fall on them to maintain an army in this way, except because the State or Government is too poor to do so?]

11. On the other hand, the proximity of an army causes prices to go up; and high prices cause the people's substance to be drained away.

[Wang Hsi says high prices occur before the army has left its own territory. Ts'ao Kung understands it of an army that has already crossed the frontier.]

12. When their substance is drained away, the peasantry will be afflicted by heavy exactions.

13, 14. With this loss of substance and exhaustion of strength, the homes of the people will be stripped bare, and three-tenths of their income will be dissipated;

[Tu Mu and Wang Hsi agree that the people are not mulcted not of 3/10, but of 7/10, of their income. But this is hardly to be extracted from our text. Ho Shih has a characteristic tag: "The people being regarded as the essential part of the State, and food as the people's heaven, is it not right that those in authority should value and be careful of both?"]

while government expenses for broken chariots, worn-out horses, breast-plates and helmets, bows and arrows, spears and shields, protective mantles, draught-oxen and heavy wagons, will amount to four-tenths of its total revenue.

15. Hence a wise general makes a point of foraging on the enemy. One cartload of the enemy's provisions is equivalent to twenty of one's own, and likewise a single picul of his provender is equivalent to twenty from one's own store.

[Because twenty cartloads will be consumed in the process of transporting one cartload to the front. A picul is a unit of measure equal to 133.3 pounds (65.5 kilograms).]

16. Now in order to kill the enemy, our men must be roused to anger; that there may be advantage from defeating the enemy, they must have their rewards.

[Tu Mu says: "Rewards are necessary in order to make the soldiers see the advantage of beating the enemy; thus, when you capture spoils from the enemy, they must be used as rewards, so that all your men may have a keen desire to fight, each on his own account."]

17. Therefore in chariot fighting, when ten or more chariots have been taken, those should be rewarded who took the first. Our own flags should be substituted for those of the enemy, and the chariots mingled and used in conjunction with ours. The captured soldiers should be kindly treated and kept.

18. This is called, using the conquered foe to augment one's own

strength.

19. In war, then, let your great object be victory, not lengthy campaigns.

[As Ho Shih remarks: "War is not a thing to be trifled with." Sun Tzu here reiterates the main lesson which this chapter is intended to enforce."]

20. Thus it may be known that the leader of armies is the arbiter of the people's fate, the man on whom it depends whether the nation shall be in peace or in peril.

CHAPTER III. ATTACK BY STRATAGEM

1. Sun Tzu said: In the practical art of war, the best thing of all is to take the enemy's country whole and intact; to shatter and destroy it is not so good. So, too, it is better to recapture an army entire than to destroy it, to capture a regiment, a detachment or a company entire than to destroy them.

[The equivalent to an army corps, according to Ssu-ma Fa, consisted nominally of 12500 men; according to Ts'ao Kung, the equivalent of a regiment contained 500 men, the equivalent to a detachment consists from any number between 100 and 500, and the equivalent of a company contains from 5 to 100 men. For the last two, however, Chang Yu gives the exact figures of 100 and 5 respectively.]

2. Hence to fight and conquer in all your battles is not supreme excellence; supreme excellence consists in breaking the enemy's resistance without fighting.

[Here again, no modern strategist but will approve the words of the old Chinese general. Moltke's greatest triumph, the capitulation of the huge French army at Sedan, was won practically without bloodshed.]

3. Thus the highest form of generalship is to balk the enemy's plans;

[Perhaps the word "balk" falls short of expressing the full force of the Chinese word, which implies not an attitude of defense, whereby one might be content to foil the enemy's stratagems one after another, but an active policy of counter-attack. Ho Shih puts this very clearly in his note: "When the enemy has made a plan of attack against us, we must anticipate him by delivering our own attack first."]

the next best is to prevent the junction of the enemy's forces;

[Isolating him from his allies. We must not forget that Sun Tzu, in speaking of hostilities, always has in mind the numerous states or principalities into which the China of his day was split up.]

the next in order is to attack the enemy's army in the field;

[When he is already at full strength.]

and the worst policy of all is to besiege walled cities.

4. The rule is, not to besiege walled cities if it can possibly be avoided.

[Another sound piece of military theory. Had the Boers acted upon it in 1899, and refrained from dissipating their strength before Kimberley, Mafeking, or even Ladysmith, it is more than probable that they would have been masters of the situation before the British were ready seriously to oppose them.]

The preparation of mantlets, movable shelters, and various implements of war, will take up three whole months;

[It is not quite clear what the Chinese word, here translated as "mantlets", described. Ts'ao Kung simply defines them as "large shields," but we get a better idea of them from Li Ch'uan, who says they were to protect the heads of those who were assaulting the city walls at close quarters. This seems to suggest a sort of Roman testudo, ready made. Tu Mu says they were wheeled vehicles used in repelling attacks, but this is denied by Ch'en Hao. See supra

II. 14. The name is also applied to turrets on city walls. Of the "movable shelters" we get a fairly clear description from several commentators. They were wooden missile-proof structures on four wheels, propelled from within, covered over with raw hides, and used in sieges to convey parties of men to and from the walls, for the purpose of filling up the encircling moat with earth. Tu Mu adds that they are now called "wooden donkeys."]

and the piling up of mounds over against the walls will take three months more.

[These were great mounds or ramparts of earth heaped up to the level of the enemy's walls in order to discover the weak points in the defense, and also to destroy the fortified turrets mentioned in the preceding note.]

5. The general, unable to control his irritation, will launch his men to the assault like swarming ants,

[This vivid simile of Ts'ao Kung is taken from the spectacle of an army of ants climbing a wall. The meaning is that the general, losing patience at the long delay, may make a premature attempt to storm the place before his engines of war are ready.]

with the result that one-third of his men are slain, while the town still remains untaken. Such are the disastrous effects of a siege.

[We are reminded of the terrible losses of the Japanese before Port Arthur, in the most recent siege which history has to record.]

6. Therefore the skillful leader subdues the enemy's troops without any fighting; he captures their cities without laying siege to them; he overthrows their kingdom without lengthy operations in the field.

[Chia Lin notes that he only overthrows the Government, but does no harm to individuals. The classical instance is Wu Wang, who after having put an end to the Yin dynasty was acclaimed "Father and mother of the people."]

7. With his forces intact he will dispute the mastery of the Empire, and thus, without losing a man, his triumph will be complete.

[Owing to the double meanings in the Chinese text, the latter part of the sentence is susceptible of quite a different meaning: "And thus, the weapon not being blunted by use, its keenness remains perfect."]

This is the method of attacking by stratagem.

8. It is the rule in war, if our forces are ten to the enemy's one, to surround him; if five to one, to attack him;

[Straightway, without waiting for any further advantage.]

if twice as numerous, to divide our army into two.

[Tu Mu takes exception to the saying; and at first sight, indeed, it appears to violate a fundamental principle of war. Ts'ao Kung, however, gives a clue to Sun Tzu's meaning: "Being two to the enemy's one, we may use one part of our army in the regular way, and the other for some special diversion." Chang Yu thus further elucidates the point: "If our force is twice as numerous as that of the enemy, it should be split up into two divisions, one to meet the enemy in front, and one to fall upon his rear; if he replies to the frontal attack, he may be crushed from behind; if to the rearward attack, he may be crushed in front." This is what is meant by saying that 'one part may be used in the regular way, and the other for some special diversion.' Tu Mu does not understand that dividing one's army is simply an irregular, just as concentrating it is the regular, strategical method, and he is too hasty in calling this a mistake."]

9. If equally matched, we can offer battle;

[Li Ch'uan, followed by Ho Shih, gives the following paraphrase: "If attackers and attacked are equally matched in strength, only the able general will fight."]

if slightly inferior in numbers, we can avoid the enemy;

[The meaning, "we can watch the enemy," is certainly a great improvement on the above; but unfortunately there appears to be no very good authority for the variant. Chang Yu reminds us that the saying only applies if the other factors are equal; a small difference in numbers is often more than counterbalanced by superior energy and discipline.]

if quite unequal in every way, we can flee from him.

10. Hence, though an obstinate fight may be made by a small force, in the end it must be captured by the larger force.

11. Now the general is the bulwark of the State; if the bulwark is complete at all points; the State will be strong; if the bulwark is defective, the State will be weak.

[As Li Ch'uan tersely puts it: "Gap indicates deficiency; if the general's ability is not perfect (i.e. if he is not thoroughly versed in his profession), his army will lack strength."]

12. There are three ways in which a ruler can bring misfortune upon his army:—

13. (1) By commanding the army to advance or to retreat, being ignorant of the fact that it cannot obey. This is called hobbling the army.

[Li Ch'uan adds the comment: "It is like tying together the legs of a thoroughbred, so that it is unable to gallop." One would naturally think of "the ruler" in this passage as being at home, and trying to direct the movements of his army from a distance. But the commentators understand just the reverse, and quote the saying of T'ai Kung: "A kingdom should not be governed from without, and army should not be directed from within." Of course it is true that, during an engagement, or when in close touch with the enemy, the general should not be in the thick of his own troops, but a little distance apart. Otherwise, he will be liable to misjudge the position as a whole, and give wrong orders.]

14. (2) By attempting to govern an army in the same way as he administers a kingdom, being ignorant of the conditions which obtain in an army. This causes restlessness in the soldier's minds.

[Ts'ao Kung's note is, freely translated: "The military sphere and the civil sphere are wholly distinct; you can't handle an army in kid gloves." And Chang Yu says: "Humanity and justice are the principles on which to govern a state, but not an army; opportunism and flexibility, on the other hand, are military rather than civil virtues to assimilate the governing of an army"—to that of a State, understood.]

15. (3) By employing the officers of his army without discrimination,

[That is, he is not careful to use the right man in the right place.]

through ignorance of the military principle of adaptation to circumstances. This shakes the confidence of the soldiers.

[I follow Mei Yao-ch'en here. The other commentators refer not to the ruler, as in §§ 13, 14, but to the officers he employs. Thus Tu Yu says: "If a general is ignorant of the principle of adaptability, he must not be entrusted with a position of authority." Tu Mu quotes: "The skillful employer of men will employ the wise man, the brave man, the covetous man, and the stupid man. For the wise man delights in establishing his merit, the brave man likes to show his courage in action, the covetous man is quick at seizing advantages, and the stupid man has no fear of death."]

16. But when the army is restless and distrustful, trouble is sure to come from the other feudal princes. This is simply bringing anarchy into the army, and flinging victory away.

17. Thus we may know that there are five essentials for victory: (1) He will win who knows when to fight and when not to fight.

[Chang Yu says: If he can fight, he advances and takes the offensive; if he cannot fight, he retreats and remains on the defensive. He will invariably conquer who knows whether it is right to take the offensive or the defensive.]

(2) He will win who knows how to handle both superior and inferior forces.

[This is not merely the general's ability to estimate numbers correctly, as Li Ch'uan and others make out. Chang Yu expounds the saying more satisfactorily: "By applying the art of war, it is possible with a lesser force to defeat a greater, and vice versa. The secret lies in an eye for locality, and in not letting the right moment slip. Thus Wu Tzu says: 'With a superior force, make for easy ground; with an inferior one, make for difficult ground.'"]

(3) He will win whose army is animated by the same spirit throughout all its ranks.

(4) He will win who, prepared himself, waits to take the enemy unprepared.

(5) He will win who has military capacity and is not interfered with by the sovereign.

[Tu Yu quotes Wang Tzu as saying: "It is the sovereign's function to give broad instructions, but to decide on battle it is the function of the general." It is needless to dilate on the military disasters which have been caused by undue interference with operations in the field on the part of the home government. Napoleon undoubtedly owed much of his extraordinary success to the fact that he was not hampered by central authority.]

18. Hence the saying: If you know the enemy and know yourself, you need not fear the result of a hundred battles. If you know yourself but not the enemy, for every victory gained you will also suffer a defeat.

[Li Ch'uan cites the case of Fu Chien, prince of Ch'in, who in 383 A.D. marched with a vast army against the Chin Emperor. When warned not to despise an enemy who could command the services of such men as Hsieh An and Huan Ch'ung, he boastfully replied: "I have the population of eight provinces at my back, infantry and horsemen to the number of one million; why, they could dam up the Yangtsze River itself by merely throwing their whips into the stream. What danger have I to fear?" Nevertheless, his forces were soon after disastrously routed at the Fei River, and he was obliged to beat a hasty retreat.]

If you know neither the enemy nor yourself, you will succumb in every battle.

[Chang Yu said: "Knowing the enemy enables you to take the offensive, knowing yourself enables you to stand on the defensive." He adds: "Attack is the secret of defense; defense is the planning of an attack." It would be hard to find a better epitome of the root-principle of war.]

CHAPTER VI. TACTICAL DISPOSITIONS

[Ts'ao Kung explains the Chinese meaning of the words for the title of this chapter: "marching and countermarching on the part of the two armies with a view to discovering each other's condition." Tu Mu says: "It is through the dispositions of an army that its condition may be discovered. Conceal your dispositions, and your condition will remain secret, which leads to victory; show your dispositions, and your condition will become patent, which leads to defeat." Wang Hsi remarks that the good general can "secure success by modifying his tactics to meet those of the enemy."]

1. Sun Tzu said: The good fighters of old first put themselves beyond the possibility of defeat, and then waited for an opportunity of defeating the enemy.

2. To secure ourselves against defeat lies in our own hands, but the opportunity of defeating the enemy is provided by the enemy himself.

[That is, of course, by a mistake on the enemy's part.]

3. Thus the good fighter is able to secure himself against defeat,

[Chang Yu says this is done, "By concealing the disposition of his troops, covering up his tracks, and taking unremitting precautions."]

but cannot make certain of defeating the enemy.

4. Hence the saying: One may know how to conquer without being able to do it.

5. Security against defeat implies defensive tactics; ability to defeat the enemy means taking the offensive.

[I retain the sense found in a similar passage in §§ 1-3, in spite of the fact that the commentators are all against me. The meaning they give, "He who cannot conquer takes the defensive," is plausible enough.]

6. Standing on the defensive indicates insufficient strength; attacking, a superabundance of strength.

7. The general who is skilled in defense hides in the most secret recesses of the earth;

[Literally, "hides under the ninth earth," which is a metaphor indicating the utmost secrecy and concealment, so that the enemy may not know his whereabouts."]

he who is skilled in attack flashes forth from the topmost heights of heaven.

[Another metaphor, implying that he falls on his adversary like a thunderbolt, against which there is no time to prepare. This is the opinion of most of the commentators.]

Thus on the one hand we have ability to protect ourselves; on the other, a victory that is complete.

8. To see victory only when it is within the ken of the common herd is not the acme of excellence.

[As Ts'ao Kung remarks, "the thing is to see the plant before it has germinated," to foresee the event before the action has begun. Li Ch'uan alludes to the story of Han Hsin who, when about to attack the vastly superior army of Chao, which was strongly entrenched in the city of Ch'eng-an, said to his officers: "Gentlemen, we are going to annihilate the enemy, and shall meet again at dinner." The officers hardly took his words seriously, and gave a very dubious assent. But Han Hsin had already worked out in his mind the details of a clever stratagem, whereby, as he foresaw, he was able to capture the city and inflict a crushing defeat on his adversary."]

9. Neither is it the acme of excellence if you fight and conquer and the whole Empire says, "Well done!"

[True excellence being, as Tu Mu says: "To plan secretly, to move surreptitiously, to foil the enemy's intentions and balk his schemes, so that at last the day may be won without shedding a drop of blood." Sun Tzu reserves his approbation for things that

"the world's coarse thumb

And finger fail to plumb."

10. To lift an autumn hair is no sign of great strength;

["Autumn hair" is explained as the fur of a hare, which is finest in autumn, when it begins to grow afresh. The phrase is a very common one in Chinese writers.]

to see the sun and moon is no sign of sharp sight; to hear the noise of thunder is no sign of a quick ear.

[Ho Shih gives as real instances of strength, sharp sight and quick hearing: Wu Huo, who could lift a tripod weighing 250 stone; Li Chu, who at a distance of a hundred paces could see objects no bigger than a mustard seed; and Shih K'uang, a blind musician who could hear the footsteps of a mosquito.]

11. What the ancients called a clever fighter is one who not only wins, but excels in winning with ease.

[The last half is literally "one who, conquering, excels in easy conquering." Mei Yao-ch'en says: "He who only sees the obvious, wins his battles with difficulty; he who looks below the surface of things, wins with ease."]

12. Hence his victories bring him neither reputation for wisdom nor credit for courage.

[Tu Mu explains this very well: "Inasmuch as his victories are gained over circumstances that have not come to light, the world as large knows nothing of them, and he wins no reputation for wisdom; inasmuch as the hostile state submits before there has been any bloodshed, he receives no credit for courage."]

13. He wins his battles by making no mistakes.

[Ch'en Hao says: "He plans no superfluous marches, he devises no futile attacks." The connection of ideas is thus explained by Chang Yu: "One who seeks to conquer by sheer strength, clever though he may be at winning pitched battles, is also liable on occasion to be vanquished; whereas he who can look into the future and discern conditions that are not yet manifest, will never make a blunder and therefore invariably win."]

Making no mistakes is what establishes the certainty of victory, for it means conquering an enemy that is already defeated.

14. Hence the skillful fighter puts himself into a position which makes defeat impossible, and does not miss the moment for defeating the enemy.

[A "counsel of perfection" as Tu Mu truly observes. "Position" need not be confined to the actual ground occupied by the troops. It includes all the arrangements and preparations which a wise general will make to increase the safety of his army.]

15. Thus it is that in war the victorious strategist only seeks battle after the victory has been won, whereas he who is destined to defeat first fights and afterwards looks for victory.

[Ho Shih thus expounds the paradox: "In warfare, first lay plans which will ensure victory, and then lead your army to battle; if you will not begin with stratagem but rely on brute strength alone, victory will no longer be assured."]

16. The consummate leader cultivates the moral law, and strictly adheres to method and discipline; thus it is in his power to control success.

17. In respect of military method, we have, firstly, Measurement; secondly, Estimation of quantity; thirdly, Calculation; fourthly, Balancing of chances; fifthly, Victory.

18. Measurement owes its existence to Earth; Estimation of quantity to Measurement; Calculation to Estimation of quantity; Balancing of chances to Calculation; and Victory to Balancing of chances.

[It is not easy to distinguish the four terms very clearly in the Chinese. The first seems to be surveying and measurement of the ground, which enable us to form an estimate of the enemy's strength, and to make calculations based on the data thus obtained; we are thus led to a general weighing-up, or comparison of the enemy's chances with our own; if the latter turn the scale, then victory ensues. The chief difficulty lies in third term, which in the Chinese some commentators take as a calculation of numbers, thereby making it nearly synonymous with the second term. Perhaps the second term should be thought of as a consideration of the enemy's general position or condition, while the third term is the estimate of his numerical strength. On the other hand, Tu Mu says: "The question of relative strength having been settled, we can bring the varied resources of cunning into play." Ho Shih seconds this interpretation, but weakens it. However, it points to the third term as being a calculation of numbers.]

19. A victorious army opposed to a routed one, is as a pound's weight placed in the scale against a single grain.

[Literally, "a victorious army is like an i (20 oz.) weighed against a shu (1/24 oz.); a routed army is a shu weighed against an i." The point is simply the enormous advantage which a disciplined force, flushed with victory, has over one demoralized by defeat. Legge, in his note on Mencius, I. 2. ix. 2, makes the i to be 24 Chinese ounces, and corrects Chu Hsi's statement that it equaled 20 oz. only. But Li Ch'uan of the T'ang dynasty here gives the same figure as Chu Hsi.]

20. The onrush of a conquering force is like the bursting of pent-up waters into a chasm a thousand fathoms deep.

CHAPTER V. ENERGY

1. Sun Tzu said: The control of a large force is the same principle as the control of a few men: it is merely a question of dividing up their numbers.

[That is, cutting up the army into regiments, companies, etc., with subordinate officers in command of each. Tu Mu reminds us of Han Hsin's famous reply to the first Han Emperor, who once said to him: "How large an army do you think I could lead?" "Not more than 100,000 men, your Majesty." "And you?" asked the Emperor. "Oh!" he answered, "the more the better."]

2. Fighting with a large army under your command is nowise different from fighting with a small one: it is merely a question of instituting signs and signals.

3. To ensure that your whole host may withstand the brunt of the enemy's attack and remain unshaken—this is effected by manœuvers direct and indirect.

[We now come to one of the most interesting parts of Sun Tzu's treatise, the discussion of the cheng and the ch'i." As it is by no means easy to grasp the full significance of these two terms, or to render them consistently by good English equivalents; it may be as well to tabulate some of the commentators' remarks on the subject before proceeding further. Li Ch'uan: "Facing the enemy is cheng, making lateral diversion is ch'i. Chia Lin: "In presence of the enemy, your troops should be arrayed in normal fashion, but in order to secure victory abnormal manœuvers must be employed." Mei Yao-ch'en: "Ch'i is active, cheng is passive; passivity means waiting for an opportunity, activity brings the victory itself." Ho Shih: "We must cause the enemy to regard our straightforward attack as one that is secretly designed, and vice versa; thus cheng may also be ch'i, and ch'i may also be cheng." He instances the famous exploit of Han Hsin, who when marching ostensibly against Lin-chin (now Chao-i in Shensi), suddenly threw a large force across the Yellow River in wooden tubs, utterly disconcerting his opponent. [Ch'ien Han Shu, ch. 3.] Here, we are told, the march on Lin-chin was cheng, and the surprise manœuver was ch'i." Chang Yu gives the following summary of opinions on the words: "Military writers do not agree with regard to the meaning of ch'i and cheng. Wei Liao Tzu [4th cent. B.C.] says: 'Direct warfare favors frontal attacks, indirect warfare attacks from the rear.' Ts'ao Kung says: 'Going straight out to join battle is a direct operation; appearing on the enemy's rear is an indirect manœuver.' Li Wei-kung [6th and 7th cent. A.D.] says: 'In war, to march straight ahead is cheng; turning movements, on the other hand, are ch'i.' These writers simply regard cheng as cheng, and ch'i as ch'i; they do not note that the two are mutually interchangeable and run into each other like the two sides of a circle [see infra, § 11]. A comment on the T'ang Emperor T'ai Tsung goes to the root of the matter: 'A ch'i manœuver may be cheng, if we make the enemy look upon it as cheng; then our real attack will be ch'i, and vice versa. The whole secret lies in confusing the enemy, so that he cannot fathom our real intent.'" To put it perhaps a little more clearly: any attack or other operation is cheng, on which the enemy has had his attention fixed; whereas that is ch'i," which takes him by surprise or comes from an unexpected quarter. If the enemy perceives a movement which is meant to be ch'i," it immediately becomes cheng."]

4. That the impact of your army may be like a grindstone dashed against an egg—this is effected by the science of weak points and strong.

5. In all fighting, the direct method may be used for joining battle, but indirect methods will be needed in order to secure victory.

[Chang Yu says: "Steadily develop indirect tactics, either by pounding the enemy's flanks or falling on his rear." A brilliant example of "indirect tactics" which decided the fortunes of a campaign was Lord Roberts' night march round the Peiwar Kotal in the second Afghan war. [1]

6. Indirect tactics, efficiently applied, are inexhausible as Heaven and Earth, unending as the flow of rivers and streams; like the sun and moon, they end but to begin anew; like the four seasons, they pass away to return once more.

[Tu Yu and Chang Yu understand this of the permutations of ch'i and cheng." But at present Sun Tzu is not speaking of cheng at all, unless, indeed, we suppose with Cheng Yu-hsien that a clause relating to it has fallen out of the text. Of course, as has already been pointed out, the two are so inextricably interwoven in all military operations, that they cannot really be considered apart. Here we simply have an expression, in figurative language, of the almost infinite resource of a great leader.]

7. There are not more than five musical notes, yet the combinations of these five give rise to more melodies than can ever be heard.

8. There are not more than five primary colors (blue, yellow, red, white, and black), yet in combination they produce more hues than can ever been seen.

9. There are not more than five cardinal tastes (sour, acrid, salt, sweet, bitter), yet combinations of them yield more flavors than can ever be tasted.

10. In battle, there are not more than two methods of attack— the direct and the indirect; yet these two in combination give rise to an endless series of manœuvers.

11. The direct and the indirect lead on to each other in turn. It is like moving in a circle—you never come to an end. Who can exhaust the possibilities of their combination?

12. The onset of troops is like the rush of a torrent which will even roll stones along in its course.

13. The quality of decision is like the well-timed swoop of a falcon which enables it to strike and destroy its victim.

[The Chinese here is tricky and a certain key word in the context it is used defies the best efforts of the translator. Tu Mu defines this word as "the measurement or estimation of distance." But this meaning does not quite fit the illustrative simile in §. 15. Applying this definition to the falcon, it seems to me to denote that instinct of self-restraint which keeps the bird from swooping on its quarry until the right moment, together with the power of judging when the right moment has arrived. The analogous quality in soldiers is the highly important one of being able to reserve their fire until the very instant at which it will be most effective. When the "Victory" went into action at Trafalgar at hardly more than drifting pace, she was for several minutes exposed to a storm of shot and shell before replying with a single gun. Nelson coolly waited until he was within close range, when the broadside he brought to bear worked fearful havoc on the enemy's nearest ships.]

14. Therefore the good fighter will be terrible in his onset, and prompt in his decision.

[The word "decision" would have reference to the measurement of distance mentioned above, letting the enemy get near before striking. But I cannot help thinking that Sun Tzu meant to use the word in a figurative sense comparable to our own idiom "short and sharp." Cf. Wang Hsi's note, which after describing the falcon's mode of attack, proceeds: "This is just how the 'psychological moment' should be seized in war."]

15. Energy may be likened to the bending of a crossbow; decision, to the releasing of a trigger.

[None of the commentators seem to grasp the real point of the simile of energy and the force stored up in the bent cross-bow until released by the finger on the trigger.]

16. Amid the turmoil and tumult of battle, there may be seeming disorder and yet no real disorder at all; amid confusion and chaos, your array may be without head or tail, yet it will be proof against defeat.

[Mei Yao-ch'en says: "The subdivisions of the army having been previously fixed, and the various signals agreed upon, the separating and joining, the dispersing and collecting which will take place in the course of a battle, may give the appearance of disorder when no real disorder is possible. Your formation may be without head or tail, your dispositions all topsy-turvy, and yet a rout of your forces quite out of the question."]

17. Simulated disorder postulates perfect discipline, simulated fear postulates courage; simulated weakness postulates strength.

[In order to make the translation intelligible, it is necessary to tone down the sharply paradoxical form of the original. Ts'ao Kung throws out a hint of the meaning in his brief note: "These things all serve to destroy formation and conceal one's condition." But Tu Mu is the first to put it quite plainly: "If you wish to feign confusion in order to lure the enemy on, you must first have perfect discipline; if you wish to display timidity in order to entrap the enemy, you must have extreme courage; if you wish to parade your weakness in order to make the enemy over-confident, you must have exceeding strength."]

18. Hiding order beneath the cloak of disorder is simply a question of subdivision;

[See supra, § 1.]

concealing courage under a show of timidity presupposes a fund of latent energy;

[The commentators strongly understand a certain Chinese word here differently than anywhere else in this chapter. Thus Tu Mu says: "seeing that we are favorably circumstanced and yet make no move, the enemy will believe that we are really afraid."]

masking strength with weakness is to be effected by tactical dispositions.

[Chang Yu relates the following anecdote of Kao Tsu, the first Han Emperor: "Wishing to crush the Hsiung-nu, he sent out spies to report on their condition. But the Hsiung-nu, forewarned, carefully concealed all their able-bodied men and well-fed horses, and only allowed infirm soldiers and emaciated cattle to be seen. The result was that spies one and all recommended the Emperor to deliver his attack. Lou Ching alone opposed them, saying: 'When two countries go to war, they are naturally inclined to make an ostentatious display of their strength. Yet our spies have seen nothing but old age and infirmity. This is surely some ruse on the part of the enemy, and it would be unwise for us to attack.' The Emperor, however, disregarding this advice, fell into the trap and found himself surrounded at Po-teng."]

19. Thus one who is skillful at keeping the enemy on the move maintains deceitful appearances, according to which the enemy will act.

[Ts'ao Kung's note is "Make a display of weakness and want." Tu Mu says: "If our force happens to be superior to the enemy's, weakness may be simulated in order to lure him on; but if inferior, he must be led to believe that we are strong, in order that he may keep off. In fact, all the enemy's movements should be determined by the signs that we choose to give him." Note the following anecdote of Sun

Pin, a descendent of Sun Wu: In 341 B.C., the Ch'i State being at war with Wei, sent T'ien Chi and Sun Pin against the general P'ang Chuan, who happened to be a deadly personal enemy of the later. Sun Pin said: "The Ch'i State has a reputation for cowardice, and therefore our adversary despises us. Let us turn this circumstance to account." Accordingly, when the army had crossed the border into Wei territory, he gave orders to show 100,000 fires on the first night, 50,000 on the next, and the night after only 20,000. P'ang Chuan pursued them hotly, saying to himself: "I knew these men of Ch'i were cowards: their numbers have already fallen away by more than half." In his retreat, Sun Pin came to a narrow defile, which he calculated that his pursuers would reach after dark. Here he had a tree stripped of its bark, and inscribed upon it the words: "Under this tree shall P'ang Chuan die." Then, as night began to fall, he placed a strong body of archers in ambush near by, with orders to shoot directly if they saw a light. Later on, P'ang Chuan arrived at the spot, and noticing the tree, struck a light in order to read what was written on it. His body was immediately riddled by a volley of arrows, and his whole army thrown into confusion. [The above is Tu Mu's version of the story; the Shih Chi, less dramatically but probably with more historical truth, makes P'ang Chuan cut his own throat with an exclamation of despair, after the rout of his army.]]

He sacrifices something, that the enemy may snatch at it.

20. By holding out baits, he keeps him on the march; then with a body of picked men he lies in wait for him.

[With an emendation suggested by Li Ching, this then reads, "He lies in wait with the main body of his troops."]

21. The clever combatant looks to the effect of combined energy, and does not require too much from individuals.

[Tu Mu says: "He first of all considers the power of his army in the bulk; afterwards he takes individual talent into account, and uses each men according to his capabilities. He does not demand perfection from the untalented."]

Hence his ability to pick out the right men and utilize combined energy.

22. When he utilizes combined energy, his fighting men become as it were like unto rolling logs or stones. For it is the nature of a log or stone to remain motionless on level ground, and to move when on a slope; if four-cornered, to come to a standstill, but if round-shaped, to go rolling down.

[Ts'au Kung calls this "the use of natural or inherent power."]

23. Thus the energy developed by good fighting men is as the momentum of a round stone rolled down a mountain thousands of feet in height. So much on the subject of energy.

[The chief lesson of this chapter, in Tu Mu's opinion, is the paramount importance in war of rapid evolutions and sudden rushes. "Great results," he adds, "can thus be achieved with small forces."]

[1] "Forty-one Years in India," chapter 46.

CHAPTER VI. WEAK POINTS AND STRONG

[Chang Yu attempts to explain the sequence of chapters as follows: "Chapter IV, on Tactical Dispositions, treated of the offensive and the defensive; chapter V, on Energy, dealt with direct and indirect methods. The good general acquaints himself first with the theory of attack and defense, and then turns his attention to direct and indirect methods. He studies the art of varying and combining these two methods before proceeding to the subject of weak and strong points. For the use of direct or indirect methods arises out of attack and defense, and the perception of weak and strong points depends again on the above methods. Hence the present chapter comes immediately after the chapter on Energy."]

1. Sun Tzu said: Whoever is first in the field and awaits the coming of the enemy, will be fresh for the fight; whoever is second in the field and has to hasten to battle will arrive exhausted.

2. Therefore the clever combatant imposes his will on the enemy, but does not allow the enemy's will to be imposed on him.

[One mark of a great soldier is that he fight on his own terms or fights not at all. [1]]

3. By holding out advantages to him, he can cause the enemy to approach of his own accord; or, by inflicting damage, he can make it impossible for the enemy to draw near.

[In the first case, he will entice him with a bait; in the second, he will strike at some important point which the enemy will have to defend.]

4. If the enemy is taking his ease, he can harass him;

[This passage may be cited as evidence against Mei Yao- Ch'en's interpretation of I. § 23.]

if well supplied with food, he can starve him out; if quietly encamped, he can force him to move.

5. Appear at points which the enemy must hasten to defend; march swiftly to places where you are not expected.

6. An army may march great distances without distress, if it marches through country where the enemy is not.

[Ts'ao Kung sums up very well: "Emerge from the void [q.d. like "a bolt from the blue"], strike at vulnerable points, shun places that are defended, attack in unexpected quarters."]

7. You can be sure of succeeding in your attacks if you only attack places which are undefended.

[Wang Hsi explains "undefended places" as "weak points; that is to say, where the general is lacking in capacity, or the soldiers in spirit; where the walls are not strong enough, or the precautions not strict enough; where relief comes too late, or provisions are too scanty, or the defenders are variance amongst themselves."]

You can ensure the safety of your defense if you only hold positions that cannot be attacked.

[I.e., where there are none of the weak points mentioned above. There is rather a nice point involved in the interpretation of this later clause. Tu Mu, Ch'en Hao, and Mei Yao-ch'en assume the meaning to be: "In order to make your defense quite safe, you must defend even those places that are not likely to be attacked;" and Tu Mu adds: "How much more, then, those that will be attacked." Taken thus, however, the clause balances less well with the preceding — always a consideration in the highly antithetical style which is natural to the Chinese. Chang Yu, therefore, seems to come nearer the mark in saying: "He who is skilled in attack flashes forth from the topmost heights of heaven [see IV.

7], making it impossible for the enemy to guard against him. This being so, the places that I shall attack are precisely those that the enemy cannot defend.... He who is skilled in defense hides in the most secret recesses of the earth, making it impossible for the enemy to estimate his whereabouts. This being so, the places that I shall hold are precisely those that the enemy cannot attack."]

8. Hence that general is skillful in attack whose opponent does not know what to defend; and he is skillful in defense whose opponent does not know what to attack.

[An aphorism which puts the whole art of war in a nutshell.]

9. O divine art of subtlety and secrecy! Through you we learn to be invisible, through you inaudible;

[Literally, "without form or sound," but it is said of course with reference to the enemy.]

and hence we can hold the enemy's fate in our hands.

10. You may advance and be absolutely irresistible, if you make for the enemy's weak points; you may retire and be safe from pursuit if your movements are more rapid than those of the enemy.

11. If we wish to fight, the enemy can be forced to an engagement even though he be sheltered behind a high rampart and a deep ditch. All we need do is attack some other place that he will be obliged to relieve.

[Tu Mu says: "If the enemy is the invading party, we can cut his line of communications and occupy the roads by which he will have to return; if we are the invaders, we may direct our attack against the sovereign himself." It is clear that Sun Tzu, unlike certain generals in the late Boer war, was no believer in frontal attacks.]

12. If we do not wish to fight, we can prevent the enemy from engaging us even though the lines of our encampment be merely traced out on the ground. All we need do is to throw something odd and unaccountable in his way.

[This extremely concise expression is intelligibly paraphrased by Chia Lin: "even though we have constructed neither wall nor ditch." Li Ch'uan says: "we puzzle him by strange and unusual dispositions;" and Tu Mu finally clinches the meaning by three illustrative anecdotes—one of Chu-ko Liang, who when occupying Yang-p'ing and about to be attacked by Ssu-ma I, suddenly struck his colors, stopped the beating of the drums, and flung open the city gates, showing only a few men engaged in sweeping and sprinkling the ground. This unexpected proceeding had the intended effect; for Ssu-ma I, suspecting an ambush, actually drew off his army and retreated. What Sun Tzu is advocating here, therefore, is nothing more nor less than the timely use of "bluff."]

13. By discovering the enemy's dispositions and remaining invisible ourselves, we can keep our forces concentrated, while the enemy's must be divided.

[The conclusion is perhaps not very obvious, but Chang Yu (after Mei Yao-ch'en) rightly explains it thus: "If the enemy's dispositions are visible, we can make for him in one body; whereas, our own dispositions being kept secret, the enemy will be obliged to divide his forces in order to guard against attack from every quarter."]

14. We can form a single united body, while the enemy must split up into fractions. Hence there will be a whole pitted against separate parts of a whole, which means that we shall be many to the enemy's few.

15. And if we are able thus to attack an inferior force with a superior one, our opponents will be in dire straits.

16. The spot where we intend to fight must not be made known; for then the enemy will have to prepare against a possible attack at several different points;

[Sheridan once explained the reason of General Grant's victories by saying that "while his opponents were kept fully employed wondering what he was going to do, he was thinking most of what he was going to do himself."]

and his forces being thus distributed in many directions, the numbers we shall have to face at any given point will be proportionately few.

17. For should the enemy strengthen his van, he will weaken his rear; should he strengthen his rear, he will weaken his van; should he strengthen his left, he will weaken his right; should he strengthen his right, he will weaken his left. If he sends reinforcements everywhere, he will everywhere be weak.

[In Frederick the Great's Instructions to his Generals we read: "A defensive war is apt to betray us into too frequent detachment. Those generals who have had but little experience attempt to protect every point, while those who are better acquainted with their profession, having only the capital object in view, guard against a decisive blow, and acquiesce in small misfortunes to avoid greater."]

18. Numerical weakness comes from having to prepare against possible attacks; numerical strength, from compelling our adversary to make these preparations against us.

[The highest generalship, in Col. Henderson's words, is "to compel the enemy to disperse his army, and then to concentrate superior force against each fraction in turn."]

19. Knowing the place and the time of the coming battle, we may

concentrate from the greatest distances in order to fight.

[What Sun Tzu evidently has in mind is that nice calculation of distances and that masterly employment of strategy which enable a general to divide his army for the purpose of a long and rapid march, and afterwards to effect a junction at precisely the right spot and the right hour in order to confront the enemy in overwhelming strength. Among many such successful junctions which military history records, one of the most dramatic and decisive was the appearance of Blucher just at the critical moment on the field of Waterloo.]

20. But if neither time nor place be known, then the left wing will be impotent to succor the right, the right equally impotent to succor the left, the van unable to relieve the rear, or the rear to support the van. How much more so if the furthest portions of the army are anything under a hundred li apart, and even the nearest are separated by several *li*!

[The Chinese of this last sentence is a little lacking in precision, but the mental picture we are required to draw is probably that of an army advancing towards a given rendezvous in separate columns, each of which has orders to be there on a fixed date. If the general allows the various detachments to proceed at haphazard, without precise instructions as to the time and place of meeting, the enemy will be able to annihilate the army in detail. Chang Yu's note may be worth quoting here: "If we do not know the place where our opponents mean to concentrate or the day on which they will join battle, our unity will be forfeited through our preparations for defense, and the positions we hold will be insecure. Suddenly happening upon a powerful foe, we shall be brought to battle in a flurried condition, and no mutual support will be possible between wings, vanguard or rear, especially if there is any great distance between the foremost and hindmost divisions of the army."]

21. Though according to my estimate the soldiers of Yueh exceed

our own in number, that shall advantage them nothing in the matter of victory. I say then that victory can be achieved.

[Alas for these brave words! The long feud between the two states ended in 473 B.C. with the total defeat of Wu by Kou Chien and its incorporation in Yueh. This was doubtless long after Sun Tzu's death. With his present assertion compare IV. § 4. Chang Yu is the only one to point out the seeming discrepancy, which he thus goes on to explain: "In the chapter on Tactical Dispositions it is said, 'One may know how to conquer without being able to do it,' whereas here we have the statement that 'victory' can be achieved.' The explanation is, that in the former chapter, where the offensive and defensive are under discussion, it is said that if the enemy is fully prepared, one cannot make certain of beating him. But the present passage refers particularly to the soldiers of Yueh who, according to Sun Tzu's calculations, will be kept in ignorance of the time and place of the impending struggle. That is why he says here that victory can be achieved."]

22. Though the enemy be stronger in numbers, we may prevent him from fighting. Scheme so as to discover his plans and the likelihood of their success.

[An alternative reading offered by Chia Lin is: "Know beforehand all plans conducive to our success and to the enemy's failure."

23. Rouse him, and learn the principle of his activity or inactivity.

[Chang Yu tells us that by noting the joy or anger shown by the enemy on being thus disturbed, we shall be able to conclude whether his policy is to lie low or the reverse. He instances the action of Cho-ku Liang, who sent the scornful present of a woman's head-dress to Ssu-ma I, in order to goad him out of his Fabian tactics.]

Force him to reveal himself, so as to find out his vulnerable spots.

24. Carefully compare the opposing army with your own, so that you may know where strength is superabundant and where it is

deficient.

[Cf. IV. § 6.]

25. In making tactical dispositions, the highest pitch you can attain is to conceal them;

[The piquancy of the paradox evaporates in translation. Concealment is perhaps not so much actual invisibility (see supra § 9) as "showing no sign" of what you mean to do, of the plans that are formed in your brain.]

conceal your dispositions, and you will be safe from the prying of the subtlest spies, from the machinations of the wisest brains.

[Tu Mu explains: "Though the enemy may have clever and capable officers, they will not be able to lay any plans against us."]

26. How victory may be produced for them out of the enemy's own tactics—that is what the multitude cannot comprehend.

27. All men can see the tactics whereby I conquer, but what none can see is the strategy out of which victory is evolved.

[I.e., everybody can see superficially how a battle is won; what they cannot see is the long series of plans and combinations which has preceded the battle.]

28. Do not repeat the tactics which have gained you one victory, but let your methods be regulated by the infinite variety of circumstances.

[As Wang Hsi sagely remarks: "There is but one root-principle underlying victory, but the tactics which lead up to it are infinite in number." With this compare Col. Henderson: "The rules of strategy are few and simple. They may be learned in a week. They may be taught by familiar illustrations or a dozen diagrams. But such knowledge will no more teach a man to lead an army like Napoleon than a knowledge of grammar will teach him to write like Gibbon."]

29. Military tactics are like unto water; for water in its natural course runs away from high places and hastens downwards.

30. So in war, the way is to avoid what is strong and to strike at what is weak.

[Like water, taking the line of least resistance.]

31. Water shapes its course according to the nature of the ground over which it flows; the soldier works out his victory in relation to the foe whom he is facing.

32. Therefore, just as water retains no constant shape, so in warfare there are no constant conditions.

33. He who can modify his tactics in relation to his opponent and thereby succeed in winning, may be called a heaven-born captain.

34. The five elements (water, fire, wood, metal, earth) are not always equally predominant;

[That is, as Wang Hsi says: "they predominate alternately."]

the four seasons make way for each other in turn.

[Literally, "have no invariable seat."]

There are short days and long; the moon has its periods of waning and waxing.

[Cf. V. § 6. The purport of the passage is simply to illustrate the want of fixity in war by the changes constantly taking place in Nature. The comparison is not very happy, however, because the regularity of the phenomena which Sun Tzu mentions is by no means paralleled in war.]

[1] See Col. Henderson's biography of Stonewall Jackson, 1902 ed., vol. II, p. 490.

CHAPTER VII. MANŒUVERING

1. Sun Tzu said: In war, the general receives his commands from the sovereign.

2. Having collected an army and concentrated his forces, he must blend and harmonize the different elements thereof before pitching his camp.

["Chang Yu says: "the establishment of harmony and confidence between the higher and lower ranks before venturing into the field;" and he quotes a saying of Wu Tzu (chap. I ad init.): "Without harmony in the State, no military expedition can be undertaken; without harmony in the army, no battle array can be formed." In an historical romance Sun Tzu is represented as saying to Wu Yuan: "As a general rule, those who are waging war should get rid of all the domestic troubles before proceeding to attack the external foe."]

3. After that, comes tactical manœuvering, than which there is nothing more difficult.

[I have departed slightly from the traditional interpretation of Ts'ao Kung, who says: "From the time of receiving the sovereign's instructions until our encampment over against the enemy, the tactics to be pursued are most difficult." It seems to me that the tactics or manœuvers can hardly be said to begin until the army has sallied forth and encamped, and Ch'ien Hao's note gives color to this view: "For levying, concentrating, harmonizing and entrenching an army, there are plenty of old rules which will serve. The real difficulty comes when we engage in tactical operations." Tu Yu also observes that "the great difficulty is to be beforehand with the enemy in seizing favorable position."]

The difficulty of tactical manœuvering consists in turning the devious into the direct, and misfortune into gain.

[This sentence contains one of those highly condensed and somewhat enigmatical expressions of which Sun Tzu is so fond. This is how it is explained by Ts'ao Kung: "Make it appear that you are a long way off, then cover the distance rapidly and arrive on the scene before your opponent." Tu Mu says: "Hoodwink the enemy, so that he may be remiss and leisurely while you are dashing along with utmost speed." Ho Shih gives a slightly different turn: "Although you may have difficult ground to traverse and natural obstacles to encounter this is a drawback which can be turned into actual advantage by celerity of movement." Signal examples of this saying are afforded by the two famous passages across the Alps—that of Hannibal, which laid Italy at his mercy, and that of Napoleon two thousand years later, which resulted in the great victory of Marengo.]

4. Thus, to take a long and circuitous route, after enticing the enemy out of the way, and though starting after him, to contrive to reach the goal before him, shows knowledge of the artifice of deviation.

[Tu Mu cites the famous march of Chao She in 270 B.C. to relieve the town of O-yu, which was closely invested by a Ch'in army. The King of Chao first consulted Lien P'o on the advisability of attempting a relief, but the latter thought the distance too great, and the intervening country too rugged and difficult. His Majesty then turned to Chao She, who fully admitted the hazardous nature of the march, but finally said: "We shall be like two rats fighting in a whole—and the pluckier one will win!" So he left the capital with his army, but had only gone a distance of 30 li when he stopped and began throwing up entrenchments. For 28 days he continued strengthening his fortifications, and took care that spies should carry the intelligence to the enemy. The Ch'in general was overjoyed, and attributed his adversary's tardiness to the fact that the beleaguered city was in the Han State, and thus not actually part of Chao territory. But the spies had no sooner departed than Chao She began a forced march lasting for two days and one night, and arrive on the scene of action with such astonishing rapidity that he was able to occupy a commanding position on the "North hill" before the enemy had got wind of his movements. A crushing defeat followed for the Ch'in forces, who were obliged to raise the siege of O-yu in all haste and retreat across the border.]

5. Manœuvering with an army is advantageous; with an undisciplined multitude, most dangerous.

[I adopt the reading of the T'ung Tien, Cheng Yu-hsien and the T'u Shu, since they appear to apply the exact nuance required in order to make sense. The commentators using the standard text take this line to mean that manœuvers may be profitable, or they may be dangerous: it all depends on the ability of the general.]

6. If you set a fully equipped army in march in order to snatch an advantage, the chances are that you will be too late. On the other hand, to detach a flying column for the purpose involves the sacrifice of its baggage and stores.

[Some of the Chinese text is unintelligible to the Chinese commentators, who paraphrase the sentence. I submit my own rendering without much enthusiasm, being convinced that there is some deep-seated corruption in the text. On the whole, it is clear that Sun Tzu does not approve of a lengthy march being undertaken without supplies. Cf. infra, § 11.]

7. Thus, if you order your men to roll up their buff-coats, and make forced marches without halting day or night, covering double the usual distance at a stretch,

[The ordinary day's march, according to Tu Mu, was 30 li; but on one occasion, when pursuing Liu Pei, Ts'ao Ts'ao is said to have covered the incredible distance of 300 li within twenty-four hours.]

doing a hundred *li* in order to wrest an advantage, the leaders of all your three divisions will fall into the hands of the enemy.

8. The stronger men will be in front, the jaded ones will fall behind, and on this plan only one-tenth of your army will reach its destination.

[The moral is, as Ts'ao Kung and others point out: Don't march a hundred li to gain a tactical advantage, either with or without impedimenta. Manœuvers of this description should be confined to short distances. Stonewall Jackson said "The hardships of forced marches are often more painful than the dangers of battle." He did not often call upon his troops for extraordinary exertions. It was only when he intended a surprise, or when a rapid retreat was imperative, that he sacrificed everything for speed. [1]]

9. If you march fifty li in order to outmanœuver the enemy, you will lose the leader of your first division, and only half your force will reach the goal.

[Literally, "the leader of the first division will be torn away."]

10. If you march thirty li with the same object, two-thirds of your army will arrive.

[In the T'ung Tien is added: "From this we may know the difficulty of manœuvering."]

11. We may take it then that an army without its baggage-train is lost; without provisions it is lost; without bases of supply it is lost.

[I think Sun Tzu meant "stores accumulated in depots." But Tu Yu says "fodder and the like," Chang Yu says "Goods in general," and Wang Hsi says "fuel, salt, foodstuffs, etc."]

12. We cannot enter into alliances until we are acquainted with

the designs of our neighbors.

13. We are not fit to lead an army on the march unless we are familiar with the face of the country—its mountains and forests, its pitfalls and precipices, its marshes and swamps.

14. We shall be unable to turn natural advantage to account unless we make use of local guides.

[§§. 12-14 are repeated in chap. XI. § 52.]

15. In war, practice dissimulation, and you will succeed.

[In the tactics of Turenne, deception of the enemy, especially as to the numerical strength of his troops, took a very prominent position. [2]]

16. Whether to concentrate or to divide your troops, must be decided by circumstances.

17. Let your rapidity be that of the wind,

[The simile is doubly appropriate, because the wind is not only swift but, as Mei Yao-ch'en points out, "invisible and leaves no tracks."]

your compactness that of the forest.

[Meng Shih comes nearer to the mark in his note: "When slowly marching, order and ranks must be preserved"—so as to guard against surprise attacks. But natural forest do not grow in rows, whereas they do generally possess the quality of density or compactness.]

18. In raiding and plundering be like fire,

[Cf. Shih Ching, IV. 3. iv. 6: "Fierce as a blazing fire which no man can check."]

in immovability like a mountain.

[That is, when holding a position from which the enemy is trying to dislodge you, or perhaps, as Tu Yu says, when he is trying to entice you into a trap.]

19. Let your plans be dark and impenetrable as night, and when you move, fall like a thunderbolt.

[Tu Yu quotes a saying of T'ai Kung which has passed into a proverb: "You cannot shut your ears to the thunder or your eyes to the lighting—so rapid are they." Likewise, an attack should be made so quickly that it cannot be parried.]

20. When you plunder a countryside, let the spoil be divided amongst your men;

[Sun Tzu wishes to lessen the abuses of indiscriminate plundering by insisting that all booty shall be thrown into a common stock, which may afterwards be fairly divided amongst all.]

when you capture new territory, cut it up into allotments for the benefit of the soldiery.

[Ch'en Hao says "quarter your soldiers on the land, and let them sow and plant it." It is by acting on this principle, and harvesting the lands they invaded, that the Chinese have succeeded in carrying out some of their most memorable and triumphant expeditions, such as that of Pan Ch'ao who penetrated to the Caspian, and in more recent years, those of Fu-k'ang-an and Tso Tsung-t'ang.]

21. Ponder and deliberate before you make a move.

[Chang Yu quotes Wei Liao Tzu as saying that we must not break camp until we have gained the resisting power of the enemy and the cleverness of the opposing general. Cf. the "seven comparisons" in I. § 13.]

22. He will conquer who has learnt the artifice of deviation.

[See supra, §§ 3, 4.]

Such is the art of manœuvering.

[With these words, the chapter would naturally come to an end. But there now follows a long appendix in the shape of an extract from an earlier book on War, now lost, but apparently extant at the time when Sun Tzu wrote. The style of this fragment is not noticeably different from that of Sun Tzu himself, but no commentator raises a doubt as to its genuineness.]

23. The Book of Army Management says:

[It is perhaps significant that none of the earlier commentators give us any information about this work. Mei Yao- Ch'en calls it "an ancient military classic," and Wang Hsi, "an old book on war." Considering the enormous amount of fighting that had gone on for centuries before Sun Tzu's time between the various kingdoms and principalities of China, it is not in itself improbable that a collection of military maxims should have been made and written down at some earlier period.]

On the field of battle,

[Implied, though not actually in the Chinese.]

the spoken word does not carry far enough: hence the institution of gongs and drums. Nor can ordinary objects be seen clearly enough: hence the institution of banners and flags.

24. Gongs and drums, banners and flags, are means whereby the ears and eyes of the host may be focused on one particular point.

[Chang Yu says: "If sight and hearing converge simultaneously on the same object, the evolutions of as many as a million soldiers will be like those of a single man."!]

25. The host thus forming a single united body, is it impossible either for the brave to advance alone, or for the cowardly to retreat alone.

[Chuang Yu quotes a saying: "Equally guilty are those who advance against orders and those who retreat against orders." Tu Mu tells a story in this connection of Wu Ch'i, when he was fighting against the Ch'in State. Before the battle had begun, one of his soldiers, a man of matchless daring, sallied forth by himself, captured two heads from the enemy, and returned to camp. Wu Ch'i had the man instantly executed, whereupon an officer ventured to remonstrate, saying: "This man was a good soldier, and ought not to have been beheaded." Wu Ch'i replied: "I fully believe he was a good soldier, but I had him beheaded because he acted without orders."]

This is the art of handling large masses of men.

26. In night-fighting, then, make much use of signal-fires and drums, and in fighting by day, of flags and banners, as a means of influencing the ears and eyes of your army.

[Ch'en Hao alludes to Li Kuang-pi's night ride to Ho-yang at the head of 500 mounted men; they made such an imposing display with torches, that though the rebel leader Shih Ssu-ming had a large army, he did not dare to dispute their passage.]

27. A whole army may be robbed of its spirit;

["In war," says Chang Yu, "if a spirit of anger can be made to pervade all ranks of an army at one and the same time, its onset will be irresistible. Now the spirit of the enemy's soldiers will be keenest when they have newly arrived on the scene, and it is therefore our cue not to fight at once, but to wait until their ardor and enthusiasm have worn off, and then strike. It is in this way that they may be robbed of their keen spirit." Li Ch'uan and others tell an anecdote (to be found in the Tso Chuan, year 10, § 1) of Ts'ao Kuei, a protege of Duke Chuang of Lu. The latter State was attacked by Ch'i, and the duke was about to join battle at Ch'ang-cho, after the first roll of the enemy's drums, when Ts'ao said: "Not just yet." Only after their drums had beaten for the third time, did he give the word for attack. Then they fought, and the men of Ch'i were utterly defeated.

Questioned afterwards by the Duke as to the meaning of his delay, Ts'ao Kuei replied: "In battle, a courageous spirit is everything. Now the first roll of the drum tends to create this spirit, but with the second it is already on the wane, and after the third it is gone altogether. I attacked when their spirit was gone and ours was at its height. Hence our victory." Wu Tzu (chap. 4) puts "spirit" first among the "four important influences" in war, and continues: "The value of a whole army—a mighty host of a million men—is dependent on one man alone: such is the influence of spirit!"]

a commander-in-chief may be robbed of his presence of mind.

[Chang Yu says: "Presence of mind is the general's most important asset. It is the quality which enables him to discipline disorder and to inspire courage into the panic-stricken." The great general Li Ching (A.D. 571-649) has a saying: "Attacking does not merely consist in assaulting walled cities or striking at an army in battle array; it must include the art of assailing the enemy's mental equilibrium."]

28. Now a soldier's spirit is keenest in the morning;

[Always provided, I suppose, that he has had breakfast. At the battle of the

Trebia, the Romans were foolishly allowed to fight fasting, whereas Hannibal's men had breakfasted at their leisure. See Livy, XXI, liv. 8, lv. 1 and 8.]

by noonday it has begun to flag; and in the evening, his mind is bent only on returning to camp.

29. A clever general, therefore, avoids an army when its spirit is keen, but attacks it when it is sluggish and inclined to return. This is the art of studying moods.

30. Disciplined and calm, to await the appearance of disorder and hubbub amongst the enemy:—this is the art of retaining self-possession.

31. To be near the goal while the enemy is still far from it, to wait at ease while the enemy is toiling and struggling, to be well-fed while the enemy is famished:—this is the art of husbanding one's strength.

32. To refrain from intercepting an enemy whose banners are in perfect order, to refrain from attacking an army drawn up in calm and confident array:—this is the art of studying circumstances.

33. It is a military axiom not to advance uphill against the enemy, nor to oppose him when he comes downhill.

34. Do not pursue an enemy who simulates flight; do not attack soldiers whose temper is keen.

35. Do not swallow bait offered by the enemy.

[Li Ch'uan and Tu Mu, with extraordinary inability to see a metaphor, take these words quite literally of food and drink that have been poisoned by the enemy. Ch'en Hao and Chang Yu carefully point out that the saying has a wider application.]

Do not interfere with an army that is returning home.

[The commentators explain this rather singular piece of advice by saying that a man whose heart is set on returning home will fight to the death against any attempt to bar his way, and is therefore too dangerous an opponent to be tackled. Chang Yu quotes the words of Han Hsin: "Invincible is the soldier who hath his desire and returneth homewards." A marvelous tale is told of Ts'ao Ts'ao's courage and resource in ch. I of the San Kuo Chi, In 198 A.D., he was besieging Chang Hsiu in Jang, when Liu Piao sent reinforcements with a view to cutting off Ts'ao's retreat. The latter was obliged to draw off his troops, only to find himself hemmed in between two enemies, who were guarding each outlet of a narrow pass in which he had engaged himself. In this desperate plight Ts'ao waited until nightfall, when he bored a tunnel into the mountain side and laid an ambush in it. As soon as the whole army had passed by, the hidden troops fell on his rear, while Ts'ao himself turned and met his pursuers in front, so that they were thrown into confusion and annihilated. Ts'ao Ts'ao said afterwards: "The brigands tried to check my army in its retreat and brought me to battle in a desperate position: hence I knew how to overcome them."]

36. When you surround an army, leave an outlet free.

[This does not mean that the enemy is to be allowed to escape. The object, as Tu Mu puts it, is "to make him believe that there is a road to safety, and thus prevent his fighting with the courage of despair." Tu Mu adds pleasantly: "After that, you may crush him."]

Do not press a desperate foe too hard.

[Ch'en Hao quotes the saying: "Birds and beasts when brought to bay will use their claws and teeth." Chang Yu says: "If your adversary has burned his boats and destroyed his cooking-pots, and is ready to stake all on the issue of a battle, he must not be pushed to extremities." Ho Shih illustrates the meaning by a story taken from the life of Yen-ch'ing. That general, together with his colleague Tu Chung-wei was surrounded by a vastly superior army of Khitans in the year 945 A.D. The country was bare and desert-like, and the little Chinese force was soon in dire straits for want of water. The wells they bored ran dry, and the men were reduced to squeezing lumps of mud and sucking out the moisture. Their ranks thinned rapidly, until at last Fu Yen-ch'ing exclaimed: "We are desperate men. Far better to die for our country than to go with fettered hands into captivity!" A strong gale happened to be blowing from the northeast and darkening the air with dense clouds of sandy dust. To Chung-wei was for waiting until this had abated before deciding on a final attack; but luckily another officer, Li Shou-cheng by name, was quicker to see an opportunity, and said: "They are many and we are few, but in the midst of this sandstorm our numbers will not be discernible; victory will go to the strenuous fighter, and the wind will be our best ally." Accordingly, Fu Yen-ch'ing made a sudden and wholly unexpected onslaught with his cavalry, routed the barbarians and succeeded in breaking through to safety.]

37. Such is the art of warfare.

See Col. Henderson, op. cit. vol. I. p. 426.

For a number of maxims on this head, see "Marshal Turenne" (Longmans, 1907), p. 29

CHAPTER VIII. VARIATION OF TACTICS

[The heading means literally "The Nine Variations," but as Sun Tzu does not appear to enumerate these, and as, indeed, he has already told us (V §§ 6-11) that such deflections from the ordinary course are practically innumerable, we have little option but to follow Wang Hsi, who says that "Nine" stands for an indefinitely large number. "All it means is that in warfare we ought to vary our tactics to the utmost degree.... I do not know what Ts'ao Kung makes these Nine Variations out to be, but it has been suggested that they are connected with the Nine Situations" - of chapt. XI. This is the view adopted by Chang Yu. The only other alternative is to suppose that something has been lost—a supposition to which the unusual shortness of the chapter lends some weight.]

1. Sun Tzu said: In war, the general receives his commands from the sovereign, collects his army and concentrates his forces.

[Repeated from VII. § 1, where it is certainly more in place. It may have been interpolated here merely in order to supply a beginning to the chapter.]

2. When in difficult country, do not encamp. In country where high roads intersect, join hands with your allies. Do not linger in dangerously isolated positions.

[The last situation is not one of the Nine Situations as given in the beginning of chap. XI, but occurs later on (ibid. § 43. q.v.). Chang Yu defines this situation as being situated across the frontier, in hostile territory. Li Ch'uan says it is "country in which there are no springs or wells, flocks or herds, vegetables or firewood;" Chia Lin, "one of gorges, chasms and precipices, without a road by which to advance."]

In hemmed-in situations, you must resort to stratagem. In desperate position, you must fight.

3. There are roads which must not be followed,

["Especially those leading through narrow defiles," says Li Ch'uan, "where an ambush is to be feared."]

armies which must be not attacked,

[More correctly, perhaps, "there are times when an army must not be attacked." Ch'en Hao says: "When you see your way to obtain a rival advantage, but are powerless to inflict a real defeat, refrain from attacking, for fear of overtaxing your men's strength."]

towns which must not be besieged,

[Cf. III. § 4 Ts'ao Kung gives an interesting illustration from his own experience. When invading the territory of Hsu-chou, he ignored the city of Hua-pi, which lay directly in his path, and pressed on into the heart of the country. This excellent strategy was rewarded by the subsequent capture of no fewer than fourteen important district cities. Chang Yu says: "No town should be attacked which, if taken, cannot be held, or if left alone, will not cause any trouble." Hsun Ying, when urged to attack Pi-yang, replied: "The city is small and well-fortified; even if I succeed intaking it, it will be no great feat of arms; whereas if I fail, I shall make myself a laughing-stock." In the seventeenth century, sieges still formed a large proportion of war. It was Turenne who directed attention to the importance of marches, countermarches and manœuvers. He said: "It is a great mistake to waste men in taking a town when the same expenditure of soldiers will gain a province." [I]] positions which must not be contested, commands of the sovereign which must not be obeyed.

[This is a hard saying for the Chinese, with their reverence for authority, and Wei Liao Tzu (quoted by Tu Mu) is moved to exclaim: "Weapons are baleful instruments, strife is antagonistic to virtue, a military commander is the negation of civil order!" The unpalatable fact remains, however, that even Imperial wishes must be subordinated to military necessity.]

4. The general who thoroughly understands the advantages that accompany variation of tactics knows how to handle his troops.

5. The general who does not understand these, may be well acquainted with the configuration of the country, yet he will not be able to turn his knowledge to practical account.

[Literally, "get the advantage of the ground," which means not only securing good positions, but availing oneself of natural advantages in every possible way. Chang Yu says: "Every kind of ground is characterized by certain natural features, and also gives scope for a certain variability of plan. How it is possible to turn these natural features to account unless topographical knowledge is supplemented by versatility of mind?"]

6. So, the student of war who is unversed in the art of war of varying his plans, even though he be acquainted with the Five Advantages, will fail to make the best use of his men.

[Chia Lin tells us that these imply five obvious and generally advantageous lines of action, namely: "if a certain road is short, it must be followed; if an army is isolated, it must be attacked; if a town is in a parlous condition, it must be besieged; if a position can be stormed, it must be attempted; and if consistent with military operations, the ruler's commands must be obeyed." But there are circumstances which sometimes forbid a general to use these advantages. For instance, "a certain road may be the shortest way for him, but if he knows that it abounds in natural obstacles, or that the enemy has laid an ambush on it, he will not follow that road. A hostile force may be open to attack, but if he knows that it is hard-pressed and likely to fight with desperation, he will refrain from striking," and so on.]

7. Hence in the wise leader's plans, considerations of advantage and of disadvantage will be blended together.

["Whether in an advantageous position or a disadvantageous one," says Ts'ao Kung, "the opposite state should be always present to your mind."]

8. If our expectation of advantage be tempered in this way, we may succeed in accomplishing the essential part of our schemes.

[Tu Mu says: "If we wish to wrest an advantage from the enemy, we must not fix our minds on that alone, but allow for the possibility of the enemy also doing some harm to us, and let this enter as a factor into our calculations."]

9. If, on the other hand, in the midst of difficulties we are always ready to seize an advantage, we may extricate ourselves from misfortune.

[Tu Mu says: "If I wish to extricate myself from a dangerous position, I must consider not only the enemy's ability to injure me, but also my own ability to gain an advantage over the enemy. If in my counsels these two considerations are properly blended, I shall succeed in liberating myself.... For instance; if I am

surrounded by the enemy and only think of effecting an escape, the nervelessness of my policy will incite my adversary to pursue and crush me; it would be far better to encourage my men to deliver a bold counter-attack, and use the advantage thus gained to free myself from the enemy's toils." See the story of Ts'ao Ts'ao, VII. § 35, note.]

10. Reduce the hostile chiefs by inflicting damage on them;

[Chia Lin enumerates several ways of inflicting this injury, some of which would only occur to the Oriental mind:—"Entice away the enemy's best and wisest men, so that he may be left without counselors. Introduce traitors into his country, that the government policy may be rendered futile. Foment intrigue and deceit, and thus sow dissension between the ruler and his ministers. By means of every artful contrivance, cause deterioration amongst his men and waste of his treasure. Corrupt his morals by insidious gifts leading him into excess. Disturb and unsettle his mind by presenting him with lovely women." Chang Yu (after Wang Hsi) makes a different interpretation of Sun Tzu here: "Get the enemy into a position where he must suffer injury, and he will submit of his own accord."]

and make trouble for them,

[Tu Mu, in this phrase, in his interpretation indicates that trouble should be made for the enemy affecting their "possessions," or, as we might say, "assets," which he considers to be "a large army, a rich exchequer, harmony amongst the soldiers, punctual fulfillment of commands." These give us a whip-hand over the enemy.]

and keep them constantly engaged;

[Literally, "make servants of them." Tu Yu says "prevent them from having any rest."]

hold out specious allurements, and make them rush to any given point.

[Meng Shih's note contains an excellent example of the idiomatic use of: "cause them to forget pien (the reasons for acting otherwise than on their first impulse), and hasten in our direction."]

11. The art of war teaches us to rely not on the likelihood of the enemy's not coming, but on our own readiness to receive him; not on the chance of his not attacking, but rather on the fact that we

have made our position unassailable.

12. There are five dangerous faults which may affect a general: (1) Recklessness, which leads to destruction;

["Bravery without forethought," as Ts'ao Kung analyzes it, which causes a man to fight blindly and desperately like a mad bull. Such an opponent, says Chang Yu, "must not be encountered with brute force, but may be lured into an ambush and slain." Cf. Wu Tzu, chap. IV. ad init.: "In estimating the character of a general, men are wont to pay exclusive attention to his courage, forgetting that courage is only one out of many qualities which a general should possess. The merely brave man is prone to fight recklessly; and he who fights recklessly, without any perception of what is expedient, must be condemned." Ssu-ma Fa, too, makes the incisive remark: "Simply going to one's death does not bring about victory."]

(2) cowardice, which leads to capture;

[Ts'ao Kung defines the Chinese word translated here as "cowardice" as being of the man "whom timidity prevents from advancing to seize an advantage," and Wang Hsi adds "who is quick to flee at the sight of danger." Meng Shih gives the closer paraphrase "he who is bent on returning alive," this is, the man who will never take a risk. But, as Sun Tzu knew, nothing is to be achieved in war unless you are willing to take risks. T'ai Kung said: "He who lets an advantage slip will subsequently bring upon himself real disaster." In 404 A.D., Liu Yu pursued the rebel Huan Hsuan up the Yangtsze and fought a naval battle with him at the island of Ch'eng-hung. The loyal troops numbered only a few thousands, while their opponents were in great force. But Huan Hsuan, fearing the fate which was in store for him should be be overcome, had a light boat made fast to the side of his war-junk, so that he might escape, if necessary, at a moment's notice. The natural result was that the fighting spirit of his soldiers was utterly quenched, and when the loyalists made an attack from windward with fireships, all striving with the utmost ardor to be first in the fray, Huan Hsuan's forces were routed, had to burn all their baggage and fled for two days and nights without stopping. Chang Yu tells a somewhat similar story of Chao Ying-ch'i, a general of the Chin State who during a battle with the army of Ch'u in 597 B.C. had a boat kept in readiness for him on the river, wishing in case of defeat to be the first to get across.]

(3) a hasty temper, which can be provoked by insults;

[Tu Mu tells us that Yao Hsing, when opposed in 357 A.D. by Huang Mei, Teng Ch'iang and others shut himself up behind his walls and refused to fight. Teng Ch'iang said: "Our adversary is of a choleric temper and easily provoked; let us make constant sallies and break down his walls, then he will grow angry and come out. Once we can bring his force to battle, it is doomed to be our prey." This plan was acted upon, Yao Hsiang came out to fight, was lured as far as San-yuan by the enemy's pretended flight, and finally attacked and slain.]

(4) a delicacy of honor which is sensitive to shame;

This need not be taken to mean that a sense of honor is really a defect in a general. What Sun Tzu condemns is rather an exaggerated sensitiveness to slanderous reports, the thin-skinned man who is stung by opprobrium, however undeserved. Mei Yao-ch'en truly observes, though somewhat paradoxically: "The seeker after glory should be careless of public opinion."]

(5) over-solicitude for his men, which exposes him to worry and trouble.

[Here again, Sun Tzu does not mean that the general is to be careless of the welfare of his troops. All he wishes to emphasize is the danger of sacrificing any important military advantage to the immediate comfort of his men. This is a shortsighted policy, because in the long run the troops will suffer more from the defeat, or, at best, the prolongation of the war, which will be the consequence. A mistaken feeling of pity will often induce a general to relieve a beleaguered city, or to reinforce a hard-pressed detachment, contrary to his military instincts. It is now generally admitted that our repeated efforts to relieve Ladysmith in the South African War were so many strategical blunders which defeated their own purpose. And in the end, relief came through the very man who started out with the distinct resolve no longer to subordinate the interests of the whole to sentiment in favor of a part. An old soldier of one of our generals who failed most conspicuously in this war, tried once, I remember, to defend him to me on the ground that he was always "so good to his men." By this plea, had he but known it, he was only condemning him out of Sun Tzu's mouth.]

13. These are the five besetting sins of a general, ruinous to the conduct of war.

14. When an army is overthrown and its leader slain, the cause will surely be found among these five dangerous faults. Let them be a subject of meditation.

[1] "Marshal Turenne," p. 50.

CHAPTER IX. THE ARMY ON THE MARCH

[The contents of this interesting chapter are better indicated in § 1 than by this heading.]

1. Sun Tzu said: We come now to the question of encamping the army, and observing signs of the enemy. Pass quickly over mountains, and keep in the neighborhood of valleys.

[The idea is, not to linger among barren uplands, but to keep close to supplies of water and grass. Cf. Wu Tzu, ch. 3: "Abide not in natural ovens," i.e. "the openings of valleys." Chang Yu tells the following anecdote: Wu-tu Ch'iang was a robber captain in the time of the Later Han, and Ma Yuan was sent to exterminate his gang. Ch'iang having found a refuge in the hills, Ma Yuan made no attempt to force a battle, but seized all the favorable positions commanding supplies of water and forage. Ch'iang was soon in such a desperate plight for want of provisions that he was forced to make a total surrender. He did not know the advantage of keeping in the neighborhood of valleys."]

2. Camp in high places,

[Not on high hills, but on knolls or hillocks elevated above the surrounding country.]

facing the sun.

[Tu Mu takes this to mean "facing south," and Ch'en Hao "facing east." Cf. infra, §§ 11, 13.

Do not climb heights in order to fight. So much for mountain warfare.

3. After crossing a river, you should get far away from it.

["In order to tempt the enemy to cross after you," according to Ts'ao Kung, and also, says Chang Yu, "in order not to be impeded in your evolutions." The T'ung Tien reads, "If the enemy crosses a river," etc. But in view of the next sentence, this is almost certainly an interpolation.]

4. When an invading force crosses a river in its onward march, do not advance to meet it in mid-stream. It will be best to let half the army get across, and then deliver your attack.

[Li Ch'uan alludes to the great victory won by Han Hsin over Lung Chu at the Wei River. Turning to the Ch'ien Han Shu, ch. 34, fol. 6 verso, we find the battle described as follows: "The two armies were drawn up on opposite sides of the river. In the night, Han Hsin ordered his men to take some ten thousand sacks filled with sand and construct a dam higher up. Then, leading half his army across, he attacked Lung Chu; but after a time, pretending to have failed in his attempt, he hastily withdrew to the other bank. Lung Chu was much elated by this unlooked-for success, and exclaiming: "I felt sure that Han Hsin was really a coward!" he pursued him and began crossing the river in his turn. Han Hsin now sent a party to cut open the sandbags, thus releasing a great volume of water, which swept down and prevented the greater portion of Lung Chu's army from getting across. He then turned upon the force which had been cut off, and annihilated it, Lung Chu himself being amongst the slain. The rest of the army, on the further bank, also scattered and fled in all directions.]

5. If you are anxious to fight, you should not go to meet the invader near a river which he has to cross.

[For fear of preventing his crossing.]

6. Moor your craft higher up than the enemy, and facing the sun.

[See supra, § 2. The repetition of these words in connection with water is very awkward. Chang Yu has the note: "Said either of troops marshaled on the river-bank, or of boats anchored in the stream itself; in either case it is essential to be higher than the enemy and facing the sun." The other commentators are not at all explicit.]

Do not move up-stream to meet the enemy.

[Tu Mu says: "As water flows downwards, we must not pitch our camp on the lower reaches of a river, for fear the enemy should open the sluices and sweep us away in a flood. Chu-ko Wu-hou has remarked that 'in river warfare we must not advance against the stream,' which is as much as to say that our fleet must not be anchored below that of the enemy, for then they would be able to take advantage of the current and make short work of us." There is also the danger, noted by other commentators, that the enemy may throw poison on the water to be carried down to us.]

So much for river warfare.

7. In crossing salt-marshes, your sole concern should be to get over them quickly, without any delay.

[Because of the lack of fresh water, the poor quality of the herbage, and last but not least, because they are low, flat, and exposed to attack.]

8. If forced to fight in a salt-marsh, you should have water and grass near you, and get your back to a clump of trees.

[Li Ch'uan remarks that the ground is less likely to be treacherous where there are trees, while Tu Mu says that they will serve to protect the rear.]

So much for operations in salt-marches.

9. In dry, level country, take up an easily accessible position with rising ground to your right and on your rear,

[Tu Mu quotes T'ai Kung as saying: "An army should have a stream or a marsh on its left, and a hill or tumulus on its right."]

so that the danger may be in front, and safety lie behind. So much for campaigning in flat country.

10. These are the four useful branches of military knowledge

[Those, namely, concerned with (1) mountains, (2) rivers, (3) marshes, and (4) plains. Compare Napoleon's "Military Maxims," no. 1.]

which enabled the Yellow Emperor to vanquish four several sovereigns.

[Regarding the "Yellow Emperor": Mei Yao-ch'en asks, with some plausibility, whether there is an error in the text as nothing is known of Huang Ti having conquered four other Emperors. The Shih Chi (ch. 1 ad init.) speaks only of his victories over Yen Ti and Ch'ih Yu. In the Liu T'ao it is mentioned that he "fought seventy battles and pacified the Empire." Ts'ao Kung's explanation is, that the Yellow Emperor was the first to institute the feudal system of vassals princes, each of whom (to the number of four) originally bore the title of Emperor. Li Ch'uan tells us that the art of war originated under Huang Ti, who received it from his Minister Feng Hou.]

11. All armies prefer high ground to low.

["High Ground," says Mei Yao-ch'en, "is not only more agreeable and salubrious, but more convenient from a military point of view; low ground is not only damp and unhealthy, but also disadvantageous for fighting."]

and sunny places to dark.

12. If you are careful of your men,

276

[Ts'ao Kung says: "Make for fresh water and pasture, where you can turn out your animals to graze."]

and camp on hard ground, the army will be free from disease of every kind,

[Chang Yu says: "The dryness of the climate will prevent the outbreak of illness."]

and this will spell victory.

13. When you come to a hill or a bank, occupy the sunny side, with the slope on your right rear. Thus you will at once act for the benefit of your soldiers and utilize the natural advantages of the ground.

14. When, in consequence of heavy rains up-country, a river which you wish to ford is swollen and flecked with foam, you must wait until it subsides.

15. Country in which there are precipitous cliffs with torrents running between, deep natural hollows,

The latter defined as "places enclosed on every side by steep banks, with pools of water at the bottom."]

confined places,

[Defined as "natural pens or prisons" or "places surrounded by precipices on three sides—easy to get into, but hard to get out of."]

tangled thickets,

[Defined as "places covered with such dense undergrowth that spears cannot be used."]

quagmires

[Defined as "low-lying places, so heavy with mud as to be impassable for chariots and horsemen."]

and crevasses,

[Defined by Mei Yao-ch'en as "a narrow difficult way between beetling cliffs." Tu Mu's note is "ground covered with trees and rocks, and intersected by numerous ravines and pitfalls." This is very vague, but Chia Lin explains it clearly enough as a defile or narrow pass, and Chang Yu takes much the same view. On the whole, the weight of the commentators certainly inclines to the rendering "defile." But the ordinary meaning of the Chinese in one place is "a crack or fissure" and the fact that the meaning of the Chinese elsewhere in the sentence indicates something in the nature of a defile, make me think that Sun Tzu is here speaking of crevasses.]

should be left with all possible speed and not approached.

16. While we keep away from such places, we should get the enemy to approach them; while we face them, we should let the enemy have them on his rear.

17. If in the neighborhood of your camp there should be any hilly country, ponds surrounded by aquatic grass, hollow basins filled with reeds, or woods with thick undergrowth, they must be carefully routed out and searched; for these are places where men in ambush or insidious spies are likely to be lurking.

[Chang Yu has the note: "We must also be on our guard against traitors who may lie in close covert, secretly spying out our weaknesses and overhearing our instructions."]

18. When the enemy is close at hand and remains quiet, he is relying on the natural strength of his position.

[Here begin Sun Tzu's remarks on the reading of signs, much of which is so good that it could almost be included in a modern manual like Gen. Baden-Powell's "Aids to Scouting."]

19. When he keeps aloof and tries to provoke a battle, he is anxious for the other side to advance.

[Probably because we are in a strong position from which he wishes to dislodge us. "If he came close up to us, says Tu Mu, "and tried to force a battle, he would seem to despise us, and there would be less probability of our responding to the challenge."]

20. If his place of encampment is easy of access, he is tendering a bait.

21. Movement amongst the trees of a forest shows that the enemy is advancing.

[Ts'ao Kung explains this as "felling trees to clear a passage," and Chang Yu says: "Every man sends out scouts to climb high places and observe the enemy. If a scout sees that the trees of a forest are moving and shaking, he may know that they are being cut down to clear a passage for the enemy's march."]

The appearance of a number of screens in the midst of thick grass means that the enemy wants to make us suspicious.

[Tu Yu's explanation, borrowed from Ts'ao Kung's, is as follows: "The presence of a number of screens or sheds in the midst of thick vegetation is a sure sign that the enemy has fled and, fearing pursuit, has constructed these hiding-places in order to make us suspect an ambush." It appears that these "screens" were hastily knotted together out of any long grass which the retreating enemy happened to come across.]

22. The rising of birds in their flight is the sign of an ambuscade.

[Chang Yu's explanation is doubtless right: "When birds that are flying along in a straight line suddenly shoot upwards, it means that soldiers are in ambush at the spot beneath."]

Startled beasts indicate that a sudden attack is coming.

23. When there is dust rising in a high column, it is the sign of chariots advancing; when the dust is low, but spread over a wide

area, it betokens the approach of infantry.

["High and sharp," or rising to a peak, is of course somewhat exaggerated as applied to dust. The commentators explain the phenomenon by saying that horses and chariots, being heavier than men, raise more dust, and also follow one another in the same wheel-track, whereas foot-soldiers would be marching in ranks, many abreast. According to Chang Yu, "every army on the march must have scouts some way in advance, who on sighting dust raised by the enemy, will gallop back and report it to the commander-in-chief." Cf. Gen. Baden-Powell: "As you move along, say, in a hostile country, your eyes should be looking afar for the enemy or any signs of him: figures, dust rising, birds getting up, glitter of arms, etc." [1]]

When it branches out in different directions, it shows that parties have been sent to collect firewood. A few clouds of dust moving to and fro signify that the army is encamping.

[Chang Yu says: "In apportioning the defenses for a cantonment, light horse will be sent out to survey the position and ascertain the weak and strong points all along its circumference. Hence the small quantity of dust and its motion."]

24. Humble words and increased preparations are signs that the enemy is about to advance.

["As though they stood in great fear of us," says Tu Mu. "Their object is to make us contemptuous and careless, after which they will attack us." Chang Yu alludes to the story of T'ien Tan of the Ch'i-mo against the Yen forces, led by Ch'i Chieh. In ch. 82 of the Shih Chi we read: "T'ien Tan openly said: 'My only fear is that the Yen army may cut off the noses of their Ch'i prisoners and place them in the front rank to fight against us; that would be the undoing of our city.' The other side being informed of this speech, at once acted on the suggestion; but those within the city were enraged at seeing their fellow-countrymen thus mutilated, and fearing only lest they should fall into the enemy's hands, were nerved to defend themselves more obstinately than ever. Once again T'ien Tan sent back converted spies who reported these words to the enemy: "What I dread most is that the men of Yen may dig up the ancestral tombs outside the town, and by inflicting this indignity on our forefathers cause us to become faint-hearted.' Forthwith the besiegers dug up all the graves and burned the corpses lying in them. And the inhabitants of Chi-mo, witnessing the outrage from the city-walls, wept passionately and were all impatient to go out and fight, their fury being increased tenfold. T'ien Tan knew then that his soldiers were ready for any enterprise. But instead of a sword, he himself took a mattock in his hands, and ordered others to be distributed amongst his best warriors, while the ranks were filled up with their wives and concubines. He then served out all the remaining rations and bade his men eat their fill. The regular soldiers were told to keep out of sight, and the walls were manned with the old and weaker men and with women. This done, envoys were dispatched to the enemy's camp to arrange terms of surrender, whereupon the Yen army began shouting for joy. T'ien Tan also collected 20,000 ounces of silver from the people, and got the wealthy citizens of Chi-mo to send it to the Yen general with the prayer that, when the town capitulated, he would not allow their homes to be plundered or their women to be maltreated. Ch'i Chieh, in high good humor, granted their prayer; but his army now became increasingly slack and careless. Meanwhile, T'ien Tan got together a thousand oxen, decked them with pieces of red silk, painted their bodies, dragon-like, with colored stripes, and fastened sharp blades on their horns and well-greased rushes on their tails. When night came on, he lighted the ends of the rushes, and drove the oxen through a number of holes which he had pierced in the walls, backing them up with a force of 5000 picked warriors. The animals, maddened with pain, dashed furiously into the enemy's camp where they caused the utmost confusion and dismay; for their tails acted as torches, showing up the hideous pattern on their bodies, and the weapons on their horns killed or wounded any with whom they came into contact. In the meantime, the band of 5000 had crept up with gags in their mouths, and now threw themselves on the enemy.

At the same moment a frightful din arose in the city itself, all those that remained behind making as much noise as possible by banging drums and hammering on bronze vessels, until heaven and earth were convulsed by the uproar. Terror-stricken, the Yen army fled in disorder, hotly pursued by the men of Ch'i, who succeeded in slaying their general Ch'i Chien.... The result of the battle was the ultimate recovery of some seventy cities which had belonged to the Ch'i State."]

Violent language and driving forward as if to the attack are signs that he will retreat.

25. When the light chariots come out first and take up a position on the wings, it is a sign that the enemy is forming for battle.

26. Peace proposals unaccompanied by a sworn covenant indicate a plot.

[The reading here is uncertain. Li Ch'uan indicates "a treaty confirmed by oaths and hostages." Wang Hsi and Chang Yu, on the other hand, simply say "without reason," "on a frivolous pretext."]

27. When there is much running about

[Every man hastening to his proper place under his own regimental banner.]

and the soldiers fall into rank, it means that the critical moment has come.

28. When some are seen advancing and some retreating, it is a lure.

29. When the soldiers stand leaning on their spears, they are faint from want of food.

30. If those who are sent to draw water begin by drinking themselves, the army is suffering from thirst.

[As Tu Mu remarks: "One may know the condition of a whole army from the behavior of a single man."]

31. If the enemy sees an advantage to be gained and makes no effort to secure it, the soldiers are exhausted.

32. If birds gather on any spot, it is unoccupied.

[A useful fact to bear in mind when, for instance, as Ch'en Hao says, the enemy has secretly abandoned his camp.]

Clamor by night betokens nervousness.

33. If there is disturbance in the camp, the general's authority is weak. If the banners and flags are shifted about, sedition is afoot. If the officers are angry, it means that the men are weary.

[Tu Mu understands the sentence differently: "If all the officers of an army are angry with their general, it means that they are broken with fatigue" owing to the exertions which he has demanded from them.]

34. When an army feeds its horses with grain and kills its cattle for food,

[In the ordinary course of things, the men would be fed on grain and the horses chiefly on grass.]

and when the men do not hang their cooking-pots over the camp-fires, showing that they will not return to their tents, you may know that they are determined to fight to the death.

[I may quote here the illustrative passage from the Hou Han Shu, ch. 71, given in abbreviated form by the P'ei Wen Yun Fu: "The rebel Wang Kuo of Liang was besieging the town of Ch'en- ts'ang, and Huang-fu Sung, who was in supreme command, and Tung Cho were sent out against him. The latter pressed for hasty measures, but Sung turned a deaf ear to his counsel. At last the rebels were utterly worn out, and began to throw down their weapons of their own accord.

Sung was not advancing to the attack, but Cho said: 'It is a principle of war not to pursue desperate men and not to press a retreating host.' Sung answered: 'That does not apply here. What I am about to attack is a jaded army, not a retreating host; with disciplined troops I am falling on a disorganized multitude, not a band of desperate men.' Thereupon he advances to the attack unsupported by his colleague, and routed the enemy, Wang Kuo being slain."]

35. The sight of men whispering together in small knots or speaking in subdued tones points to disaffection amongst the rank and file.

36. Too frequent rewards signify that the enemy is at the end of his resources;

[Because, when an army is hard pressed, as Tu Mu says, there is always a fear of mutiny, and lavish rewards are given to keep the men in good temper.]

too many punishments betray a condition of dire distress.

[Because in such case discipline becomes relaxed, and unwonted se verity is necessary to keep the men to their duty.]

37. To begin by bluster, but afterwards to take fright at the enemy's numbers, shows a supreme lack of intelligence.

[I follow the interpretation of Ts'ao Kung, also adopted by Li Ch'uan, Tu Mu, and Chang Yu. Another possible meaning set forth by Tu Yu, Chia Lin, Mei Tao-ch'en and Wang Hsi, is: "The general who is first tyrannical towards his men, and then in terror lest they should mutiny, etc." This would connect the sentence with what went before about rewards and punishments.]

38. When envoys are sent with compliments in their mouths, it is a sign that the enemy wishes for a truce.

[Tu Mu says: "If the enemy open friendly relations be sending hostages, it is a sign that they are anxious for an armistice, either because their strength is exhausted or for some other reason." But it hardly needs a Sun Tzu to draw such an obvious inference.]

39. If the enemy's troops march up angrily and remain facing ours for a long time without either joining battle or taking themselves off again, the situation is one that demands great vigilance and circumspection.

[Ts'ao Kung says a manœuver of this sort may be only a ruse to gain time for an unexpected flank attack or the laying of an ambush.]

40. If our troops are no more in number than the enemy, that is amply sufficient; it only means that no direct attack can be made.

[Literally, "no martial advance." That is to say, cheng tactics and frontal attacks must be eschewed, and stratagem resorted to instead.]

What we can do is simply to concentrate all our available strength, keep a close watch on the enemy, and obtain reinforcements.

[This is an obscure sentence, and none of the commentators succeed in squeezing very good sense out of it. I follow Li Ch'uan, who appears to offer the simplest explanation: "Only the side that gets more men will win." Fortunately we have Chang Yu to expound its meaning to us in language which is lucidity itself: "When the numbers are even, and no favorable opening presents itself, although we may not be strong enough to deliver a sustained attack, we can find additional recruits amongst our sutlers and camp-followers, and then, concentrating our forces and keeping a close watch on the enemy, contrive to snatch the victory. But we must avoid borrowing foreign soldiers to help us." He then quotes from Wei Liao Tzu, ch. 3: "The nominal strength of mercenary troops may be 100,000, but their real value will be not more than half that figure."]

41. He who exercises no forethought but makes light of his opponents is sure to be captured by them.

[Ch'en Hao, quoting from the Tso Chuan, says: "If bees and scorpions carry

poison, how much more will a hostile state! Even a puny opponent, then, should not be treated with contempt."]

42. If soldiers are punished before they have grown attached to you, they will not prove submissive; and, unless submissive, then will be practically useless. If, when the soldiers have become attached to you, punishments are not enforced, they will still be useless.

43. Therefore soldiers must be treated in the first instance with humanity, but kept under control by means of iron discipline.

[Yen Tzu [B.C. 493] said of Ssu-ma Jang-chu: "His civil virtues endeared him to the people; his martial prowess kept his enemies in awe." Cf. Wu Tzu, ch. 4 init.: "The ideal commander unites culture with a warlike temper; the profession of arms requires a combination of hardness and tenderness."]

This is a certain road to victory.

44. If in training soldiers commands are habitually enforced, the army will be well-disciplined; if not, its discipline will be bad.

45. If a general shows confidence in his men but always insists on his orders being obeyed,

[Tu Mu says: "A general ought in time of peace to show kindly confidence in his men and also make his authority respected, so that when they come to face the enemy, orders may be executed and discipline maintained, because they all trust and look up to him." What Sun Tzu has said in § 44, however, would lead one rather to expect something like this: "If a general is always confident that his orders will be carried out," etc."]

the gain will be mutual.

[Chang Yu says: "The general has confidence in the men under his command, and the men are docile, having confidence in him. Thus the gain is mutual." He quotes a pregnant sentence from Wei Liao Tzu, ch. 4: "The art of giving orders is not to try to rectify minor blunders and not to be swayed by petty doubts." Vacillation and fussiness are the surest means of sapping the confidence of an army.]

[1] "Aids to Scouting," p. 26.

CHAPTER X. TERRAIN

[Only about a third of the chapter, comprising §§ 1-13, deals with "terrain," the subject being more fully treated in ch. XI. The "six calamities" are discussed in §§ 14-20, and the rest of the chapter is again a mere string of desultory remarks, though not less interesting, perhaps, on that account.]

1. Sun Tzu said: We may distinguish six kinds of terrain, to wit: (1) Accessible ground;

[Mei Yao-ch'en says: "plentifully provided with roads and means of communications."]

(2) entangling ground;

[The same commentator says: "Net-like country, venturing into which you become entangled."]

(3) temporizing ground;

[Ground which allows you to "stave off" or "delay."]

(4) narrow passes; (5) precipitous heights; (6) positions at a great distance from the enemy.

[It is hardly necessary to point out the faultiness of this classification. A strange lack of logical perception is shown in the Chinaman's unquestioning acceptance of glaring cross-divisions such as the above.]

2. Ground which can be freely traversed by both sides is called accessible.

3. With regard to ground of this nature, be before the enemy in occupying the raised and sunny spots, and carefully guard your line of supplies.

[The general meaning of the last phrase is doubtlessly, as Tu Yu says, "not to allow the enemy to cut your communications." In view of Napoleon's dictum, "the secret of war lies in the communications," [1] we could wish that Sun Tzu had done more than skirt the edge of this important subject here and in I. § 10, VII. § 11. Col. Henderson says: "The line of supply may be said to be as vital to the existence of an army as the heart to the life of a human being. Just as the duelist who finds his adversary's point menacing him with certain death, and his own guard astray, is compelled to conform to his adversary's movements, and to content himself with warding off his thrusts, so the commander whose communications are suddenly threatened finds himself in a false position, and he will be fortunate if he has not to change all his plans, to split up his force into more or less isolated detachments, and to fight with inferior numbers on ground which he has not had time to prepare, and where defeat will not be an ordinary failure, but will entail the ruin or surrender of his whole army." [2]

Then you will be able to fight with advantage.

4. Ground which can be abandoned but is hard to re-occupy is called entangling.

5. From a position of this sort, if the enemy is unprepared, you may sally forth and defeat him. But if the enemy is prepared for your coming, and you fail to defeat him, then, return being impossible, disaster will ensue.

6. When the position is such that neither side will gain by making the first move, it is called temporizing ground.

[Tu Mu says: "Each side finds it inconvenient to move, and the situation remains at a deadlock."]

7. In a position of this sort, even though the enemy should offer us an attractive bait,

[Tu Yu says, "turning their backs on us and pretending to flee." But this is only one of the lures which might induce us to quit our position.]

it will be advisable not to stir forth, but rather to retreat, thus enticing the enemy in his turn; then, when part of his army has come out, we may deliver our attack with advantage.

8. With regard to narrow passes, if you can occupy them first, let them be strongly garrisoned and await the advent of the enemy.

[Because then, as Tu Yu observes, "the initiative will lie with us, and by making sudden and unexpected attacks we shall have the enemy at our mercy."]

9. Should the army forestall you in occupying a pass, do not go after him if the pass is fully garrisoned, but only if it is weakly garrisoned.

10. With regard to precipitous heights, if you are beforehand with your adversary, you should occupy the raised and sunny spots, and there wait for him to come up.

[Ts'ao Kung says: "The particular advantage of securing heights and defiles is that your actions cannot then be dictated by the enemy." [For the enunciation of the grand principle alluded to, see VI. § 2]. Chang Yu tells the following anecdote of P'ei Hsing-chien (A.D. 619-682), who was sent on a punitive expedition against the Turkic tribes. "At night he pitched his camp as usual, and it had already been completely fortified by wall and ditch, when suddenly he gave orders that the army should shift its quarters to a hill near by. This was highly displeasing to his officers, who protested loudly against the extra fatigue which it would entail on the men. P'ei Hsing-chien, however, paid no heed to their remonstrances and had the camp moved as quickly as possible. The same night, a terrific storm came on, which flooded their former place of encampment to the depth of over twelve feet. The recalcitrant officers were amazed at the sight, and owned that they had been in the wrong. 'How did you know what was going to happen?' they asked. P'ei Hsing-chien replied: 'From this time forward be content to obey orders without asking unnecessary questions.' From this it may be seen," Chang Yu continues, "that high and sunny places are advantageous not only for fighting, but also because they are immune from disastrous floods."]

11. If the enemy has occupied them before you, do not follow him, but retreat and try to entice him away.

[The turning point of Li Shih-min's campaign in 621 A.D. against the two rebels, Tou Chien-te, King of Hsia, and Wang Shih-ch'ung, Prince of Cheng, was his seizure of the heights of Wu-lao, in spite of which Tou Chien-te persisted in his attempt to relieve his ally in Lo-yang, was defeated and taken prisoner. See Chiu T'ang Shu, ch. 2, fol. 5 verso, and also ch. 54.]

12. If you are situated at a great distance from the enemy, and the strength of the two armies is equal, it is not easy to provoke a battle,

[The point is that we must not think of undertaking a long and wearisome march, at the end of which, as Tu Yu says, "we should be exhausted and our adversary fresh and keen."]

and fighting will be to your disadvantage.

13. These six are the principles connected with Earth.

[Or perhaps, "the principles relating to ground." See, however, I. § 8.]

The general who has attained a responsible post must be careful to study them.

14. Now an army is exposed to six several calamities, not arising from natural causes, but from faults for which the general is responsible. These are: (1) Flight; (2) insubordination; (3) collapse; (4) ruin; (5) disorganization; (6) rout.

15. Other conditions being equal, if one force is hurled against another ten times its size, the result will be the flight of the former.

16. When the common soldiers are too strong and their officers too weak, the result is insubordination.

[Tu Mu cites the unhappy case of T'ien Pu [Hsin T'ang Shu, ch. 148], who was sent to Wei in 821 A.D. with orders to lead an army against Wang T'ing-ts'ou. But the whole time he was in command, his soldiers treated him with the utmost contempt, and openly flouted his authority by riding about the camp on donkeys, several thousands at a time. T'ien Pu was powerless to put a stop to this conduct, and when, after some months had passed, he made an attempt to engage the enemy, his troops turned tail and dispersed in every direction. After that, the unfortunate man committed suicide by cutting his throat.]

When the officers are too strong and the common soldiers too weak, the result is collapse.

[Ts'ao Kung says: "The officers are energetic and want to press on, the common soldiers are feeble and suddenly collapse."]

17. When the higher officers are angry and insubordinate, and on meeting the enemy give battle on their own account from a feeling of resentment, before the commander-in-chief can tell whether or no he is in a position to fight, the result is ruin.

[Wang Hsi's note is: "This means, the general is angry without cause, and at the same time does not appreciate the ability of his subordinate officers; thus he arouses fierce resentment and brings an avalanche of ruin upon his head."]

18. When the general is weak and without authority; when his orders are not clear and distinct;

[Wei Liao Tzu (ch. 4) says: "If the commander gives his orders with decision, the soldiers will not wait to hear them twice; if his moves are made without vacillation, the soldiers will not be in two minds about doing their duty." General Baden-Powell says, italicizing the words: "The secret of getting successful work out of your trained men lies in one nutshell—in the clearness of the instructions they receive." [3] Cf. also Wu Tzu ch. 3: "the most fatal defect in a military leader is difference; the worst calamities that befall an army arise from hesitation."]

when there are no fixes duties assigned to officers and men,

[Tu Mu says: "Neither officers nor men have any regular routine."]

and the ranks are formed in a slovenly haphazard manner, the result is utter disorganization.

19. When a general, unable to estimate the enemy's strength, allows an inferior force to engage a larger one, or hurls a weak detachment against a powerful one, and neglects to place picked soldiers in the front rank, the result must be rout.

[Chang Yu paraphrases the latter part of the sentence and continues: "Whenever there is fighting to be done, the keenest spirits should be appointed to serve in the front ranks, both in order to strengthen the resolution of our own men and to demoralize the enemy." Cf. the primi ordines of Caesar ("De Bello Gallico," V. 28, 44, et al.).]

20. These are six ways of courting defeat, which must be carefully noted by the general who has attained a responsible post.

[See supra, § 13.]

21. The natural formation of the country is the soldier's best ally;

[Ch'en Hao says: "The advantages of weather and season are not equal to those connected with ground."]

but a power of estimating the adversary, of controlling the forces of victory, and of shrewdly calculating difficulties, dangers and distances, constitutes the test of a great general.

22. He who knows these things, and in fighting puts his knowledge into practice, will win his battles. He who knows them not, nor practices them, will surely be defeated.

23. If fighting is sure to result in victory, then you must fight, even though the ruler forbid it; if fighting will not result in victory, then you must not fight even at the ruler's bidding.

[Cf. VIII. § 3 fin. Huang Shih-kung of the Ch'in dynasty, who is said to have been the patron of Chang Liang and to have written the San Lueh, has these words attributed to him: "The responsibility of setting an army in motion must devolve on the general alone; if advance and retreat are controlled from the Palace, brilliant results will hardly be achieved. Hence the god-like ruler and the enlightened monarch are content to play a humble part in furthering their country's cause [lit., kneel down to push the chariot wheel]." This means that "in matters lying outside the zenana, the decision of the military commander must be absolute." Chang Yu also quote the saying: "Decrees from the Son of Heaven do not penetrate the walls of a camp."]

24. The general who advances without coveting fame and retreats without fearing disgrace,

[It was Wellington, I think, who said that the hardest thing of all for a soldier is to retreat.]

whose only thought is to protect his country and do good service for his sovereign, is the jewel of the kingdom.

[A noble presentiment, in few words, of the Chinese "happy

warrior." Such a man, says Ho Shih, "even if he had to suffer punishment, would not regret his conduct."]

25. Regard your soldiers as your children, and they will follow you into the deepest valleys; look upon them as your own beloved sons, and they will stand by you even unto death.

[Cf. I. § 6. In this connection, Tu Mu draws for us an engaging picture of the famous general Wu Ch'i, from whose treatise on war I have frequently had occasion to quote: "He wore the same clothes and ate the same food as the meanest of his soldiers, refused to have either a horse to ride or a mat to sleep on, carried his own surplus rations wrapped in a parcel, and shared every hardship with his men. One of his soldiers was suffering from an abscess, and Wu Ch'i himself sucked out the virus. The soldier's mother, hearing this, began wailing and lamenting. Somebody asked her, saying: 'Why do you cry? Your son is only a common soldier, and yet the commander-in-chief himself has sucked the poison from his sore.' The woman replied, 'Many years ago, Lord Wu performed a similar service for my husband, who never left him afterwards, and finally met his death at the hands of the enemy. And now that he has done the same for my son, he too will fall fighting I know not where.'" Li Ch'uan mentions the Viscount of Ch'u, who invaded the small state of Hsiao during the winter. The Duke of Shen said to him: "Many of the soldiers are suffering severely from the cold." So he made a round of the whole army, comforting and encouraging the men; and straightway they felt as if they were clothed in garments lined with floss silk.]

26. If, however, you are indulgent, but unable to make your authority felt; kind-hearted, but unable to enforce your commands; and incapable, moreover, of quelling disorder: then your soldiers must be likened to spoilt children; they are useless for any practical purpose.

[Li Ching once said that if you could make your soldiers afraid of you, they would not be afraid of the enemy. Tu Mu recalls an instance of stern military discipline which occurred in 219 A.D., when Lu Meng was occupying the town of Chiang-ling. He had given stringent orders to his army not to molest the inhabitants nor take anything from them by force. Nevertheless, a certain officer serving under his banner, who happened to be a fellow-townsman, ventured to appropriate a bamboo hat belonging to one of the people, in order to wear it over his regulation helmet as a protection against the rain. Lu Meng considered that the fact of his being also a native of Ju-nan should not be allowed to palliate a clear breach of discipline, and accordingly he ordered his summary execution, the tears rolling down his face, however, as he did so. This act of severity filled the army with wholesome awe, and from that time forth even articles dropped in the highway were not picked up.]

27. If we know that our own men are in a condition to attack, but are unaware that the enemy is not open to attack, we have gone only halfway towards victory.

[That is, Ts'ao Kung says, "the issue in this case is uncertain."]

28. If we know that the enemy is open to attack, but are unaware that our own men are not in a condition to attack, we have gone only halfway towards victory.

[Cf. III. § 13 (1).]

29. If we know that the enemy is open to attack, and also know that our men are in a condition to attack, but are unaware that the nature of the ground makes fighting impracticable, we have still gone only halfway towards victory.

30. Hence the experienced soldier, once in motion, is never bewildered; once he has broken camp, he is never at a loss.

[The reason being, according to Tu Mu, that he has taken his measures so thoroughly as to ensure victory beforehand. "He does not move recklessly," says Chang Yu, "so that when he does move, he makes no mistakes."]

31. Hence the saying: If you know the enemy and know yourself, your victory will not stand in doubt; if you know Heaven and know Earth, you may make your victory complete.

[Li Ch'uan sums up as follows: "Given a knowledge of three things—the affairs of men, the seasons of heaven and the natural advantages of earth—, victory will invariably crown your battles."]

[1] See "Pensees de Napoleon 1er," no. 47.

[2] "The Science of War," chap. 2.

[3] "Aids to Scouting," p. xii.

CHAPTER XI. THE NINE SITUATIONS

1. Sun Tzu said: The art of war recognizes nine varieties of ground:

(1) Dispersive ground; (2) facile ground; (3) contentious ground; (4) open ground; (5) ground of intersecting highways; (6) serious ground; (7) difficult ground; (8) hemmed-in ground; (9) desperate ground.

2. When a chieftain is fighting in his own territory, it is dispersive ground.

[So called because the soldiers, being near to their homes and anxious to see their wives and children, are likely to seize the opportunity afforded by a battle and scatter in every direction. "In their advance," observes Tu Mu, "they will lack the valor of desperation, and when they retreat, they will find harbors of refuge."]

3.When he has penetrated into hostile territory, but to no great distance, it is facile ground.

[Li Ch'uan and Ho Shih say "because of the facility for retreating," and the other commentators give similar explanations. Tu Mu remarks: "When your army has crossed the border, you should burn your boats and bridges, in order to make it clear to everybody that you have no hankering after home."]

4. Ground the possession of which imports great advantage to either side, is contentious ground.

[Tu Mu defines the ground as ground "to be contended for." Ts'ao

Kung says: "ground on which the few and the weak can defeat the many and the strong," such as "the neck of a pass," instanced by Li Ch'uan. Thus, Thermopylae was of this classification because the possession of it, even for a few days only, meant holding the entire invading army in check and thus gaining invaluable time. Cf. Wu Tzu, ch. V. ad init.: "For those who have to fight in the ratio of one to ten, there is nothing better than a narrow pass." When Lu Kuang was returning from his triumphant expedition to Turkestan in 385 A.D., and had got as far as I-ho, laden with spoils, Liang Hsi, administrator of Liang-chou, taking advantage of the death of Fu Chien, King of Ch'in, plotted against him and was for barring his way into the province. Yang Han, governor of Kao-ch'ang, counseled him, saying: "Lu Kuang is fresh from his victories in the west, and his soldiers are vigorous and mettlesome. If we oppose him in the shifting sands of the desert, we shall be no match for him, and we must therefore try a different plan. Let us hasten to occupy the defile at the mouth of the Kao-wu pass, thus cutting him off from supplies of water, and when his troops are prostrated with thirst, we can dictate our own terms without moving. Or if you think that the pass I mention is too far off, we could make a stand against him at the I-wu pass, which is nearer. The cunning and resource of Tzu-fang himself would be expended in vain against the enormous strength of these two positions." Liang Hsi, refusing to act on this advice, was overwhelmed and swept away by the invader.]

5. Ground on which each side has liberty of movement is open ground.

[There are various interpretations of the Chinese adjective for this type of ground. Ts'ao Kung says it means "ground covered with a network of roads," like a chessboard. Ho Shih suggested: "ground on which intercommunication is easy."]

6. Ground which forms the key to three contiguous states,

[Ts'au Kung defines this as: "Our country adjoining the enemy's and a third country conterminous with both." Meng Shih instances the small principality of Cheng, which was bounded on the north-east by Ch'i, on the west by Chin, and on the south by Ch'u.]

so that he who occupies it first has most of the Empire at his command,

[The belligerent who holds this dominating position can constrain most of them to become his allies.]

is a ground of intersecting highways.

7. When an army has penetrated into the heart of a hostile country, leaving a number of fortified cities in its rear, it is serious ground.

[Wang Hsi explains the name by saying that "when an army has reached such a point, its situation is serious."]

8. Mountain forests,

[Or simply "forests."]

rugged steeps, marshes and fens—all country that is hard to traverse: this is difficult ground.

9. Ground which is reached through narrow gorges, and from which we can only retire by tortuous paths, so that a small number of the enemy would suffice to crush a large body of our men: this is hemmed in ground.

10. Ground on which we can only be saved from destruction by fighting without delay, is desperate ground.

[The situation, as pictured by Ts'ao Kung, is very similar to the "hemmed-in ground" except that here escape is no longer possible: "A lofty mountain in front, a large river behind, advance impossible, retreat blocked." Ch'en Hao says: "to be on 'desperate ground' is like sitting in a leaking boat or crouching in a burning house." Tu Mu quotes from Li Ching a vivid description of the plight of an army thus entrapped: "Suppose an army invading hostile territory without the aid of local guides:—it falls into a fatal snare and is at the enemy's mercy. A ravine on the left, a mountain on the right, a pathway so perilous that the horses have to be roped together and the chariots carried in slings, no passage open in front, retreat cut off behind, no choice but to proceed in single file. Then, before there is time to range our soldiers in order of battle, the enemy is overwhelming strength suddenly appears on the scene. Advancing, we can nowhere take a breathing-space; retreating, we have no haven of refuge. We seek a pitched battle, but in vain; yet standing on the defensive, none of us has a moment's respite. If we simply maintain our ground, whole days and months will crawl by; the moment we make a move, we have to sustain the enemy's attacks on front and rear. The country is wild, destitute of water and plants; the army is lacking in the necessaries of life, the horses are jaded and the men worn-out, all the resources of strength and skill unavailing, the pass so narrow that a single man defending it can check the onset of ten thousand; all means of offense in the hands of the enemy, all points of vantage already forfeited by ourselves:—in this terrible plight, even though we had the most valiant soldiers and the keenest of weapons, how could they be employed with the slightest effect?" Students of Greek history may be reminded of the awful close to the Sicilian expedition, and the agony of the Athenians under Nicias and Demonsthenes. [See Thucydides, VII. 78 sqq.].]

11. On dispersive ground, therefore, fight not. On facile ground, halt not. On contentious ground, attack not.

[But rather let all your energies be bent on occupying the advantageous position first. So Ts'ao Kung. Li Ch'uan and others, however, suppose the meaning to be that the enemy has already forestalled us, sot that it would be sheer madness to attack. In the Sun Tzu Hsu Lu, when the King of Wu inquires what should be done in this case, Sun Tzu replies: "The rule with regard to contentious ground is that those in possession have the advantage over the other side. If a position of this kind is secured first by the enemy, beware of attacking him. Lure him away by pretending to flee—show your banners and sound your drums—make a dash for other places that he cannot afford to lose—trail brushwood and raise a dust—confound his ears and eyes—detach a body of your best troops, and place it secretly in ambuscade. Then your opponent will sally forth to the rescue."]

12. On open ground, do not try to block the enemy's way.

[Because the attempt would be futile, and would expose the blocking force itself to serious risks. There are two interpretations available here. I follow that of Chang Yu. The other is indicated in Ts'ao Kung's brief note: "Draw closer together"—i.e., see that a portion of your own army is not cut off.]

On the ground of intersecting highways, join hands with your allies.

[Or perhaps, "form alliances with neighboring states."]

13. On serious ground, gather in plunder.

[On this, Li Ch'uan has the following delicious note: "When an army penetrates far into the enemy's country, care must be taken not to alienate the people by unjust treatment. Follow the example of the Han Emperor Kao Tsu, whose march into Ch'in territory was marked by no violation of women or looting of valuables. [Nota bene: this was in 207 B.C., and may well cause us to blush for the Christian armies that entered Peking in 1900 A.D.] Thus he won the hearts of all. In the present passage, then, I think that the true reading must be, not 'plunder,' but 'do not plunder.'" Alas, I fear that in this instance the worthy commentator's feelings outran his judgment. Tu Mu, at least, has no such illusions. He says: "When encamped on 'serious ground,' there being no inducement as yet to advance further, and no possibility of retreat, one ought to take measures for a protracted resistance by bringing in provisions from all sides, and keep a close watch on the enemy."]

In difficult ground, keep steadily on the march.

[Or, in the words of VIII. § 2, "do not encamp."]

14. On hemmed-in ground, resort to stratagem.

[Ts'au Kung says: "Try the effect of some unusual artifice;" and Tu Yu amplifies this by saying: "In such a position, some scheme must be devised which will suit the circumstances, and if we can succeed in deluding the enemy, the peril may be escaped." This is exactly what happened on the famous occasion when Hannibal was hemmed in among the mountains on the road to Casilinum, and to all appearances entrapped by the dictator Fabius. The stratagem which Hannibal devised to baffle his foes was remarkably like that which T'ien Tan had also employed with success exactly 62 years before. [See IX. § 24, note.] When night came on, bundles of twigs were fastened to the horns of some 2000 oxen and set on fire, the terrified animals being then quickly driven along the mountain side towards the passes which were beset by the enemy. The strange spectacle of these rapidly moving lights so alarmed and discomfited the Romans that they withdrew from their position, and Hannibal's army passed safely through the defile. [See Polybius, III. 93, 94; Livy, XXII. 16 17.]

On desperate ground, fight.

[For, as Chia Lin remarks: "if you fight with all your might, there is a chance of life; where as death is certain if you cling to your corner."]

15. Those who were called skillful leaders of old knew how to drive a wedge between the enemy's front and rear;

[More literally, "cause the front and rear to lose touch with each other."]

to prevent co-operation between his large and small divisions; to hinder the good troops from rescuing the bad, the officers from rallying their men.

6. When the enemy's men were united, they managed to keep them in disorder.

17. When it was to their advantage, they made a forward move; when otherwise, they stopped still.

[Mei Yao-ch'en connects this with the foregoing: "Having succeeded in thus dislocating the enemy, they would push forward in order to secure any advantage to be gained; if there was no advantage to be gained, they would remain where they were."]

18. If asked how to cope with a great host of the enemy in orderly array and on the point of marching to the attack, I should say: "Begin by seizing something which your opponent holds dear; then he will be amenable to your will."

[Opinions differ as to what Sun Tzu had in mind. Ts'ao Kung thinks it is "some strategical advantage on which the enemy is depending." Tu Mu says: "The three things which an enemy is anxious to do, and on the accomplishment of which his success depends, are: (1) to capture our favorable positions; (2) to ravage our cultivated land; (3) to guard his own communications." Our object then must be to thwart his plans in these three directions and thus render him helpless. [Cf. III. § 3.] By boldly seizing the initiative in this way, you at once throw the other side on the defensive.]

19. Rapidity is the essence of war:

[According to Tu Mu, "this is a summary of leading principles in warfare," and he adds: "These are the profoundest truths of military science, and the chief business of the general." The following anecdotes, told by Ho Shih, shows the importance attached to speed by two of China's greatest generals. In 227 A.D., Meng Ta, governor of Hsin-ch'eng under the Wei Emperor Wen Ti, was meditating defection to the House of Shu, and had entered into correspondence with Chu-ko Liang, Prime Minister of that State.

The Wei general Ssu-ma I was then military governor of Wan, and getting wind of Meng Ta's treachery, he at once set off with an army to anticipate his revolt, having previously cajoled him by a specious message of friendly import. Ssu-ma's officers came to him and said: "If Meng Ta has leagued himself with Wu and Shu, the matter should be thoroughly investigated before we make a move." Ssu-ma I replied: "Meng Ta is an unprincipled man, and we ought to go and punish him at once, while he is still wavering and before he has thrown off the mask." Then, by a series of forced marches, be brought his army under the walls of Hsin-ch'eng with in a space of eight days. Now Meng Ta had previously said in a letter to Chu-ko Liang: "Wan is 1200 li from here. When the news of my revolt reaches Ssu-ma I, he will at once inform his imperial master, but it will be a whole month before any steps can be taken, and by that time my city will be well fortified. Besides, Ssu-ma I is sure not to come himself, and the generals that will be sent against us are not worth troubling about." The next letter, however, was filled with consternation: "Though only eight days have passed since I threw off my allegiance, an army is already at the city-gates. What miraculous rapidity is this!" A fortnight later, Hsin- ch'eng had fallen and Meng Ta had lost his head. [See Chin Shu, ch. 1, f. 3.] In 621 A.D., Li Ching was sent from K'uei-chou in Ssu-ch'uan to reduce the successful rebel Hsiao Hsien, who had set up as Emperor at the modern Ching-chou Fu in Hupeh. It was autumn, and the Yangtsze being then in flood, Hsiao Hsien never dreamt that his adversary would venture to come down through the gorges, and consequently made no preparations. But Li Ching embarked his army without loss of time, and was just about to start when the other generals implored him to postpone his departure until the river was in a less dangerous state for navigation. Li Ching replied: "To the soldier, overwhelming speed is of paramount importance, and he must never miss opportunities. Now is the time to strike, before Hsiao Hsien even knows that we have got an army together. If we seize the present moment when the river is in flood, we shall appear before his capital with startling suddenness, like the thunder which is heard before you have time to stop your ears against it. [See VII. § 19, note.] This is the great principle in war. Even if he gets to know of our approach, he will have to levy his soldiers in such a hurry that they will not be fit to oppose us. Thus the full fruits of victory will be ours." All came about as he predicted, and Hsiao Hsien was obliged to surrender, nobly stipulating that his people should be spared and he alone suffer the penalty of death.]

take advantage of the enemy's unreadiness, make your way by unexpected routes, and attack unguarded spots.

20. The following are the principles to be observed by an invading force: The further you penetrate into a country, the greater will be the solidarity of your troops, and thus the defenders will not prevail against you.

21. Make forays in fertile country in order to supply your army with food.

[Cf. supra, § 13. Li Ch'uan does not venture on a note here.]

22. Carefully study the well-being of your men,

[For "well-being", Wang Hsi means, "Pet them, humor them, give them plenty of food and drink, and look after them generally."]

and do not overtax them. Concentrate your energy and hoard your strength.

[Ch'en recalls the line of action adopted in 224 B.C. by the famous general Wang Chien, whose military genius largely contributed to the success of the First Emperor. He had invaded the Ch'u State, where a universal levy was made to oppose him. But, being doubtful of the temper of his troops, he declined all invitations to fight and remained strictly on the defensive. In vain did the Ch'u general try to force a battle: day after day Wang Chien kept inside his walls and would not come out, but devoted his whole time and energy to winning the affection and confidence of his men. He took care that they should be well fed, sharing his own meals with them, provided facilities for bathing, and employed every method of judicious indulgence to weld them into a loyal and homogenous body. After some time had elapsed, he told off certain persons to find out how the men were amusing themselves. The answer was, that they were contending with one another in putting the weight and long-jumping. When Wang Chien heard that they were engaged in these athletic pursuits, he knew that their spirits had been strung up to the required pitch and that they were now ready for fighting. By this time the Ch'u army, after repeating their challenge again and again, had marched away eastwards in disgust. The Ch'in general immediately broke up his camp and followed them, and in the battle that ensued they were routed with great slaughter. Shortly afterwards, the whole of Ch'u was conquered by Ch'in, and the king Fu-ch'u led into captivity.]

Keep your army continually on the move,

[In order that the enemy may never know exactly where you are. It has struck me, however, that the true reading might be "link your army together."]

and devise unfathomable plans.

23. Throw your soldiers into positions whence there is no escape, and they will prefer death to flight. If they will face death, there is nothing they may not achieve.

[Chang Yu quotes his favorite Wei Liao Tzu (ch. 3): "If one man were to run amok with a sword in the market-place, and everybody else tried to get our of his way, I should not allow that this man alone had courage and that all the rest were contemptible cowards. The truth is, that a desperado and a man who sets some value on his life do not meet on even terms."]

Officers and men alike will put forth their uttermost strength.

[Chang Yu says: "If they are in an awkward place together, they will surely exert their united strength to get out of it."]

24. Soldiers when in desperate straits lose the sense of fear. If there is no place of refuge, they will stand firm. If they are in hostile country, they will show a stubborn front. If there is no help for it, they will fight hard.

25. Thus, without waiting to be marshaled, the soldiers will be constantly on the qui vive; without waiting to be asked, they will do your will;

[Literally, "without asking, you will get."]

without restrictions, they will be faithful; without giving orders, they can be trusted.

26. Prohibit the taking of omens, and do away with superstitious doubts. Then, until death itself comes, no calamity need be feared.

[The superstitious, "bound in to saucy doubts and fears," degenerate into cowards and "die many times before their deaths." Tu Mu quotes Huang Shih-kung: "'Spells and incantations should be strictly forbidden, and no officer allowed to inquire by divination into the fortunes of an army, for fear the soldiers' minds should be seriously perturbed.' The meaning is," he continues, "that if all doubts and scruples are discarded, your men will never falter in their resolution until they die."]

27. If our soldiers are not overburdened with money, it is not because they have a distaste for riches; if their lives are not unduly long, it is not because they are disinclined to longevity.

[Chang Yu has the best note on this passage: "Wealth and long life are things for which all men have a natural inclination. Hence, if they burn or fling away valuables, and sacrifice their own lives, it is not that they dislike them, but simply that they have no choice." Sun Tzu is slyly insinuating that, as soldiers are but human, it is for the general to see that temptations to shirk fighting and grow rich are not thrown in their way.]

28. On the day they are ordered out to battle, your soldiers may weep,

[The word in the Chinese is "snivel." This is taken to indicate more genuine grief than tears alone.]

those sitting up bedewing their garments, and those lying down letting the tears run down their cheeks.

[Not because they are afraid, but because, as Ts'ao Kung says, "all have embraced the firm resolution to do or die." We may remember that the heroes of the Iliad were equally childlike in showing their emotion. Chang Yu alludes to the mournful parting at the I River between Ching K'o and his friends, when the former was sent to attempt the life of the King of Ch'in (afterwards First Emperor) in 227 B.C. The tears of all flowed down like rain as he bade them farewell and uttered the following lines: "The shrill blast is blowing, Chilly the burn; Your champion is going—Not to return." [1]]

But let them once be brought to bay, and they will display the courage of a Chu or a Kuei.

[Chu was the personal name of Chuan Chu, a native of the Wu State and contemporary with Sun Tzu himself, who was employed by Kung-tzu Kuang, better known as Ho Lu Wang, to assassinate his sovereign Wang Liao with a dagger which he secreted in the belly of a fish served up at a banquet. He succeeded in his attempt, but was immediately hacked to pieces by the king's bodyguard. This was in 515 B.C. The other hero referred to, Ts'ao Kuei (or Ts'ao Mo), performed the exploit which has made his name famous 166 years earlier, in 681 B.C. Lu had been thrice defeated by Ch'i, and was just about to conclude a treaty surrendering a large slice of territory, when Ts'ao Kuei suddenly seized Huan Kung, the Duke of Ch'i, as he stood on the altar steps and held a dagger against his chest. None of the duke's retainers dared to move a muscle, and Ts'ao Kuei proceeded to demand full restitution, declaring the Lu was being unjustly treated because she was a smaller and a weaker state. Huan Kung, in peril of his life, was obliged to consent, whereupon Ts'ao Kuei flung away his dagger and quietly resumed his place amid the terrified assemblage without having so much as changed color. As was to be expected, the Duke wanted afterwards to repudiate the bargain, but his wise old counselor Kuan Chung pointed out to him the impolicy of breaking his word, and the upshot was that this bold stroke regained for Lu the whole of what she had lost in three pitched battles.]

29. The skillful tactician may be likened to the shuai-jan. Now the shuai-jan is a snake that is found in the Ch'ang mountains.

["Shuai-jan" means "suddenly" or "rapidly," and the snake in question was doubtless so called owing to the rapidity of its movements. Through this passage, the term in the Chinese has now come to be used in the sense of "military manœuvers."]

Strike at its head, and you will be attacked by its tail; strike at its tail, and you will be attacked by its head; strike at its middle, and you will be attacked by head and tail both.

30. Asked if an army can be made to imitate the shuai-jan,

[That is, as Mei Yao-ch'en says, "Is it possible to make the front and rear of an army each swiftly responsive to attack on the other, just as though they were part of a single living body?"]

I should answer, Yes. For the men of Wu and the men of Yueh are enemies;

[Cf. VI. § 21.]

yet if they are crossing a river in the same boat and are caught by a storm, they will come to each other's assistance just as the left hand helps the right.

[The meaning is: If two enemies will help each other in a time of common peril, how much more should two parts of the same army, bound together as they are by every tie of interest and fellow-feeling. Yet it is notorious that many a campaign has been ruined through lack of cooperation, especially in the case of allied armies.]

31. Hence it is not enough to put one's trust in the tethering of horses, and the burying of chariot wheels in the ground.

[These quaint devices to prevent one's army from running away recall the Athenian hero Sophanes, who carried the anchor with him at the battle of Plataea, by means of which he fastened himself firmly to one spot. [See Herodotus, IX. 74.] It is not enough, says Sun Tzu, to render flight impossible by such mechanical means. You will not succeed unless your men have tenacity and unity of purpose, and, above all, a spirit of sympathetic cooperation. This is the lesson which can be learned from the shuai-jan.]

32. The principle on which to manage an army is to set up one standard of courage which all must reach.

[Literally, "level the courage [of all] as though [it were that of] one." If the ideal army is to form a single organic whole, then it follows that the resolution and spirit of its component parts must be of the same quality, or at any rate must not fall below a certain standard. Wellington's seemingly ungrateful description of his army at Waterloo as "the worst he had ever commanded" meant no more than that it was deficient in this important particular—unity of spirit and courage. Had he not foreseen the Belgian defections and carefully kept those troops in the background, he would almost certainly have lost the day.]

33. How to make the best of both strong and weak—that is a question involving the proper use of ground.

[Mei Yao-ch'en's paraphrase is: "The way to eliminate the differences of strong and weak and to make both serviceable is to utilize accidental features of the ground." Less reliable troops, if posted in strong positions, will hold out as long as better troops on more exposed terrain. The advantage of position neutralizes the inferiority in stamina and courage. Col. Henderson says: "With all respect to the text books, and to the ordinary tactical teaching, I am inclined to think that the study of ground is often overlooked, and that by no means sufficient importance is attached to the selection of positions... and to the immense advantages that are to be derived, whether you are defending or attacking, from the proper utilization of natural features." [2]]

34. Thus the skillful general conducts his army just as though he were leading a single man, willy-nilly, by the hand.

[Tu Mu says: "The simile has reference to the ease with which he does it."]

35. It is the business of a general to be quiet and thus ensure secrecy; upright and just, and thus maintain order.

36. He must be able to mystify his officers and men by false reports and appearances,

[Literally, "to deceive their eyes and ears."]

and thus keep them in total ignorance.

[Ts'ao Kung gives us one of his excellent apophthegms: "The troops must not be allowed to share your schemes in the beginning; they may only rejoice with you over their happy outcome." "To mystify, mislead, and surprise the enemy," is one of the first principles in war, as had been frequently pointed out. But how about the other process—the mystification of one's own men? Those who may think that Sun Tzu is over-emphatic on this point would do well to read Col. Henderson's remarks on Stonewall Jackson's Valley campaign: "The infinite pains," he says, "with which Jackson sought to conceal, even from his most trusted staff officers, his movements, his intentions, and his thoughts, a commander less thorough would have pronounced useless"—etc. etc. [3] In the year 88 A.D., as we read in ch. 47 of the Hou Han Shu, "Pan Ch'ao took the field with 25,000 men from Khotan and other Central Asian states with the object of crushing Yarkand. The King of Kutcha replied by dispatching his chief commander to succor the place with an army drawn from the kingdoms of Wen-su, Ku-mo, and Wei-t'ou, totaling 50,000 men. Pan Ch'ao summoned his officers and also the King of Khotan to a council of war, and said: 'Our forces are now outnumbered and unable to make head against the enemy. The best plan, then, is for us to separate and disperse, each in a different direction. The King of Khotan will march away by the easterly route, and I will then return myself towards the west. Let us wait until the evening drum has sounded and then start.' Pan Ch'ao now secretly released the prisoners whom he had taken alive, and the King of Kutcha was thus informed of his plans. Much elated by the news, the latter set off at once at the head of 10,000 horsemen to bar Pan Ch'ao's retreat in the west, while the King of Wen-su rode eastward with 8000 horse in order to intercept the King of Khotan. As soon as Pan Ch'ao knew that the two chieftains had gone, he called his divisions together, got them well in hand, and at cock-crow hurled them against the army of Yarkand, as it lay encamped. The barbarians, panic-stricken, fled in confusion, and were closely pursued by Pan Ch'ao. Over 5000 heads were brought back as trophies, besides immense spoils in the shape of horses and cattle and valuables of every description. Yarkand then capitulating, Kutcha and the other kingdoms drew off their respective forces. From that time forward, Pan Ch'ao's prestige completely overawed the countries of the west." In this case, we see that the Chinese general not only kept his own officers in ignorance of his real plans, but actually took the bold step of dividing his army in order to deceive the enemy.]

37. By altering his arrangements and changing his plans,

[Wang Hsi thinks that this means not using the same stratagem twice.]

he keeps the enemy without definite knowledge.

[Chang Yu, in a quotation from another work, says: "The axiom, that war is based on deception, does not apply only to deception of the enemy. You must deceive even your own soldiers. Make them follow you, but without letting them know why."]

By shifting his camp and taking circuitous routes, he prevents the enemy from anticipating his purpose.

38. At the critical moment, the leader of an army acts like one who has climbed up a height and then kicks away the ladder behind him. He carries his men deep into hostile territory before he shows his hand.

[Literally, "releases the spring" (see V. § 15), that is, takes some decisive step which makes it impossible for the army to return—like Hsiang Yu, who sunk his ships after crossing a river. Ch'en Hao, followed by Chia Lin, understands the words less well as "puts forth every artifice at his command."]

39. He burns his boats and breaks his cooking-pots; like a shepherd driving a flock of sheep, he drives his men this way and that, and nothing knows whither he is going.

[Tu Mu says: "The army is only cognizant of orders to advance or retreat; it is ignorant of the ulterior ends of attacking and conquering."]

40. To muster his host and bring it into danger:—this may be termed the business of the general.

[Sun Tzu means that after mobilization there should be no delay in aiming a blow at the enemy's heart. Note how he returns again and again to this point. Among the warring states of ancient China, desertion was no doubt a much more present fear and serious evil than it is in the armies of today.]

41. The different measures suited to the nine varieties of ground;

[Chang Yu says: "One must not be hide-bound in interpreting the rules for the nine varieties of ground."]

the expediency of aggressive or defensive tactics; and the fundamental laws of human nature: these are things that must most certainly be studied.

42. When invading hostile territory, the general principle is, that penetrating deeply brings cohesion; penetrating but a short way means dispersion.

[Cf. supra, § 20.]

43. When you leave your own country behind, and take your army across neighborhood territory, you find yourself on critical ground.

[This "ground" is curiously mentioned in VIII. § 2, but it does not figure among the Nine Situations or the Six Calamities in chap. X. One's first impulse would be to translate it distant ground," but this, if we can trust the commentators, is precisely what is not meant here. Mei Yao-ch'en says it is "a position not far enough advanced to be called 'facile,' and not near enough to home to be 'dispersive,' but something between the two." Wang Hsi says: "It is ground separated from home by an interjacent state, whose territory we have had to cross in order to reach it. Hence, it is incumbent on us to settle our business there quickly." He adds that this position is of rare occurrence, which is the reason why it is not included among the Nine Situations.]

When there are means of communication on all four sides, the ground is one of intersecting highways.

44. When you penetrate deeply into a country, it is serious ground.

When you penetrate but a little way, it is facile ground.

45. When you have the enemy's strongholds on your rear, and

narrow passes in front, it is hemmed-in ground. When there is no place of refuge at all, it is desperate ground.

46. Therefore, on dispersive ground, I would inspire my men with unity of purpose.

[This end, according to Tu Mu, is best attained by remaining on the defensive, and avoiding battle. Cf. supra, § 11.]

On facile ground, I would see that there is close connection between all parts of my army.

[As Tu Mu says, the object is to guard against two possible contingencies: "(1) the desertion of our own troops; (2) a sudden attack on the part of the enemy." Cf. VII. § 17. Mei Yao-ch'en says: "On the march, the regiments should be in close touch; in an encampment, there should be continuity between the fortifications."]

47. On contentious ground, I would hurry up my rear.

[This is Ts'ao Kung's interpretation. Chang Yu adopts it, saying: "We must quickly bring up our rear, so that head and tail may both reach the goal." That is, they must not be allowed to straggle up a long way apart. Mei Yao-ch'en offers another equally plausible explanation: "Supposing the enemy has not yet reached the coveted position, and we are behind him, we should advance with all speed in order to dispute its possession." Ch'en Hao, on the other hand, assuming that the enemy has had time to select his own ground, quotes VI. § 1, where Sun Tzu warns us against coming exhausted to the attack. His own idea of the situation is rather vaguely expressed: "If there is a favorable position lying in front of you, detach a picked body of troops to occupy it, then if the enemy, relying on their numbers, come up to make a fight for it, you may fall quickly on their rear with your main body, and victory will be assured." It was thus, he adds, that Chao She beat the army of Ch'in. (See p. 57.)]

48. On open ground, I would keep a vigilant eye on my defenses.

On ground of intersecting highways, I would consolidate my alliances.

49. On serious ground, I would try to ensure a continuous stream of supplies.

[The commentators take this as referring to forage and plunder, not, as one might expect, to an unbroken communication with a home base.]

On difficult ground, I would keep pushing on along the road.

50. On hemmed-in ground, I would block any way of retreat.

[Meng Shih says: "To make it seem that I meant to defend the position, whereas my real intention is to burst suddenly through the enemy's lines." Mei Yao-ch'en says: "in order to make my soldiers fight with desperation." Wang Hsi says, "fearing lest my men be tempted to run away." Tu Mu points out that this is the converse of VII. § 36, where it is the enemy who is surrounded. In 532 A.D., Kao Huan, afterwards Emperor and canonized as Shen-wu, was surrounded by a great army under Erh-chu Chao and others. His own force was comparatively small, consisting only of 2000 horse and something under 30,000 foot. The lines of investment had not been drawn very closely together, gaps being left at certain points. But Kao Huan, instead of trying to escape, actually made a shift to block all the remaining outlets himself by driving into them a number of oxen and donkeys roped together. As soon as his officers and men saw that there was nothing for it but to conquer or die, their spirits rose to an extraordinary pitch of exaltation, and they charged with such desperate ferocity that the opposing ranks broke and crumbled under their onslaught.]

On desperate ground, I would proclaim to my soldiers the hopelessness of saving their lives.

Tu Yu says: "Burn your baggage and impedimenta, throw away your stores and provisions, choke up the wells, destroy your cooking-stoves, and make it plain to your men that they cannot survive, but must fight to the death." Mei Yao-ch'en says: "The only chance of life lies in giving up all hope of it." This concludes what Sun Tzu has to say about "grounds" and the "variations" corresponding to them. Reviewing the passages which bear on this important subject, we cannot fail to be struck by the desultory and unmethodical fashion in which it is treated. Sun Tzu begins abruptly in VIII. § 2 to enumerate "variations" before touching on "grounds" at all, but only mentions five, namely nos. 7, 5, 8 and 9 of the subsequent list, and one that is not included in it. A few varieties of ground are dealt with in the earlier portion of chap. IX, and then chap. X sets forth six new grounds, with six variations of plan to match. None of these is mentioned again, though the first is hardly to be distinguished from ground no. 4 in the next chapter. At last, in chap. XI, we come to the Nine Grounds par excellence, immediately followed by the variations. This takes us down to § 14. In §§ 43-45, fresh definitions are provided for nos. 5, 6, 2, 8 and 9 (in the order given), as well as for the tenth ground noticed in chap. VIII; and finally, the nine variations are enumerated once more from beginning to end, all, with the exception of 5, 6 and 7, being different from those previously given. Though it is impossible to account for the present state of Sun Tzu's text, a few suggestive facts maybe brought into prominence: (1) Chap. VIII, according to the title, should deal with nine variations, whereas only five appear. (2) It is an abnormally short chapter. (3) Chap. XI is entitled The Nine Grounds. Several of these are defined twice over, besides which there are two distinct lists of the corresponding variations. (4) The length of the chapter is disproportionate, being double that of any other except IX. I do not propose to draw any inferences from these facts, beyond the general conclusion that Sun Tzu's work cannot have come down to us in the shape in which it left his hands: chap. VIII is obviously defective and probably out of place, while XI seems to contain matter that has either been added by a later hand or ought to appear elsewhere.]

51. For it is the soldier's disposition to offer an obstinate resistance

when surrounded, to fight hard when he cannot help himself, and to obey promptly when he has fallen into danger.

[Chang Yu alludes to the conduct of Pan Ch'ao's devoted followers in 73 A.D. The story runs thus in the Hou Han Shu, ch. 47: "When Pan Ch'ao arrived at Shan-shan, Kuang, the King of the country, received him at first with great politeness and respect; but shortly afterwards his behavior underwent a sudden change, and he became remiss and negligent. Pan Ch'ao spoke about this to the officers of his suite: 'Have you noticed,' he said, 'that Kuang's polite intentions are on the wane? This must signify that envoys have come from the Northern barbarians, and that consequently he is in a state of indecision, not knowing with which side to throw in his lot. That surely is the reason. The truly wise man, we are told, can perceive things before they have come to pass; how much more, then, those that are already manifest!' Thereupon he called one of the natives who had been assigned to his service, and set a trap for him, saying: 'Where are those envoys from the Hsiung-nu who arrived some day ago?' The man was so taken aback that between surprise and fear he presently blurted out the whole truth. Pan Ch'ao, keeping his informant carefully under lock and key, then summoned a general gathering of his officers, thirty-six in all, and began drinking with them. When the wine had mounted into their heads a little, he tried to rouse their spirit still further by addressing them thus: 'Gentlemen, here we are in the heart of an isolated region, anxious to achieve riches and honor by some great exploit. Now it happens that an ambassador from the Hsiung-no arrived in this kingdom only a few days ago, and the result is that the respectful courtesy extended towards us by our royal host has disappeared. Should this envoy prevail upon him to seize our party and hand us over to the Hsiung-no, our bones will become food for the wolves of the desert. What are we to do?' With one accord, the officers replied: 'Standing as we do in peril of our lives, we will follow our commander through life and death.' For the sequel of this adventure, see chap. XII. § 1, note.]

52. We cannot enter into alliance with neighboring princes until we are acquainted with their designs. We are not fit to lead an army on the march unless we are familiar with the face of the country—its mountains and forests, its pitfalls and precipices, its marshes and swamps. We shall be unable to turn natural advantages to account unless we make use of local guides.

[These three sentences are repeated from VII. §§ 12-14—in order to emphasize their importance, the commentators seem to think. I prefer to regard them as interpolated here in order to form an antecedent to the following words. With regard to local guides, Sun Tzu might have added that there is always the risk of going wrong, either through their treachery or some misunderstanding such as Livy records (XXII. 13): Hannibal, we are told, ordered a guide to lead him into the neighborhood of Casinum, where there was an important pass to be occupied; but his Carthaginian accent, unsuited to the pronunciation of Latin names, caused the guide to understand Casilinum instead of Casinum, and turning from his proper route, he took the army in that direction, the mistake not being discovered until they had almost arrived.]

53. To be ignored of any one of the following four or five principles does not befit a warlike prince.

54. When a warlike prince attacks a powerful state, his generalship shows itself in preventing the concentration of the enemy's forces. He overawes his opponents, and their allies are prevented from joining against him.

[Mei Tao-ch'en constructs one of the chains of reasoning that are so much affected by the Chinese: "In attacking a powerful state, if you can divide her forces, you will have a superiority in strength; if you have a superiority in strength, you will overawe the enemy; if you overawe the enemy, the neighboring states will be frightened; and if the neighboring states are frightened, the enemy's allies will be prevented from joining her." The following gives a stronger meaning: "If the great state has once been defeated (before she has had time to summon her allies), then the lesser states will hold aloof and refrain from massing their forces." Ch'en Hao and Chang Yu take the sentence in quite another way. The former says: "Powerful though a prince may be, if he attacks a large state, he will be unable to raise enough troops, and must rely to some extent on external aid; if he dispenses with this, and with overweening confidence in his own strength, simply tries to intimidate the enemy, he will surely be defeated." Chang Yu puts his view thus: "If we recklessly attack a large state, our own people will be discontented and hang back. But if (as will then be the case) our display of military force is inferior by half to that of the enemy, the other chieftains will take fright and refuse to join us."]

55. Hence he does not strive to ally himself with all and sundry, nor does he foster the power of other states. He carries out his own secret designs, keeping his antagonists in awe.

[The train of thought, as said by Li Ch'uan, appears to be this: Secure against a combination of his enemies, "he can afford to reject entangling alliances and simply pursue his own secret designs, his prestige enable him to dispense with external friendships."]

Thus he is able to capture their cities and overthrow their kingdoms.

[This paragraph, though written many years before the Ch'in State became a serious menace, is not a bad summary of the policy by which the famous Six Chancellors gradually paved the way for her final triumph under Shih Huang Ti. Chang Yu, following up his previous note, thinks that Sun Tzu is condemning this attitude of cold-blooded selfishness and haughty isolation.]

56. Bestow rewards without regard to rule,

[Wu Tzu (ch. 3) less wisely says: "Let advance be richly rewarded and retreat be heavily punished."]

issue orders

[Literally, "hang" or post up."]

without regard to previous arrangements;

["In order to prevent treachery," says Wang Hsi. The general meaning is made clear by Ts'ao Kung's quotation from the Ssu-ma Fa: "Give instructions only on sighting the enemy; give rewards when you see deserving deeds." Ts'ao Kung's paraphrase: "The final instructions you give to your army should not correspond with those that have been previously posted up." Chang Yu simplifies this into "your arrangements should not be divulged beforehand." And Chia Lin says: "there should be no fixity in your rules and arrangements." Not only is there danger in letting your plans be known, but war often necessitates the entire reversal of them at the last moment.]

and you will be able to handle a whole army as though you had to do with but a single man.

[Cf. supra, § 34.]

57. Confront your soldiers with the deed itself; never let them know your design.

[Literally, "do not tell them words;" i.e. do not give your reasons for any order. Lord Mansfield once told a junior colleague to "give no reasons" for his decisions, and the maxim is even more applicable to a general than to a judge.]

When the outlook is bright, bring it before their eyes; but tell them nothing when the situation is gloomy.

58. Place your army in deadly peril, and it will survive; plunge it into desperate straits, and it will come off in safety.

[These words of Sun Tzu were once quoted by Han Hsin in explanation of the tactics he employed in one of his most brilliant battles, already alluded to on p.

In 204 B.C., he was sent against the army of Chao, and halted ten miles from the mouth of the Ching-hsing pass, where the enemy had mustered in full force. Here, at midnight, he detached a body of 2000 light cavalry, every man of which was furnished with a red flag. Their instructions were to make their way through narrow defiles and keep a secret watch on the enemy. "When the men of Chao see me in full flight," Han Hsin said, "they will abandon their fortifications and give chase. This must be the sign for you to rush in, pluck down the Chao standards and set up the red banners of Han in their stead." Turning then to his other officers, he remarked: "Our adversary holds a strong position, and is not likely to come out and attack us until he sees the standard and drums of the commander-in-chief, for fear I should turn back and escape through the mountains." So saying, he first of all sent out a division consisting of 10,000 men, and ordered them to form in line of battle with their backs to the River Ti. Seeing this manœuver, the whole army of Chao broke into loud laughter. By this time it was broad daylight, and Han Hsin, displaying the generalissimo's flag, marched out of the pass with drums beating, and was immediately engaged by the enemy. A great battle followed, lasting for some time; until at length Han Hsin and his colleague Chang Ni, leaving drums and banner on the field, fled to the division on the river bank, where another fierce battle was raging. The enemy rushed out to pursue them and to secure the trophies, thus denuding their ramparts of men; but the two generals succeeded in joining the other army, which was fighting with the utmost desperation. The time had now come for the 2000 horsemen to play their part. As soon as they saw the men of Chao following up their advantage, they galloped behind the deserted walls, tore up the enemy's flags and replaced them by those of Han. When the Chao army looked back from the pursuit, the sight of these red flags struck them with terror. Convinced that the Hans had got in and overpowered their king, they broke up in wild disorder, every effort of their leader to stay the panic being in vain. Then the Han army fell on them from both sides and completed the rout, killing a number and capturing the rest, amongst whom was King Ya himself.... After the battle, some of Han Hsin's officers came to him and said: "In the Art of War we are told to have a hill or tumulus on the right rear, and a river or marsh on the left front. [This appears to be a blend of Sun Tzu and T'ai Kung. See IX § 9, and note.] You, on the contrary, ordered us to draw up our troops with the river at our back. Under these conditions, how did you manage to gain the victory?" The general replied: "I fear you gentlemen have not studied the Art of War with sufficient care. Is it not written there: 'Plunge your army into desperate straits and it will come off in safety; place it in deadly peril and it will survive'? Had I taken the usual course, I should never have been able to bring my colleague round. What says the Military Classic—'Swoop down on the market-place and drive the men off to fight.' [This passage does not occur in the present text of Sun Tzu.] If I had not placed my troops in a position where they were obliged to fight for their lives, but had allowed each man to follow his own discretion, there would have been a general débandade, and it would have been impossible to do anything with them." The officers admitted the force of his argument, and said: "These are higher tactics than we should have been capable of." [See Ch'ien Han Shu, ch. 34, ff. 4, 5.]]

59. For it is precisely when a force has fallen into harm's way that is capable of striking a blow for victory.

[Danger has a bracing effect.]

60. Success in warfare is gained by carefully accommodating ourselves to the enemy's purpose.

[Ts'ao Kung says: "Feign stupidity"—by an appearance of yielding and falling in with the enemy's wishes. Chang Yu's note makes the meaning clear: "If the enemy shows an inclination to advance, lure him on to do so; if he is anxious to retreat, delay on purpose that he may carry out his intention." The object is to make him remiss and contemptuous before we deliver our attack.]

61. By persistently hanging on the enemy's flank,

[I understand the first four words to mean "accompanying the enemy in one direction." Ts'ao Kung says: "unite the soldiers and make for the enemy." But such a violent displacement of characters is quite indefensible.]

we shall succeed in the long run

[Literally, "after a thousand li."]

in killing the commander-in-chief.

[Always a great point with the Chinese.]

62. This is called ability to accomplish a thing by sheer cunning.

63. On the day that you take up your command, block the frontier passes, destroy the official tallies,

[These were tablets of bamboo or wood, one half of which was issued as a permit or passport by the official in charge of a gate. Cf. the "border-warden" of Lun Yu III. 24, who may have had similar duties. When this half was returned to him, within a fixed period, he was authorized to open the gate and let the traveler through.]

and stop the passage of all emissaries.

[Either to or from the enemy's country.]

64. Be stern in the council-chamber,

[Show no weakness, and insist on your plans being ratified by the sovereign.]

so that you may control the situation.

[Mei Yao-ch'en understands the whole sentence to mean: Take the strictest precautions to ensure secrecy in your deliberations.]

65. If the enemy leaves a door open, you must rush in.

66. Forestall your opponent by seizing what he holds dear,

[Cf. supra, § 18.]

and subtly contrive to time his arrival on the ground.

[Ch'en Hao's explanation: "If I manage to seize a favorable position, but the enemy does not appear on the scene, the advantage thus obtained cannot be turned to any practical account. He who intends therefore, to occupy a position of importance to the enemy, must begin by making an artful appointment, so to speak, with his antagonist, and cajole him into going there as well." Mei Yao-ch'en explains that this "artful appointment" is to be made through the medium of the enemy's own spies, who will carry back just the amount of information that we choose to give them. Then, having cunningly disclosed our intentions, "we must manage, though starting after the enemy, to arrive before him (VII. § 4). We must start after him in order to ensure his marching thither; we must arrive before him in order to capture the place without trouble. Taken thus, the present passage lends some support to Mei Yao-ch'en's interpretation of § 47.]

67. Walk in the path defined by rule,

[Chia Lin says: "Victory is the only thing that matters, and this cannot be achieved by adhering to conventional canons." It is unfortunate that this variant rests on very slight authority, for the sense yielded is certainly much more satisfactory. Napoleon, as we know, according to the veterans of the old school whom he defeated, won his battles by violating every accepted canon of warfare.]

and accommodate yourself to the enemy until you can fight a decisive battle.

[Tu Mu says: "Conform to the enemy's tactics until a favorable opportunity offers; then come forth and engage in a battle that shall prove decisive."]

68. At first, then, exhibit the coyness of a maiden, until the enemy gives you an opening; afterwards emulate the rapidity of a running

hare, and it will be too late for the enemy to oppose you.

[As the hare is noted for its extreme timidity, the comparison hardly appears felicitous. But of course Sun Tzu was thinking only of its speed. The words have been taken to mean: You must flee from the enemy as quickly as an escaping hare; but this is rightly rejected by Tu Mu.]

[1] Giles' Biographical Dictionary, no. 399.

[2] "The Science of War," p. 333.

[3] "Stonewall Jackson," vol. I, p. 421.

CHAPTER XII. THE ATTACK BY FIRE

[Rather more than half the chapter (§§ 1-13) is devoted to the subject of fire, after which the author branches off into other topics.]

1. Sun Tzu said: There are five ways of attacking with fire. The first is to burn soldiers in their camp;

[So Tu Mu. Li Ch'uan says: "Set fire to the camp, and kill the soldiers" (when they try to escape from the flames). Pan Ch'ao, sent on a diplomatic mission to the King of Shan-shan [see XI. § 51, note], found himself placed in extreme peril by the unexpected arrival of an envoy from the Hsiung-nu [the mortal enemies of the Chinese]. In consultation with his officers, he exclaimed: "Never venture, never win! [1] The only course open to us now is to make an assault by fire on the barbarians under cover of night, when they will not be able to discern our numbers. Profiting by their panic, we shall exterminate them completely; this will cool the King's courage and cover us with glory, besides ensuring the success of our mission.' The officers all replied that it would be necessary to discuss the matter first with the Intendant. Pan Ch'ao then fell into a passion: 'It is today,' he cried, 'that our fortunes must be decided! The Intendant is only a humdrum civilian, who on hearing of our project will certainly be afraid, and everything will be brought to light. An inglorious death is no worthy fate for valiant warriors.' All then agreed to do as he wished. Accordingly, as soon as night came on, he and his little band quickly made their way to the barbarian camp. A strong gale was blowing at the time. Pan Ch'ao ordered ten of the party to take drums and hide behind the enemy's barracks, it being arranged that when they saw flames shoot up, they should begin drumming and yelling with all their might. The rest of his men, armed with bows and crossbows, he posted in ambuscade at the gate of the camp. He then set fire to the place from the windward side, whereupon a deafening noise of drums and shouting arose on the front and rear of the Hsiung-nu, who rushed out pell-mell in frantic disorder. Pan Ch'ao slew three of them with his own hand, while his companions cut off the heads of the envoy and thirty of his suite. The remainder, more than a hundred in all, perished in the flames. On the following day, Pan Ch'ao, divining his thoughts, said with uplifted hand: 'Although you did not go with us last night, I should not think, Sir, of taking sole credit for our exploit.' This satisfied Kuo Hsun, and Pan Ch'ao, having sent for Kuang, King of Shan-shan, showed him the head of the barbarian envoy. The whole kingdom was seized with fear and trembling, which Pan Ch'ao took steps to allay by issuing a public proclamation. Then, taking the king's sons as hostage, he returned to make his report to Tou Ku." Hou Han Shu, ch. 47, ff. 1, 2.]]

the second is to burn stores;

[Tu Mu says: "Provisions, fuel and fodder." In order to subdue the rebellious population of Kiangnan, Kao Keng recommended Wen Ti of the Sui dynasty to make periodical raids and burn their stores of grain, a policy which in the long run proved entirely successful.]

the third is to burn baggage trains;

[An example given is the destruction of Yuan Shao's wagons and impedimenta by Ts'ao Ts'ao in 200 A.D.]

the fourth is to burn arsenals and magazines;

[Tu Mu says that the things contained in "arsenals" and "magazines" are the same. He specifies weapons and other implements, bullion and clothing. Cf. VII. § 11.]

the fifth is to hurl dropping fire amongst the enemy.

[Tu Yu says in the T'ung Tien: "To drop fire into the enemy's camp. The method by which this may be done is to set the tips of arrows alight by dipping them into a brazier, and then shoot them from powerful crossbows into the enemy's lines."]

2. In order to carry out an attack, we must have means available.

[T'sao Kung thinks that "traitors in the enemy's camp" are referred to. But Ch'en Hao is more likely to be right in saying: "We must have favorable circumstances in general, not merely traitors to help us." Chia Lin says: "We must avail ourselves of wind and dry weather."]

the material for raising fire should always be kept in readiness.

[Tu Mu suggests as material for making fire: "dry vegetable matter, reeds, brushwood, straw, grease, oil, etc." Here we have the material cause. Chang Yu says: "vessels for hoarding fire, stuff for lighting fires."]

3. There is a proper season for making attacks with fire, and special days for starting a conflagration.

4. The proper season is when the weather is very dry; the special days are those when the moon is in the constellations of the Sieve, the Wall, the Wing or the Cross-bar;

[These are, respectively, the 7th, 14th, 27th, and 28th of the Twenty-eight Stellar Mansions, corresponding roughly to Sagittarius, Pegasus, Crater and Corvus.]

for these four are all days of rising wind.

5. In attacking with fire, one should be prepared to meet five possible developments:

6. (1) When fire breaks out inside to enemy's camp, respond at once with an attack from without.

7. (2) If there is an outbreak of fire, but the enemy's soldiers remain quiet, bide your time and do not attack.

[The prime object of attacking with fire is to throw the enemy into confusion. If this effect is not produced, it means that the enemy is ready to receive us. Hence the necessity for caution.]

8. (3) When the force of the flames has reached its height, follow it up with an attack, if that is practicable; if not, stay where you are.

[Ts'ao Kung says: "If you see a possible way, advance; but if you find the difficulties too great, retire."]

9. (4) If it is possible to make an assault with fire from without, do not wait for it to break out within, but deliver your attack at a favorable moment.

[Tu Mu says that the previous paragraphs had reference to the fire breaking out (either accidentally, we may suppose, or by the agency of incendiaries) inside the enemy's camp. "But," he continues, "if the enemy is settled in a waste place littered with quantities of grass, or if he has pitched his camp in a position which can be burnt out, we must carry our fire against him at any seasonable opportunity, and not await on in hopes of an outbreak occurring within, for fear our opponents should themselves burn up the surrounding vegetation, and thus render our own attempts fruitless." The famous Li Ling once baffled the leader of the Hsiung-nu in this way. The latter, taking advantage of a favorable wind, tried to set fire to the Chinese general's camp, but found that every scrap of combustible vegetation in the neighborhood had already been burnt down. On the other hand, Po-ts'ai, a general of the Yellow Turban rebels, was badly defeated in 184 A.D. through his neglect of this simple precaution. "At the head of a large army he was besieging Ch'ang-she, which was held by Huang-fu Sung. The garrison was very small, and a general feeling of nervousness pervaded the ranks; so Huang-fu Sung called his officers together and said: "In war, there are various indirect methods of attack, and numbers do not count for everything. [The commentator here quotes Sun Tzu, V. §§ 5, 6 and 10.] Now the rebels have pitched their camp in the midst of thick grass which will easily burn when the wind blows. If we set fire to it at night, they will be thrown into a panic, and we can make a sortie and attack them on all sides at once, thus emulating the achievement of T'ien Tan.' [See p. 90.] That same evening, a strong breeze sprang up; so Huang-fu Sung instructed his soldiers to bind reeds together into torches and mount guard on the city walls, after which he sent out a band of daring men, who stealthily made their way through the lines and started the fire with loud shouts and yells. Simultaneously, a glare of light shot up from the city walls, and Huang-fu Sung, sounding his drums, led a rapid charge, which threw the rebels into confusion and put them to headlong flight." [Hou Han Shu, ch. 71.]]

10. (5) When you start a fire, be to windward of it. Do not attack from the leeward.

[Chang Yu, following Tu Yu, says: "When you make a fire, the enemy will retreat away from it; if you oppose his retreat and attack him then, he will fight desperately, which will not conduce to your success." A rather more obvious explanation is given by Tu Mu: "If the wind is in the east, begin burning to the east of the enemy, and follow up the attack yourself from that side. If you start the fire on the east side, and then attack from the west, you will suffer in the same way as your enemy."]

11. A wind that rises in the daytime lasts long, but a night breeze soon falls.

[Cf. Lao Tzu's saying: "A violent wind does not last the space of a morning." (Tao Te Ching, chap. 23.) Mei Yao-ch'en and Wang Hsi say: "A day breeze dies down at nightfall, and a night breeze at daybreak. This is what happens as a general rule." The phenomenon observed may be correct enough, but how this sense is to be obtained is not apparent.]

12. In every army, the five developments connected with fire must be known, the movements of the stars calculated, and a watch kept for the proper days.

[Tu Mu says: "We must make calculations as to the paths of the stars, and watch for the days on which wind will rise, before making our attack with fire." Chang Yu seems to interpret the text differently: "We must not only know how to assail our opponents with fire, but also be on our guard against similar attacks from them."]

13. Hence those who use fire as an aid to the attack show intelligence; those who use water as an aid to the attack gain an accession of strength.

14. By means of water, an enemy may be intercepted, but not robbed of all his belongings.

[Ts'ao Kung's note is: "We can merely obstruct the enemy's road or divide his army, but not sweep away all his accumulated stores." Water can do useful service, but it lacks the terrible destructive power of fire. This is the reason, Chang Yu concludes, why the former is dismissed in a couple of sentences, whereas the attack by fire is discussed in detail. Wu Tzu (ch. 4) speaks thus of the two elements: "If an army is encamped on low-lying marshy ground, from which the water cannot run off, and where the rainfall is heavy, it may be submerged by a flood. If an army is encamped in wild marsh lands thickly overgrown with weeds and brambles, and visited by frequent gales, it may be exterminated by fire."]

15. Unhappy is the fate of one who tries to win his battles and succeed in his attacks without cultivating the spirit of enterprise; for the result is waste of time and general stagnation.

[This is one of the most perplexing passages in Sun Tzu. Ts'ao Kung says: "Rewards for good service should not be deferred a single day." And Tu Mu: "If you do not take opportunity to advance and reward the deserving, your subordinates will not carry out your commands, and disaster will ensue." For several reasons, however, and in spite of the formidable array of scholars on the other side, I prefer the interpretation suggested by Mei Yao-ch'en alone, whose words I will quote: "Those who want to make sure of succeeding in their battles and assaults must seize the favorable moments when they come and not shrink on occasion from heroic measures: that is to say, they must resort to such means of attack of fire, water and the like. What they must not do, and what will prove fatal, is to sit still and simply hold to the advantages they have got."]

16. Hence the saying: The enlightened ruler lays his plans well ahead; the good general cultivates his resources.

[Tu Mu quotes the following from the San Lueh, ch. 2: "The warlike prince controls his soldiers by his authority, kits them together by good faith, and by rewards makes them serviceable. If faith decays, there will be disruption; if rewards are deficient, commands will not be respected."]

17. Move not unless you see an advantage; use not your troops unless there is something to be gained; fight not unless the position is critical.

[Sun Tzu may at times appear to be over-cautious, but he never goes so far in that direction as the remarkable passage in the Tao Te Ching, ch. 69. "I dare not take the initiative, but prefer to act on the defensive; I dare not advance an inch, but prefer to retreat a foot."]

18. No ruler should put troops into the field merely to gratify his own spleen; no general should fight a battle simply out of pique.

19. If it is to your advantage, make a forward move; if not, stay where you are.

[This is repeated from XI. § 17. Here I feel convinced that it is an interpolation, for it is evident that § 20 ought to follow immediately on § 18.]

20. Anger may in time change to gladness; vexation may be succeeded by content.

21. But a kingdom that has once been destroyed can never come again into being;

[The Wu State was destined to be a melancholy example of this saying.]

nor can the dead ever be brought back to life.

22. Hence the enlightened ruler is heedful, and the good general full of caution. This is the way to keep a country at peace and an army intact.

[1] "Unless you enter the tiger's lair, you cannot get hold of the tiger's cubs."

CHAPTER XIII. THE USE OF SPIES

1. Sun Tzu said: Raising a host of a hundred thousand men and marching them great distances entails heavy loss on the people and a drain on the resources of the State. The daily expenditure will amount to a thousand ounces of silver.

[Cf. II. §§ 1, 13, 14.]

There will be commotion at home and abroad, and men will drop down exhausted on the highways.

[Cf. Tao Te Ching, ch. 30: "Where troops have been quartered, brambles and thorns spring up. Chang Yu has the note: "We may be reminded of the saying: 'On serious ground, gather in plunder.' Why then should carriage and transportation cause exhaustion on the highways?—The answer is, that not victuals alone, but all sorts of munitions of war have to be conveyed to the army. Besides, the injunction to 'forage on the enemy' only means that when an army is deeply engaged in hostile territory, scarcity of food must be provided against. Hence, without being solely dependent on the enemy for corn, we must forage in order that there may be an uninterrupted flow of supplies. Then, again, there are places like salt deserts where provisions being unobtainable, supplies from home cannot be dispensed with."]

As many as seven hundred thousand families will be impeded in their labor.

[Mei Yao-ch'en says: "Men will be lacking at the plough-tail."

The allusion is to the system of dividing land into nine parts, each consisting of about 15 acres, the plot in the center being cultivated on behalf of the State by the tenants of the other eight. It was here also, so Tu Mu tells us, that their cottages were built and a well sunk, to be used by all in common. [See II. § 12, note.] In time of war, one of the families had to serve in the army, while the other seven contributed to its support. Thus, by a levy of 100,000 men (reckoning one able-bodied soldier to each family) the husbandry of 700,000 families would be affected.]

2. Hostile armies may face each other for years, striving for the victory which is decided in a single day. This being so, to remain in ignorance of the enemy's condition simply because one grudges the outlay of a hundred ounces of silver in honors and emoluments,

["For spies" is of course the meaning, though it would spoil the effect of this curiously elaborate exordium if spies were actually mentioned at this point.]

is the height of inhumanity.

[Sun Tzu's agreement is certainly ingenious. He begins by adverting to the frightful misery and vast expenditure of blood and treasure which war always brings in its train. Now, unless you are kept informed of the enemy's condition, and are ready to strike at the right moment, a war may drag on for years. The only way to get this information is to employ spies, and it is impossible to obtain trustworthy spies unless they are properly paid for their services. But it is surely false economy to grudge a comparatively trifling amount for this purpose, when every day that the war lasts eats up an incalculably greater sum. This grievous burden falls on the shoulders of the poor, and hence Sun Tzu concludes that to neglect the use of spies is nothing less than a crime against humanity.]

3. One who acts thus is no leader of men, no present help to his sovereign, no master of victory.

[This idea, that the true object of war is peace, has its root in the national temperament of the Chinese. Even so far back as 597 B.C., these memorable words were uttered by Prince Chuang of the Ch'u State: "The [Chinese] character for 'prowess' is made up of [the characters for] 'to stay' and 'a spear' (cessation of hostilities). Military prowess is seen in the repression of cruelty, the calling in of weapons, the preservation of the appointment of Heaven, the firm establishment of merit, the bestowal of happiness on the people, putting harmony between the princes, the diffusion of wealth."]

. Thus, what enables the wise sovereign and the good general to strike and conquer, and achieve things beyond the reach of ordinary men, is foreknowledge.

[That is, knowledge of the enemy's dispositions, and what he means to do.]

5. Now this foreknowledge cannot be elicited from spirits; it cannot be obtained inductively from experience,

[Tu Mu's note is: "[knowledge of the enemy] cannot be gained by reasoning from other analogous cases."]

nor by any deductive calculation.

[Li Ch'uan says: "Quantities like length, breadth, distance and magnitude, are susceptible of exact mathematical determination; human actions cannot be so calculated."]

6. Knowledge of the enemy's dispositions can only be obtained from other men.

[Mei Yao-ch'en has rather an interesting note: "Knowledge of the spirit-world is to be obtained by divination; information in natural science may be sought by inductive reasoning; the laws of the universe can be verified by mathematical calculation: but the dispositions of an enemy are ascertainable through spies and spies alone."]

7. Hence the use of spies, of whom there are five classes: (1) Local spies; (2) inward spies; (3) converted spies; (4) doomed spies; (5) surviving spies.

8. When these five kinds of spy are all at work, none can discover the secret system. This is called "divine manipulation of the threads." It is the sovereign's most precious faculty.

[Cromwell, one of the greatest and most practical of all cavalry leaders, had officers styled 'scout masters,' whose business it was to collect all possible information regarding the enemy, through scouts and spies, etc., and much of his success in war was traceable to the previous knowledge of the enemy's moves thus gained." [1]]

9. Having *local* spies means employing the services of the inhabitants of a district.

[Tu Mu says: "In the enemy's country, win people over by kind treatment, and use them as spies."]

10. Having inward spies, making use of officials of the enemy.

[Tu Mu enumerates the following classes as likely to do good service in this respect: "Worthy men who have been degraded from office, criminals who have undergone punishment; also, favorite concubines who are greedy for gold, men who are aggrieved at being in subordinate positions, or who have been passed over in the distribution of posts, others who are anxious that their side should be defeated in order that they may have a chance of displaying their ability and talents, fickle turncoats who always want to have a foot in each boat. Officials of these several kinds," he continues, "should be secretly approached and bound to one's interests by means of rich presents. In this way you will be able to find out the state of affairs in the enemy's country, ascertain the plans that are being formed against you, and moreover disturb the harmony and create a breach between the sovereign and his ministers." The necessity for extreme caution, however, in dealing with "inward spies," appears from an historical incident related by Ho Shih: "Lo Shang, Governor of I-Chou, sent his general Wei Po to attack the rebel Li Hsiung of Shu in his stronghold at P'i. After each side had experienced a number of victories and defeats, Li Hsiung had recourse to the services of a certain P'o-t'ai, a native of Wu-tu. He began to have him whipped until the blood came, and then sent him off to Lo Shang, whom he was to delude by offering to cooperate with him from inside the city, and to give a fire signal at the right moment for making a general assault. Lo Shang, confiding in these promises, march out all his best troops, and placed Wei Po and others at their head with orders to attack at P'o-t'ai's bidding. Meanwhile, Li Hsiung's general, Li Hsiang, had prepared an ambuscade on their line of march; and P'o-t'ai, having reared long scaling-ladders against the city walls, now lighted the beacon-fire. Wei Po's men raced up on seeing the signal and began climbing the ladders as fast as they could, while others were drawn up by ropes lowered from above. More than a hundred of Lo Shang's soldiers entered the city in this way, every one of whom was forthwith beheaded. Li Hsiung then charged with all his forces, both inside and outside the city, and routed the enemy completely." [This happened in 303 A.D. I do not know where Ho Shih got the story from. It is not given in the biography of Li Hsiung or that of his father Li T'e, Chin Shu, ch. 120, 121.]

11. Having *converted spies*, getting hold of the enemy's spies and using them for our own purposes.

[By means of heavy bribes and liberal promises detaching them from the enemy's service, and inducing them to carry back false information as well as to spy in turn on their own countrymen. On the other hand, Hsiao Shih-hsien says that we pretend not to have detected him, but contrive to let him carry away a false impression of what is going on. Several of the commentators accept this as an alternative definition; but that it is not what Sun Tzu meant is conclusively proved by his subsequent remarks about treating the converted spy generously (§ 21 sqq.). Ho Shih notes three occasions on which converted spies were used with conspicuous success: (1)

by T'ien Tan in his defense of Chi-mo (see supra, p. 90); (2) by Chao She on his march to O-yu (see p. 57); and by the wily Fan Chu in 260 B.C., when Lien P'o was conducting a defensive campaign against Ch'in. The King of Chao strongly disapproved of Lien P'o's cautious and dilatory methods, which had been unable to avert a series of minor disasters, and therefore lent a ready ear to the reports of his spies, who had secretly gone over to the enemy and were already in Fan Chu's pay. They said: "The only thing which causes Ch'in anxiety is lest Chao Kua should be made general. Lien P'o they consider an easy opponent, who is sure to be vanquished in the long run." Now this Chao Kua was a son of the famous Chao She. From his boyhood, he had been wholly engrossed in the study of war and military matters, until at last he came to believe that there was no commander in the whole Empire who could stand against him. His father was much disquieted by this overweening conceit, and the flippancy with which he spoke of such a serious thing as war, and solemnly declared that if ever Kua was appointed general, he would bring ruin on the armies of Chao. This was the man who, in spite of earnest protests from his own mother and the veteran statesman Lin Hsiang-ju, was now sent to succeed Lien P'o. Needless to say, he proved no match for the redoubtable Po Ch'i and the great military power of Ch'in. He fell into a trap by which his army was divided into two and his communications cut; and after a desperate resistance lasting 46 days, during which the famished soldiers devoured one another, he was himself killed by an arrow, and his whole force, amounting, it is said, to 400,000 men, ruthlessly put to the sword.]

12. Having *doomed spies*, doing certain things openly for purposes of deception, and allowing our spies to know of them and report them to the enemy.

[Tu Yu gives the best exposition of the meaning: "We ostentatiously do things calculated to deceive our own spies, who must be led to believe that they have been unwittingly disclosed. Then, when these spies are captured in the enemy's lines, they will make an entirely false report, and the enemy will take measures accordingly, only to find that we do something quite different. The spies will thereupon be put to death." As an example of doomed spies, Ho Shih mentions the prisoners released by Pan Ch'ao in his campaign against Yarkand. (See p. 132.) He also refers to T'ang Chien, who in 630 A.D. was sent by T'ai Tsung to lull the Turkish Kahn Chieh-li into fancied security, until Li Ching was able to deliver a crushing blow against him. Chang Yu says that the Turks revenged themselves by killing T'ang Chien, but this is a mistake, for we read in both the old and the New T'ang History (ch. 58, fol. 2 and ch. 89, fol. 8 respectively) that he escaped and lived on until 656. Li I-chi played a somewhat similar part in 203 B.C., when sent by the King of Han to open peaceful negotiations with Ch'i. He has certainly more claim to be described a "doomed spy", for the king of Ch'i, being subsequently attacked without warning by Han Hsin, and infuriated by what he considered the treachery of Li I-chi, ordered the unfortunate envoy to be boiled alive.]

13. *Surviving spies*, finally, are those who bring back news from the enemy's camp.

[This is the ordinary class of spies, properly so called, forming a regular part of the army. Tu Mu says: "Your surviving spy must be a man of keen intellect, though in outward appearance a fool; of shabby exterior, but with a will of iron. He must be active, robust, endowed with physical strength and courage; thoroughly accustomed to all sorts of dirty work, able to endure hunger and cold, and to put up with shame and ignominy." Ho Shih tells the following story of

Ta'hsi Wu of the Sui dynasty: "When he was governor of Eastern Ch'in, Shen-wu of Ch'i made a hostile movement upon Sha-yuan. The Emperor T'ai Tsu [? Kao Tsu] sent Ta-hsi Wu to spy upon the enemy. He was accompanied by two other men. All three were on horseback and wore the enemy's uniform. When it was dark, they dismounted a few hundred feet away from the enemy's camp and stealthily crept up to listen, until they succeeded in catching the passwords used in the army. Then they got on their horses again and boldly passed through the camp under the guise of night-watchmen; and more than once, happening to come across a soldier who was committing some breach of discipline, they actually stopped to give the culprit a sound cudgeling! Thus they managed to return with the fullest possible information about the enemy's dispositions, and received warm commendation from the Emperor, who in consequence of their report was able to inflict a severe defeat on his adversary."]

14. Hence it is that which none in the whole army are more intimate relations to be maintained than with spies.

[Tu Mu and Mei Yao-ch'en point out that the spy is privileged to enter even the general's private sleeping-tent.]

None should be more liberally rewarded. In no other business should greater secrecy be preserved.

[Tu Mu gives a graphic touch: all communication with spies should be carried "mouth-to-ear." The following remarks on spies may be quoted from Turenne, who made perhaps larger use of them than any previous commander: "Spies are attached to those who give them most, he who pays them ill is never served. They should never be known to anybody; nor should they know one another. When they propose anything very material, secure their persons, or have in your possession their wives and children as hostages for their fidelity. Never communicate anything to them but what is absolutely necessary that they should know. [2]]

15. Spies cannot be usefully employed without a certain intuitive sagacity.

[Mei Yao-ch'en says: "In order to use them, one must know fact from falsehood, and be able to discriminate between honesty and double-dealing." Wang Hsi in a different interpretation thinks more along the lines of "intuitive perception" and "practical intelligence." Tu Mu strangely refers these attributes to the spies themselves: "Before using spies we must assure ourselves as to their integrity of character and the extent of their experience and skill." But he continues: "A brazen face and a crafty disposition are more dangerous than mountains or rivers; it takes a man of genius to penetrate such." So that we are left in some doubt as to his real opinion on the passage."]

16. They cannot be properly managed without benevolence and straightforwardness.

[Chang Yu says: "When you have attracted them by substantial offers, you must treat them with absolute sincerity; then they will work for you with all their might."]

17. Without subtle ingenuity of mind, one cannot make certain of the truth of their reports.

[Mei Yao-ch'en says: "Be on your guard against the possibility of spies going over to the service of the enemy."]

18. Be subtle! be subtle! and use your spies for every kind of business.

[Cf. VI. § 9.]

19. If a secret piece of news is divulged by a spy before the time is ripe, he must be put to death together with the man to whom the secret was told.

[Word for word, the translation here is: "If spy matters are heard before [our plans] are carried out," etc. Sun Tzu's main point in this passage is: Whereas you kill the spy himself "as a punishment for letting out the secret," the object of killing the other man is only, as Ch'en Hao puts it, "to stop his mouth" and prevent news leaking any further. If it had already been repeated to others, this object would not be gained. Either way, Sun Tzu lays himself open to the charge of inhumanity, though Tu Mu tries to defend him by saying that the man deserves to be put to death, for the spy would certainly not have told the secret unless the other had been at pains to worm it out of him."]

20. Whether the object be to crush an army, to storm a city, or to assassinate an individual, it is always necessary to begin by finding out the names of the attendants, the aides-de- camp,

[Literally "visitors", is equivalent, as Tu Yu says, to "those whose duty it is to keep the general supplied with information," which naturally necessitates frequent interviews with him.]

and door-keepers and sentries of the general in command. Our spies must be commissioned to ascertain these.

[As the first step, no doubt towards finding out if any of these important functionaries can be won over by bribery.]

21. The enemy's spies who have come to spy on us must be sought out, tempted with bribes, led away and comfortably housed. Thus they will become converted spies and available for our service.

22. It is through the information brought by the converted spy that we are able to acquire and employ local and inward spies.

[Tu Yu says: "through conversion of the enemy's spies we learn the enemy's condition." And Chang Yu says: "We must tempt the converted spy into our service, because it is he that knows which of the local inhabitants are greedy of gain, and which of the officials are open to corruption."]

223. It is owing to his information, again, that we can cause the doomed spy to carry false tidings to the enemy.

[Chang Yu says, "because the converted spy knows how the enemy can best be deceived."]

24. Lastly, it is by his information that the surviving spy can be used on appointed occasions.

25. The end and aim of spying in all its five varieties is knowledge

of the enemy; and this knowledge can only be derived, in the first instance, from the converted spy.

[As explained in §§ 22-24. He not only brings information himself, but makes it possible to use the other kinds of spy to advantage.]

Hence it is essential that the converted spy be treated with the utmost liberality.

26. Of old, the rise of the Yin dynasty

[Sun Tzu means the Shang dynasty, founded in 1766 B.C. Its name was changed to Yin by P'an Keng in 1401.

was due to I Chih

[Better known as I Yin, the famous general and statesman who took part in Ch'eng T'ang's campaign against Chieh Kuei.]

who had served under the Hsia. Likewise, the rise of the Chou dynasty was due to Lu Ya

[Lu Shang rose to high office under the tyrant Chou Hsin, whom he afterwards helped to overthrow. Popularly known as T'ai Kung, a title bestowed on him by Wen Wang, he is said to have composed a treatise on war, erroneously identified with the Liu T'ao.]

who had served under the Yin.

[There is less precision in the Chinese than I have thought it well to introduce into my translation, and the commentaries on the passage are by no means explicit. But, having regard to the context, we can hardly doubt that Sun Tzu is holding up I Chih and Lu Ya as illustrious examples of the converted spy, or something closely analogous. His suggestion is, that the Hsia and Yin dynasties were upset owing to the intimate knowledge of their weaknesses and shortcoming which these former ministers were able to impart to the other side. Mei Yao-ch'en appears to resent any such aspersion on these historic names: "I Yin and Lu Ya," he says, "were not rebels against the Government. Hsia could not employ the former, hence Yin employed him. Yin could not employ the latter, hence Hou employed him. Their great achievements were all for the good of the people." Ho Shih is also indignant: "How should two divinely inspired men such as I and Lu have acted as common spies? Sun Tzu's mention of them simply means that the proper use of the five classes of spies is a matter which requires men of the highest mental caliber like I and Lu, whose wisdom and capacity qualified them for the task. The above words only emphasize this point." Ho Shih believes then that the two heroes are mentioned on account of their supposed skill in the use of spies. But this is very weak.]

27. Hence it is only the enlightened ruler and the wise general who will use the highest intelligence of the army for purposes of spying and thereby they achieve great results.

[Tu Mu closes with a note of warning: "Just as water, which carries a boat from bank to bank, may also be the means of sinking it, so reliance on spies, while production of great results, is oft-times the cause of utter destruction."]

Spies are a most important element in war, because on them depends an army's ability to move.

[Chia Lin says that an army without spies is like a man with ears or eyes.]

[1] "Aids to Scouting," p. 2.

[2] "Marshal Turenne," p. 311.

BUSHIDO,
THE SOUL OF JAPAN

Inazo Nitobe: Inazo Nitobe was a Japanese economist, diplomat and writer. He was a major actor in the League of Nations, and served in the Japanese parliament. His important work Bushido: The Soul of Japan is one of the best early explorations of Japanese culture and samurai ethics written in the English language.

To my beloved uncle
Tokitoshi Ota
Who taught me to revere the past
and
To admire the deeds of the Samurai
I dedicate
this little book

PREFACE TO THE FIRST EDITION

ABOUT ten years ago, while spending a few days under the hospitable roof of the distinguished Belgian jurist, the lamented M. de Laveleye, our conversation turned during one of our rambles, to the subject of religion. "Do you mean to say," asked the venerable professor, "that you have no religious instruction in your schools?" On my replying in the negative, he suddenly halted in astonishment, and in a voice which I shall not easily forget, he repeated "No religion! How do you impart moral education?" The question stunned me at the time. I could give no ready answer, for the moral precepts I learned in my childhood days were not given in schools; and not until I began to analyse the different elements that formed my notions of right and wrong, did I find that it was Bushido that breathed them into my nostrils.

The direct inception of this little book is due to the frequent queries put by my wife as to the reasons why such and such ideas and customs prevail in Japan.

In my attempts to give satisfactory replies to M. de Laveleye and to my wife, I found that without understanding feudalism and Bushido,[1] the moral ideas of present Japan are a sealed volume.

1 Pronounced Boóshee-doh'. In putting Japanese words and names into English, Hepburn's rule is followed, that the vowels should be used as in European languages, and the consonants as in English.

Taking advantage of enforced idleness on account of long illness, I put down in the order now presented to the public some of the answers given in our household conversation. They consist mainly of what I was taught and told in my youthful days, when feudalism was still in force.

Between Lafcadio Hearn and Mrs. Hugh Fraser on one side and Sir Ernest Satow and Professor Chamberlain on the other, it is indeed discouraging to write anything Japanese in English. The only advantage I have over them is that I can assume the attitude of a personal defendant, while these distinguished writers are at best solicitors and attorneys. I have often thought,—"Had I their gift of language, I would present the cause of Japan in more eloquent terms!" But one who speaks in a borrowed tongue should be thankful if he can just make himself intelligible.

All through the discourse I have tried to illustrate whatever points I have made with parallel examples from European history and literature, believing that these will aid in bringing the subject nearer to the comprehension of foreign readers.

Should any of my allusions to religious subjects and to religious workers be thought slighting, I trust my attitude toward Christianity itself will not be questioned. It is with ecclesiastical methods and with the forms which obscure the teachings of Christ, and not with the teachings themselves, that I have little sympathy. I believe in the religion taught by Him and handed down to us in the New Testament, as well as in the law written in the heart. Further, I believe that God hath made a testament which may be called "old" with every people and nation,—Gentile or Jew, Christian or Heathen. As to the rest of my theology, I need not impose upon the patience of the public.

In concluding this preface, I wish to express my thanks to my friend Anna C. Hartshome for many valuable suggestions.

— *Inazo Nitobe*

INTRODUCTION

At the request of his publishers, to whom Dr. Nitobe has left some freedom of action concerning prefatory matter, I am glad to offer a few sentences of introduction to this new edition of *Bushido*, for readers of English everywhere. I have been acquainted with the author for over fifteen years, indeed, but, in a measure at least, with his subject during forty-five years.

It was in 1860, in Philadelphia (where, in 1847, I saw the Susquehanna, Commodore Perry's flagship launched), that I looked on my first Japanese and met members of the Embassy from Yedo. I was mightily impressed with these strangers, to whom Bushido was a living code of ideals and manners. Later, during three years at Rutgers College, New Brunswick, N. J., I was among scores of young men from Nippon, whom I taught or knew as fellow-students. I found that Bushido, about which we often talked, was a superbly winsome thing. As illustrated in the lives of these future governors, diplomatists, admirals, educators, and bankers, yes, even in the dying hours of more than one who "fell on sleep" in Willow Grove Cemetery, the perfume of this most fragrant flower of far-off Japan was very sweet. Never shall I forget how the dying samurai lad, Kusakabe, when invited to the noblest of services and the greatest of hopes, made answer: "Even if I could know your Master, Jesus, I should not offer Him only the dregs of a life." So, "on the banks of the old Raritan," in athletic sports, in merry jokes at the supper table when contrasting things Japanese and Yankee, and in the discussion of ethics and ideals, I felt quite willing to take the "covert missionary retort," about which my friend Charles Dudley Warner once wrote. At some points, codes of ethics and proprieties differed, but rather in dots or tangents than as occultation or eclipse. As their own poet wrote—was it a thousand years ago?--when in crossing a moor the dew-laden flowers brushed by his robe left their glittering drops on his brocade, "On account of its perfume, I brush not this moisture from my sleeve." Indeed, I was glad to get out of ruts, which are said to differ from graves only by their length. For, is not comparison the life of science and culture? Is it not true that, in the study of languages, ethics, religions, and codes of manners, "he who knows but one knows none"?

Called, in 1870, to Japan as pioneer educator to introduce the methods and spirit of the American public-school system, how glad I was to leave the capital, and at Fukui, in the province of Echizen, see pure feudalism in operation! There I looked on Bushido, not as an exotic, but in its native soil. In daily life I realised that Bushido, with its *cha-no-yu,jū- jmtsm* ("jiu-jitsu"), *hara-kiri*, polite prostrations on the mats and genuflections on the street, rules of the sword and road, all leisurely salutations and politest moulds of speech, canons of art and conduct, as well as heroisms for wife, maid, and child, formed the universal creed and praxis of all the gentry in the castled city and province. In it, as a living school of thought and life, girl and boy alike were trained. What Dr. Nitobe received as an inheritance, had breathed into his nostrils, and writes about so gracefully and forcibly, with such grasp, insight, and breadth of view, I saw. Japanese feudalism "died without the sight" of its ablest exponent and most convincing defender. To him it is as wafted fragrance. To me it was "the plant and flower of light."

Hence, living under and being in at the death of feudalism, the body of Bushido, I can bear witness to the essential truth of Dr. Nitobe's descriptions, so far as they go, and to the faithfulness of his analysis and generalisations. He has limned with masterly art and reproduced the colouring of the picture which a thousand years of Japanese literature reflects so gloriously. The Knightly Code grew up during a millenium of evolution, and our author lovingly notes the blooms that have starred the path trodden by millions of noble souls, his countrymen.

Critical study has but deepened my own sense of the potency and value of Bushido to the nation. He who would understand twentieth-century Japan must know something of its roots in the soil of the past. Even if now as invisible to the present generation in Nippon as to the alien, the philosophic student reads the results of to-day in the stored energies of ages gone. The sunbeams of unrecorded time have laid the strata out of which Japan now digs her foot-pounds of impact for war or peace. All the spiritual senses are keen in those nursed by Bushido. The crystalline lump has dissolved in the sweetened cup, but the delicacy of the flavour remains to cheer. In a word, Bushido has obeyed the higher law enunciated by One whom its own exponent salutes and confesses his Master—"Except a grain of corn die, it abideth alone; but if it die it bringeth forth much fruit."

Has Dr. Nitobe idealised Bushido? Rather, we ask, how could he help doing so? He calls himself "defendant." In all creeds, cults, and systems, while the ideal grows, exemplars and exponents vary. Gradual cumulation and slow attainment of harmony is the law. Bushido never reached a final goal. It was too much alive, and it died at last only in its splendour and strength. The clash of the world's movement—for so we name the rush of influences and events which followed Perry and Harris—with feudalism in Japan, did not find Bushido an embalmed mummy, but a living soul. What it really met was the quickening spirit of humanity. Then the less was blessed of the greater. Without losing the best in her own history and civilisation, Japan, following her own noble precedents, first adopted and then adapted the choicest the world had to offer. Thus her opportunity to bless Asia and the race became unique, and grandly she has embraced it—"in diffusion ever more intense." To-day, not only are our gardens, our art, our homes enriched by the flowers, the pictures, and the pretty things of Japan, whether "trifles of a moment or triumphs for all time," but in physical culture, in public hygiene, in lessons for peace and war, Japan has come to us with her hands gift-laden.

Not only in his discourse as advocate and counsel for the defence, but as prophet and wise householder, rich in things new and old, our author is able to teach us. No man in Japan has united the precepts and practice of his own Bushido more harmoniously in life and toil, labour and work, craft of hand and of pen, culture of the soil and of the soul. Illuminator of Dai Nippon's past, Dr. Nitobe is a true maker of the New Japan. In Formosa, the empire's new accretion, as in Kioto, he is the scholar and practical man, at home in newest science and most ancient diligence.

This little book on Bushido is more than a weighty message to the Anglo- Saxon nations. It is a notable contribution to the solution of this century's grandest problem—the reconciliation and unity of the East and the West. There were of old many civilisations: in the better world coming there will be one. Already the terms "Orient" and "Occident," with all their freight of mutual ignorance and insolence, are ready to pass, away. As the efficient middle term between the wisdom and communism of Asia and the energy and individualism of Europe and America, Japan is already working with resistless power.

Instructed in things ancient and modern and cultured in the literatures of the world, Dr. Nitobe herein shows himself admirably fitted for a congenial task. He is a true interpreter and reconciler. He need not and does not apologise for his own attitude toward the Master whom he has long loyally followed. What scholar, familiar with the ways of the Spirit and with the history of the race as led by man's Infinite Friend, but must in all religions put difference between the teachings of the Founder and the original documents and the ethnic, rationalistic, and ecclesiastical additions and accretions? The doctrine of the testaments, hinted at in the author's preface, is the teaching of Him who came not to destroy, but to fulfil. Even in Japan, Christianity, unwrapped from its foreign mould and matting, will cease being an exotic and strike its roots deep in the soil on which Bushido has grown. Stripped alike of its swaddling bands and its foreign regimentals, the church of the Founder will be as native as the air.

— *William Elliot Grippis.*
Ithaca,
May, 1905.

EPIGRAMS

"That way
Over the mountain, which who stands upon
Is apt to doubt if it be indeed a road;
While if he views it from the waste itself,
Up goes the line there, plain from base to brow,
Not vague, mistakable! What's a break or two
Seen from the unbroken deserts either side?
And then (to bring in fresh philosophy)
What if the breaks themselves should prove at last
The most consummate of contrivances
To train a man's eye, teach him what is faith?

— Robert Browning,
Bishop Blougram's Apology.

"There are, if I may so say, three powerful spirits, which have, from time to time, moved on the face of the waters, and given a predominant impulse to the moral sentiments and energies of mankind. These are the spirits of liberty, of religion, and of honor.
HALLAM,
Europe in the Middle Ages.
"Chivalry is itself the poetry of life."
SCHLEGEL,
Philosophy of History.

CHAPTER 1

BUSHIDO AS AN ETHICAL SYSTEM

Chivalry is a flower no less indigenous to the soil of Japan than its emblem, the cherry blossom; nor is it a dried-up specimen of an antique virtue preserved in the herbarium of our history. It is still a living object of power and beauty among us; and if it assumes no tangible shape or form, it not the less scents the moral atmosphere, and makes us aware that we are still under its potent spell. The conditions of society which brought it forth and nourished it have long disappeared; but as those far- off stars which once were and are not, still continue to shed their rays upon us, so the light of chivalry, which was a child of feudalism, still illuminates our moral path, surviving its mother institution. It is a pleasure to me to reflect upon this subject in the language of Burke, who uttered the well-known touching eulogy over the neglected bier of its European prototype.

It argues a sad defect of information concerning the Far East, when so erudite a scholar as Dr. George Miller did not hesitate to affirm that, chivalry, or any other similar institution, has never existed either among the nations of antiquity or among the modern Orientals.[1] Such ignorance, however, is amply excusable, as the third edition of the good Doctor's, work appeared the same year that Commodore Perry was knocking at the portals of our

---

1 *History Philosophically Illustrated* (3d ed., 1853). vol. ii., p. 2.

exclusivism. More than a decade later, about the time that our feudalism was in the last throes of existence, Carl Marx, writing his *Capital*, called the attention of his readers to the peculiar advantage of studying the social and political institutions of feudalism, as then to be seen in living form only in Japan. I would likewise point the Western historical and ethical student to the study of chivalry in the Japan of the present.

Enticing as is an historical disquisition on the comparison between European and Japanese feudalism and chivalry, it is not the purpose of this paper to enter into it at length. My attempt is rather to relate firstly, the origin and sources of our chivalry; secondly, its character and teaching; thirdly, its influence among the masses; and, fourthly, the continuity and permanence of its influence. Of these several points, the first will be only brief and cursory, or else I should have to take my readers into the devious paths of our national history; the second will be dwelt upon at greater length, as being most likely to interest students of International Ethics and Comparative Ethology in our ways of thought and action; and the rest will be dealt with as corollaries.

The Japanese word which I have roughly rendered Chivalry, is, in the original, more expressive than Horsemanship. *Bu-shi-do* means literally Military-Knight-Ways—the ways which fighting nobles should observe in their daily life as well as in their vocation; in a word, the "Precepts of Knighthood," the *noblesse oblige* of the warrior class. Having thus given its literal significance, I may be allowed henceforth to use the word in the original. The use of the original term is also advisable for this reason, that a teaching so circumscribed and unique, engendering a cast of mind and character so peculiar, so local, must wear the badge of its singularity on its face; then, some words have a national *timbre* so expressive of race characteristics that the best of translators can do them but scant justice, not to say positive injustice and grievance. Who can improve by translation what the

German "*Gemŭth*" signifies, or who does not feel the difference between the two words verbally so closely allied as the English gentleman and the French *gentilhomme*?

Bushido, then, is the code of moral principles which the knights were required or instructed to observe. It is not a written code; at best it consists of a few maxims handed down from mouth to mouth or coming from the pen of some well-known warrior or savant. More frequently it is a code unuttered and unwritten, possessing all the more the powerful sanction of veritable deed, and of a law written on the fleshly tablets of the heart. It was founded not on the creation of one brain, however able, or on the life of a single personage, however renowned. It was an organic growth of decades and centuries of military career. It, perhaps, fills the same position in the history of ethics that the English Constitution does in political history; yet it has had nothing to compare with the Magna Charta or the Habeas Corpus Act. True, early in the seventeenth century Military Statutes (*Buké Hatto*) were promulgated; but their thirteen short articles were taken up mostly with marriages, castles, leagues, etc., and didactic regulations were but meagerly touched upon. We cannot, therefore, point out any definite time and place and say, "Here is its fountainhead." Only as it attains consciousness in the feudal age, its origin, in respect to time, may be identified with feudalism. But feudalism itself is woven of many threads, and Bushido shares its intricate nature. As in England the political institutions of feudalism may be said to date from the Norman Conquest, so we may say that in Japan its rise was simultaneous with the ascendancy of Yoritomo, late in the twelfth century. As, however, in England, we find the social elements of feudalism far back in the period previous to William the Conqueror, so, too, the germs of feudalism in Japan had been long existent before the period I have mentioned.

Again, in Japan as in Europe, when feudalism was formally inaugurated, the professional class of warriors naturally came into prominence. These were known as *samurai*, meaning literally, like the old English *cniht* (knecht, knight), guards or attendants— resembling in character the *soldurii*, whom Cæsar mentioned as existing in Aquitania, or the *comitati*, who, according to Tacitus, followed Germanic chiefs in his time; or, to take a still later parallel, the *milites medii* that one reads about in the history of Mediæval Europe. A Sinico-Japanese word *Bu- ké* or *Bu-shi* (Fighting Knights) was also adopted in common use. They were a privileged class, and must originally have been a rough breed who made fighting their vocation. This class was naturally recruited, in a long period of constant warfare, from the manliest and the most adventurous, and all the while the process of elimination went on, the timid and the feeble being sorted out, and only "a rude race, all masculine, with brutish strength," to borrow Emerson's phrase, surviving to form families and the ranks of the samurai. Coming to profess great honour and great privileges, and correspondingly great responsibilities, they soon felt the need of a common standard of behaviour, especially as they were always on a belligerent footing and belonged to different clans. just as physicians limit competition among themselves by professional courtesy, just as lawyers sit in courts of honour in cases of violated etiquette; so must also warriors possess some resort for final judgment on their misdemeanours.

Fair play in fight! What fertile germs of morality lie in this primitive sense of savagery and childhood. Is it not the root of all military and civic virtue? We smile (as if we had outgrown it!) at the boyish desire of the small Britisher, Tom Brown, "to leave behind him the name of a fellow who never bullied a little boy or turned his back on a big one." And yet, who does not know that this desire is the corner-stone on which moral structures of mighty dimensions can be reared? May I not go even so far as to say that the gentlest and most peace-loving of religions endorses this aspiration? The desire of Tom is the basis on which the greatness of England is largely built, and it will not take us long to discover that Bushido does not stand on a lesser pedestal. If fighting in itself, be it offensive or defensive, is, as Quakers rightly testify, brutal and wrong, we can still say with Lessing, "We know from what failings our virtue springs."[2] "Sneaks" and "cowards" are epithets of the worst opprobrium to healthy, simple natures. Childhood begins life with these notions, and knighthood also; but, as life grows larger and its relations many-sided, the early faith seeks sanction from higher authority and more rational sources for its own justification, satisfaction, and development. If military systems had operated alone, without higher moral support, how far short of chivalry would the ideal of knighthood have fallen! In Europe, Christianity, interpreted with concessions convenient to chivalry, infused it nevertheless with spiritual data. "Religion, war, and glory were the three souls of a perfect Christian knight," says Lamartine. In Japan there were several sources of Bushido.

---

2   Ruskin was one of the most gentle-hearted and peace-loving men that ever lived. Yet he believed in war with all the fervor of a worshipper of the strenuous life. "When I tell you," he says in the *Crown of Wild Olive*, "that war is the foundation of all the arts, I mean also that it is the foundation of all the high virtues and faculties of men. It is very strange to me to discover this, and very dreadful, but I saw it to be quite an undeniable fact I found, in brief, that all great nations learned their truth of word and strength of thought in war; that they were nourished in war and wasted by peace; taught by war and deceived by peace; trained by war and betrayed by peace; in a word, that they were born in war and expired in peace."

CHAPTER 2

SOURCES OF BUSHIDO

I may begin with Buddhism. It furnished a sense of calm trust in Fate, a quiet submission to the inevitable, that stoic composure in sight of danger or calamity, that disdain of life and friendliness with death. A foremost teacher of swordsmanship, when he saw his pupil master the utmost of his art, told him, "Beyond this my instruction must give way to Zen teaching." "Zen" is the Japanese equivalent for the Dhyâna, which "represents human effort to reach through meditation zones of thought beyond the range of verbal expression."[3] Its method is contemplation, and its purport, so far as I understand it, to be convinced of a principle that underlies all phenomena, and, if it can, of the Absolute itself, and thus to put oneself in harmony with this Absolute. Thus defined, the teaching was more than the dogma of a sect, and whoever attains to the perception of the Absolute raises himself above mundane things and awakes "to a new Heaven and a new Earth."

What Buddhism failed to give, Shintoism offered. in abundance. Such loyalty to the sovereign, such reverence for ancestral memory, and such filial piety as are not taught by any other creed, were inculcated by the Shinto doctrines, imparting passivity to the otherwise arrogant character of the samurai. Shinto theology has no place for the dogma of "original sin." On

3 Lafcadio Hearn, *Exotics and Retrospectives*, p. 84.

the contrary, it believes in the innate goodness and Godlike purity of the human soul, adoring it as the adytum from which divine oracles are proclaimed. Everybody has observed that the Shinto shrines are conspicuously devoid of objects and instruments of worship, and that a plain mirror hung in the sanctuary forms the essential part of its furnishing. The presence of this article is easy to explain: it typifies the human heart, which, when perfectly placid and clear, reflects the very image of the Deity. When you stand, therefore, in front of the shrine to worship, you see your own image reflected on its shining surface, and the act of worship is tantamount to the old Delphic injunction, "Know Thyself." But self-knowledge does not imply, either in the Greek or Japanese teaching, knowledge of the physical part of man, not his anatomy or his psycho-physics; knowledge was to be of a moral kind, the introspection of our moral nature. Mommsen, comparing the Greek and the Roman, says that when the former worshipped he raised his eyes to Heaven, for his prayer was contemplation, while the latter veiled his head, for his was reflection. Essentially like the Roman conception of religion, our reflection brought into prominence not so much the moral as the national consciousness of the individual. Its nature-worship endeared the country to our inmost souls, while its ancestor-worship, tracing from lineage to lineage, made the Imperial family the fountain- head of the whole nation. To us the country is more than land and soil from which to mine gold or to reap grain—it is the sacred abode of the gods, the spirits of our forefathers: to us the Emperor is more than the Arch Constable of a *Rechtsstaat*, or even the Patron of a *Culturstaat*—he is the bodily representative of Heaven on earth, blending in his person its power and its mercy. If what M. Boutmy[4] says is true of English royalty—that it "is not only the image of authority, but the author and symbol of national unity," as I believe it to be, doubly and trebly may this be affirmed of royalty in Japan.

4 The English People, p. 188.

The tenets of Shintoism cover the two predominating features of the emotional life of our race.—Patriotism and Loyalty. Arthur May Knapp very truly says: "In Hebrew literature it is often difficult to tell whether the writer is speaking of God or of the Commonwealth; of Heaven or of Jerusalem; of the Messiah or of the Nation itself."[5] A similar confusion may be noticed in the nomenclature of our national faith. I said confusion, because it will be so deemed by a logical intellect on account of its verbal ambiguity; still, being a frame work of national instinct and race feelings, it never pretends to systematic philosophy or a rational theology. This religion—or, is it not more correct to say, the race emotions which this religion expressed?—thoroughly imbued Bushido with loyalty to the sovereign and love of country. These acted more as impulses than as doctrines; for Shintoism, unlike the Mediæval Christian Church, prescribed to its votaries scarcely any *credenda*, furnishing them at the same time with *agenda* of a straightforward and simple type.

As to strictly ethical doctrines, the teachings of Confucius were the most prolific source of Bushido. His enunciation of the five moral relations between master and servant (the governing and the governed), father and son, husband and wife, older and younger brother, and between friend and friend, was but a confirmation of what the race instinct had recognised before his writings were introduced from China. The calm, benignant and worldly-wise character of his politico-ethical precepts was particularly well suited to the samurai, who formed the ruling class. His aristocratic and conservative tone was well adapted to the requirements of these warrior statesmen. Next to Confucius, Mencius exercised an immense authority over Bushido. His forcible and often quite democratic theories were exceedingly taking to sympathetic natures, and they were even thought dangerous to, and subversive of, the existing social order, hence his works were for a long

5   *Feudal and Modern Japan*, vol. i., p. 183

time under censure. Still, the words of this master mind found permanent lodgment in the heart of the samurai.

The writings of Confucius and Mencius formed the principal text-books for youths and the highest authority in discussion among the old. A mere acquaintance with the classics of these two sages was held, however, in no high esteem. A common proverb ridicules one who has only an intellectual knowledge of Confucius, as a man ever studious but ignorant of *Analects*. A typical samurai calls a literary savant a book-smelling sot. Another compares learning to an ill-smelling vegetable that must be boiled and boiled before it is fit for use. A man who has read little smells a little pedantic, and a man who has read much smells yet more so; both are alike unpleasant. The writer meant thereby that knowledge becomes really such only when it is assimilated in the mind of the learner and shows in his character. An intellectual specialist was considered a machine. Intellect itself was considered subordinate to ethical emotion. Man and the universe were conceived to be alike spiritual and ethical.Bushido could not accept the judgment of Huxley, that the cosmic process was unmoral.

Bushido made light of knowledge of such. It was not pursued as an end in itself, but as a means to the attainment of wisdom. Hence, he who stopped short of this end was regarded no higher than a convenient machine, which could turn out poems and maxims at bidding. Thus, knowledge was conceived as identical with its practical application in life; and this Socratic doctrine found its greatest exponent in the Chinese philosopher, Wan Yang Ming, who never wearies of repeating, "To know and to act are one and the same."

I beg leave for a moment's digression while I am on this subject, inasmuch as some of the noblest types of *bushi* were strongly influenced by the teachings of this sage. Western readers will easily recognise in his writings many parallels to the New Testament. Making allowance for the terms peculiar to either teaching, the passage, "Seek ye first the kingdom of God and his righteousness; and all these things shall be added unto you," conveys a thought that may be found on almost any page of Wan Yang Ming. A Japanese disciple[6] of his says—"The lord of heaven and earth, of all living beings, dwelling in the heart of man, becomes his mind (*Kokoro*); hence a mind is a living thing, and is ever luminous": and again, "The spiritual light of our essential being is pure, and is not affected by the will of man. Spontaneously springing up in our mind, it shows what is right and wrong: it is then called conscience; it is even the light that proceedeth from the god of heaven." How very much do these words sound like some passages from Isaac Pennington or other philosophic mystics! I am inclined to think that the Japanese mind, as expressed in the simple tenets of the Shinto religion, was particularly open to the reception of Yang Ming's precepts. He carried his doctrine of the infallibility of conscience to extreme transcendentalism, attributing to it the faculty to perceive, not only the distinction between right and wrong, but also the nature of psychical facts and physical phenomena.

He went as far as, if not farther than, Berkeley and Fichte, in Idealism, denying the existence of things outside of human ken. If his system had all the logical errors charged to Solipsism, it had all the efficacy of strong conviction, and its moral import in developing individuality of character and equanimity of temper cannot be gainsaid.

Thus, whatever the sources, the essential principles which *Bushido* imbibed from them and assimilated to itself, were few and simple. Few and simple as these were, they were sufficient to furnish a safe conduct of life even through the unsafest days of the most unsettled period of our nation's history. The wholesome unsophisticated nature of our warrior ancestors derived ample food for their spirit from a sheaf of commonplace and fragmentary

6   Miwa Shissai.

teachings, gleaned as it were on the highways and byways of ancient thought, and, stimulated by the demands of the age, formed from these gleanings a new and unique type of manhood. An acute French savant, M. de la Mazelière, thus sums up his impressions of the sixteenth century: "Toward the middle of the sixteenth century, all is confusion in Japan, in the government, in society, in the church. But the civil wars the manners returning to barbarism, the necessity for each to execute justice for himself,—these formed men comparable to those Italians of the sixteenth century, in whom Taine praises 'the vigorous initiative, the habit of sudden resolutions and desperate undertakings, the grand capacity to do and to suffer.' In Japan as in Italy 'the rude manners of the Middle Ages' made of man a superb animal, 'wholly militant and wholly resistant.' And this is why the sixteenth century displays in the highest degree the principal quality of the Japanese race, that great diversity which one finds there between minds (*esprits*) as well as between temperaments. While in India and even in China men seem to differ chiefly in degree of energy or intelligence, in Japan they differ by originality of character as well. Now, individuality is the sign of superior races and of civilisations already developed. If we make use of an expression dear to Nietzsche, we might say that in Asia, to speak of humanity is to speak of its plains; in Japan as in Europe, one represents it above all by its mountains."

To the pervading characteristics of the men of whom M. de la Mazelière writes, let us now address ourselves. I shall begin with Rectitude.

CHAPTER 3

RECTITUDE OR JUSTICE

Here we discern the most cogent precept in the code of the samurai. Nothing is more loathsome to him than underhand dealings and crooked undertakings. The conception of Rectitude may be erroneous—it may be narrow. A well-known bushi defines it as a power of resolution:— "Rectitude is the power of deciding upon a certain course of conduct in accordance with reason, without wavering,—to die when it is right to die, to strike when to strike is right." Another speaks of it in the following terms: "Rectitude is the bone that gives firmness and stature. As without bones the head cannot rest on the top of the spine, nor hands move nor feet stand, so without rectitude neither talent nor learning can make of a human frame a samurai. With it the lack of accomplishments is as nothing." Mencius calls Benevolence man's mind, and Rectitude or Righteousness his path. "How lamentable," he exclaims, "is it to neglect the path and not pursue it, to lose the mind and not know to seek it again! When men's fowls and dogs are lost, they know to seek for them again, but they lose their mind and do not know to seek for it." Have we not here "as in a glass darkly" a parable propounded three hundred years later in another clime and by a greater Teacher, Who called Himself *the* Way of righteousness, through whom the lost could be found? But I stray from my point. Righteousness, according to Mencius, is a straight and narrow path which a man ought to take to regain the lost paradise.

Even in the latter days of feudalism, when the long continuance of peace brought leisure into the life of the warrior class, and with it dissipations of all kinds and accomplishments of gentle arts, the epithet *Gishi* (a man of rectitude) was considered superior to any name that signified mastery of learning or art. The Forty-seven Faithfuls—of whom so much is made in our popular education-- are known in common parlance as the Forty- seven *Gishi*.

In times when cunning artifice was liable to pass for military tact and downright falsehood for *ruse de guerre*, this manly virtue, frank and honest, was a jewel that shone the brightest and was most highly praised. Rectitude is a twin brother to Valour, another martial virtue. But before proceeding to speak of Valour, let me linger a little while on what I may term a derivation from Rectitude, which, at first deviating slightly from its original, became more and more removed from it, until its meaning was perverted in the popular acceptance. I speak of *Gi-ri*, literally the Right Reason, but which came in time to mean a vague sense of duty which public opinion expects an incumbent to fulfil. In its original and unalloyed sense, it meant duty, pure and simple,— hence, we speak of the *Giri* we owe to parents, to superiors, to inferiors, to society at large, and so forth. In these instances *Giri* is duty; for what else is duty than what Right Reason demands and commands us to do? Should not Right Reason be our categorical imperative?

Giri primarily meant no more than duty, and I dare say its etymology was derived from the fact, that in our conduct, say to our parents, though love should be the only motive, lacking that, there must be some other authority to enforce filial piety; and they formulated this authority in *Giri*. Very rightly did they formulate this authority—*Giri*—since if love does not rush to deeds of virtue, recourse must be had to man's intellect and his reason must be quickened to convince him of the necessity of acting aright. The same is true of any other moral obligation. The instant Duty becomes onerous, Right Reason steps in to prevent our shirking it. *Giri* thus understood is a severe taskmaster, with a birch-rod in his hand to make sluggards perform their part. It is a secondary power in ethics; as a motive it is infinitely inferior to the Christian doctrine of love, which should be *the* law. I deem it a product of the conditions of an artificial society—of a society in which accident of birth and unmerited favour instituted class distinctions, in which the family was the social unit, in which seniority of age was of more account than superiority of talents, in which natural affections had often to succumb before arbitrary man-made customs. Because of this very artificiality, *Giri* in time degenerated into a vague sense of propriety called up to explain this and sanction that,—as, for example, why a mother must, if need be, sacrifice all her other children in order to save the first-born; or why a daughter must sell her chastity to get funds to pay for the father's dissipation, and the like. Starting as Right Reason, *Giri* has, in my opinion, often stooped to casuistry. It has even degenerated into cowardly fear of censure. I might say of *Giri* what Scott wrote of patriotism, that "as it is the fairest, so it is often the most suspicious, mask of other feelings." Carried beyond or below Right Reason, *Giri* became a monstrous misnomer. It harboured under its wings every sort of sophistry and hypocrisy. It would have been easily turned into a nest of cowardice, if Bushido had not a keen and correct sense of courage, the spirit of daring and bearing.

CHAPTER 4

COURAGE, THE SPIRIT OF
DARING AND BEARING

Courage was scarcely deemed worthy to be counted among virtues, unless it was exercised in the cause of Righteousness. In his *Analects* Confucius defines Courage by explaining, as is often his wont, what its negative is. "Perceiving what is right," he says, "and doing it not, argues lack of courage." Put this epigram into a positive statement, and it runs, "Courage is doing what is right." To run all kinds of hazards, to jeopard one's self, to rush into the jaws of death—these are too often identified with Valour, and in the profession of arms such rashness of conduct—what Shakespeare calls "valour misbegot"—is unjustly applauded; but not so in the Precepts of Knighthood. Death for a cause unworthy of dying for, was called a "dog's death." "To rush into the thick of battle and to be slain in it," says a Prince of Mito, "is easy enough, and the merest churl is equal to the task; but," he continues, "it is true courage to live when it is right to live, and to die only when it is right to die"—and yet the prince had not even heard of the name of Plato, who defines courage as "the knowledge of things that a man should fear and that he should not fear." A distinction which is made in the West between moral and physical courage has long been recognised among us. What samurai youth has not heard of "Great Valour" and the "Valour of a Villain?"

Valour, Fortitude, Bravery, Fearlessness, Courage, being the qualities of soul which appeal most easily to juvenile minds, and which can be trained by exercise and example, were, so to speak, the most popular virtues, early emulated among the youth. Stories of military exploits were repeated almost before boys left their mother's breast. Does a little booby cry for any ache? The mother scolds him in this fashion: "What a coward to cry for a trifling pain! What will you do when your arm is cut off in battle? What when you are called upon to commit *hara-kiri*?" We all know the pathetic fortitude of a famished little boy-prince of Sendai, who in the drama is made to say to his little page, "Seest thou those tiny sparrows in the nest, how their yellow bills are opened wide, and now see! there comes their mother with worms to feed them. How eagerly and happily the little ones eat! but for a samurai, when his stomach is empty, it is a disgrace to feel hungry." Anecdotes of fortitude and bravery abound in nursery tales, though stories of this kind are not by any means the only method of early imbuing the spirit with daring and fearlessness. Parents, with sternness sometimes verging on cruelty, set their children to tasks that called forth all the pluck that was in them. "Bears hurl their cubs down the gorge," they said. Samurai's sons were let down to steep valleys of hardship, and spurred to Sisyphus-like tasks.

Occasional deprivation of food or exposure to cold, was considered a highly efficacious test for inuring them to endurance. Children of tender age were sent among utter strangers with some message to deliver, were made to rise before the sun, and before breakfast attend to their reading exercises, walking to their teachers with bare feet in the cold of winter; they frequently—once or twice a month, as on the festival of a god of learning,—came together in small groups and passed the night without sleep, in reading aloud by turns. Pilgrimages to all sorts of uncanny places—to execution grounds, to graveyards, to houses reputed of being haunted, were favourite pastimes of the young. In the days when decapitation was public, not only were small boys sent to witness the ghastly scene, but they were made to visit alone the place in the darkness of night and there to leave a mark of their visit on the trunkless head.

Does this ultra-Spartan system[7] of "drilling the nerves" strike

---

7 The spiritual aspect of valour is evidenced by composure—calm presence of mind. Tranquillity is courage in repose. It is a statical manifestation of valour, as daring deeds are a dynamical. A truly brave man is ever serene; he is never taken by surprise; nothing ruffles the equanimity of his spirit. In the heat of battle he remains cool; in the midst of catastrophes he keeps level his mind. Earthquakes do not shake him, he laughs at storms. We admire him as truly great, who, in the menacing presence of danger or death, retains his self-possession; who, for instance, can compose a poem under impending peril, or hum a strain in the face of death. Such indulgence betraying no tremor in the writing or in the voice is taken as an infallible index of a large nature—of what we call a capacious mind (*yoyu*), which, far from being pressed or crowded, has always room for something more. It passes current among us as a piece of authentic history, that as Ota Dokan, the great builder of the castle of Tokyo, was pierced through with a spear, his assassin, knowing the poetical predilection of his victim, accompanied his thrust with this couplet:

"Ah! how in moments like these Our heart doth grudge the light of life"; whereupon the expiring hero, not one whit daunted by the mortal wound in his side, added the lines: "Had not in hours of peace, It learned to lightly look on life."

There is even a sportive element in a courageous nature. Things which are serious to ordinary people, may be but play to the valiant. Hence in old warfare it was not at all rare for the parties to a conflict to exchange repartee or to begin a rhetorical contest. Combat was not solely a matter of brute force; it was, as well, an intellectual engagement.

Of such character was the battle fought on the banks of the Koromo River, late in the eleventh century. The eastern army routed, its leader, Sadato, took to flight. When the pursuing general pressed him hard and called aloud, "It is a disgrace for a warrior to show his back to the enemy," Sadato reined his horse; upon this the conquering chief shouted an impromptu verse:

"Torn into shreds is the warp of the cloth" (*koromo*).

Scarcely had the words escaped his lips when the defeated warrior, undismayed, completed the couplet:

"Since age has worn its threads by use."

Yoshiie, whose bow had all the while been bent, suddenly unstrung it and turned away, leaving his prospective victim to do as he pleased. When asked the reason of his strange behaviour, he replied that he could not bear to put to shame one who had kept his presence of mind while hotly pursued by his enemy.

The sorrow which overtook Antony and Octavius at the death of Brutus, has been the general experience of brave men. Kenshin, who fought for fourteen years with Shingen, when he heard of the latter's death, wept aloud at the loss of "the best of enemies." It was this same Kenshin who had set a noble example for all time in his treatment of Shingen, whose provinces lay in a mountainous region quite away from the sea, and who had consequently depended upon the Hôjô provinces of the Tokaido for salt. The Hôjô prince wishing to weaken him, although not openly at war with him, had cut off from Shingen all traffic in this important article. Kenshin, hearing of his enemy's dilemma and able to obtain his salt from the coast of his own dominions, wrote Shingen that in his opinion the Hôjô lord had committed a very mean act, and that although he (Kenshin) was at war with him (Shingen) he had ordered his subjects to furnish him with plenty of salt—adding, "I do not fight with salt, but with the sword," affording more than a parallel to the words of Camillus, "We Romans do not fight with gold, but with iron." Nietzsche spoke for the Samurai heart tendency would not be brutalising, nipping in the bud the tender emotions of the heart?

Let us see in another chapter what other concepts Bushido had of Valour.

---

when he wrote, "You are to be proud of your enemy; then the success of your enemy is your success also." Indeed, valour and honour alike required that we should own as enemies in war only such as prove worthy of being friends in peace. When valour attains this height, it becomes akin to Benevolence.

CHAPTER 5

BENEVOLENCE,
THE FEELING OF DISTRESS

Love, magnanimity, affection for others, sympathy and pity, were ever recognised to be supreme virtues, the highest of all the attributes of the human soul. It was deemed a princely virtue in a twofold sense: princely among the manifold attributes of a noble spirit; princely as particularly befitting a princely profession. We needed no Shakespeare to feel— though, perhaps, like the rest of the world, we needed him to express it— that mercy became a monarch better than his crown, that it was above his sceptered sway. How often both Confucius and Mencius repeat the highest requirement of a ruler of men to consist in benevolence.

Confucius would say,—"Let but a prince cultivate virtue, people will flock to him; with people will come to him lands; lands will bring forth for him wealth; wealth will give him the benefit of right uses. Virtue is the root, and wealth an outcome." Again, "Never has there been a case of a sovereign loving benevolence, and the people not loving righteousness." Mencius follows close at his heels and says, "Instances are on record where individuals attained to supreme power in a single state, without benevolence, but never have I heard of a whole empire falling into the hands of one who lacked this virtue. Also,—It is impossible that any one should become ruler of the people to whom they have not yielded the subjection of their hearts. Both defined this indispensable requirement in a ruler by saying, "Benevolence—benevolence is Man."

Under the regime of feudalism, which could easily degenerate into militarism it was to benevolence that we owed our deliverance from despotism of the worst kind. An utter surrender of "life and limb" on the part of the governed would have left nothing for the governing but self- will, and this has for its natural consequence the growth of that absolutism so often called "oriental despotism," as though there were no despots of occidental history!

Let it be far from me to uphold despotism of any sort; but it is a mistake to identify feudalism with it. When Frederick the Great wrote that "Kings are the first servants of the State," jurists thought rightly that a new era was reached in the development of freedom. Strangely coinciding in time, in the backwoods of North-western Japan, Yozan of Yonézawa made exactly the same declaration, showing that feudalism was not all tyranny and oppression. A feudal prince, although unmindful of owing reciprocal obligations to his vassals, felt a higher sense of responsibility to his ancestors and to Heaven. He was a father to his subjects, whom Heaven entrusted to his care. According to the ancient *Chinese Book of Poetry*, "Until the house of Yin lost the hearts of the people, they could appear before Heaven." And Confucius in his *Great Learning* taught: "When the prince loves what the people love and hates what the people hate, then is he what is called the parent of the people." Thus are public opinion and monarchical will or democracy and absolutism merged one in the other. Thus also, in a sense not usually assigned to the term, Bushido accepted and corroborated paternal government—paternal also as opposed to the less interested avuncular government. (Uncle Sam's, to wit!) The difference between a despotic and a paternal government lies in this, that in the one the people obey reluctantly, while in the other they do so with "that proud submission, that dignified obedience, that subordination of heart which kept alive, even in servitude itself, the spirit of exalted freedom."[8] The old saying is not entirely false which called the king of England the "king of devils, because of his subjects' often insurrections against, and depositions of, their princes," and which made the French monarch the "king of asses, because of their infinite taxes and impositions," but which gave the title of the king of men to the sovereign of Spain "because of his subjects' willing obedience." But enough!

Virtue and absolute power may strike the Anglo-Saxon mind as terms which it is impossible to harmonise. Pobyedonostseff has clearly set forth before us the contrast in the foundations of English and other European communities; namely, that these were organised on the basis of common interest, while that was distinguished by a strongly developed independent personality. What this Russian statesman says of the personal dependence of individuals on some social alliance and in the end of ends on the State, among the continental nations of Europe and particularly among Slavonic peoples, is doubly true of the Japanese. Hence not only is a free exercise of monarchical power not felt as heavily by us as in Europe, but it is generally moderated by paternal consideration for the feelings of the people. "Absolutism," says Bismarck, "primarily demands in the ruler impartiality, honesty, devotion to duty, energy and inward humility." If I may be allowed to make one more quotation on this subject, I will cite from the speech of the German Emperor at Coblenz, in which he spoke of "Kingship, by the grace of God, with its heavy duties, its tremendous responsibilities to the Creator alone, from which no man, no minister, no parliament, can release the monarch."

We knew benevolence was a tender virtue and mother-like. If upright Rectitude and stem justice were peculiarly masculine, Mercy had the gentleness and the persuasiveness of a feminine nature. We were warned against indulging in indiscriminate

8 Burke, *French Revolution.*

charity, without seasoning it with justice and rectitude. Masamuné expressed it well in his oft-quoted aphorism—"Rectitude carried to excess hardens into stiffness; benevolence indulged beyond measure sinks into weakness." Fortunately mercy was not so rare as it was beautiful, for it is universally true that "The bravest are the tenderest, the loving are the daring." "*Bushi no nasaké*"—the tenderness of a warrior—had a sound which appealed at once to whatever was noble in us; not that the mercy of a samurai was generically different from the mercy of any other being, but because it implied mercy where mercy was not a blind impulse, but where it recognised due regard to justice, and where mercy did not remain merely a certain state of mind, but where it was backed with power to save or kill. As economists speak of demand as being effectual or ineffectual, similarly we may call the mercy of Bushi effectual, since it implied the power of acting for the good or detriment of the recipient.

Priding themselves as they did in their brute strength and privileges to turn it into account, the samurai gave full consent to what Mencius taught concerning the power of love. "Benevolence," he says, "brings under its sway whatever hinders its power, just as water subdues fire: they only doubt the power of water to quench flames who try to extinguish with a cupful a whole burning waggon-load of fagots." He also says that "the feeling of distress is the root of benevolence," therefore a benevolent man is ever mindful of those who are suffering and in distress. Thus did Mencius long anticipate Adam Smith who founds his ethical philosophy on sympathy.

It is indeed striking how closely the code of knightly honour of one country coincides with that of others; in other words, how the much- abused oriental ideas of morals find their counterparts in the noblest maxims of European literature. If the well-known lines,

Hæ tibi erunt artes—pacisque imponere morem,
Parcere subjectis, et debellare superbos,

were shown a Japanese gentleman, he might readily accuse the Mantuan bard of plagiarising from the literature of his own country.

Benevolence to the weak, the down-trodden or the vanquished, was ever extolled as peculiarly becoming to a samurai. Lovers of Japanese art must be familiar with the representation of a priest riding backwards on a cow. The rider was once a warrior who in his day made his name a by- word of terror. In that terrible battle of Sumano-ura, (1184 A. D.) which was one of the most decisive in our history, he overtook an enemy and in single combat had him in the clutch of his gigantic arms. Now the etiquette of war required that on such occasions no blood should be spilt, unless the weaker party proved to be a man of rank or ability equal to that of the stronger. The grim combatant would have the name of the man under him; but he refusing to make it known, his helmet was ruthlessly torn off, when the sight of a juvenile face, fair and beardless, made the astonished knight relax his hold. Helping the youth to his feet, in paternal tones he bade the stripling go: "Off, young prince, to thy mother's side! The sword of Kumagayé shall never be tarnished by a drop of thy blood. Haste and flee o'er yon pass before thine enemies come in sight!" The young warrior refused to go and begged Kumagayé, for the honour of both, to dispatch him on the spot. Above the hoary head of the veteran gleams the cold blade, which many a time before has sundered the chords of life, but his stout heart quails; there flashes athwart his mental eye the vision of his own boy, who this self-same day marched to the sound of bugle to try his maiden arms; the strong hand of the warrior quivers; again he begs his victim to flee for his life. Finding all his entreaties vain and hearing the approaching steps of his comrades, he exclaims: "If thou art overtaken, thou mayst fall at a more ignoble hand than mine. O thou Infinite! receive his soul!" In an instant the sword flashes in the air, and when it falls it is red with adolescent blood. When the war is ended, we find our soldier returning in triumph, but little cares he now for honour or fame; he renounces his warlike career, shaves his head, dons a priestly garb, devotes the rest of his days to holy pilgrimage, never turning his back to the West where lies the Paradise whence salvation comes and whither the sun hastes daily for his rest.

Critics may point out flaws in this story, which is casuistically vulnerable. Let it be: all the same it shows that Tenderness, Pity, and Love were traits which adorned the most sanguinary exploits of a samurai. It was an old maxim among them that "It becometh not the fowler to slay the bird which takes refuge in his bosom." This in a large measure explains why the Red Cross movement, considered so peculiarly Christian, so readily found a firm footing among us. Decades before we heard of the Geneva Convention, Bakin, our greatest novelist, had familiarised us with the medical treatment of a fallen foe. In the principality of Satsuma, noted for its martial spirit and education, the custom prevailed for young men to practise music; not the blast of trumpets or the beat of drums,— "those clamorous harbingers of blood and death"—stirring us to imitate the actions of a tiger, but sad and tender melodies on the *biwa*,[9] soothing our fiery spirits, drawing our thoughts away from scent of blood and scenes of carnage. Polybius tells us of the Constitution of Arcadia, which required all youths under thirty to practise music, in order that this gentle art might alleviate the rigours of the inclement region. It is to its influence that he attributes the absence of cruelty in that part of the Arcadian mountains.

Nor was Satsuma the only place in Japan where gentleness was inculcated among the warrior class. A Prince of Shirakawa jots down his random thoughts, and among them is the following: "Though they come stealing to your bedside in the silent watches of the night, drive not away, but rather cherish these—

---

9   A musical instrument, resembling the guitar.

the fragrance of flowers, the sound of distant bells, the insect hummings of a frosty night." And again, "Though they may wound your feelings, these three you have only to forgive, the breeze that scatters your flowers, the cloud that hides your moon, and the man who tries to pick quarrels with you."

It was ostensibly to express, but actually to cultivate, these gentler emotions that the writing of verses was encouraged. Our poetry has therefore a strong undercurrent of pathos and tenderness. A well-known anecdote of a rustic samurai illustrates the case in point. When he was told to learn versification, and "The Warbler's Notes"[10] was given him for the subject of his first attempt, his fiery spirit rebelled and he flung at the feet of his master this uncouth production, which ran

"The brave warrior keeps
apart The ear that might listen
To the warbler's song."

His master, undaunted by the crude sentiment, continued to encourage the youth, until one day the music of his soul was awakened to respond to the sweet notes of the *uguisu*, and he wrote

"Stands the warrior, mailed and strong,
To hear the uguisu's song,
Warbled sweet the trees among."

We admire and enjoy the heroic incident in Körner's short life, when, as he lay wounded on the battle-field, he scribbled his famous *Farewell to Life*. Incidents of a similar kind were not at all unusual in our warfare.

Our pithy, epigrammatic poems were particularly well suited

10 The uguisu or warbler, sometimes called the nightingale of Japan.

to the improvisation of a single sentiment. Everybody of any education was either a poet or a poetaster. Not infrequently a marching soldier might be seen to halt, take his writing utensils from his belt, and compose an ode,—and such papers were found afterward in the helmets or the breastplates when these were removed from their lifeless wearers.

What Christianity has done in Europe toward rousing compassion in the midst of belligerent horrors, love of music and letters has done in Japan. The cultivation of tender feelings breeds considerate regard for the sufferings of others. Modesty and complaisance, actuated by respect for others' feelings, are at the root of politeness.

CHAPTER 6

POLITENESS

Courtesy and urbanity of manners have been noticed by every foreign tourist as a marked Japanese trait. Politeness is a poor virtue, if it is actuated only by a fear of offending good taste, whereas it should be the outward manifestation of a sympathetic regard for the feelings of others. It also implies a due regard for the fitness of things, therefore due respect to social positions; for these latter express no plutocratic distinctions, but were originally distinctions for actual merit.

In its highest form, politeness almost approaches love. We may reverently say, politeness "suffereth long, and is kind; envieth not, vaunteth not itself, is not puffed up; doth not behave itself unseemly, seeketh so not her own, is not easily provoked, taketh not account of evil." Is it any wonder that Professor Dean, in speaking of the six elements of humanity, accords to politeness an exalted position, inasmuch as it is the ripest fruit of social intercourse?

While thus extolling politeness, far be it from me to put it in the front rank of virtues. If we analyse it, we shall find it correlated with other virtues of a higher order; for what virtue stands alone? While—or rather because—it was exalted as peculiar to the profession of arms, and as such esteemed in a degree higher than its deserts, there came into existence its counterfeits. Confucius himself has repeatedly taught that external appurtenances are as little a part of propriety as sounds are of music.

When propriety was elevated to the *sine qua non* of social intercourse, it was only to be expected that an elaborate system of etiquette should come into vogue to train youth in correct social behaviour. How one must bow in accosting others, how he must walk and sit, were taught and learned with utmost care. Table manners grew to be a science. Tea serving and drinking were raised to ceremony. A man of education is, of course, expected to be master of all these. Very fitly does Mr. Veblen, in his interesting book,[11] call decorum "a product and an exponent of the leisure-class life."

I have heard slighting remarks made by Europeans upon our elaborate discipline of politeness. It has been criticised as absorbing too much of our thought and in so far a folly to observe strict obedience to it. I admit that there may be unnecessary niceties in ceremonious etiquette, but whether it partakes as much of folly as the adherence to ever-changing fashions of the West, is a question not very clear to my mind. Even fashions I do not consider solely as freaks of vanity; on the contrary, I look upon these as a ceaseless search of the human mind for the beautiful. Much less do I consider elaborate ceremony as altogether trivial; for it denotes the result of long observation as to the most appropriate method of achieving a certain result. If there is anything to do, there is certainly a best way to do it, and the best way is both the most economical and the most graceful. Mr. Spencer defines grace as the most economical manner of motion. The tea ceremony presents certain definite ways of manipulating a bowl, a spoon, a napkin, etc. To a novice it looks tedious. But one soon discovers that the way prescribed is, after all, the most saving of time and labour; in other words, the most economical use of force,—hence, according to Spencer's dictum, the most graceful.

---

11 *Theory of the Leisure Class*, N. Y., 1899, p. 46.

The spiritual significance of social decorum—or, I might say, to borrow from the vocabulary of the "Philosophy of Clothes," the spiritual discipline of which etiquette and ceremony are mere outward garments— is out of all proportion to what their appearance warrants us in believing. I might follow the example of Mr. Spencer and trace in our ceremonial institutions their origins and the moral motives that gave rise to them; but that is not what I shall endeavour to do in this book. It is the moral training involved in strict observance of propriety, that I wish to emphasise.

I have said that etiquette was elaborated into the finest niceties, so much so that different schools, advocating different systems, came into existence. But they all united in the ultimate essential, and this was put by a great exponent of the best known school of etiquette, the Ogasawara, in the following terms: "The end of all etiquette is to so cultivate your mind that even when you are quietly seated, not the roughest ruffian can dare make onset on your person." It means, in other words, that by constant exercise in correct manners, one brings all the parts and faculties of his body into perfect order and into such harmony with itself and its environment as to express the mastery of spirit over the flesh. What a new and deep significance the French word *biensèance*[12], comes to contain.

If the promise is true that gracefulness means economy of force, then it follows as a logical sequence that a constant practice of graceful deportment must bring with it a reserve and storage of force. Fine manners, therefore, mean power in repose. When the barbarian Gauls, during the sack of Rome, burst into the assembled Senate and dared pull the beards of the venerable Fathers, we think the old gentlemen were to blame, inasmuch as they lacked dignity and strength of manners. Is lofty spiritual attainment really possible through etiquette? Why not?—All roads lead to Rome!

---

12 Etymologically, well-seatedness.

As an example of how the simplest thing can be made into an art and then become spiritual culture, I may take *Cha-no-yu*, the tea ceremony. Tea-sipping as a fine art! Why should it not be? In the children drawing pictures on the sand, or in the savage carving on a rock, was the promise of a Raphael or a Michael Angelo. How much more is the drinking of a beverage, which began with the transcendental contemplation of a Hindoo anchorite, entitled to develop into a handmaid of Religion and Morality? That calmness of mind, that serenity of temper, that composure and quietness of demeanour which are the first essentials of *Cha-no-yu*, are without doubt the first conditions of right thinking and right feeling. The scrupulous cleanliness of the little room, shut off from sight and sound of the madding crowd, is in itself conducive to direct one's thoughts from the world. The bare interior does not engross one's attention like the innumerable pictures and bric-a-brac of a Western parlour; the presence of *kakémono*[13] calls our attention more to grace of design than to beauty of colour. The utmost refinement of taste is the object aimed at; whereas anything like display is banished with religious horror. The very fact that it was invented by a contemplative recluse, in a time when wars and the rumours of wars were incessant, is well calculated to show that this institution was more than a pastime.

Before entering the quiet precincts of the tea-room, the company assembling to partake of the ceremony laid aside, together with their swords, the ferocity of battle-field or the cares of government, there to find peace and friendship.

Cha-no-yu is more than a ceremony—it is a fine art; it is poetry, with articulate gestures for rhythms: it is a *modus operandi* of soul discipline. Its greatest value lies in this last phase. Not infrequently the other phases preponderated in the mind of its votaries, but that does not prove that its essence was not of a spiritual nature.

---

13 Hanging scrolls, which may be either paintings or ideograms, used for decorative purposes.

Politeness will be a great acquisition, if it does no more than impart grace to manners; but its function does not stop here. For propriety, springing as it does from motives of benevolence and modesty, and actuated by tender feelings toward the sensibilities of others, is ever a graceful expression of sympathy. Its requirement is that we should weep with those that weep and rejoice with those that rejoice. Such didactic requirement, when reduced into small everyday details of life, expresses itself in little acts scarcely noticeable, or, if noticed, is, as one missionary lady of twenty years' residence once said to me, "awfully funny." You are out in the hot, glaring sun with no shade over you; a Japanese acquaintance passes by; you accost him, and instantly his hat is off—well, that is perfectly natural, but the "awfully funny" performance is, that all the while he talks with you his parasol is down and he stands in the glaring sun also. How foolish!—Yes, exactly so, provided the motive were less than this: "You are in the sun; I sympathise with you; I would willingly take you under my parasol if it were large enough, or if we were familiarly acquainted; as I cannot shade you, I will share your discomforts." Little acts of this kind, equally or more amusing, are not mere gestures or conventionalities. They are the "bodying forth" of thoughtful feelings for the comfort of others.

Another "awfully funny" custom is dictated by our canons of Politeness; but many superficial writers on Japan have dismissed it by simply attributing it to the general topsy-turvyness of the nation. Every foreigner who has observed it will confess the awkwardness he felt in making proper reply upon the occasion. In America, when you make a gift, you sing its praises to the recipient; in Japan we depreciate or slander it. The underlying idea with you is, "This is a nice: gift if it were not nice I would not dare give it to you; for it will be an insult to give you anything but what is nice." In contrast to this, our logic runs: "You are a nice person, and no gift is nice enough for you. You will not accept anything I can lay at your feet except as a token of my good will; so accept this, not for its intrinsic value, but as a token. It will be an insult to your worth to call the best gift good enough for you." Place the two ideas side by side, and we see that the ultimate idea is one and the same. Neither is "awfully funny." The American speaks of the material which makes the gift; the Japanese speaks of the spirit which prompts the gift.

It is perverse reasoning to conclude, because our sense of propriety shows itself in all the smallest ramifications of our deportment, to take the least important of them and uphold it as the type, and pass judgment upon the principle itself. Which is more important, to eat or to observe rules of propriety about eating? A Chinese sage answers, "If you take a case where the eating is all-important, and the observing the rules of propriety is of little importance, and compare them together, why not merely say that the eating is of the more importance?" "Metal is heavier than feathers," but does that saying have reference to a single clasp of metal and a waggon-load of feathers? Take a piece of wood a foot thick and raise it above the pinnacle of a temple, none would call it taller than the temple. To the question, "Which is the more important, to tell the truth or to be polite?" the Japanese are said to give an answer diametrically opposite to what the American will say,—but I forbear any comment until I come to speak of veracity and sincerity.

CHAPTER 7

VERACITY AND SINCERITY

Without veracity and sincerity, politeness is a farce and a show. "Propriety carried beyond right bounds," says Masamuné, "becomes a lie." An ancient poet has outdone Polonius in the advice he gives: "To thyself be faithful: if in thy heart thou strayest not from truth, without prayer of thine the Gods will keep thee whole." The apotheosis of Sincerity to which Confucius gives expression in the *Doctrine of the Mean*, attributes to it transcendental powers, almost identifying them with the Divine. "Sincerity is the end and the beginning of all things; without Sincerity there would be nothing." He then dwells with eloquence on its far-reaching and long-enduring nature, its power to produce changes without movement and by its mere presence to accomplish its purpose without effort. From the Chinese ideogram for Sincerity, which is a combination of "Word" and "Perfect," one is tempted to draw a parallel between it and the Neo-Platonic doctrine of *Logos*—to such height does the sage soar in his unwonted mystic flight.

Lying or equivocation were deemed equally cowardly. The bushi held that his high social position demanded a loftier standard of veracity than that of the tradesman and peasant. *Bushi no ichi-gon*—the word of a samurai, or in exact German equivalent, *Ritterwort*—was sufficient guaranty for the truthfulness of an assertion. His word carried such weight with it that promises were generally made and fulfilled without a written pledge, which would have been deemed quite beneath his dignity. Many thrilling anecdotes were told of those who atoned by death for *ni-gon*, a double tongue.

The regard for veracity was so high that, unlike the generality of Christians who persistently violate the plain commands of the Teacher not to swear, the best of samurai looked upon an oath as derogatory to their honour. I am well aware that they did swear by different deities or upon their swords; but never has swearing degenerated into wanton form and irreverent interjection. To emphasise our words a practice was sometimes resorted to of literally sealing with blood. For the explanation of such a practice, I need only refer my readers to Goethe's *Faust*.

A recent American writer is responsible for this statement, that if you ask an ordinary Japanese which is better, to tell a falsehood or be impolite, he will not hesitate to answer, "To tell a falsehood!" Dr. Peery[14] is partly right and partly wrong; right in that an ordinary Japanese, even a samurai, may answer in the way ascribed to him, but wrong in attributing too much weight to the term he translates "falsehood." This word (in Japanese, *uso*) is employed to denote anything which is not a truth (*makoto*) or fact (*honto*). Lowell tells us that Wordsworth could not distinguish between truth and fact, and an ordinary Japanese is in this respect as good as Wordsworth. Ask a Japanese, or even an American of any refinement, to tell you whether he dislikes you or whether he is sick at his stomach, and he will not hesitate long to tell falsehoods and answer "I like you much," or, "I am quite well, thank you." To sacrifice truth merely for the sake of politeness was regarded as an "empty form" (*kyo-rei*) and "deception by sweet words."

I own I am speaking now of the Bushido idea of veracity: but it may not be amiss to devote a few words to our commercial

14 Peery, *The Gist of Japan*, p. 86.

integrity, of which I have heard much complaint in foreign books and journals. A loose business morality has indeed been the worst blot on our national reputation; but before abusing it or hastily condemning the whole race for it, let us calmly study it and we shall be rewarded with consolation for the future.

Of all the great occupations of life, none was farther removed from the profession of arms than commerce. The merchant was placed lowest in the category of vocations,—the knight, the tiller of the soil, the mechanic, the merchant. The samurai derived his income from land and could even indulge, if he had a mind to, in amateur farming; but the counter and abacus were abhorred. We know the wisdom of this social arrangement. Montesquieu has made it clear that the debarring of the nobility from mercantile pursuits was an admirable social policy, in that it prevented wealth from accumulating in the hands of the powerful. The separation of power and riches kept the distribution of the latter more nearly equable. Professor Dill, the author of *Roman Society in the Last Century of the Western Empire*, has brought afresh to our mind that one cause of the decadence of the Roman Empire, was the permission given to the nobility to engage in trade, and the consequent monopoly of wealth and power by a minority of the senatorial families.

Commerce, therefore, in feudal Japan did not reach that degree of development which it would have attained under freer conditions. The obloquy attached to the calling naturally brought within its pale such as cared little for social repute. "Call one a thief and he will steal." Put a stigma on a calling and its followers adjust their morals to it, for it is natural that "the normal conscience," as Hugh Black says, "rises to the demands made on it, and easily falls to the limit of the standard expected from it." It is unnecessary to add that no business, commercial or otherwise, can be transacted without a code of morals. Our merchants of the feudal period had one among themselves, without which they could never have developed, as they did in embryo, such fundamental mercantile institutions as the guild, the bank, the bourse, insurance, checks, bills of exchange, etc.; but in their relations with people outside their vocation, the tradesmen lived too true to the reputation of their order.

This being the case, when the country was opened to foreign trade, only the most adventurous and unscrupulous rushed to the ports, while the respectable business houses declined for some time the repeated requests of the authorities to establish branch houses. Was Bushido powerless to stay the current of commercial dishonour? Let us see.

Those who are well acquainted with our history will remember that only a few years after our treaty ports were opened to foreign trade, feudalism was abolished, and when with it the samurai's fiefs were taken and bonds issued to them in compensation, they were given liberty to invest them in mercantile transactions. Now you may ask, "Why could they not bring their much boasted veracity into their new business relations and so reform the old abuses?" Those who had eyes to see could not weep enough, those who had hearts to feel could not sympathise enough, with the fate of many a noble and honest samurai who signally and irrevocably failed in his new and unfamiliar field of trade and industry, through sheer lack of shrewdness in coping with his artful plebeian rival. When we know that eighty per cent. of the business houses fail in so industrial a country as America, is it any wonder that scarcely one among a hundred samurai who went into trade could succeed in his new vocation? It will be long before it will be recognised how many fortunes were wrecked in the attempt to apply Bushido ethics to business methods; but it was soon patent to every observing mind that the ways of wealth were not the ways of honour. In what respects, then, were they different?

Of the three incentives to veracity that Lecky enumerates, viz., the industrial, the political, and the philosophical, the first was altogether lacking in Bushido. As to the second, it could develop little in a political community under a feudal system. It is in its philosophical and, as Lecky says, in its highest aspect, that honesty attained elevated rank in our catalogue of virtues. With all my sincere regard for the high commercial integrity of the Anglo-Saxon race, when I ask for the ultimate ground, I am told that "honesty is the best policy,"—that it pays to be honest. Is not this virtue, then, its own reward? If it is followed because it brings in more cash than falsehood, I am afraid Bushido would rather indulge in lies!

If Bushido rejects a doctrine of *quid pro quo* rewards, the shrewder tradesman will readily accept it. Lecky has very truly remarked that veracity owes its growth largely to commerce and manufacture; as Nietzsche puts it, honesty is the youngest of the virtues--in other words, it is the foster-child of modern industry. Without this mother, veracity was like a blue-blood orphan whom only the most cultivated mind could adopt and nourish. Such minds were general among the samurai, but, for want of a more democratic and utilitarian foster-mother, the tender child failed to thrive. Industries advancing, veracity will prove an easy, nay, a profitable virtue to practise. Just think—as late as November, 1880, Bismarck sent a circular to the professional consuls of the German Empire, warning them of "a lamentable lack of reliability with regard to German shipments *inter alia*, apparent both as to quality and quantity." Nowadays we hear comparatively little of German carelessness and dishonesty in trade. In twenty years her merchants have learned that in the end honesty pays. Already our merchants have found that out. For the rest I recommend the reader to two recent writers for well-weighed judgment on this point.15   It is interesting to remark in this connection that integrity and honour were the surest

15 Knapp, *Feudal and Modern Japan*, Vol. I., ch. iv.; Ransome, *Japan in Transition*, ch. viii.

guaranties which even a merchant debtor could present in the form of promissory notes. It was quite a usual thing to insert such clauses as these: "In default of the repayment of the sum lent to me, I shall say nothing against being ridiculed in public"; or, "In case I fail to pay you back, you may call me a fool," and the like.

Often have I wondered whether the veracity of Bushido had any motive higher than courage. In the absence of any positive commandment against bearing false witness, lying was not condemned as sin, but simply denounced as weakness, and, as such, highly dishonourable. As a matter of fact, the idea of honesty is so intimately blended, and its Latin and its German etymology so identified with honour, that it is high time I should pause a few moments for the consideration of this feature of the Precepts of Knighthood.

CHAPTER 8

HONOUR

The sense of honour, implying a vivid consciousness of personal dignity and worth, could not fail to characterise the samurai, born and bred to value the duties and privileges of their profession. Though the word ordinarily given nowadays as the translation of honour was not used freely, yet the idea was conveyed by such terms as *na* (name) *men- moku*(countenance), *guai-bun* (outside hearing), reminding us respectively of the biblical use of "name," of the evolution of the term "personality" from the Greek mask, and of "fame." A good name—one's reputation, "the immortal part of one's self, what remains being bestial"—assumed as a matter of course, any infringement upon its integrity was felt as shame, and the sense of shame (*Ren-chi-shin*) was one of the earliest to be cherished in juvenile education. "You will be laughed at," "It will disgrace you," "Are you not ashamed?" were the last appeal to correct behaviour on the part of a youthful delinquent. Such a recourse to his honour touched the most sensitive spot in the child's heart, as though it had been nursed on honour while he was in his mother's womb; for most truly is honour a pre-natal influence, being closely bound up with strong family consciousness. "In losing the solidarity of families," says Balzac, "society has lost the fundamental force which Montesquieu named Honour." Indeed, the sense of shame seems to me to be the earliest indication of the moral consciousness of the race. The first and worst punishment which befell humanity in consequence of tasting "the fruit of that forbidden tree" was, to my mind, not the sorrow of child-birth, nor the thorns and thistles, but the awakening of the sense of shame. Few incidents in history excel in pathos the scene of the first mother plying, with heaving breast and tremulous fingers, her crude needle on the few fig leaves which her dejected husband plucked for her. This first fruit of disobedience clings to us with a tenacity that nothing else does. All the sartorial ingenuity of mankind has not yet succeeded in sewing an apron that will efficaciously hide our sense of shame. That samurai was right who refused to compromise his character by a slight humiliation in his youth; "because," he said, "dishonour is like a scar on a tree, which time, instead of effacing, only helps to enlarge." Mencius had taught centuries before, in almost the identical phrase, what Carlyle has latterly expressed,—namely, that "Shame is the soil of all Virtue, of good manners and good morals."

The fear of disgrace was so great that if our literature lacks such eloquence as Shakespeare puts into the mouth of Norfolk, it nevertheless hung like Damocles' sword over the head of every samurai and often assumed a morbid character. In the name of honour, deeds were perpetrated which can find no justification in the code of Bushido. At the slightest, nay—imaginary insult—the quick-tempered braggart took offence, resorted to the use of the sword, and many an unnecessary strife was raised and many an innocent life lost. The story of a well-meaning citizen who called the attention of a bushi to a flea jumping on his back, and who was forthwith cut in two, for the simple and questionable reason, that inasmuch as fleas are parasites which feed on animals, it was an unpardonable insult to identify a noble warrior with a beast--I say, stories like these are too frivolous to believe. Yet, the circulation of such stories implies three things: (1) that they were invented to overawe common people; (2) that abuses were really made of the samurai's profession of honour; and (3) that a very strong sense of shame was developed among them. It is plainly unfair to take an abnormal case to cast blame upon the precepts, any more than to judge of the true teachings of Christ from the fruits of religious fanaticism and extravagance,--inquisitions and hypocrisy. But, as in religious monomania there is something touchingly noble as compared with the delirium tremens of a drunkard, so in that extreme sensitiveness of the samurai about their honour do we not recognise the substratum of a genuine virtue?

The morbid excess into which the delicate code of honour was inclined to run was strongly counterbalanced by preaching magnanimity and patience. To take offence at slight provocation was ridiculed as "short- tempered." The popular adage said: "To bear what you think you cannot bear is really to bear." The great Iyéyasu left to posterity a few maxims, among which are the following:—"The life of man is like going a long distance with a heavy load upon the shoulders. Haste not . . . Reproach none, but be forever watchful of thine own short-comings . . . Forbearance is the basis of length of days." He proved in his life what he preached. A literary wit put a characteristic epigram into the mouths of three well-known personages in our history: to Nobunaga he attributed, "I will kill her, if the nightingale sings not in time"; to Hidéyoshi, "I will force her to sing for me"; and to Iyéyasu, "I will wait till she opens her lips."

Patience and long-suffering were also highly commended by Mencius. In one place he writes to this effect: "Though you denude yourself and insult me, what is that to me? You cannot defile my soul by your outrage." Elsewhere he teaches that anger at a petty offence is unworthy a superior man, but indignation for a great cause is righteous wrath.

To what height of unmartial and unresisting meekness Bushido could reach in some of its votaries, may be seen in their utterances. Take, for instance, this saying of Ogawa: "When others speak all manner of evil things against thee, return not evil for evil, but rather reflect that thou wast not more faithful in the discharge of thy duties." Take another of Kumazawa:—"When others blame thee, blame them not; when others are angry at thee, return not anger. joy cometh only as Passion and Desire part." Still another instance I may cite from Saigo, upon whose overhanging brows "Shame is ashamed to sit":—"The Way is the way of Heaven and Earth; Man's place is to follow it; therefore make it the object of thy life to reverence Heaven. Heaven loves me and others with equal love; therefore with the love wherewith thou lovest thyself, love others. Make not Man thy partner but Heaven, and making Heaven thy partner do thy best. Never condemn others; but see to it that thou comest not short of thine own mark." Some of these sayings remind us of Christian expostulations, and show us how far in practical morality natural religion can approach the revealed. Not only did these sayings remain as utterances, but they were really embodied in acts.

It must be admitted that very few attained this sublime height of magnanimity, patience and forgiveness. It was a great pity that nothing clear and general was expressed as to what constitutes honour, only a few enlightened minds being aware that it "from no condition rises," but that it lies in each acting well his part; for nothing was easier than for youths to forget in the heat of action what they had learned in Mencius in their calmer moments. Said this sage: "'Tis in every man's mind to love honour; but little doth he dream that what is truly honourable lies within himself and not elsewhere. The honour which men confer is not good honour. Those whom Châo the Great ennobles, he can make mean again." For the most part, an insult was quickly resented and repaid by death, as we shall see later, while honour—too often nothing higher than vainglory or worldly approbation—was prized as the *summum bonum* of earthly existence. Fame, and not wealth or knowledge, was the goal toward which youths had to strive.

Many a lad swore within himself as he crossed the threshold of his paternal home, that he would not recross it until he had made a name in the world; and many an ambitious mother refused to see her sons again unless they could "return home," as the expression is, "caparisoned in brocade." To shun shame or win a name, samurai boys would submit to any privations and undergo severest ordeals of bodily or mental suffering. They knew that honour won in youth grows with age. In the memorable seige of Osaka, a young son of Iyéyasu, in spite of his earnest entreaties to be put in the vanguard, was placed at the rear of the army. When the castle fell, he was so chagrined and wept so bitterly that an old councillor tried to console him with all the resources at his command; "Take comfort, Sire," said he, "at the thought of the long future before you. In the many years that you may live, there will come divers occasions to distinguish yourself." The boy fixed his indignant gaze upon the man and said—"How foolishly you talk! Can ever my fourteenth year come round again?" Life itself was thought cheap if honour and fame could be attained therewith: hence, whenever a cause presented itself which was considered dearer than life, with utmost serenity and celerity was life laid down.

Of the causes in comparison with which no life was too dear to sacrifice, was the duty of loyalty, which was the key-stone making feudal virtues a symmetrical arch.

CHAPTER 9

THE DUTY OF LOYALTY

Feudal morality shares other virtues in common with other systems of ethics, with other classes of people, but this virtue—homage and fealty to a superior—is its distinctive feature. I am aware that personal fidelity is a moral adhesion existing among all sorts and conditions of men,—a gang of pickpockets owe allegiance to a Fagin; but it is only in the code of chivalrous honour that loyalty assumes paramount importance.

In spite of Hegel's criticism[16] that the fidelity of feudal vassals, being an obligation to an individual and not to a commonwealth, is a bond established on totally unjust principles, a great compatriot of his made it his boast that personal loyalty was a German virtue. Bismarck had good reasons to do so, not because the *Treue* he boasts of was the monopoly of his Fatherland or of any single nation or race, but because this favoured fruit of chivalry lingers latest among the people where feudalism has lasted longest. In America, where "everybody is as good as anybody else," and, as the Irishman added, "better too," such exalted ideas of loyalty as we feel for our sovereign may be deemed "excellent within certain bounds," but preposterous as encouraged among us. Montesquieu complained long ago that right on one side of the Pyrenees was wrong on the other, and

16 *Philosophy of History* (Eng. trans. by Sibree), Pt. IV., sec. ii., ch. i.

the recent Dreyfus trial proved the truth of his remark, save that the Pyrenees were not the sole boundary beyond which French justice finds no accord. Similarly, loyalty as we conceive it may find few admirers elsewhere, not because our conception is wrong, but because it is, I am afraid, forgotten, and also because we carry it to a degree not reached in any other country. Griffis[17] was quite right in stating that whereas in China Confucian ethics made obedience to parents the primary human duty, in Japan precedence was given to loyalty. At the risk of shocking some of my good readers, I will relate of one "who could endure to follow a fall'n lord" and who thus, as Shakespeare assures, "earned a place i' the story."

The story is of one of the greatest characters of our history, Michizané, who, falling a victim to jealousy and calumny, is exiled from the capital. Not content with this, his unrelenting enemies are now bent upon the extinction of his family. Strict search for his son—not yet grown—reveals the fact of his being secreted in a village school kept by one Genzo, a former vassal of Michizané. When orders are dispatched to the schoolmaster to deliver the head of the juvenile offender on a certain day, his first idea is to find a suitable substitute for it. He ponders over his school-list, scrutinises with careful eyes all the boys, as they stroll into the class-room, but none among the children born of the soil bears the least resemblance to his protégé. His despair, however, is but for a moment; for, behold, a new scholar is announced—a comely boy of the same age as his master's son, escorted by a mother of noble mien.

No less conscious of the resemblance between infant lord and infant retainer, were the mother and the boy himself. In the privacy of home both had laid themselves upon the altar; the one his life—the other her heart, yet without sign to the outer world. Unwitting of what had passed between them, it is the teacher from whom comes the suggestion.

---

17 *Religions of Japan.*

Here, then, is the scapegoat!—The rest of the narrative may be briefly told.—On the day appointed, arrives the officer commissioned to identify and receive the head of the youth. Will he be deceived by the false head? The poor Genzo's hand is on the hilt of the sword, ready to strike a blow either at the man or at himself, should the examination defeat his scheme. The officer takes up the gruesome object before him, goes calmly over each feature, and in a deliberate, business-like tone, pronounces it genuine.—That evening in a lonely home awaits the mother we saw in the school. Does she know the fate of her child? It is not for his return that she watches with eagerness for the opening of the wicket. Her father-in-law has been for a long time a recipient of Michizané's bounties, but since his banishment, circumstances have forced her husband to follow the service of the enemy of his family's benefactor. He himself could not be untrue to his own cruel master; but his son could serve the cause of the grandsire's lord. As one acquainted with the exile's family, it was he who had been entrusted with the task of identifying the boy's head. Now the day's—yea, the life's—hard work is done, he returns home and as he crosses its threshold, he accosts his wife, saying: "Rejoice, my wife, our darling son has proved of service to his lord!"

"What an atrocious story!" I hear my readers exclaim. "Parents deliberately sacrificing their own innocent child to save the life of another man's!" But this child was a conscious and willing victim: it is a story of vicarious death—as significant as, and not more revolting than, the story of Abraham's intended sacrifice of Isaac. In both cases was obedience to the call of duty, utter submission to the command of a higher voice, whether given by a visible or an invisible angel, or heard by an outward or an inward ear;—but I abstain from preaching.

The individualism of the West, which recognises separate interests for father and son, husband and wife, necessarily brings into strong relief the duties owed by one to the other; but Bushido held that the interest of the family and of the members thereof is intact,—one and inseparable.

This interest it bound up with affection—natural, instinctive, irresistible; hence, if we die for one we love with natural love (which animals themselves possess), what is that? "For if ye love them that love you, what reward have ye? Do not even the publicans the same?"

In his great history, Sanyo relates in touching language the heart struggle of Shigemori concerning his father's rebellious conduct. "If I be loyal, my father must be undone; if I obey my father, my duty to my sovereign must go amiss." Poor Shigemori! We see him afterward praying with all his soul that kind Heaven may visit him with death, that he may be released from this world where it is hard for purity and righteousness to dwell.

Many a Shigemori has his heart tom by the conflict between duty and affection. Indeed, neither Shakespeare nor the Old Testament itself contains an adequate rendering of *ko*, our conception of filial piety, and yet in such conflicts Bushido never wavered in its choice of loyalty.

Women, too, encouraged their offspring to sacrifice all for the king. Even as resolute as Widow Windham and her illustrious consort, the samurai matron stood ready to give up her boys for the cause of loyalty.

Since Bushido, like Aristotle and some modern sociologists, conceived the state as antedating the individual,—the latter being born into the former as part and parcel thereof,—he must live and die for it or for the incumbent of its legitimate authority. Readers of Crito will remember the argument with which Socrates represents the laws of the city as pleading with him on the subject of his escape. Among others he makes them (the laws or the state) say: "Since you were begotten and nurtured and educated under us, dare you once to say you are not our offspring and servant, you and your fathers before you?" These are words which do not impress us as any thing extraordinary; for the same thing has long been on the lips of Bushido, with this modification, that the laws and the state were represented with us by a personal being. Loyalty is an ethical outcome of this political theory.

I am not entirely ignorant of Mr. Spencer's view according to which political obedience--loyalty—is accredited with only a transitional function.[18] It may be so. Sufficient unto the day is the virtue thereof. We may complacently repeat it, especially as we believe *that* day to be a long space of time, during which, so our national anthem says, "tiny pebbles grow into mighty rocks draped with moss."

We may remember at this juncture that even among so democratic a people as the English, "the sentiment of personal fidelity to a man and his posterity which their Germanic ancestors felt for their chiefs, has," as Monsieur Boutmy recently said, "only passed more or less into their profound loyalty to the race and blood of their princes, as evidenced in their extraordinary attachment to the dynasty."

Political subordination, Mr. Spencer predicts, will give place to loyalty, to the dictates of conscience. Suppose his induction is realised—will loyalty and its concomitant instinct of reverence disappear forever? We transfer our allegiance from one master to another, without being unfaithful to either: from being subjects of a ruler that wields the temporal sceptre we become servants of the monarch who sits enthroned in the penetralia of our hearts. A few years ago a very stupid controversy, started by the misguided disciples of Spencer, made havoc among the reading class of Japan. In their zeal to uphold the claim of the throne to undivided loyalty, they charged Christians with treasonable propensity in that they avow fidelity to their Lord

18 *Principles of Ethics*, Vol. I., pt. ii., ch. x.

and Master. They arrayed forth sophistical arguments without the wit of Sophists, and scholastic tortuosities minus the niceties of the Schoolmen. Little did they know that we can, in a sense, "serve two masters without holding to the one or despising the other," "rendering unto Cæsar the things that are Cæsar's and unto God the things that are God's." Did not Socrates, all the while he unflinchingly refused to concede one iota of loyalty to his *dæmon*, obey with equal fidelity and equanimity the command of his earthly master, the State? His conscience he followed, alive; his country he served, dying. Alack the day when a state grows so powerful as to demand of its citizens the dictates of their conscience!

Bushido did not require us to make our conscience the slave of any lord or king. Thomas Mowbray was a veritable spokesman for us when he said:

> *"Myself I throw, dread sovereign, at thy foot.*
> *My life thou shall command, but not my shame.*
> *The one my duty owes; but my fair name,*
> *Despite of death, that lives upon my grave,*
> *To dark dishonour's use, thou shall not have."*
> *A man who sacrificed his own conscience to*

the capricious will or freak or fancy of a sovereign was accorded a low place in the estimate of the Precepts. Such an one was despised as *nei- shin*, a cringeling, who makes court by unscrupulous fawning, or as *chô- shin*, a favourite who steals his master's affections by means of servile compliance; these two species of subjects corresponding exactly to those which Iago describes,—the one, a duteous and knee-crooking knave, doting on his own obsequious bondage, wearing out his time much like his master's ass; the other trimming in forms and visages of duty, keeping yet his heart attending on himself.

When a subject differed from his master, the loyal path for him to pursue was to use every available means to persuade him of his error, as Kent did to King Lear. Failing in this, let the master deal with him as he wills. In cases of this kind, it was quite a usual course for the samurai to make the last appeal to the intelligence and conscience of his lord by demonstrating the sincerity of his words with the shedding of his own blood.

Life being regarded as the means whereby to serve his master, and its ideal being set upon honour, the whole education and training of a samurai were conducted accordingly.

CHAPTER 10

THE EDUCATION AND TRAINING OF A SAMURAI

The first point to observe in knightly pedagogics was to build up character, leaving in the shade the subtler faculties of prudence, intelligence and dialectics. We have seen the important part æsthetic accomplishments played in his education. Indispensable as they were to a man of culture, they were accessories rather than essentials of samurai training. Intellectual superiority was, of course, esteemed; but the word *Chi*, which was employed to denote intellectuality, meant wisdom in the first instance and gave knowledge only a very subordinate place.

The tripod which supported the framework of Bushido was said to be *Chi*, *Jin*, *Yu*, respectively, Wisdom, Benevolence, and Courage. A samurai was essentially a man of action. Science was without the pale of his activity. He took advantage of it in so far as it concerned his profession of arms. Religion and theology were relegated to the priests; he concerned himself with them in so far as they helped to nourish courage. Like an English poet the samurai believed "'tis not the creed that saves the man; but it is the man that justifies the creed." Philosophy and literature formed the chief part of his intellectual training; but even in the pursuit of these, it was not objective truth that he strove after,— literature was pursued mainly as a pastime, and philosophy as a practical aid in the formation of character, if not for the exposition of some military or political problem.

From what has been said, it will not surprising to note that the curriculum of studies, according to the pedagogics of Bushido, consisted mainly of the following:--fencing, archery, *jiujutsu*[19] or *yawara*, horsemanship, the use of the spear, tactics, caligraphy, ethics, literature, and history. Of these, *jiujutsu* and caligraphy may require a few words of explanation. Great stress was laid on good writing, probably because our logograms, partaking as they do of the nature of pictures, possess artistic value, and also because chirography was accepted as indicative of one's personal character. *Jiujutsu* may be briefly defined as an application of anatomical knowledge to the purpose of offence or defence. It differs from wrestling, in that it does not depend upon muscular strength. It differs from other forms of attack in that it uses no weapons. Its feat consists in clutching or striking such part of the enemy's body as will make him numb and incapable of resistance. Its object is not to kill, but to incapacitate one for action for the time being.

A subject of study which one would expect to find in military education and which is rather conspicuous by its absence in the Bushido course of instruction, is mathematics. This, however, can be readily explained in part by the fact that feudal warfare was not carried on with scientific precision. Not only that, but the whole training of the samurai was unfavourable to fostering numerical notions.

Chivalry is uneconomical: it boasts of penury. It says with Ventidius that "ambition, the soldier's virtue, rather makes choice of loss, than gain which darkens him." Don Quixote takes more pride in his rusty spear and skin-and-bone horse than in gold and lands, and a samurai is in hearty sympathy with his exaggerated confrère of La Mancha. He disdains money itself,—the art of

19 The same word as that misspelled jiu-jitsu in common English parlance. It is the gentle art. It "uses no weapon." (W. E. G.)

making or hoarding it. It was to him veritably filthy lucre. The hackneyed expression to describe the decadence of an age was "that the civilians loved money and the soldiers feared death." Niggardliness of gold and of life excited as much disapprobation as their lavish use was panegyrised. "Less than all things," says a current precept, "men must grudge money: it is by riches that wisdom is hindered." Hence children were brought up with utter disregard of economy. It was considered bad taste to speak of it, and ignorance of the value of different coins was a token of good breeding.

Knowledge of numbers was indispensable in the mustering of forces as well as in distribution of benefices and fiefs; but the counting of money was left to meaner hands. In many feudatories, public finance was administered by a lower kind of samurai or by priests. Every thinking bushi knew well enough that money formed the sinews of war; but he did not think of raising the appreciation of money to a virtue. It is true that thrift was enjoined by Bushido, but not for economical reasons so much as for the exercise of abstinence. Luxury was thought the greatest menace to manhood and severest simplicity of living was required of the warrior class, sumptuary laws being enforced in many of the clans.

We read that in ancient Rome the farmers of revenue and other financial agents were gradually raised to the rank of knights, the State thereby showing its appreciation of their service and of the importance of money itself. How closely this is connected with the luxury and avarice of the Romans may be imagined. Not so with the Precepts of Knighthood. It persisted in systematically regarding finance as something low—low as compared with moral and intellectual vocations.

Money and the love of it being thus diligently ignored, Bushido itself could long remain free from a thousand and one evils of which money is the root. This is sufficient reason for the fact that our public men have long been free from corruption; but alas! how fast plutocracy is making its way in our time and generation.

The mental discipline which would nowadays be chiefly aided by the study of mathematics, was supplied by literary exegesis and deontological discussions. Very few abstract subjects troubled the mind of the young, the chief aim of their education being, as I have said, decision of character. People whose minds were simply stored with information found no great admirers. Of the three services of studies that Bacon gives,—for delight, ornament, and ability,—Bushido had decided preference for the last, where their use was "in judgment and the disposition of business." Whether it was for the disposition of public business or for the exercise of self-control, it was with a practical end in view that education was conducted. "Learning without thought," said Confucius, "is labour lost; thought without learning is perilous."

When character and not intelligence, when the soul and not the head, is chosen by a teacher for the material to work upon and to develop, his vocation partakes of a sacred character. "It is the parent who has borne me: it is the teacher who makes me man." With this idea, therefore, the esteem in which one's preceptor was held was very high. A man to evoke such confidence and respect from the young, must necessarily be endowed with superior personality, without lacking erudition. He was a father to the fatherless, and an adviser to the erring. "Thy father and thy mother."—so runs our maxim—"are like heaven and earth; thy teacher and thy lord are like the sun and moon."

The present system of paying for every sort of service was not in vogue among the adherents of Bushido. It believed in a service which can be rendered only without money and without price. Spiritual service, be it of priest or teacher, was not to be repaid in gold or silver, not because it was valueless but because it was invaluable. Here the non-arithmetical honour-instinct of

Bushido taught a truer lesson than modern Political Economy; for wages and salaries can be paid only for services whose results are definite, tangible, and measurable, whereas the best service done in education,—namely, in soul development (and this includes the services of a pastor), is not definite, tangible, or measurable. Being immeasurable, money, the ostensible measure of value, is of inadequate use. Usage sanctioned that pupils brought to their teachers money or goods at different seasons of the year; but these were not payments but offerings, which indeed were welcome to the recipients as they were usually men of stern calibre, boasting of honourable penury, too dignified to work with their hands and too proud to beg. They were grave personifications of high spirits undaunted by adversity. They were an embodiment of what was considered as an end of all learning, and were thus a living example of that discipline of disciplines, self-control, which was universally required of samurai.

CHAPTER 11

SELF-CONTROL

The discipline of fortitude on the one hand, inculcating endurance without a groan, and the teaching of politeness on the other, requiring us not to mar the pleasure or serenity of another by expressions of our own sorrow or pain, combined to engender a stoical turn of mind, and eventually to confirm it into a national trait of apparent stoicism. I say apparent stoicism, because I do not believe that true stoicism can ever become the characteristic of a whole nation, and also because some of our national manners and customs may seem to a foreign observer hard- hearted. Yet we are really as susceptible to tender emotion as any race under the sky.

I am inclined to think that in one sense we have to feel more than others—yes, doubly more since the very attempt to restrain natural promptings entails suffering. Imagine boys—and girls, too—brought up not to resort to the shedding of a tear or the uttering of a groan for the relief of their feelings,—and there is a physiological problem whether such effort steels their nerves or makes them more sensitive.

It was considered unmanly for a samurai to betray his emotions on his face. "He shows no sign of joy or anger," was a phrase used, in describing a great character. The most natural affections were kept under control. A father could embrace his son only at the expense of his dignity; a husband would not kiss his wife,—no, not in the presence of other people, whatever he might do in private! There may be some truth in the remark of a witty youth when he said, "American husbands kiss their wives in public and beat them in private; Japanese husbands beat theirs in public and kiss them in private."

Calmness of behaviour, composure of mind, should not be disturbed by passion of any kind. I remember when, during the late war with China, a regiment left a certain town, a large concourse of people flocked to the station to bid farewell to the general and his army. On this occasion an American resident resorted to the place, expecting to witness loud demonstrations, as the nation itself was highly excited and there were fathers, mothers, wives, and sweethearts of the soldiers in the crowd.

The American was strangely disappointed; for as the whistle blew and the train began to move, the hats of thousands of people were silently taken off and their heads bowed in reverential farewell; no waving of handkerchiefs, no word uttered, but deep silence in which only an attentive ear could catch a few broken sobs. In domestic life, too, I know of a father who spent whole nights listening to the breathing of a sick child, standing behind the door that he might not be caught in such an act of parental weakness! I know of a mother who, in her last moments, refrained from sending for her son, that he might not be disturbed in his studies. Our history and everyday life are replete with examples of heroic matrons who can well bear comparison with some of the most touching pages of Plutarch. Among our peasantry an Ian Maclaren would be sure to find many a Marget Howe.

It is the same discipline of self-restraint which is accountable for the absence of more frequent revivals in the Christian churches of Japan. When a man or woman feels his or her soul stirred, the first instinct is quietly to suppress the manifestation of it. In rare instances is the tongue set free by an irresistible spirit, when we have eloquence of sincerity and fervour. It is putting a premium upon a breach of the third commandment to encourage speaking lightly of spiritual experience. It is truly jarring to Japanese ears to hear the most sacred words, the most secret heart experiences, thrown out in promiscuous audiences. "Dost thou feel the soil of thy soul stirred with tender thoughts? It is time for seeds to sprout. Disturb it not with speech; but let it work alone in quietness and secrecy,"—writes a young samurai in his diary.

To give in so many articulate words one's inmost thoughts and feelings— notably the religious—is taken among us as an unmistakable sign that they are neither very profound nor very sincere. "Only a pomegranate is he"—so runs a popular saying "who, when he gapes his mouth, displays the contents of his heart."

It is not altogether perverseness of oriental minds that the instant our emotions are moved, we try to guard our lips in order to hide them. Speech is very often with us, as the Frenchman defines it, "the art of concealing thought."

Call upon a Japanese friend in time of deepest affliction and he will invariably receive you laughing, with red eyes or moist cheeks. At first you may think him hysterical. Press him for explanation and you will get a few broken commonplaces— "Human life has sorrow"; "They who meet must part"; "He that is born must die"; "It is foolish to count the years of a child that is gone, but a woman's heart will indulge in follies"; and the like. So the noble words of a noble Hohenzollern—"Lerne zu leiden ohne klagen"—had found many responsive minds among us long before they were uttered.

Indeed, the Japanese have recourse to risibility whenever the frailties of human nature are put to severest test. I think we possess a better reason than Democritus himself for our Abderian tendency, for laughter with us oftenest veils an effort to regain balance of temper when disturbed by any untoward circumstance. It is a counterpoise of sorrow or rage.

The suppression of feelings being thus steadily insisted upon, they find their safety-valve in poetical aphorisms. A poet of the tenth century writes "In Japan and China as well, humanity, when moved by sorrow, tells its bitter grief inverse." Another who tries to console her broken heart by fancying her departed child absent on his wonted chase after the dragon-fly hums,

> *"How far to-day in chase, I wonder,*
> *Has gone my hunter of the dragon-fly!"*

I refrain from quoting other examples, for I know I could do only scant justice to the pearly gems of our literature, were I to render into a foreign tongue the thoughts which were wrung drop by drop from bleeding hearts and threaded into beads of rarest value. I hope I have in a measure shown that inner working of our minds which often presents an appearance of callousness or of an hysterical mixture of laughter and dejection, and whose sanity is sometimes called in question.

It has also been suggested that our endurance of pain and indifference to death are due to less sensitive nerves. This is plausible as far as it goes. The next question is,—Why are our nerves less tightly strung? It may be our climate is; not so stimulating as the American. It may be our monarchical form of government does not excite us so much as the Republic does the Frenchman. It may be that we do not read *Sartor Resartus* so zealously as the Englishman. Personally, I believe it was our very excitability and sensitiveness which made it a necessity to recognise and enforce constant self-repression; but whatever may be the explanation, without taking into account long years of discipline in self- control, none can be correct.

Discipline in self-control can easily go too far. It can well repress the genial current of the soul. It can force pliant natures into distortions and monstrosities. It can beget bigotry, breed hypocrisy, or hebetate affections. Be a virtue never so noble, it has its counterpart and counterfeit. We must recognise in each virtue its own positive excellence and follow its positive ideal, and the ideal of self-restraint is to keep the mind level—as our expression is—or, to borrow a Greek term, attain the state of *euthymia*, which Democritus called the highest good.

The acme and pitch of self-control is reached and best illustrated in the first of the two institutions which we shall now bring to view, namely, the institutions of suicide and redress.

CHAPTER 12

THE INSTITUTIONS OF
SUICIDE AND REDRESS

Of these two institutions (the former known as *hara-kiri* and the latter as *kataki-uchi*), many foreign writers have treated more or less fully.

To begin with suicide, let me state that I confine my observations only to *seppuku* or *kappuku*, popularly known as *hara-kiri*—which means self-immolation by disembowelment. "Ripping the abdomen? How absurd!"—so cry those to whom the name is new. Absurdly odd as it may sound at first to foreign ears, it cannot be so very foreign to students of Shakespeare, who puts these words in Brutus's mouth—"Thy [Caesar's] spirit walks abroad and turns our swords into our proper entrails."

Listen to a modern English poet who, in his *Light of Asia*, speaks of a sword piercing the bowels of a queen;—none blames him for bad English or breach of modesty. Or, to take still another example, look at Guercino's painting of Cato's death in the Palazzo Rossa, in Genoa.

Whoever has read the swan-song which Addison makes Cato sing, will not jeer at the sword half-buried in his abdomen. In our minds this mode of death is associated with instances of noblest deeds and of most touching pathos, so that nothing repugnant, much less ludicrous, mars our conception of it. So wonderful is the transforming power of virtue, of greatness. of tenderness, that the vilest form of death assumes a sublimity and becomes a symbol of new life, or else the sign which Constantine beheld would not conquer the world!

Not for extraneous associations only does *seppuku* lose in our mind any taint of absurdity; for the choice of this particular part of the body to operate upon, was based on an old anatomical belief as to the seat of the soul and of the affections. When Moses wrote of Joseph's "bowels yearning upon his brother," or David prayed the Lord not to forget his bowels, or when Isaiah, Jeremiah, and other inspired men of old spoke of the "sounding" or the "troubling" of bowels, they all and each endorsed the belief prevalent among the Japanese that in the abdomen was enshrined the soul. The Semites habitually spoke of the liver and kidneys and surrounding fat as the seat of emotion and of life. The term *"hara"* was more comprehensive than the Greek *phren* or *thumos*, and the Japanese and Hellenese alike thought the spirit of man to dwell somewhere in that region. Such a notion is by no means confined to the peoples of antiquity. The French, in spite of the theory propounded by one of their most distinguished philosophers, Descartes, that the soul is located in the pineal gland, still insist in using the term *ventre* in a sense which, if anatomically too vague, is nevertheless physiologically significant. Similarly, *entrailles* stands in their language for affection and compassion. Nor is such a belief mere superstition, being more scientific than the general idea of making the heart the centre of the feelings.

Without asking a friar, the Japanese knew better than Romeo "in what vile part of this anatomy one's name did lodge." Modern neurologists speak of the abdominal and pelvic brains, denoting thereby sympathetic nerve centres in those parts which are strongly affected by any psychical action. This view of mental physiology once admitted, the syllogism of *seppuku* is easy to construct. "I will open the seat of my soul and show you how it fares with it. See for yourself whether it is polluted or clean."

I do not wish to be understood as asserting religious or even moral justification of suicide, but the high estimate placed upon honour was ample excuse with many for taking one's own life. How many acquiesced in the sentiment expressed by Garth,

> "When honour's lost, 't is a relief to die;
> Death's but a sure retreat from infamy,"

and have smilingly surrendered their souls to oblivion! Death involving a question of honour, was accepted in Bushido as a key to the solution of many complex problems, so that to an ambitious samurai a natural departure from life seemed a rather tame affair and a consummation not devoutly to be wished for. I dare say that many good Christians, if only they are honest enough, will confess the fascination of, if not positive admiration for, the sublime composure with which Cato, Brutus, Petronius, and a host of other ancient worthies terminated their own earthly existence. Is it too bold to hint that the death of the first of the philosophers was partly suicidal? When we are told so minutely by his pupils how their master willingly submitted to the mandate of the state—which he knew was morally mistaken—in spite of the possibilities of escape, and how he took the cup of hemlock in his own hand, even offering libation from its deadly contents, do we not discern, in his whole proceeding and demeanour, an act of self-immolation? No physical compulsion here, as in ordinary cases of execution. True, the verdict of the judges was compulsory: it said, "Thou shalt die,—and that by thine own hand." If suicide meant no more than dying by one's own hand, Socrates was a clear case of suicide. But nobody would charge him with the crime; Plato, who was averse to it, would not call his master a suicide.

Now my readers will understand that *seppuku* was not a mere suicidal process. It was an institution, legal and ceremonial. An invention of the middle ages, it was a process by which warriors could expiate their crimes, apologise for errors, escape from disgrace, redeem their friends, or prove their sincerity. When enforced as a legal punishment, it was practised with due ceremony. It was a refinement of self-destruction, and none could perform it without the utmost coolness of temper and composure of demeanour, and for these reasons it was particularly befitting the profession of bushi.

Antiquarian curiosity, if nothing else, would tempt me to give here a description of this obsolete ceremony; but seeing that such a description was made by a far abler writer, whose book is not much read nowadays, I am tempted to make a somewhat lengthy quotation. Mitford, in his *Tales of Old Japan*, after giving a translation of a treatise on *seppuku* from a rare Japanese manuscript, goes on to describe an instance of such an execution of which he was an eye-witness:

"We (seven foreign representatives) were invited to follow the Japanese witnesses into the *hondo* or main hall of the temple, where the ceremony was to be performed. It was an imposing scene. A large hall with a high roof supported by dark pillars of wood. From the ceiling hung a profusion of those huge gilt lamps and ornaments peculiar to Buddhist temples. In front of the high altar, where the floor, covered with beautiful white mats, is raised some three or four inches from the ground, was laid a rug of scarlet felt. Tall candles placed at regular intervals gave out a dim mysterious light, just sufficient to let all the proceedings be seen. The seven Japanese took their places on the left of the raised floor, the seven foreigners on the right. No other person was present.

"After the interval of a few minutes of anxious suspense, Taki Zenzaburo, a stalwart man thirty-two years of age, with a noble air, walked into the hall attired in his dress of ceremony, with the peculiar hempen-cloth wings which are worn on great occasions. He was accompanied by a *kaishaku* and three officers, who wore the *jimbaori* or war surcoat with gold tissue facings. The word *kaishaku*, it should be observed, is one to which our word executioner is no equivalent term. The office is that of a gentleman; in many cases it is performed by a kinsman or friend of the condemned, and the relation between them is rather that of principal and second than that of victim and executioner. In this instance, the *kaishaku* was a pupil of Taki Zenzaburo, and was selected by friends of the latter from among their own number for his skill in swordsmanship.

"With the *kaishaku* on his left hand, Taki Zenzaburo advanced slowly toward the Japanese witnesses, and the two bowed before them, then drawing near to the foreigners they saluted us in the same way, perhaps even with more deference; in each case the salutation was ceremoniously returned. Slowly and with great dignity the condemned man mounted on to the raised floor, prostrated himself before the high altar twice, and seated[20] himself on the felt carpet with his back to the high altar, the *kaishaku* crouching on his left-hand side. One of the three attendant officers then came forward, bearing a stand of the kind used in the temple for offerings, on which, wrapped in paper, lay the *wakizashi*, the short sword or dirk of the Japanese, nine inches and a half in length, with a point and an edge as sharp as a razor's. This he handed, prostrating himself, to the condemned man, who received it reverently raising it to his head with both hands, and placed it in front of himself.

"After another profound obeisance, Taki Zenzaburo, in a voice which betrayed just so much emotion and hesitation as might be

20 Seated himself-that is, in the Japanese fashion, his knees and toes touching the ground and his body resting on his heels. In this position, which is one of respect, he remained until his death.

expected from a man who is making a painful confession, but with no sign of either in his face or manner, spoke as follows:—

"'I, and I alone, unwarrantably gave the order to fire on the foreigners at Kobe, and again as they tried to escape. For this crime I disembowel myself, and I beg you who are present to do me the honour of witnessing the act.'

"Bowing once more, the speaker allowed his upper garments to slip down to his girdle, and remained naked to the waist. Carefully, according to custom, he tucked his sleeves under his knees to prevent himself from falling backward; for a noble Japanese gentleman should die falling forwards. Deliberately, with a steady hand he took the dirk that lay before him; he looked at it wistfully, almost affectionately; for a moment he seemed to collect his thoughts for the last time, and then stabbing himself deeply below the waist in the left-hand side, he drew the dirk slowly across to his right side, and turning it in the wound, gave a slight cut upwards. During this sickeningly painful operation he never moved a muscle of his face. When he drew out the dirk, he leaned forward and stretched out his neck; an expression of pain for the first time crossed his face, but he uttered no sound. At that moment the *kaishaku*, who, still crouching by his side, had been keenly watching his every movement, sprang to his feet, poised his sword for a second in the air; there was a flash, a heavy, ugly thud, a crashing fall; with one blow the head had been severed from the body.

"A dead silence followed, broken only by the hideous noise of the blood throbbing out of the inert heap before us, which but a moment before had been a brave and chivalrous man. It was horrible.

"The *kaishaku* made a low bow, wiped his sword with a piece of paper which he had ready for the purpose, and retired from the raised floor; and the stained dirk was solemnly borne away, a bloody proof of the execution.

"The two representatives of the Mikado then left their places, and crossing over to where the foreign witnesses sat, called to us to witness that the sentence of death upon Taki Zenzaburo had been faithfully carried out. The ceremony being at an end, we left the temple."

I might multiply any number of descriptions of *seppuku* from literature or from the relations of eye-witnesses; but one more instance will suffice.

Two brothers, Sakon and Naiki, respectively twenty-four and seventeen years of age, made an effort to kill Iyéyasu in order to avenge their father's wrongs; but before they could enter the camp they were made prisoners. The old general admired the pluck of the youths who dared an attempt on his life and ordered that they should be allowed to die an honourable death. Their little brother Hachimaro, a mere infant of eight summers, was condemned to a similar fate, as the sentence was pronounced on all the male members of the family, and the three were taken to a monastery where it was to be executed. A physician who was present on the occasion has left us a diary, from which the following scene is translated:

"When they were all seated in a row for final despatch, Sakon turned to the youngest and said—'Go thou first, for I wish to be sure that thou doest it aright.' Upon the little one's replying that, as he had never seen *seppuku* performed, he would like to see his brothers do it and then he could follow them, the older brothers smiled between their tears:— 'Well said, little fellow! So canst thou well boast of being our father's child.' When they had placed him between them, Sakon thrust the dagger into the left side of his abdomen and said—'Look brother! Dost understand now? Only, don't push the dagger too far, lest thou fall back. Lean forward, rather, and keep thy knees well composed.' Naiki did likewise and said to the boy—'Keep thine eyes open or else thou mayst look like a dying woman. If thy dagger feels anything within and thy strength fails, take courage and double thy effort to cut across.'

The child looked from one to the other, and, when both had expired, he calmly half denuded himself and followed the example set him on either hand."

The glorification of *seppuku* offered, naturally enough, no small temptation to its unwarranted committal. For causes entirely incompatible with reason, or for reasons entirely undeserving of death, hot-headed youths rushed into it as insects fly into fire; mixed and dubious motives drove more samurai to this deed than nuns into convent gates. Life was cheap--cheap as reckoned by the popular standard of honour. The saddest feature was that honour, which was always in

the *agio*, so to speak, was not always solid gold, but alloyed with baser metals. No one circle in the Inferno will boast of greater density of Japanese population than the seventh, to which Dante consigns all victims of self-destruction!

And yet, for a true samurai to hasten death or to court it, was alike cowardice. A typical fighter, when he lost battle after battle and was pursued from plain to hill and from bush to cavern, found himself hungry and alone in the dark hollow of a tree, his sword blunt with use, his bow broken and arrows exhausted—did not the noblest of the Romans fall upon his own sword in Philippi under like circumstances?— deemed it cowardly to die, but, with a fortitude approaching a Christian martyr's, cheered himself with an impromptu verse:

> *"Come! evermore come,*
> *Ye dread sorrows and pains!*
> *And heap on my burden'd back;*
> *That I not one test may lack*
> *Of what strength in me remains!"*

This, then, was the Bushido teaching—Bear and face all calamities and adversities with patience and a pure conscience;

for, as Mencius[21] taught, "When Heaven is about to confer a great office on anyone, it first exercises his mind with suffering and his sinews and bones with toil; it exposes his body to hunger and subjects him to extreme poverty: and it confounds his undertakings. In all these ways it stimulates his mind, hardens his nature, and supplies his incompetencies." True honour lies in fulfilling Heaven's decree and no death incurred in so doing is ignominious, whereas, death to avoid what Heaven has in store is cowardly indeed! In that quaint book of Sir Thomas Browne's, *Religio Medici*, there is an exact English equivalent for what is repeatedly taught in our Precepts. Let me quote it: "It is a brave act of valour to contemn death, but where life is more terrible than death, it is then the truest valour to dare to live." A renowned priest of the seventeenth century satirically observed--"Talk as he may, a samurai who ne'er has died is apt in decisive moments to flee or hide." Again— "Him who once has died in the bottom of his breast, no spears of Sanada nor all the arrows of Tametomo can pierce." How near we come to the portals of the temple whose Builder taught "He that loseth his life for my sake shall find it"! These are but a few of the numerous examples that tend to confirm the moral identity of the human species, notwithstanding an attempt so assiduously made to render the distinction between Christian and Pagan as great as possible.

We have thus seen that the Bushido institution of suicide was neither so irrational nor barbarous as its abuse strikes us at first sight. We will now see whether its sister institution of Redress— or call it Revenge, if you will—has its mitigating features. I hope I can dispose of this question in a few words, since a similar institution, or call it custom, if that suits you better, prevailed among all peoples and has not yet become entirely obsolete, as attested by the continuance of duelling and lynching. Why, has not an American captain recently challenged Esterhazy, that the

21 I use Dr. Legge's translation verbatim.

wrongs of Dreyfus be avenged? Among a savage tribe which has no marriage, adultery is not a sin, and only the jealousy of a lover protects a woman from abuse; so in a time which has no criminal court, murder is not a crime, and only the vigilant vengeance of the victim's people preserves social order. "What is the most beautiful thing on earth?" said Osiris to Horus. The reply was, "To avenge a parent's wrongs,"—to which a Japanese would have added "and a master's."

In revenge there is something which satisfies one's sense of justice. The avenger reasons:—"My good father did not deserve death. He who killed him did great evil. My father, if he were alive, would not tolerate a deed like this: Heaven itself hates wrongdoing. It is the will of my father; it is the will of Heaven that the evil-doer cease from his work. He must perish by my hand; because he shed my father's blood, I, who am his flesh and blood, must shed the murderer's. The same Heaven shall not shelter him and me." The ratiocination is simple and childish (though we know Hamlet did not reason much more deeply); nevertheless it shows an innate sense of exact balance and equal justice. "An eye for an eye, a tooth for a tooth." Our sense of revenge is as exact as our mathematical faculty, and until both terms of the equation are satisfied we cannot get over the sense of something left undone.

In Judaism, which believed in a jealous God, or in Greek mythology, which provided a Nemesis, vengeance may be left to superhuman agencies; but common sense furnished Bushido with the institution of redress as a kind of ethical court of equity, where people could take cases not to be judged in accordance with ordinary law. The master of the forty-seven Ronins was condemned to death; he had no court of higher instance to appeal to; his faithful retainers addressed themselves to vengeance, the only Supreme Court existing; they in their turn were condemned by common law,—but the popular instinct passed a different judgment, and hence their memory is still kept as green and fragrant as are their graves at Sengakuji to this day.

Though Lâo-tse taught to recompense injury with kindness, the voice of Confucius was very much louder, which taught that injury must be recompensed with justice;—and yet revenge was justified only when it was undertaken in behalf of our superiors and benefactors. One's own wrongs, including injuries done to wife and children, were to be borne and forgiven. A samurai could therefore fully sympathise with Hannibal's oath to avenge his country's wrongs, but he scorns James Hamilton for wearing in his girdle a handful of earth from his wife's grave, as an eternal incentive to avenge her wrongs on the Regent Murray.

Both of these institutions of suicide and redress lost their *raison d'être* at the promulgation of the Criminal Code. No more do we hear of romantic adventures of a fair maiden as she tracks in disguise the murderer of her parent. No more can we witness tragedies of family vendetta enacted.

The knight errantry of Miyamoto Musashi is now a tale of the past. The well-ordered police spies out the criminal for the injured party and the law metes out justice. The whole state and society will see that wrong is righted. The sense of justice satisfied, there is no need of *kataki-uchi*. If this had meant that "hunger of the heart which feeds upon the hope of glutting that hunger with the life blood of the victim," as a New England divine has described it, a few paragraphs in the Criminal Code would not so entirely have made an end of it.

As to *seppuku*, though it too has no *existence de jure*, we still hear of it from time to time, and shall continue to hear, I am afraid, as long as the past is remembered. Many painless and time-saving methods of self- immolation will come in vogue, as its votaries are increasing with fearful rapidity throughout the world; but Professor Morselli will have to concede to *seppuku* an aristocratic position among them. He maintains that "when suicide is accomplished by very painful means or at the cost of prolonged agony, in ninety-nine cases out of a hundred, it may be assigned as the act of a mind disordered by fanaticism, by madness, or by morbid excitement."[22] But a normal *seppuku* does not savour of fanaticism, or madness or excitement, utmost *sang froid* being necessary to its successful accomplishment. Of the two kinds into which Dr. Strahan [23]divides suicide, the Rational or Quasi, and the Irrational or True, *seppuku* is the best example of the former type.

From these bloody institutions, as well as from the general tenor of Bushido, it is easy to infer that the sword played an important part in social discipline and life. The saying passed as an axiom which called the sword the soul of the samurai.

---

22 Morselli, *Suicide*, p. 314

23 *Suicide and Insanity.*

CHAPTER 13

THE SWORD, THE SOUL OF
THE SAMURAI

Bushido made the sword its emblem of power and prowess. When Mahomet proclaimed that "the sword is the key of Heaven and of Hell," he only echoed a Japanese sentiment. Very early the samurai boy learned to wield it. It was a momentous occasion for him when at the age of five he was apparelled in the paraphernalia of samurai costume, placed upon a *go*-board[24] and initiated into the rights of the military profession, by having thrust into his girdle a real sword instead of the toy dirk with which he had been playing. After this first ceremony of *adoptio per arma*, he was no more to be seen outside his father's gates without this badge of his status, even though it was usually substituted for everyday wear by a gilded wooden dirk. Not many years pass before he wears constantly the genuine steel, though blunt, and then the sham arms are thrown aside and with enjoyment keener than his newly acquired blades, he marches out to try their edge on wood and stone. When he reaches man's estate, at the age of fifteen, being given independence of action, he can now pride himself

---

24 The game of *go* is sometimes called Japanese checkers, but is much more intricate than the English game. The go-board contains 361 squares and is supposed to represent a battle-field--the object of the game being to occupy as much space as possible.

upon the possession of arms sharp enough for any work. The very possession of the dangerous instrument imparts to him a feeling and an air of self-respect and, responsibility. "He beareth not the sword in vain." What he carries in his belt is a symbol of what he carries in his mind and heart,—loyalty and honour. The two swords, the longer and the shorter,—called respectively *daito* and *shoto* or *katana* and *wakizashi*,—never leave his side. When at home, they grace the most conspicuous place in the study or parlour; by night they guard his pillow within easy reach of his hand. Constant companions, they are beloved, and proper names of endearment given them. Being venerated, they are well-nigh worshipped. The Father of History has recorded as a curious piece of information that the Scythians sacrificed to an iron scimitar. Many a temple and many a family in Japan hoards a sword as an object of adoration. Even the commonest dirk has due respect paid to it. Any insult to it is tantamount to personal affront. Woe to him who carelessly steps over a weapon lying on the floor!

So precious an object cannot long escape the notice and the skill of artists nor the vanity of its owner, especially in times of peace, when it is worn with no more use than a crosier by a bishop or a sceptre by a king. Sharkskin and finest silk for hilt, silver and gold for guard, lacquer of varied hues for scabbard, robbed the deadliest weapon of half its terror; but these appurtenances are playthings compared with the blade itself.

The swordsmith was not a mere artisan but an inspired artist and his workshop a sanctuary. Daily he commenced his craft with prayer and purification, or, as the phrase was, "he committed his soul and spirit into the forging and tempering of the steel." Every swing of the sledge, every plunge into water, every friction on the grindstone, was a religious act of no slight import. Was it the spirit of the master or of his tutelary god that cast a formidable spell over our sword? Perfect as a work of art, setting at defiance its Toledo and Damascus rivals, there was more than art could impart. Its cold blade, collecting on its surface the moment it is drawn the vapour of the atmosphere; its immaculate texture, flashing light of bluish hue; its matchless edge, upon which histories and possibilities hang; the curve of its back, uniting exquisite grace with utmost strength;—all these thrill us with mixed feelings of power and beauty, of awe and terror. Harmless were its mission, if it only remained a thing of beauty and joy! But, ever within reach of the hand, it presented no small temptation for abuse. Too often did the blade flash forth from its peaceful sheath. The abuse sometimes went so far as to try the acquired steel on some harmless creature's neck.

The question that concerns us most is, however,—Did Bushido justify the promiscuous use of the weapon? The answer is unequivocally, no! As it laid great stress on its proper use, so did it denounce and abhor its misuse. A dastard or a braggart was he who brandished his weapon on undeserved occasions. A self-possessed man knows the right time to use it, and such times come but rarely. Let us listen to the late Count Katsu, who passed through one of the most turbulent times of our history, when assassinations, suicides, and other sanguinary practices were the order of the day. Endowed as he once was with almost dictatorial powers, chosen repeatedly as an object of assassination, he never tarnished his sword with blood. In relating some of his reminiscences to a friend he says, in a quaint, plebeian way peculiar to him: "I have a great dislike for killing people and so I haven't killed one single man. I have released those whose heads should have been chopped off. A friend said to me one day, 'You don't kill enough. Don't you eat pepper and egg-plants?' Well, some people are no better! But you see that fellow was slain himself. My escape may be due to my dislike of killing. I had the hilt of my sword so tightly fastened to the scabbard that it was hard to draw the blade. I made up my mind that though they cut me, I would not cut. Yes, yes! some people are truly like fleas and mosquitoes and they bite—but what does their biting amount to? It itches a little, that's all; it won't endanger life." These are the words of one whose Bushido training was tried in the fiery furnace of adversity and triumph. The popular apothegm—"To be beaten is to conquer," meaning true conquest consists in not opposing a riotous foe; and "The best won victory is that obtained without shedding of blood," and others of similar import—will show that after all the ultimate ideal of knighthood was peace.

It was a great pity that this high ideal was left exclusively to priests and moralists to preach, while the samurai went on practising and extolling martial traits. In this they went so far as to tinge the ideals of womanhood with Amazonian character. Here we may profitably devote a few paragraphs to the subject of the training and position of woman.

CHAPTER 14

THE TRAINING AND
POSITION OF WOMAN

The female half of our species has sometimes been called the paragon of paradoxes, because the intuitive working of its mind is beyond the comprehension of men's "arithemetical understanding." The Chinese ideogram denoting "the mysterious," "the unknowable," consists of two parts, one meaning "young" and the other "woman," because the physical charms and delicate thoughts of the fair sex are above the coarse mental calibre of our sex to explain.

In the Bushido ideal of woman, however, there is little mystery and only a seeming paradox. I have said that it was Amazonian, but that is only half the truth. Ideographically the Chinese represent wife by a woman holding a broom—certainly not to brandish it offensively or defensively against her conjugal ally, neither for witchcraft, but for the more harmless uses for which the besom was first invented—the idea involved being thus not less homely than the etymological derivation of the English wife (weaver) and daughter (*duhitar*, milkmaid). Without confining the sphere of woman's activity to *Kmche, Kirche, Kinder*, as the present German Kaiser is said to do, the Bushido ideal of womanhood was pre-eminently domestic. These seeming contradictions—domesticity and Amazonian traits—are not inconsistent with the Precepts of Knighthood, as we shall see.

Bushido being a teaching primarily intended for the masculine sex, the virtues it prized in woman were naturally far from being distinctly feminine. Winckelmann remarks that "the supreme beauty of Greek art is rather male than female," and Lecky adds that it was true in the moral conception of the Greeks as in their art. Bushido similarly praised those women most "who emancipated themselves from the frailty of their sex and displayed an heroic fortitude worthy of the strongest and the bravest of men."[25] Young girls, therefore, were trained to repress their feelings, to indurate their nerves, to manipulate weapons,— especially the long-handled sword called *nagi-nata*, so as to be able to hold their own against unexpected odds. Yet the primary motive for exercise of this martial character was not for use in the field; it was twofold-personal and domestic. Woman owning no suzerain of her own, formed her own body-guard. With her weapon she guarded her personal sanctity with as much zeal as her husband did his master's. The domestic utility of her warlike training was in the education of her sons, as we shall see later.

Fencing and similar exercises, if rarely of practical use, were a wholesome counterbalance to the otherwise sedentary habits of women. But these exercises were not followed only for hygienic purposes. They could be turned into use in times of need. Girls, when they reached womanhood, were presented with dirks (*kai-ken*, pocket poniards), which might be directed to the bosom of their assailants, or, if advisable, to their own. The latter was very often the case; and yet I will not judge them severely. Even the Christian conscience with its horror of self- immolation, will not be harsh with them, seeing Pelagia and Dominina, two suicides, were canonised for their purity and piety. When a Japanese Virginia saw her chastity menaced, she did not wait for her father's dagger. Her own weapon lay always in her bosom. It was a disgrace to her not to know the proper way in which she had to

25 Lecky, *History of European Morals*, ii., P. 383.

perpetrate self- destruction. For example, little as she was taught in anatomy, she must know the exact spot to cut in her throat; she must know how to tie her lower limbs together with a belt so that, whatever the agonies of death might be, her corpse be found in utmost modesty with the limbs properly composed. Is not a caution like this worthy of the Christian Perpetua or the Vestal Cornelia? I would not put such an abrupt interrogation were it not for a misconception, based on our bathing customs and other trifles, that chastity is unknown among us.[26] On the contrary, chastity was a pre-eminent virtue of the samurai woman, held above life itself. A young woman, taken prisoner, seeing herself in danger of violence at the hands of the rough soldiery, says she will obey their pleasure, provided she be first allowed to write a line to her sisters, whom war has dispersed in every direction. When the epistle is finished, off she runs to the nearest well and saves her honour by drowning. The letter she leaves behind ends with these verses:

"For fear lest clouds may dim her light,
Should she but graze this nether sphere,
The young moon poised above the height
Doth hastily betake to flight."

It would be unfair to give my readers an idea that masculinity alone was our highest ideal for woman. Far from it! Accomplishments and the gentler graces of life were required of them. Music, dancing, and literature were not neglected. Some of the finest verses in our literature were expressions of feminine sentiments; in fact, woman played an important rôle in the history of Japanese *belles-lettres*. Dancing was taught (I am speaking of samurai girls and not of *geisha*) only to smooth the angularity of their movements. Music was to regale the weary hours of their fathers and husbands; hence it was not for the technique, the art as such, that music was learned; for the ultimate object was

26 For a very sensible explanation of nudity and bathing see Finck's *Lotos Time in Japan*, pp. 286-297.

purification of heart, since it was said that no harmony of sound is attainable without the player's heart being in harmony with itself. Here again we see the same idea prevailing which we notice in the training of youths—that accomplishments were ever kept subservient to moral worth. just enough of music and dancing to add grace and brightness to life, but never to foster vanity and extravagance. I sympathise with the Persian Prince, who, when taken into a ballroom in London and asked to take part in the merriment, bluntly remarked that in his country they provided a particular set of girls to do that kind of business for them.

The accomplishments of our women were not acquired for show or social ascendancy. They were a home diversion; and if they shone in social parties, it was as the attributes of a hostess,— in other words, as a part of the household contrivance for hospitality. Domesticity guided their education. It may be said that the accomplishments of the women of Old Japan, be they martial or pacific in character, were mainly intended for the home; and, however far they might roam, they never lost sight of the hearth as the centre. It was to maintain its honour and integrity that they slaved, drudged, and gave up their lives. Night and day, in tones at once firm and tender, brave and plaintive, they sang to their little nests. As daughter, woman sacrificed herself for her father, as wife for her husband, and as mother for her son. Thus from earliest youth she was taught to deny herself. Her life was not one of independence, but of dependent service. Man's helpmeet, if her presence is helpful she stays on the stage with him: if it hinders his work, she retires behind the curtain. Not infrequently does it happen that a youth becomes enamoured of a maiden who returns his love with equal ardour, but, when she realises his interest in her makes him forgetful of his duties, disfigures her person that her attractions may cease. Adzuma, the ideal wife in the minds of samurai girls, finds herself loved by a man who is conspiring against her husband. Upon pretence of joining in the guilty plot, she manages in the dark to take her husband's place, and the sword of the lover-assassin descends upon her own devoted head. The following epistle written by the wife of a young daimio, before taking her own life, needs no comment:

"I have heard that no accident or chance ever mars the march of events here below, and that all is in accordance with a plan. To take shelter under a common bough or a drink of the same river, is alike ordained from ages prior to our birth. Since we were joined in ties of eternal wedlock, now two short years ago, my heart hath followed thee, even as its shadow followeth an object, inseparably bound heart to heart, loving and being loved. Learning but recently, however, that the coming battle is to be the last of thy labour and life, take the farewell greeting of thy loving partner. I have heard that Kowu, the mighty warrior of ancient China, lost a battle, loth to part with his favorite Gu. Yoshinaka, too, brave as he was, brought disaster to his cause, too weak to bid prompt farewell to his wife. Why should I, to whom earth no longer offers hope or joy--Why should 1 detain thee or thy thoughts by living? Why should I not, rather, await thee on the road which all mortal kind must sometime tread? Never, prithee, never, forget the many benefits which our good master Hidéyori hath heaped upon thee. The gratitude we owe him is as deep as the sea and as high as the hills."

Woman's surrender of herself to the good of her husband, home, and family, was as willing and honourable as the man's self-surrender to the good of his lord and country. Self-renunciation, without which no life- enigma can be solved, was the key-note of the loyalty of man as well as of the domesticity of woman. She was no more the slave of man than was her husband of his liege-lord, and the part she played was recognised as *naijo*, "the inner help." In the ascending scale of service stood woman, who annihilated herself for man, that he might annihilate himself for the master, that he in turn might obey Heaven. I know the weakness of this teaching and that the superiority of Christianity is nowhere more manifested than here, in that it requires of each and every living soul direct responsibility to its Creator. Nevertheless, as far as the doctrine of service—the serving of a cause higher than one's own self, even at the sacrifice of one's individuality; I say the doctrine of service, which is the greatest that Christ preached and was the sacred key-note of His mission—so far as that is concerned, Bushido was based on eternal truth.

My readers will not accuse me of undue prejudice in favour of slavish surrender of volition. I accept in a large measure the view advanced and defended with breadth of learning and profundity of thought by Hegel, that history is the unfolding and realisation of freedom. The point I wish to make is that the whole teaching of Bushido was so thoroughly imbued with the spirit of self-sacrifice, that it was required not only of woman but of man. Hence, until the influence of its precepts is entirely done away with, our society will not realise the view rashly expressed by an American exponent of woman's rights, who exclaimed, "May all the daughters of Japan rise in revolt against ancient customs!" Can such a revolt succeed? Will it improve the female status? Will the rights they gain by such a summary process repay the loss of that sweetness of disposition, that gentleness of manner, which are their present heritage? Was not the loss of domesticity on the part of Roman matrons followed by moral corruption too gross to mention? Can the American reformer assure us that a revolt of our daughters is the true course for their historical development to take? These are grave questions. Changes must and will come without revolts! In the meantime let us see whether the status of the fair sex under the Bushido regimen was really so bad as to justify a revolt.

We hear much of the outward respect European knights paid to "God and the ladies,"—the incongruity of the two terms making, Gibbon blush; we are also told by Hallam that the morality of chivalry was coarse, that gallantry implied illicit love. The effect of chivalry on the weaker vessel was food for reflection on the part of philosophers, M. Guizot contending that feudalism and chivalry wrought wholesome influences, while Mr. Spencer tells us that in a militant society (and what is feudal society if not militant?) the position of woman is necessarily low, improving only as society becomes more industrial. Now is M. Guizot's theory true of Japan, or is Mr. Spencer's? In reply I might aver that both are right. The military class in Japan was restricted to the samurai, comprising nearly two million souls. Above them were the military nobles, the *daimio*, and the court nobles, the *kugé*—these higher, sybaritical nobles being fighters only in name. Below them were masses of the common people— mechanics, tradesmen, and peasants—whose life was devoted to arts of peace. Thus what Herbert Spencer gives as the characteristics of a militant type of society may be said to have been exclusively confined to the samurai class, while those of the industrial type were applicable to the classes above and below it. This is well illustrated by the position of woman; for in no class did she experience less freedom than among the samurai. Strange to say, the lower the social class—as, for instance, among small artisans—the more equal was the position of husband and wife. Among the higher nobility, too, the difference in the relations of the sexes was less marked, chiefly because there were few occasions to bring the differences of sex into prominence, the leisurely nobleman having become literally effeminate. Thus Spencer's dictum was fully exemplified in Old Japan. As to Guizot's, those who read his presentation of a feudal community will remember that he had the higher nobility especially under consideration, so that his generalisation applies to the *daimio* and the *kugé*.

I shall be guilty of gross injustice to historical truth if my words give one a very low opinion of the status of woman under Bushido. I do not hesitate to state that she was not treated as man's equal; but, until we learn to discriminate between differences and inequalities, there will always be misunderstandings upon this subject.

When we think in how few respects men are equal among themselves, *e. g.*, before law courts or voting polls, it seems idle to trouble ourselves with a discussion on the equality of sexes. When the American Declaration of Independence said that all men were created equal, it had no reference to their mental or physical gifts; it simply repeated what Ulpian long ago announced, that before the law all men are equal. Legal rights were in this case the measure of their equality. Were the law the only scale by which to measure the position of woman in a community, it would be as easy to tell where she stands as to give her avoirdupois in pounds and ounces. But the question is: Is there a correct standard in comparing the relative social position of the sexes? Is it right, is it enough, to compare woman's status to man's, as the value of silver is compared with that of gold, and give the ratio numerically? Such a method of calculation excludes from consideration the most important kind of value which a human being possesses, namely, the intrinsic. In view of the manifold variety of requisites for making each sex fulfil its earthly mission, the standard to be adopted in measuring its relative position must be of a composite character; or to borrow from economic language, it must be a multiple standard. Bushido had a standard of its own and it was binomial. It tried to gauge the value of woman on the battle-field and by the hearth. There she counted for very little; here for all. The treatment accorded her corresponded to this double measurement:—as a social-political unit not much, while as wife and mother she received highest respect and deepest affection. Why, among so military a nation as the Romans, were their matrons so highly venerated? Was it not because they were *matrona*, mothers? Not as fighters or lawgivers, but as their mothers did men bow before them. So with us. While fathers and husbands were absent in field or camp, the government of the household was left entirely in the hands of mothers and wives. The education of the young, even their defence, was entrusted to them. The warlike exercises of women, of which I have spoken, were primarily to enable them intelligently to direct and follow the education of their children.

I have noticed a rather superficial notion prevailing among half-informed foreigners, that because the common Japanese expression for one's wife is "my rustic wife" and the like, she is despised and held in little esteem. When it is told that such phrases as "my foolish father," "my swinish son," "my awkward self," etc., are in current use, is not the answer clear enough?

To me it seems that our idea of marital union goes in some ways farther than the so-called Christian. "Man and woman shall be one flesh." The individualism of the Anglo-Saxon cannot let go of the idea that husband and wife are two persons;—hence when they disagree, their separate *rights* are recognised, and when they agree, they exhaust their vocabulary in all sorts of silly pet-names and nonsensical blandishments. It sounds highly irrational to our ears, when a husband or wife speaks to a third party of his or her other half—better or worse—as being lovely, bright, kind, and what not. Is it good taste to speak of one's self as "my bright self," "my lovely disposition," and so forth? We think praising one's own wife is praising a part of one's own self, and self-praise is regarded, to say the least, as bad taste among us,—and I hope, among Christian nations too! I have diverged at some length because the polite debasement of one's consort was a usage most in vogue among the samurai.

The Teutonic races beginning their tribal life with a superstitious awe of the fair sex (though this is really wearing off in Germany!), and the Americans beginning their social life under the painful consciousness of the numerical insufficiency of women[27] (who, now increasing, are, I am afraid, fast losing the

27 I refer to those days when girls were imported from England

prestige their colonial mothers enjoyed), the respect man pays to woman has in Western civilisation become the chief standard of morality. But in the martial ethics of Bushido, the main watershed dividing the good and the bad was sought elsewhere. It was located along the line of duty which bound man to his own divine soul and then to other souls in the five relations I 'have mentioned in the early part of this paper. Of these, we have brought to our reader's notice loyalty, the relation between one man as vassal and another as lord. Upon the rest, I have only dwelt incidentally as occasion presented itself; because they were not peculiar to Bushido. Being founded on natural affections, they could but be common to all mankind, though in some particulars they may have been accentuated by conditions which its teachings induced. In this connection there comes before me the peculiar strength and tenderness of friendship between man and man, which often added to the bond of brotherhood a romantic attachment doubtless intensified by the separation of the sexes in youth,—a separation which denied to affection the natural channel open to it in Western chivalry or in the free intercourse of Anglo-Saxon lands. I might fill pages with Japanese versions of the story of Damon and Pythias or Achilles and Patroclos, or tell in Bushido parlance of ties as sympathetic as those which bound David and Jonathan.

It is not surprising, however, that the virtues and teachings unique in the Precepts of Knighthood did not remain circumscribed to the military class.

This makes us hasten to the consideration of the influence of Bushido on the nation at large.

---

and given in marriage for so many pounds of tobacco, etc.

CHAPTER 15

THE INFLUENCE OF BUSHIDO

Thus far we have brought into view only a few of the more prominent peaks which rise above the range of knightly virtues, in themselves so much more elevated then the general level of our national life. As the sun in its rising first tips the highest peaks with russet hue, and then gradually casts its rays on the valley below, so the ethical system which first enlightened the military order drew in course of time followers from amongst the masses. Democracy raises up a natural prince for its leader, and aristocracy infuses a princely spirit among the people. Virtues are no less contagious than vices. "There needs but one wise man in a company, and all are wise, so rapid is the contagion," says Emerson. No social class or caste can resist the diffusive power of moral influence.

Prate as we may of the triumphant march of Anglo-Saxon liberty, rarely has it received impetus from the masses. Was it not rather the work of the squires and *gentlemen*? Very truly does M. Taine say, "These three syllables, as used across the channel, summarise the history of English society." Democracy may make self-confident retorts to such a statement and fling back the question—"When Adam delved and Eve span, where then was the gentleman?" All the more pity that a gentleman was not present in Eden! The first parents missed him sorely and paid a high price for his absence. Had he been there, not only would the garden have been more tastefully dressed, but they would have learned without painful experience that disobedience to Jehovah was disloyalty and dishonour, treason and rebellion.

What Japan was she owed to the samurai. They were not only the flower of the nation, but its root as well. All the gracious gifts of Heaven flowed through them. Though they kept themselves socially aloof from the populace, they set a moral standard for them and guided them by their example. I admit Bushido had its esoteric and exoteric teachings; these were eudemonic, looking after the welfare and happiness of the commonalty; those were aretaic, emphasising the practice of virtues for their own sake.

In the most chivalrous days of Europe, knights formed numerically but a small fraction of the population, but, as Emerson says,—"In English literature half the drama and all the novels, from Sir Philip Sidney to Sir Walter Scott, paint this figure (gentleman)." Write in place of Sidney and Scott, Chikamatsu and Bakin, and you have in a nutshell the main features of the literary history of Japan.

The innumerable avenues of popular amusement and instruction-the theatres, the story-tellers' booths, the preacher's dais, the musical recitations, the novels,—have taken for their chief theme the stories of the samurai. The peasants around the open fire in their huts never tire of repeating the achievements of Yoshitsuné and his faithful retainer Benkéi, or of the two brave Soga brothers; the dusky urchins listen with gaping mouths until the last stick bums out and the fire dies in its embers, still leaving their hearts aglow with tale that is told. The clerks and the shop boys, after their day's work is over and the *amado*[28] of the store are closed, gather together to relate the story of Nobunaga and Hidéyoshi far into the night, until slumber overtakes their weary eyes and transports them from the drudgery of the counter to the exploits of the field. The very babe just beginning to toddle is taught to lisp the adventures of Momotaro, the daring conqueror of

28 Outside shutters.

ogreland. Even girls are so imbued with the love of knightly deeds and virtues that, like Desdemona, they would seriously incline to devour with greedy ear the romance of the samurai.

The samurai grew to be the *beau ideal* of the whole race. "As among flowers the cherry is queen, so among men the samurai is lord," so sang the populace. Debarred from commercial pursuits, the military class itself did not aid commerce; but there was no channel of human activity, no avenue of thought, which did not receive in some measure an impetus from Bushido. Intellectual and moral Japan was directly or indirectly the work of Knighthood.

Mr. Mallock, in his exceedingly suggestive book, *Aristocracy and Evolution*, has eloquently told us that "social evolution, in so far as it is other than biological, may be defined as the unintended result of the intentions of great men"; further, that historical progress is produced by a struggle "not among the community generally, to live, but a struggle amongst a small section of the community to lead, to direct, to employ, the majority in the best way." Whatever may be said about the soundness of his argument, these statements are amply verified in the part played by bushi in the social progress, so far as it went, of our Empire.

How the spirit of Bushido permeated all social classes is also shown in the development of a certain order of men, known as *otoko-daté*, the natural leaders of democracy. Staunch fellows were they, every inch of them strong with the strength of massive manhood. At once the spokesmen and the guardians of popular rights, they had each a following of hundreds and thousands of souls who proffered, in the same fashion that samurai did to *daimio*, the willing service of "limb and life, of body, chattels, and earthly honour." Backed by a vast multitude of rash and impetuous working men, these born "bosses" formed a formidable check to the rampancy of the two-sworded order.

In manifold ways has Bushido filtered down from the social class where it originated, and acted as leaven among the masses, furnishing a moral standard for the whole people. The Precepts of Knighthood, begun at first as the glory of the *élite*, became in time an aspiration and inspiration to the nation at large; and though the populace could not attain the moral height of those loftier souls, yet *Yamato Damashii*, the Soul of Japan, ultimately came to express the *Volksgeist* of the Island Realm. If religion is no more than "Morality touched by emotion," as Matthew Arnold defines it, few ethical systems are better entitled to the rank of religion than Bushido. Motoöri has put the mute utterance of the nation into words when he sings:

> *"Isles of blest Japan!*
> *Should your Yamato spirit*
> *Strangers seek to scan,*
> *Say—scenting morn's sunlit air,*
> *Blows the cherry wild and fair!"*

Yes, the *sakura*[29] has for ages been the favourite of our people and the emblem of our character. Mark particularly the terms of definition which the poet uses, the words the *wild cherry flower scenting the morning sun*.

The Yamato spirit is not a tame, tender plant, but a wild—in the sense of natural—growth; it is indigenous to the soil; its accidental qualities it may share with the flowers of other lands, but in its essence it remains the original, spontaneous outgrowth of our clime. But its nativity is not its sole claim to our affection. The refinement and grace of its beauty appeal to *our* æsthetic sense as no other flower can. We cannot share the admiration of the Europeans for their roses, which lack the simplicity of our flower. Then, too, the thorns that are hidden beneath the sweetness of the rose, the tenacity with which she clings to life, as though loth or afraid to die rather than drop untimely, preferring to rot on her stem; her showy colours and heavy odours—all these are traits so unlike our flower, which carries no dagger or poison under

---

29 *Cerasus pseudo-cerasus*, Lindley.

its beauty, which is ever ready to depart life at the call of nature, whose colours are never gorgeous, and whose light fragrance never palls. Beauty of colour and of form is limited in its showing; it is a fixed quality of existence, whereas fragrance is volatile, ethereal as the breathing of life. So in all religious ceremonies frankincense and myrrh play a prominent part. There is something spirituelle in redolence. When the delicious perfume of the sakura quickens the morning air, as the sun in its course rises to illumine first the isles of the Far East, few sensations are more serenely exhilarating than to inhale, as it were, the very breath of beauteous day.

When the Creator Himself is pictured as making new resolutions in His heart upon smelling a sweet savour (Gen. viii. 21), is it any wonder that the sweet-smelling season of the cherry blossom should call forth the whole nation from their little habitations? Blame them not, if for a time their limbs forget their toil and moil and their hearts their pangs and sorrows. Their brief pleasure ended, they return to their daily task with new strength and new resolutions. Thus in ways more than one is the sakura the flower of the nation.

Is, then, this flower, so sweet and evanescent, blown whithersoever the wind listeth, and, shedding a puff of perfume, ready to vanish forever, is this flower the type of the Yamato-spirit? Is the soul of Japan so frailly mortal?

CHAPTER 16

IS BUSHIDO STILL ALIVE?

Has Western civilisation, in its march through our land, already wiped out every trace of its ancient discipline? It were a sad thing if a nation's soul could die so fast. That were a poor soul that could succumb so easily to extraneous influences.

The aggregate of psychological elements which constitute a national character is as tenacious as the "irreducible elements of species, of the fins of the fish, of the beak of the bird, of the tooth of the carnivorous animal." In his recent book, full of shallow asseverations and brilliant generalisations, M. LeBon[30] says: "The discoveries due to the intelligence are the common patrimony of humanity; qualities or defects of character constitute the exclusive patrimony of each people: they are the firm rock which the waters must wash day by day for centuries before they can wear away even its external asperities." These are strong words and would be highly worth pondering over, provided there were qualities and defects of character which *constitute the exclusive patrimony* of each people. Schematising theories of this sort had been advanced long before LeBon began to write his book, and they were exploded long ago by Theodor Waitz and Hugh Murray. In studying the various virtues instilled by Bushido, we have drawn upon European sources for comparison and illustrations, and

30 *The Psychology of Peoples*, p. 33.

we have seen that no one quality of character was its *exclusive* patrimony. It is true the aggregate of moral qualities presents a quite unique aspect. It is this aggregate which Emerson names a "compound result into which every great force enters as an ingredient." But, instead of making it, as LeBon does, an exclusive patrimony of a race or people, the Concord philosopher calls it "an element which unites the most forcible persons of every country; makes them intelligible and agreeable to each other; and is somewhat so precise that it is at once felt if an individual lack the Masonic sign."

The character which Bushido stamped on our nation and on the samurai in particular, cannot be said to form "an irreducible element of species," but nevertheless as to the vitality which it retains there is no doubt. Were Bushido a mere physical force, the momentum it has gained in the last seven hundred years could not stop so abruptly. Were it transmitted only by heredity, its influence must be immensely widespread. Just think, as M. Cheysson, a French economist, has calculated, that, supposing there be three generations in a century, "each of us would have in his veins the blood of at least twenty millions of the people living in the year 1000 A.D." The merest peasant that grubs the soil, "bowed by the weight of centuries," has in his veins the blood of ages, and is thus brother to us as much as "to the ox."

An unconscious and irresistible power, Bushido has been moving the nation and individuals. It was an honest confession of the race when Yoshida Shôin, one of the most brilliant pioneers of Modern Japan, wrote on the eve of his execution the following stanza:

> *"Full well I knew this course must end in death;*
> *It was Yamato spirit urged me on*
> *To dare whate'er betide."*

Unformulated, Bushido was and still is the animating spirit, the motor force of our country.

Mr. Ransome says that "there are three distinct Japans in existence side by side today,—the old, which has not wholly died out; the new, hardly yet born except in spirit; and the transition, passing now through its most critical throes." While this is very true in most respects, and particularly as regards tangible and concrete institutions, the statement, as applied to fundamental ethical notions, requires some modification; for Bushido, the maker and product of Old Japan, is still the guiding principle of the transition and will prove the formative force of the new era.

The great statesmen who steered the ship of our state through the hurricane of the Restoration and the whirlpool of national rejuvenation, were men who knew no other moral teaching than the Precepts of Knighthood. Some writers[31] have lately tried to prove that the Christian missionaries contributed an appreciable quota to the making of New Japan. I would fain render honour to whom honour is due; but this honour can as yet hardly be accorded to the good missionaries. More fitting it will be to their profession to stick to the scriptural injunction of preferring one another in honour, than to advance a claim in which they have no proofs to back them. For myself, I believe that Christian missionaries are doing great things for Japan—in the domain of education, and especially of moral education:—only, the mysterious though not the less certain working of the Spirit is still hidden in divine secrecy. Whatever they do is still of indirect effect. No, as yet Christian missions have effected but little visible in moulding the character of New Japan. No, it was Bushido, pure and simple, that urged us on for weal or woe. Open the biographies of the makers of Modern Japan--of Sakuma, of Saigo, of Okubo, of Kido, not

31 Speer: *Missions and Politics in Asia*, Lecture IV., pp. 189-192; Dennis: *Christian Missions and Social Progress*, vol. i., p. 32, vol. ii., 70, etc.

to mention the reminiscences of living men such as Ito, Okuma, Itagaki, etc.,—and you will find that it was under the impetus of samuraihood that they thought and wrought. When Mr. Henry Norman declared, after his study and observation of the Far East, that the only respect in which Japan differed from other oriental despotisms lay in "the ruling influence among her people of the strictest, loftiest, and the most punctilious codes of honour that man has ever devised," he touched the mainspring which has made New Japan what she is, and which will make her what she is destined to be.[32]

The transformation of Japan is a fact patent to the whole world. Into a work of such magnitude various motives naturally entered; but if one were to name the principal, one would not hesitate to name Bushido. When we opened the whole country to foreign trade, when we introduced the latest improvements in every department of life, when we began to study Western politics and sciences, our guiding motive was not the development of our physical resources and the increase of wealth; much less was it a blind imitation of Western customs.

A close observer of oriental institutions and peoples has written:

"We are told every day how Europe has influenced Japan, and forget that the change in those islands was entirely self-generated, that Europeans did not teach Japan, but that Japan of herself chose to learn from Europe methods of organisation, civil and military, which have so far proved successful. She imported European mechanical science, as the Turks years before imported European artillery. That is not exactly influence," continues Mr. Townsend, "unless, indeed, England is influenced by purchasing tea in China. Where is the European apostle," asks our author, "or philosopher or statesman or agitator, who has re-made Japan?"[33]

32 *The Far East*, p. 375.

33 Meredith Townsend, *Asia and Europe*, p. 28.

Mr. Townsend has well perceived that the spring of action which brought about the changes in Japan lay entirely within our own selves; and if he had only probed into our psychology, his keen powers of observation would easily have convinced him that this spring was no other than Bushido. The sense of honour which cannot bear being looked down upon as an inferior power,—that was the strongest of motives. Pecuniary or industrial considerations were awakened later in the process of transformation.

The influence of Bushido is still so palpable that he who runs may read. A glimpse into Japanese life will make it manifest. Read Hearn, the most eloquent and truthful interpreter of the Japanese mind, and you see the working of that mind to be an example of the working of Bushido. The universal politeness of the people, which is the legacy of knightly ways, is too well known to be repeated anew. The physical endurance, fortitude, and bravery that "the little Jap" possesses, were sufficiently proved in the Chino-Japanese war.[34] "Is there any nation more loyal and patriotic?" is a question asked by many; and for the proud answer, "There is not," we must thank the Precepts of Knighthood.

On the other hand, it is fair to recognise that for the very faults and defects of our character, Bushido is largely responsible. Our lack of abstruse philosophy—while some of our young men have already gained international reputation in scientific researches, not one has achieved anything in philosophical lines—is traceable to the neglect of metaphysical training under Bushido's regimen of education. Our sense of honour is responsible for our exaggerated sensitiveness and touchiness; and if there is the conceit in us with which some foreigners charge us, that, too, is a pathological outcome of honour.

---

34 Among other works on the subject, read Eastlake and Yamada on *Heroic Japan*, and Diosy on *The New Far East*.

Have you seen in your tour of Japan many a young man with unkempt hair, dressed in shabbiest garb, carrying in his hand a large cane or a book, stalking about the streets with an air of utter indifference to mundane things? He is the *shoéi* (student), to whom the earth is too small and the heavens are not high enough. He has his own theories of the universe and of life. He dwells in castles of air and feeds on ethereal words of wisdom. In his eyes beams the fire of ambition; his mind is athirst for knowledge. Penury is only a stimulus to drive him onward; worldly goods are in his sight shackles to his character. He is the repository of loyalty and patriotism. He is the self-imposed guardian of national honour. With all his virtues and his faults, he is the last fragment of Bushido.

Deep-rooted and powerful as is still the effect of Bushido, I have said that it is an unconscious and mute influence. The heart of the people responds, without knowing a reason why, to any appeal made to what it has inherited, and hence the same moral idea expressed in a newly translated term and in an old Bushido term, has a vastly different degree of efficacy. A backsliding Christian, whom no pastoral persuasion could help from downward tendency, was reverted from his course by an appeal made to his loyalty, the fidelity he once swore to his Master. The word "Loyalty" revived all the noble sentiments that were permitted to grow lukewarm. A party of unruly youths engaged in a long-continued "students' strike" in a college, on account of their dissatisfaction with a certain teacher, disbanded at two simple questions put by the Director,— "Is your professor a worthy character? If so, you ought to respect him and keep him in the school. Is he weak? If so, it is not manly to push a falling man." The scientific incapacity of the professor, which was the beginning of the trouble, dwindled into insignificance in comparison with the moral issues hinted at. By arousing the sentiments nurtured by Bushido, moral renovation of great magnitude can be accomplished.

One cause of the failure of mission work is that most of the missionaries are entirely ignorant of our history—"What do we care for heathen records?" some say—and consequently estrange their religion from the habits of thought we and our forefathers have been accustomed to for centuries past. Mocking a nation's history?—as though the career of any people even of the lowest African savages possessing no record—were not a page in the general history of mankind, written by the hand of God Himself. The very lost races are a palimpsest to be deciphered by a seeing eye. To a philosophic and pious mind the races themselves are marks of Divine chirography clearly traced in black and white as on their skin; and if this simile holds good, the yellow race forms a precious page inscribed in hieroglyphics of gold! Ignoring the past career of a people, missionaries claim that Christianity is a new religion, whereas, to my mind, it is an "old, old story," which, if presented in intelligible words,— that is to say, if expressed in the vocabulary familiar in the moral development of a people,— will find easy lodgment in their hearts, irrespective of race or nationality. Christianity in its American or English form—with more of Anglo-Saxon freaks and fancies than grace and purity of its Founder—is a poor scion to graft on Bushido stock. Should the propagator of the new faith uproot the entire stock, root, and branches, and plant the seeds of the Gospel on the ravaged soil? Such a heroic process may be possible—in Hawaii, where, it is alleged, the Church militant had complete success in amassing spoils of wealth itself, and in annihilating the aboriginal race; such a process is most decidedly impossible in Japan—nay, it is a process which Jesus Himself would never have adopted in founding His kingdom on earth.

It behooves us to take more to heart the following words of a saintly man, devout Christian, and profound scholar:

"Men have divided the world into heathen and Christian, without considering how much good may have been hidden in the one or how much evil may have been mingled with the other. They have compared the best part of themselves with the worst of their neighbours, the ideal of Christianity with the corruption of Greece or of the East. They have not aimed at impartiality, but have been contented to accumulate all that could be said in praise of their own, and in dispraise of other forms of religion."[35]

But, whatever may be the error committed by individuals, there is little doubt that the fundamental principle of the religion they profess is a power which we must take into account in reckoning the future of Bushido, whose days seem to be already numbered. Ominous signs are in the air that betoken its future. Not only signs, but redoubtable forces are at work to threaten it.

---

35 Jowett, *Sermons on Faith and Doctrine*, ii.

CHAPTER 17

THE FUTURE OF BUSHIDO

Few historical comparisons can be more judiciously made than between the Chivalry of Europe and the Bushido of Japan, and, if history repeats itself, it certainly will do with the fate of the latter what it did with that of the former. The particular and local causes for the decay of chivalry which St. Palaye gives, have, of course, little application to Japanese conditions; but the larger and more general causes that helped to undermine knighthood and chivalry in and after the Middle Ages are as surely working for the decline of Bushido.

One remarkable difference between the experience of Europe and of Japan is, that whereas in Europe, when chivalry was weaned from feudalism and was adopted by the Church, it obtained a fresh lease of life, in Japan no religion was large enough to nourish it; hence, when the mother institution, feudalism, was gone, Bushido, left an orphan, had to shift for itself. The present elaborate military organisation might take it under its patronage, but we know that modern warfare can afford little room for its continuous growth. Shintoism, which fostered it in its infancy, is itself superannuated. The hoary sages of ancient China are being supplanted by the intellectual parvenu of the type of Bentham and Mill. Moral theories of a comfortable kind, flattering to the Chauvinistic tendencies of the time, and therefore thought well adapted to the need of this day, have been invented and propounded; but as yet we hear only their shrill voices echoing through the columns of yellow journalism.

Principalities and powers are arrayed against the Precepts of Knighthood. Already, as Veblen says, "the decay of the ceremonial code—or, as it is otherwise called, the vulgarisation of life—among the industrial classes proper, has become one of the chief enormities of latter-day civilisation in the eyes of all persons of delicate sensibilities." The irresistible tide of triumphant democracy, which can tolerate no form or shape of trust,—and Bushido was a trust organised by those who monopolised reserve capital of intellect and culture, fixing the grades and value of moral qualities,—is alone powerful enough to engulf the remnant of Bushido. The present societary forces are antagonistic to petty class spirit, and chivalry is, as Freeman severely criticises, a class spirit. Modem society, if it pretends to any unity, cannot admit "purely personal obligations devised in the interests of an exclusive class."36 Add to this the progress of popular instruction, of industrial arts and habits, of wealth and city-life,—then we can easily see that neither the keenest cuts of samurai sword nor the sharpest shafts shot from Bushido's boldest bows can aught avail. The state built upon the rock of Honour and fortified by the same shall we call it the *Ehrenstaat*, or, after the manner of Carlyle, the Heroarchy?—is fast falling into the hands of quibbling lawyers and gibbering politicians armed with logic-chopping engines of war. The words which a great thinker used in speaking of Theresa and Antigone may aptly be repeated of the samurai, that "the medium in which their ardent deeds took shape is forever gone."

Alas for knightly virtues! alas for samurai pride! Morality ushered into the world with the sound of bugles and drums, is destined to fade away as "the captains and the kings depart."

---

36 *Norman Conquest*, vol. v., p. 482.

If history can teach us anything, the state built on martial virtues—be it a city like Sparta or an Empire like Rome—can never make on earth a "continuing city." Universal and natural as is the fighting instinct in man, fruitful as it has proved to be of noble sentiments and manly virtues, it does not comprehend the whole man. Beneath the instinct to fight there lurks a diviner instinct—to love. We have seen that Shintoism, Mencius, and Wan Yang Ming, have all clearly taught it; but Bushido and all other militant types of ethics, engrossed doubtless, with questions of immediate practical need, too often forgot duly to emphasise this fact.

Life has grown larger in these latter times. Callings nobler and broader than a warrior's claim our attention to-day. With an enlarged view of life, with the growth of democracy, with better knowledge of other peoples and nations, the Confucian idea of benevolence—dare I also add the Buddhist idea of pity?—will expand into the Christian conception of love. Men have become more than subjects, having grown to the estate of citizens; nay, they are more than citizens —being men. Though war clouds hang heavy upon our horizon, we will believe that the wings of the angel of peace can disperse them. The history of the world confirms the prophecy that "the meek shall inherit the earth." A nation that sells its birthright of peace, and backslides from the front rank of industrialism into the file of fillibusterism, makes a poor bargain indeed!

When the conditions of society are so changed that they have become not only adverse but hostile to Bushido, it is time for it to prepare for an honourable burial. It is just as difficult to point out when chivalry dies, as to determine the exact time of its inception. Dr. Miller says that chivalry was formally abolished in the year 1559, when Henry II. of France was slain in a tournament. With us, the edict formally abolishing feudalism in 1870 was the signal to toll the knell of Bushido. The edict, issued five years later, prohibiting the wearing of swords, rang out the old, "the unbought grace of life, the cheap defence of nations, the nurse of manly sentiment and heroic enterprise," it rang in the new age of "sophisters, economists, and calculators."

It has been said that Japan won her late war with China by means of Murata guns and Krupp cannon; it has been said the victory was the work of a modern school-system; but these are less than half-truths. Does ever a piano, be it of the choicest workmanship of Ehrbar or Steinway burst forth into the Rhapsodies of Liszt or the Sonatas of Beethoven, without a master's hand? Or, if guns win battles, why did not Louis Napoleon beat the Prussians with his *Mitrailleuse*, or the Spaniards with their Mausers the Filipinos, whose arms were no better than the old-fashioned Remingtons? Needless to repeat what has grown a trite saying,—that it is the spirit that quickeneth, without which the best of implements profiteth but little. The most improved guns and cannon do not shoot of their own accord; the most modern educational system does not make a coward a hero. No! What won the battles on the Yalu, in Corea and Manchuria, were the ghosts of our fathers, guiding our hands and beating in our hearts. They are not dead, those ghosts, the spirits of our warlike ancestors. To those who have eyes to see, they are clearly visible. Scratch a Japanese of the most advanced ideas, and he will show a samurai. The great inheritance of honour, of valour, and of all martial virtues is, as Professor Cramb very fitly expresses it, "but ours on trust, the fief inalienable of the dead and of the generations to come," and the summons of the present is to guard this heritage, nor to bate one jot of the ancient spirit; the summons of the future will be so to widen its scope as to apply it in all walks and relations of life.

It has been predicted—and predictions have been corroborated by the events of the last half-century—that the moral system of Feudal Japan, like its castles and its armouries, will crumble into dust, and new ethics rise phoenix-like to lead New Japan in her path of progress. Desirable and probable as the fulfilment of such a prophecy is, we must not forget that a phœnix rises only from its own ashes, and that it is not a bird of passage, neither does it fly on pinions borrowed from other birds. "The Kingdom of God is within you." It does not come rolling down the mountains, however lofty; it does not come sailing across the seas, however broad. "God has granted," says the Koran, "to every people a prophet in its own tongue." The seeds of the Kingdom, as vouched for and apprehended by the Japanese mind, blossomed in Bushido. Now its days are closing—sad to say, before its full fruition—and we turn in every direction for other sources of sweetness and light, of strength and comfort, but among them there is as yet nothing found to take its place. The profit-and-loss philosophy of utilitarians and materialists finds favour among logic-choppers with half a soul. The only other ethical system which is powerful enough to cope with utilitarianism and materialism is Christianity, in comparison with which Bushido, it must be confessed, is like "a dimly burning wick" which the Messiah was proclaimed not to quench, but to fan into a flame. Like His Hebrew precursors, the prophets—notably Isaiah, Jeremiah, Amos, and Habakkuk— Bushido laid particular stress on the moral conduct of rulers and public men and of nations, whereas the ethics of Christ, which deal almost solely with individuals and His personal followers, will find more and more practical application as individualism, in its capacity of a moral factor, grows in potency. The domineering, self-assertive, so- called master-morality of Nietsche, itself akin in some respects to Bushido, is, if I am not greatly mistaken, a passing phase or temporary reaction against what he terms, by morbid distortion, the humble, self- denying slave-morality of the Nazarene.

Christianity and materialism (including utilitarianism)—or will the future reduce them to still more archaic forms of Hebraism and

Hellenism?—will divide the world between them. Lesser systems of morals will ally themselves to either side for their preservation. On which side will Bushido enlist? Having no set dogma or formula to defend, it can afford to disappear as an entity; like the cherry blossom. it is willing to die at the first gust of the morning breeze. But a total extinction will never be its lot. Who can say that stoicism is dead? It is dead as a system; but it is alive as a virtue: its energy and vitality are still felt through many channels of life—in the philosophy of Western nations, in the jurisprudence of all the civilised world. Nay, wherever man struggles to raise himself above himself, wherever his spirit masters his flesh by his own exertions, there we see the immortal discipline of Zeno at work.

Bushido as an independent code of ethics may vanish, but its power will not perish from the earth; its schools of martial prowess or civic honour may be demolished, but its light and its glory will long survive their ruins. Like its symbolic flower, after it is blown to the four winds, it will still bless mankind with the perfume with which it will enrich life. Ages after, when its customaries will have been buried and its very name forgotten, its odours will come floating in the air as from a far-off, unseen hill, "the wayside gaze beyond";—then in the beautiful language of the Quaker poet,

> "The traveller owns the grateful sense
> Of sweetness near, he knows not whence,
> And, pausing, takes with forehead bare
> The benediction of the air."

LIST OF TITLES WITH ISBN NO.

ISBN	TITLE
9788194914129	1984
9789390575220	1984 & Animal Farm (2In1)
9789390575572	1984 & Animal Farm (2In1): The International Best-Selling Classics
9789390575848	35 Sonnets
9789390575329	A Clergyman's Daughter
9789390575923	A Study In Scarlet
9789390896097	A Tale Of Two Cities
9789390896837	Abide in Christ
9789390896202	Abraham Lincoln
9789390896912	Absolute Surrender
9789390896608	African American Classic Collection
9789390575305	Aldous Huxley: The Collected Works
9789390896141	An Autobiography of M. K. Gandhi
9789390575886	Animal Farm
9789390575619	Animal Farm & The Great Gatsby (2In1)
9789390575626	Animal Farm & We
9789390896158	Anna Karenina
9789390575534	Antic Hay
9789390896165	Antony & Cleopatra
9789390896172	As I Lay Dying
9789390896226	As You like it
9789390575671	At Your Command
9789390575350	Awakened Imagination
9789390575114	Be What You Wish
9789390896233	Believe In yourself
9789390896998	Best of Charles Darwin: The Origin of Species & Autobiography
9789390896684	Best Of Horror : Dracula And Frankenstein
9789390575503	Best Of Mark Twain (The Adventures of Tom Sawyer AND The Adventures of Huckleberry Finn)
9789390896769	Black History Collection
9789390575756	Brave New World, Animal Farm & 1984 (3in1)

9789390896240	Brother Karamzov
9789390575053	Bulleh Shah Poetry
9789390575725	Burmese Days
9789390896257	Bushido
9789390896066	Can't Hurt Me
9788194914112	Chanakya Neeti: With The Complete Sutras
9789390896042	Crime and Punishment
9789390575527	Crome Yellow
9789390575046	Down and Out in Paris and London
9789390896844	Dracula
9789390575442	Emersons Essays: The Complete First & Second Series (Self-Reliance & Other Essays)
9789390575749	Emma
9789390575817	Essential Tozer Collection - The Pursuit of God & The Purpose of Man
9789390896578	Fascism What It Is and How to Fight It
9789390575688	Feeling is the Secret
9789390575190	Five Lessons
9789390575954	Frankenstein
9789390575237	Franz Kafka: Collected Works
9789390575282	Franz Kafka: Short Stories
9789390575060	George Orwell Collected Works
9789390575077	George Orwell Essays
9789390575213	George Orwell Poems
9788194914150	Greatest Poetry Ever Written Vol 1
9788194914143	Greatest Poetry Ever Written Vol 1
9789390896301	Gulliver's Travel
9789390575961	Gunaho Ka Devta
9789390575893	H. P. Lovecraft Selected Stories Vol 1
9789390575978	H. P. Lovecraft Selected Stories Vol 2
9789390896059	Hamlet
9789390575022	His Last Bow: Some Reminiscences of Sherlock Holmes
9789390896134	History of Western Philosophy
9789390575121	Homage To Catalonia

9789390896219	How to develop self-confidence and Improve public Speaking
9789390896295	How to enjoy your life and your Job
9789390575633	How to own your own mind
9789390896318	How to read Human Nature
9789390896325	How to sell your way through the life
9789390896370	How to use the laws of mind
9789390896387	How to use the power of prayer
9789390896028	How to win friends & Influence People
9788194824176	How To Win Friends and Influence People
9789390896103	Humility The Beauty of Holiness
9789390896653	Imperialism the Highest Stage of Capitalism
9789390575084	In Our Time
9789390575169	In Our Time & Three Stories and Ten poems
9789390575145	James Allen: The Collected Works
9789390896189	Jesus Himself
9789390575480	Jo's Boys
9789390896394	Julius Caesar
9789390575404	Keep the Aspidistra Flying
9789390896400	Kidnapped
9789390896424	King Lear
9789390575824	Lady Susan
9789390896455	Law of Success
9789390896264	Lincoln The Unknown
9789390575565	Little Men
9789390575640	Little Women
9788194914174	Lost Horizon
9789390896462	Macbeth
9789390896929	Man Eaters of Kumaon
9789390896523	Man The Dwelling Place of God
9789390896349	Man The Dwelling Place of God
9789390575909	Mansfield Park
9788194914136	Manto Ki 25 Sarvshreshth Kahaniya
9789390896509	Marxism, Anarchism, Communism
9789390575664	Mathematical Principles of Natural Philosophy

9788194914198	Meditations
9789390575800	Mein Kampf
9789390575794	Memory How To Develop, Train, And Use It
9789390896486	Mind Power
9789390896585	Money
9789390575039	Mortal Coils
9789390575770	My Life and Work
9789390896035	Narrative of the Life of Frederick Douglass
9789390575152	Neville Goddard: The Collected Works
9789390575985	Northanger Abbey
9789390896530	Notes From Underground
9789390896547	Oliver Twist
9789390575459	On War
9789390575541	One, None and a Hundred Thousand
9789390896554	Othelo
9789390575435	Out Of This World
9789390575015	Persuasion
9789390575510	Prayer The Art Of Believing
9789390575091	Pride and Prejudice
9789390896561	Psychic Perception
9789390575381	Rabindranath Tagore - 5 Best Short Stories Vol 2
9789390575367	Rabindranath Tagore - Short Stories (Masters Collections Including The Childs Return)
9789390575374	Rabindranath Tagore 5 Best Short Stories Vol 1 (Including The Childs Return
9789390896622	Romeo & Juliet
9789390896127	Sanatana Dharma
9789390575596	Seedtime & Harvest
9789390896639	Selected Stories of Guy De Maupassant
9789390575206	Self-Reliance & Other Essays
9789390575176	Sense and Sensibility
9789390575299	Shyamchi Aai
9789390896738	Socialism Utopian and Scientific
9789390896646	Success Through a Positive Mental Attitude
9789390575428	The Adventures of Huckleberry Finn

9789390575183	The Adventures of Sherlock Holmes
9789390575343	The Adventures of Tom Sawyer
9789390896691	The Alchemy Of Happiness
9789390575862	The Art Of Public Speaking
9789390896288	The Autobiography Of Charles Darwin
9788194914181	The Best of Franz Kafka: The Metamorphosis & The Trial
9789390575008	The Call Of Cthulhu and Other Weird Tales
9789390575107	The Case-Book of Sherlock Holmes
9789390896110	The Castle Of Otranto
9789390896745	The Communist Manifesto
9789390575589	The Complete Fiction of H. P. Lovecraft
9789390575497	The Complete Works of Florence Scovel Shinn
9789390896820	The Conquest of Breard
9789390896813	The Diary of a Young Girl
9789390896332	The Diary of a Young Girl The Definitive Edition of the Worlds Most Famous Diary
9789390575701	The Great Gatsby, Animal Farm & 1984 (3In1)
9789390575312	The Greatest Works Of George Orwell (5 Books) Including 1984 & Non-Fiction
9789390575992	The Hound of Baskervilles
9789390896707	The Idiot
9789390896714	The Invisible Man
9789390575657	The Knowledge of the holy
9789390575558	The Law & the Promise
9789390896721	The Law Of Attraction
9789390896776	The Leader in you
9789390896363	The Life of Christ
9789390896196	The Man-Eating Leopard of Rudraprayag
9789390896783	The Master Key to Riches
9789390575268	The Memoirs Of Sherlock Holmes
9789390896479	The Midsummer Night's Dream
9789390575466	The Mill On The Floss
9789390896790	The Miracles of your mind
9789390896660	The Mutual Aid A Factor in Evolution
9789390896448	The Origin of Species

ISBN	Title
9789390896905	The Peter Kropotkin Anthology The Conquest of Bread & Mutual Aid A Factor of Evolution
9789390896806	The Picture of Dorian Gray
9789390896271	The Picture of Dorian Gray
9789390575275	The Power Of Awareness
9789390896356	The Power of Concentration
9788194824169	The Power of Positive Thinking
9789390575411	The Power of the Spoken Word
9788194914105	The Power Of Your Subconscious Mind
9789390896899	The Power of Your Subconscious Mind
9789390896417	The Principles of Communism
9789390575787	The Psychology Of Mans Possible Evolution
9789390896615	The Psychology of Salesmanship
9789390575732	The Pursuit of God
9789390575398	The Pursuit of Happiness
9789390896851	The Quick and Easy Way to effective Speaking
9789390575947	The Return Of Sherlock Holmes
9789390575138	The Road To Wigan Pier
9789390896981	The Root of the Righteous
9789390575855	The Science Of Being Well
9788194914167	The Science Of Getting Rich, The Science Of Being Great & The Science Of Being Well (3In1)
9789390896011	The Screwtape Letters
9789390896073	The Screwtape Letters
9789390575336	The Secret Door to Success
9789390575695	The Secret Of Imagining
9789390896868	The Secret Of Success
9789390896431	The Seven Last Words
9789390575930	The Sign of the Four
9789390896004	The Sonnets
9789390896516	The Souls of Black Folk
9789390896875	The Sound and The Fury
9789390575244	The State and Revolution
9789390896882	The Story of My Life
9789390896936	The Story Of Oriental Philosophy

9789390896752	The Strange Case of Dr. Jekyll and Mr. Hyde
9789390896943	The Tempest
9789390575916	The Valley Of Fear
9789390575879	The Wind in the willows
9789390896080	The Wind in the willows
9789390575763	Their eyes were watching gofd
9789390575831	Three Stories
9789390896950	Twelfth Night
9789390896592	Twelve Years a Slave
9789390896677	Up from Slavery
9789390896974	Value Price and Profit
9789390896967	Wake Up and Live
9789390896493	With Christ in the School of Prayer
9789390575602	Your Faith is Your Fortune
9789390575473	Your Infinite Power To Be Rich
9789390575251	Your Word is Your Wand
9789390575718	Youth
9789391316099	A Christmas Carol
9789391316105	A Doll's House
9789391316501	A Passage to India
9789391316709	A Portrait of the Artist as a Young Man
9789391316112	A Tale of Two Cities
9789391316747	A Tear and a Smile
9789391316167	Agnes Gray
9789391316174	Alice's Adventures in Wonderland
9789391316136	Anandamath
9789391316181	Anne Of Green Gables
9789391316754	Anthem
9789391316198	Around The World in 80 Days
9789391316013	As A Man Thinketh
9789391316242	Autobiography of a Yogi
9789391316266	Beyond Good and Evil
9789391316761	Bleak House
9789391316778	Chitra, a Play in One Act
9789391316310	David Copperfield

9789391316075	Demian
9789391316785	Dubliners
9789391316051	Favourite Tales from the Arabian Nights
9789391316235	Gitanjali
9789391316068	Gravity
9789391316150	Great Speeches of Abraham Lincoln
9789391316662	Guerilla Warfare
9789391316839	Kim
9789391316822	Mother
9789391316211	My Childhood
9789391316846	Nationalism
9789391316327	Oliver Twist
9789391316853	Pygmalion
9789391316334	Relativity: The Special and the General Theory
9789391316389	Scientific Healing Affirmation
9789391316341	Sons and Lovers
9789391316587	Tales from India
9789391316372	Tess of The D'Urbervilles
9789391316396	The Awakening and Selected Stories
9789391316402	The Bhagvad Gita
9789391316303	The Book of Enoch
9789391316228	The Canterville Ghost
9789391316907	The Dynamic Laws of Prosperity
9789391316006	The Great Gatsby
9789391316860	The Hungry Stones and Other Stories
9789391316433	The Idiot
9789391316440	The Importance of Being Earnest
9789391316297	The Light of Asia
9789391316914	The Madman His Parables and Poems
9789391316457	The Odyssey
9789391316921	The Picture of Dorian Gray
9789391316464	The Prince
9789391316938	The Prophet
9789391316945	The Republic
9789391316518	The Scarlet Letter

9789391316143	The Seven Laws of Teaching
9789391316525	The Story of My Experiments with Truth
9789391316532	The Tales of the Mother Goose
9789391316549	The Thirty Nine Steps
9789391316594	The Time Machine
9789391316600	The Turn of the Screw
9789391316983	The Upanishads
9789391316617	The Yellow Wallpaper
9789391316426	The Yoga Sutras of Patanjali
9789391316990	Ulysses
9789391316624	Utopia
9789391316679	Vanity Fair
9789391316020	What Is To Be Done
9789391316686	Within A Budding Grove
9789391316693	Women in Love